Database Systems: Design, Implementation and Management

Database Systems: Design, Implementation and Management

Edited by Bella Cunningham

CLANRYE
INTERNATIONAL
www.clanryeinternational.com

Clanrye International,
750 Third Avenue, 9th Floor,
New York, NY 10017, USA

ISBN: 978-1-63240-792-4

Cataloging-in-Publication Data

Database systems : design, implementation and management / edited by Bella Cunningham.
    p. cm.
Includes bibliographical references and index.
ISBN 978-1-63240-792-4
1. Databases. 2. Databases--Design. 3. Databases--Design--Data processing.
4. Database management. I. Cunningham, Bella.
QA76.9.D32 D38 2019
005.74--dc23

For information on all Clanrye International publications
visit our website at www.clanryeinternational.com

Contents

Preface...VII

Chapter 1   **Efficient and Secure Storage for Outsourced Data: A Survey**...............................1
             Jianfeng Wang and Xiaofeng Chen

Chapter 2   **Formal Modelling of Data Integration Systems Security Policies**.......................12
             Fatimah Akeel, Asieh Salehi Fathabadi, Federica Paci Andrew Gravell and
             Gary Wills

Chapter 3   **Efficient Breadth-First Search on Massively Parallel and Distributed-Memory
             Machines**..22
             Koji Ueno, Toyotaro Suzumura, Naoya Maruyama, Katsuki Fujisawa and
             Satoshi Matsuoka

Chapter 4   **Efficient Maximal Clique Enumeration over Graph Data**.................................36
             Boyi Hou, Zhuo Wang, Qun Chen, Bo Suo, Chao Fang, Zhanhuai Li and
             Zachary G. Ives

Chapter 5   **Context-Aware Recommendations with Random Partition Factorization
             Machines**..48
             Shaoqing Wang, Cuiping Li, Kankan Zhao and Hong Chen

Chapter 6   **Big Data Reduction Methods: A Survey**...59
             Muhammad Habib ur Rehman, Chee Sun Liew, Assad Abbas, Prem Prakash
             Jayaraman, Teh Ying Wah and Samee U. Khan

Chapter 7   **Fine-Grained Access Control Within NoSQL Document-Oriented Datastores**............79
             Pietro Colombo and Elena Ferrari

Chapter 8   **Graph Partitioning for Distributed Graph Processing**.....................................90
             Makoto Onizuka, Toshimasa Fujimori and Hiroaki Shiokawa

Chapter 9   **Private Blocking Technique for Multi-party Privacy-Preserving Record
             Linkage**..102
             Shumin Han, Derong Shen, Tiezheng Nie, Yue Kou and Ge Yu

Chapter 10   **An I/O-Efficient Buffer Batch Replacement Policy for Update-Intensive
             Graph**..112
             Ningnan Zhou, Xuan Zhou, Xiao Zhang and Shan Wang

Chapter 11   **Time for Addressing Software Security Issues: Prediction Models and
             Impacting Factors**..122
             Lotfi Ben Othmane, Golriz Chehrazi, Eric Bodden, Petar Tsalovski and
             Achim D. Brucker

Chapter 12   **Homomorphic Pattern Mining from a Single Large Data Tree**..140
Xiaoying Wu and Dimitri Theodoratos

Chapter 13   **Investigating TSP Heuristics for Location-Based Services**..156
Weihuang Huang and Jeffrey Xu Yu

Chapter 14   **Distance-Aware Selective Online Query Processing Over Large Distributed
Graphs**..179
Xiaofei Zhang and Lei Chen

Permissions

List of Contributors

Index

Preface

Databases are structured accumulations of data, built for easy access and retrieval of data as per requirement. Such data frameworks are constructed according to industrial or organizational needs. Large databases require elaborate and efficient database management systems. They are of two types- general and special purpose. It has applications across a number of fields such as library systems, website management, inventory management, etc. This book sheds light on the modern techniques and methods of database system design, their applications and management. It elucidates concepts and innovative models around prospective developments with respect to database systems. This book will serve as a valuable source of reference for professionals, researchers and students in the fields of computer science and engineering, information science, knowledge management and software engineering.

This book is a result of research of several months to collate the most relevant data in the field.

When I was approached with the idea of this book and the proposal to edit it, I was overwhelmed. It gave me an opportunity to reach out to all those who share a common interest with me in this field. I had 3 main parameters for editing this text:

1. Accuracy – The data and information provided in this book should be up-to-date and valuable to the readers.

2. Structure – The data must be presented in a structured format for easy understanding and better grasping of the readers.

3. Universal Approach – This book not only targets students but also experts and innovators in the field, thus my aim was to present topics which are of use to all.

Thus, it took me a couple of months to finish the editing of this book.

I would like to make a special mention of my publisher who considered me worthy of this opportunity and also supported me throughout the editing process. I would also like to thank the editing team at the back-end who extended their help whenever required.

Editor

Efficient and Secure Storage for Outsourced Data: A Survey

Jianfeng Wang[1] · Xiaofeng Chen[1]

Abstract With the growing popularity of cloud computing, more and more enterprises and individuals tend to store their sensitive data on the cloud in order to reduce the cost of data management. However, new security and privacy challenges arise when the data stored in the cloud due to the loss of data control by the data owner. This paper focuses on the techniques of verifiable data storage and secure data deduplication. We firstly summarize and classify the state-of-the-art research on cloud data storage mechanism. Then, we present some potential research directions for secure data outsourcing.

Keywords Outsourced storage · Verifiable search · Data auditing · Secure data deduplication

1 Introduction

Cloud computing, the new term for the long-dreamed vision of computing as a utility, can offer plenty of benefits for real-world applications, such as on-demand self-service, ubiquitous network access, rapid resource elasticity, usage-based pricing, outsourcing, etc. One of the fundamental advantages of cloud computing is the so-called outsourcing paradigm. That is, the resource-constrained users can enjoy high-quality data storage services by outsourcing their data to the cloud server.

Despite the tremendous benefits, the outsourcing paradigm brings some new security challenges. On the one hand, the cloud server may be not fully trusted, and face both internal and external security threats, such as software/hardware failures, compromised employees, hacker. A query on data stored on a cloud server may return an invalid search result. What's more, the cloud server may be "semi-honest-but-curious" and intentionally execute partial search operations in order to save its computation and communication overhead. Thus, one significant security challenge is how to achieve the *verifiability* of search results for data stored in the cloud. It means that the client should efficiently check the validation for the results returned by the cloud server. Specifically, the following two security requirements should be meet: (1) correctness: the result is the original data and has not been modified; (2) completeness: the result includes all the matched data satisfying the client's search request.

On the other hand, with the rapid popularity of cloud computing, an increasing amount of data is being outsourced to the cloud in a exponential growth manner. Inevitably, this leads to a cost explosion of data storage. This concerns not only the cost of the hardware and software necessary for storing data, but also the rapidly growing energy consumption in storage systems. As a promising solution, data deduplication has attracted increasing attention from both academic and industrial community. Deduplication can eliminate redundant data by storing one single copy for duplicate data.

In this paper, we present a comprehensive survey of solutions for verifiability of search results and secure data deduplication. Specifically, we first review the state of the art for verifiable data search and secure data deduplication techniques, and introduce a classification of these techniques. Then, we present current research directions, with the aim of promoting further research of data security in the cloud.

✉ Jianfeng Wang
  wjf01@163.com

[1] State Key Laboratory of Integrated Service Networks (ISN), Xidian University, Xi'an, People's Republic of China

The rest of the paper is organized as follows. In Sect. 2, we briefly present an brief overview of verifiable cloud storage, including security threats and the corresponding solutions. A summary of secure data deduplication in cloud environments is presented in Sect. 3. Finally, we discuss some future research directions for secure data outsourcing and conclude this paper in Sect. 4.

2 Verifiable Storage on Outsourced Databases

Database outsourcing has recently attracted considerable interest. The concept of database outsourcing was first implicitly introduced by Hacigümüş et al. [22]. Their approach allows the data owner to delegate the database management to a cloud service provider (CSP) that provides various database services to users. More specifically, in the outsourced database (ODB) scenario, the data owner locally encrypts its own database and then outsources the encrypted database with additional metadata (i.e., index) to the CSP, which hosts the database and provides various database services to the users on behalf of data owner. The data users can issue query to the CSP and receive the corresponding results from the CSP.

Despite the tremendous benefits, the outsourced database paradigm inevitably suffers from some new security challenges. Specifically, due to self-interest and hardware/software failures, cloud servers may execute only a fraction of the search operations honestly and/or return an incorrect and/or incomplete query result. What is worst is that, since users no longer locally possess a copy of the data, it is difficult to check the integrity of search result. Therefore, one of the most critical challenges is to effectively audit the integrity of outsourced databases.

2.1 System Model

As shown in Fig. 1, an ODB system consists of three entities: the data owner, the data user, and the cloud service provider. The data owner outsources its encrypted database to the cloud service provider, and an (authorized) data user can issue encrypted queries to the CSP. It is worth nothing that the CSP should be able to process queries over encrypted data. In addition, the data user should be able to verify the search result. Verifiability includes the following two security goals: (1) correctness: the result is the original data and has not been modified; (2) completeness: the result includes all valid data items satisfying the search condition.

2.2 Threat Model

In an ODB system, the CSP refers to a "semi-honest-but-curious" server. That is, the CSP may not honestly follow the proposed protocol but return incomplete search result and/or execute only partial search operations honestly. Thus, two types of attacker are considered: (1) external attacker: a party which wants to obtain knowledge on the database beyond what the party is authorized to obtain, i.e., a revoked user or hacker. (2) internal attacker: a party may have some knowledge about database (i.e., the CSP). The goal of the attacker is to return incomplete/incorrect search results without being detected.

2.3 Integrity Auditing for Outsourced Databases

Several researchers have investigated techniques for verifiable database outsourcing in the past decade. The existing approaches can be categorized into two types according to the verification approach adotped.

2.3.1 Authenticated Data Structure-Based Integrity Verification

The first approach is based on authenticated data structures (e.g., Merkle hash tree [36]) [8, 16, 17, 27, 34, 38, 47]. Devanbu et al. [17] firstly investigated the problem of integrity auditing on outsourced databases. Their solution does not require the results pre-computation (signature) of all the possible queries nor deliver the whole database to the user. The basic idea is that an index based on the Merkle hash tree (MHT) is generated, and then, the search result can be verified by re-computing the signature of the root of the MHT. Note that the leaf nodes of a MHT should be ordered. Such requirement makes frequent data updates costly. More importantly, the size of verification object (VO) is linear in the cardinality of the query result and logarithmic in the scale of the database. Pang et al. [47] proposed the notion of verifiable B-trees (VB-tree), where each internal node is assigned with a signed hash value derived from all the data items in the subtree rooted at the current node. In processing a query, the cloud server first locates the smallest subtree covering all the query results. It then computes the VO as the hash values for all the data items in the subtree that are not included in the result. Trivially, the size of VO is independent of the database size. Nuckolls [45] presented a flexible verification structure called hybrid authentication tree (HAT) by incorporating one-way accumulator. The proposed solution enables a consolidated proof to reduce the size of the VO. Later, Li et al. [27] introduced a novel notion of Embedded Merkle B-tree (EMB-tree). The basic idea is to embed a B^+-tree into an MHT. To verify the completeness of a range query, the VO includes all the sibling hash out of scope of two immediately neighboring records in the ordered sequence.

Fig. 1 Architecture of an
outsourced database system
model

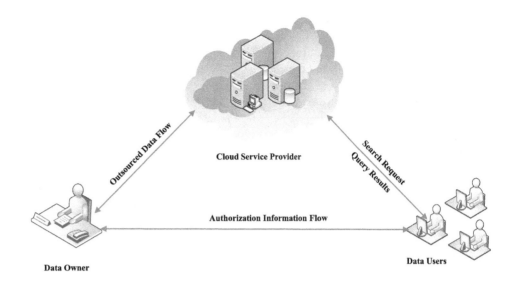

2.3.2 Signature Chaining-Based Integrity Verification

The second approach is based on the signature chaining technique [40, 41, 43, 46]. Mykletun et al. [40] investigated the notion of signature aggregation which allows one to combine multiple signatures into a single one, thereby reducing verification overhead for search results. However, their mechanism ensures correctness for search results and does not provide completeness guarantee. Later, Narasimha et al. [43] addressed completeness by integrating signature aggregation and chaining techniques. Specifically, the client generates a signature for each data item containing all the immediate predecessors in different dimensions. Then, given a range query, their technique requires two boundary data items to be returned along with the target data items. The completeness of the search result can be verified using the chained signature. Pang et al. [46, 48] give two solutions to the completeness problem for static and dynamic outsourced database, respectively. In their solutions, all data items are assumed to be ordered with respect to certain searchable attributes, and the data owner creates a signature for each item that consists of information about the two neighboring items in the ordered sequence. Note that there is no need for additional boundary data items. Nevertheless, the case when non-continuous regions are queried is intractable. Recently, Yuan and Yu [59] presented a new verifiable aggregation query scheme for outsourced databases. Specifically, each data item is assigned an authentication tag based on a polynomial, which can be used to check the integrity of query result for certain aggregation queries.

Notice that none of the existing solutions ensure the completeness of result when the cloud server intentionally returns an empty result. Wang et al. [55] proposed a novel verifiable outsourced database scheme based on Bloom filters. In their construction, the data user can check the integrity of the search result even if the CSP intentionally returns an empty set. Their technique allows the data user to ensure the correctness of search result by checking whether the search request belongs to the Bloom filters.

Remark 1 As a complementary solution, a probabilistic integrity verification methods have been proposed by Xie at al. [57] and Sion [50]. The main idea of such methods is that the data owner inserts some faked data items in the database beforehand. The disadvantages of such methods are twofold: On the one hand, the fake data items must be shared by all authorized data users and this makes the methods vulnerable to compromise attacks. On the other hand, the methods requires the cloud server to return all attributes of the data items and thus the method cannot support some common database operations such as projection.

Remark 2 Another concern about data integrity auditing is related storage integrity for outsourced data. Storage integrity refers to the ability to check whether the outsourced data are lost or corrupted without retrieving it. The pioneer works include the Provable Data Possession (PDP) protocol [3] and the Proof of Retrievability (POR) protocol [26]. Since the definition of such protocols, several researchers have investigated the problem of remote data auditing.

It should be pointed out that there are some differences between storage and query integrity for outsourced data. First, in the storage integrity setting, the user must have beforehand knowledge about the database (e.g., the hash value of data blocks). By contrast, in the query integrity setting, the user is not required to have knowledge about the database. Furthermore, storage integrity only focuses on query correctness whereas query integrity must ensure both the correctness and completeness of the query.

2.4 Verifiable Databases with Updates

Benabbas et al. [7] proposed a useful cryptographic primitive for verifiable databases with efficient updates (VDB). That is, a resource-constrained client may outsource a large-scale database to a cloud server and later efficiently performs verification of query results in a dynamic database scenario. If a dishonest cloud server tampers with any data item in the database, the misbehavior will be detected with an overwhelming probability (once the tampered data item is queried). In addition, the cost of query processing and query result verification should be independent of the size of the database.

For the case of static databases, the above problem can be addressed by trivially adopting message authentication or digital signature technique. Namely, the client signs each data item before uploading it to the cloud server, and the cloud server is required to return the requested data item together with its valid signature. Nevertheless, this solution cannot work well when the database is updated. The main challenge is related to how to revoke the valid signatures given to the cloud server for the previous values of the modified data item. A naive solution is that the client locally keeps track of every change. However, such a solution negates the advantages of database outsourcing. Although existing techniques such as accumulators [10, 11, 44], and authentication data structures [35, 42, 49, 52] that can be adopted to address such problem, these solutions either rely on nonconstant size assumptions (e.g., the q-Strong Diffie-Hellman assumptions) or require expensive operations such as the generation of primes and re-shuffling procedures.

Benabbas et al. [7] proposed the first efficient VDB scheme under the subgroup membership assumption in composite order bilinear groups. The main idea is to apply a verifiable polynomial evaluation scheme constructed with algebraic pseudo-random functions. However, their solution can only achieve private verifiability. In other words, only the data owner can perform verification of search results. As the data users have limited resources, it is critical that any data user verify the validity of data updated by the server. Here, we introduce the formal definition of VDB [7]. In the definition, the term "client" refers to the notion of "data owner" that we use in our discussion throughout the paper.

Definition 1 A verifiable database scheme $\mathsf{VDB} = (\mathsf{Setup}, \mathsf{Query}, \mathsf{Verify}, \mathsf{Update})$ consists of four algorithms defined as follows.

- $\mathsf{Setup}(1^k, DB) \to (\mathsf{S}, \mathsf{PK}, \mathsf{SK})$: On input the security parameter k and a database DB, the setup algorithm is run by the client to generate a database encoding S that

is given to the server, a public key PK that is distributed to all users, and a secret key SK that is secretly stored at the client.

- $\mathsf{Query}(\mathsf{PK}, \mathsf{S}, x) \to \sigma$: The query algorithm takes as input an index x and returns a pair $\sigma = (v, \pi)$, which is run by the server.
- $\mathsf{Verify}(\mathsf{PK}/\mathsf{SK}, x, \sigma) \to v$: The public verification algorithm outputs a value v if σ is correct with respect to x, and an special symbol $\perp$ otherwise.
- $\mathsf{Update}(\mathsf{SK}, x, v_x') \to \mathsf{PK}'$: In the update algorithm, the client firstly generates a token t_x' with its own secret key SK and then sends the pair (t_x', v_x') to the server. Then, the server uses v_x' to update the database record of index x, and outputs the updated public key PK' according to t_x'.

2.4.1 Vector Commitment-Based VDB Framework

Catalano and Fiore [12] formalized a powerful cryptographic primitive named vector commitment. Informally speaking, the notion of vector commitment allows one to commit to an vector $(m_1, \ldots, m_q)$ in such a way that the committer can later open the commitment at specific positions. Also, nobody should be able to open a commitment to two different values at the same position (this is called *position binding*). Besides, the vector commitment should be *concise*, i.e., the size of the commitment string and the opening are both independent of the vector commitment q. Additionally, the vector commitment should be updatable for constructing a VDB scheme. That is, it is required that the committer is able to update the original commitment value by changing a specific component of the vector and the opening would still be valid for the updated commitment. The detailed formal definition of vector commitment can be found in [12].

Catalano and Fiore [12] constructed a novel VDB scheme from the vector commitment. The proposed construction does not only rely on the standard constant-size cryptographic assumption (Computational Diffie-Hellman), but also satisfies the property of public verifiability. Formally, the framework consists of the following algorithms:

- $\mathsf{Setup}(1^k, DB) \to (\mathsf{S}, \mathsf{PK}, \mathsf{SK}$: Let the database be $DB = (i, v_i)$ for $1 \le i \le q$. Run the key generation and committing algorithms of vector commitment to obtain the public parameters $\mathsf{PP} \leftarrow \mathsf{VC.KeyGen}(1^k, q)$ and the initial commitment and auxiliary information $(C, \mathsf{aux}) \leftarrow \mathsf{VC.Com}_{PP}(v_1, \cdots, v_q)$, respectively. It outputs the database encoding $\mathsf{S} = (\mathsf{PP}, \mathsf{aux}, DB)$, the system public key $\mathsf{PK} = (\mathsf{PP}, C)$ and the client's secret key $\mathsf{SK} = \perp$.

- Query(PK, S, x) → σ: On input an index x, the server firstly runs the opening algorithm to compute $\pi_x \leftarrow$ VC.Open$_{PP}(v_x, x, \mathsf{aux})$ and then returns $\sigma = (v_x, \pi_x)$.
- Verify(PK, x, σ) → v_x: Parse the proofs σ as (v_x, π_x). If VC.Ver$_{PP}(C, x, v_x, \pi_x) = 1$, then return v_x, and an special symbol $\perp$ otherwise.
- Update(SK, x, v'_x): To update the record of index x, the client firstly retrieves the current record v_x from the server. That is, the client obtains $\sigma \leftarrow$ Query(PK, S, x) from the server and checks that Verify(PK, x, σ) = $v_x \neq \perp$. Then the client computes $(C', U) \leftarrow$ VC. Update$_{PP}(C, v_x, x, v'_x)$ and outputs PK' = (PP, C') and $t'_x = ($PK'$, v'_x, U)$. Finally, the server uses v'_x to update the database record of index x, PK' to update the public key, and U to update the auxiliary information.

2.4.2 Weaknesses of Catalano–Fiore's VDB Scheme

Chen et al. [14] described two types of attack for the Catalano–Fiore's VDB scheme, namely the Forward Automatic Update (FAU) attack and the Backward Substitution Update (BSU) attack. We revisit them in what follows:

2.4.2.1 Forward Automatic Update (FAU) Attack
In the Catalano–Fiore's VDB scheme [12], anyone (include a malicious cloud server) can update the data in the same manner of the data owner. To be specific, an adversary first retrieves a record v_x. Then, the adversary generates the new public key PK' and the token t' based on a new data record value v' (without involving any knowledge of secret key). Finally, the cloud server updates the corresponding data record as well as the public key. Interestingly, any query issued to the cloud server can be replied to with a valid proof based on the forward updated public key PK'. As a consequence, the above misbehavior would not be detected. The result is that an auditor cannot determine with certainty that the cloud server has been dishonest.

2.4.2.2 Backward Substitution Update (BSU) Attack
The so-called BSU attack means that anyone can substitute the current public key with the previous one. As noted above, anyone is allowed to update the public key. Therefore, if the client does not locally store a copy of the public key; it is difficult for him to distinguish the past public key from the latest one. On the other hand, even if the client has stored the latest public key, it is still to be difficult for the client to prove that the locally stored public key is the latest one.

Remark 3 The main reason of the above attacks is that the client's secret key is not be involved in the update of the

public key. Note that it is useless to append the signature on the public key. If the cloud server generates the signature, it has the ability to compute the signature on any public key. On the other hand, if the signature is computed by the client, the original question arises again: How to efficiently revoke the previous (valid) signature?

2.4.3 VDB Framework from Commitment Binding

To achieve public verifiability and protect against the FAU/BSU attacks simultaneously, Chen et al. [14] proposed a novel VDB framework for vector commitment based on the idea of commitment binding (see Fig. 2). That is, the client uses the secret key to generate a signature on some binding information. This information consists of the latest public key, the commitment on the current database, and a global counter. Assume that the client's signature on the binding information is $H_T = \text{SIGN}_{sk}(C_{T-1}, C^{(T)}, T)$, then we obtain the current public key as $C_T = H_T C^{(T)}$. Thus, this method recursively binds the commitment C_T to a 3-tuple $(C_{T-1}, C^{(T)}, T)$. As a consequence, an adversary (i.e., the cloud server) cannot update the database and public key without the client's secret key.

Chen et al. [15] also introduced the notion of verifiable database with incremental updates (Inc-VDB), i.e., the client can efficiently update the ciphertext with the previous one, rather than from scratch. It is useful for large database settings, especially when there are frequent slight modifications. Note that in traditional encryption schemes the ciphertext needs to be totally recomputed even if only one single bit is changed in plaintext, resulting in very high overhead for the resources-constrained clients. To address this challenge, the Inc-VDB framework incorporates vector commitment and encrypt-then-incremental MAC mode of encryption [9]. The main trick is that the updated ciphertext v'_x is generated in an incremental manner as follows: we define $v'_x = (v_x, P_x)$, where $P_x = (p_1, p_2, \ldots, p_k)$ denotes the location of bit positions with different values between the original and updated plaintext message. Given $v' = (v_x, P_x)$, the client first decrypts v_x to

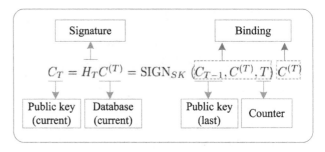

Fig. 2 Commitment binding technique

obtain m_x and then performs the bit flipping operation on the positions of P_x to obtain the final plaintext m'_x.

It worth noting that the existing VDB schemes cannot fully support data update operations. Specifically, the existing solutions can only support data replacement and deletion operations while they are not applicable of the insertion operation. The main reason is that the number of index of the database must be fixed in advance and published as the system parameters in both schemes. On the other hand, when the client performs an insertion/deletion operation on an outsourced database, the number of the index will be increased/ decreased by 1. Therefore, it seems to be a paradox to design a VDB scheme that supports all update operations using the existing solutions, such as delegating high-degree polynomial function and vector commitment.

Miao et al. [37] utilized the idea of hierarchical (vector) commitment to address the above dilemma. The hierarchical commitment consists of multiple levels, and the maximum number of data items for each level is the dimension q of vector in a vector commitment. When a level is a full (i.e., the number of data items in this level is q), a new inserted data record will be located in a new level.

3 Secure Cloud Data Deduplication Technique

According to the latest analysis by IDC [54], the volume of data we create and copy annually is doubling in size every 2 years, and will reach 44 trillion gigabytes in 2020. With the dramatic increase in data volumes, how to efficiently store the ever-increasing data becomes a critical challenge for cloud servers. Data deduplication, as a specialized data compression technique, has been adopted widely to save storage costs by only storing a single copy of repeating data and replacing with links to that copy. Data deduplication can achieve more than 50 % storage reduction [2] and has been deployed by many cloud storage providers, such as Dropbox, Google Drive, Bitcasa and Mozy.

However, conventional encryption is incompatible with deduplication. Specifically, encrypting the same data with different encryption keys results into distinct ciphertexts corresponding to the same source data. Thus, it makes cross-user deduplication impossible.

To fill the above gap, convergent encryption (CE) [19], an elegant cryptographic primitive, is proposed. Essentially speaking, CE is a deterministic symmetric encryption scheme and its encryption key is derived from the cryptographic hash value of the file content. Then, each identical data item generates the same ciphertext, which achieves deduplication and encryption simultaneously. Bellare et al. [6] defined a new cryptographic primitive called message-locked encryption (MLE), which can be

viewed as a generalization of CE. Furthermore, to enhance performance of deduplication, a randomized convergent encryption (RCE) scheme has been proposed. It is characterized by the efficiency of the relevant operations, i.e., key generation, message encryption, and tag production. However, RCE is vulnerable to what is called duplicate faking attack. Specifically, an honest user cannot retrieve his original message because it can be undetectably replaced by a fake one. To tackle this problem, an interactive version of RCE, called interactive randomized convergent encryption (IRCE) [4], has been proposed. In IRCE, an honest user can check tag consistency by interacting with the server and thus verify that the original ciphertext is stored. If an adversary may upload a modified ciphertext, this ciphertext will be inconsistent with respect to the corresponding file tag. Such a mismatch allows one to detect that the ciphertext is incorrect.

3.1 Deduplication Classification

According to the granularity and architecture, deduplication can be categorized into different types. With respect to granularity, there are two deduplication strategies. (1) File-level deduplication: The data redundancy is exploited at the file level. Only one copy of the identical data file is saved and subsequent copies are replaced with a link that points to the original file. (2) Block-level deduplication: each file is divided into multiple blocks (or segments, chunks) and the data redundancy is exploited at the block level. Note that the block size can be either fixed or variable in practice. Despite achieving higher deduplication ratio, block-level deduplication inevitably requires more metadata and needs longer processing times.

With respect to the architecture, there are two deduplication strategies. (1) Server-side deduplication (known as target-based deduplication): All clients upload their data to the CSP and are unaware of deduplication that might occur. The CSP is responsible for deleting the duplicate copies. This strategy reduces storage costs, but does not save bandwidth costs. (2) Client-side deduplication (known as source-based deduplication): The client first sends a tag of the data (e.g., a hash value) to the CSP to check whether the data to be uploaded are already in the cloud. If yes, the data does not need to be uploaded. This strategy can save both bandwidth and storage costs, but is prone to side channel attacks since a client can learn if another client already uploaded a given file. The details will be discussed later.

3.2 Security Challenges and Solutions

Without loss of generality, we focus on client-side, cross-user deduplication. Cross-user deduplication means that the deduplication operations are performed across all data uploaded by all users. Such method increases the effectiveness of deduplication, as deduplication is executed not only when a single user repeatedly uploads the same data but also when different users upload the same data.

Despite its benefits in reducing storage and communication costs, client-side cross-user deduplication suffers from several privacy threats [5, 24, 58].

3.2.1 Brute-Force Attack

As discuss above, CE protocols can be used to ensure data privacy in deduplication. However, it is vulnerable to brute-force attacks. That is, suppose the target message is drawn from a finite space of size n $S = \{M_1, \ldots, M_n\}$. Then, any attacker can generate the convergent key of each message and compute the corresponding ciphertext as in off-line encryption. If one computed ciphertext is equal to the target ciphertext, the target message is inferred. The basic reason is that CE is a deterministic symmetric encryption scheme, and the key space is limited. It implies that no MLE (CE) scheme can achieve traditional semantic security [21]. The ideal security for MLE scheme, PRV$-CDA [6], refers to an encryption scheme that can achieve semantic security when the messages are unpredictable (i.e., have high min-entropy).

Bellare et al. [5] proposed a novel secure deduplication system resisting brute-force attacks, called DupLESS, which can transform the predictable message into an unpredictable one with the help of an additional key server. More specifically, DupLESS introduces an additional key server that generates the convergent key based on two inputs: the hash of message and a system-wide key. The client obtains the convergent key by interactively running an oblivious pseudorandom function (OPRF) with the key server. As long as the key server is secure, the convergent key is derived from a random large key space. It implies that DupLESS can ensure confidentiality for the predictable message. Furthermore, to prevent online brute-force attacks by compromised client, a per-client rate-limiting strategy is applied to limit the total number of queries a client can make during each epoch. It implies that DupLESS can achieve the same security of MLE at worst even the key server is compromised. Duan [20] proposed a distributed version of DupLESS, where the client must interact with the threshold of other clients to generate the convergent key before uploading a file. Moreover, a trusted dealer should be included to distribute key shares for each client. We argue that the trusted dealer has similar role of the key server in DupLESS. Thus, this scheme still suffers from online brute-force attacks in the case in which the dealer is comprised.

Recently, Liu et al. [33] proposed a secure single-server cross-user deduplication scheme that resists brute-force attacks. The client who wants to upload a given file runs a password authenticated key exchange (PAKE) protocol with the CSP to obtain the encryption key from the original client who had previously uploaded the identical file. Suppose the client wants to upload a file, the client first sends a short hash of the uploading file as "password." Upon receiving the uploading request, the CSP firstly identifies all the candidate clients with the same short hash value and asks the client to engage in a Same-Input-PAKE protocol with each candidate client. Note that as the Same-Input-PAKE protocol is run between the CSP and the client, the client does not need direct communications among themselves. To protect against brute-force attacks, two additional mechanisms are introduced. First, it uses the randomized threshold strategy [24] to assign a random threshold for each file and perform client-side deduplication once the number of the file is higher than the threshold value, so that the attacker cannot determine whether the file being uploaded already exists at the CSP. Second, a per-file rate-limiting strategy is used to protect against online brute-force attacks. Compared with the per-client rate-limiting strategy in DupLESS, the proposed strategy enhances security of deduplication and reduces communication overhead (i.e., the run time of PAKE).

3.2.2 Duplicate Faking Attacks

In a duplicate faking attack, an honest user might be unable to retrieve his original file, since it can be replaced by a fake one and the replacement cannot be detected. That is, suppose that users Alice and Bob possess two different files F_a and F_b, respectively. The malicious user Alice may upload a modified ciphertext $C_a = (E(H(F_b), F_a))$ and the corresponding tag $T_a = H(E(H(F_b), F_b))$ into the CSP. Later, when the honest user Bob uploads the ciphertext $C_b = (E(H(F_b), F_b))$ and its tag $T_b = H(E(H(F_b), F_b))$, the CSP wrongly determines that the plaintexts of C_b and C_a are identical, and thus deletes C_b. As a result, Bob cannot retrieve his original plaintext. The main reason is that the CSP cannot check tag consistency [6] without knowing the hash value of the file.

To address this drawback, a variant of MLE called randomized convergent encryption (RCE) has been introduced [6]. RCE introduces a checking mechanism, called guarded decryption, by which the client can check the integrity of the returned ciphertext. The RCE scheme is described as follows: the client first picks at random a key L and then computes ciphertext $C_1 = E(L, F)$ and $C_2 = L \oplus K$, where K is the hash value of file $H(F)$. The tag is generated from the file by a double hash, i.e., $T = H(K)$. Upon receiving the ciphertexts C_1 and C_2, the tag T, the client can obtain the random key $L = C_2 \oplus K$ using the hash of file, and the plaintext F by decrypting C_1 with L. Then, the client regenerates a tag $T' = H(H(F))$ and checks whether T' is equal to T. Furthermore, an interactive version of RCE, called interactive randomized convergent encryption (IRCE), has been proposed [4], by which a client can check the consistency of a file tag by interacting with the CSP. In this way, the client can ensure that the original ciphertext is stored by the CSP. However, the cloud server cannot check consistency between the tag and the ciphertext, since it has no access to the original plaintext. Thus, the CSP cannot determine which user is dishonest. From the point of view of practical applications, this is a major drawback. Preferably, it should be possible not only to identify which users are malicious, but also to trace these users—i.e., identify all ciphertexts uploaded by these. This is nontrivial, if a CSP or the data owners allow users to remain anonymous or appear under different identities. Wang et al. [56] designed a novel deduplication scheme, called TrDup, which makes it possible to trace malicious users. Specifically, each user generates a kind of anonymous signature for the uploaded file—a variant of the traceable signature scheme is used. Once a duplicate faking attack is detected, the tracing agent can determine the identity of the malicious user without revealing identities of other users or linking their files in the cloud.

3.2.3 Hash Manipulation Attack

Harnik et al. [24] pointed out that client-side deduplication is vulnerable to side channel attacks. That is, whenever receiving an upload request, the CSP will tell whether the uploading file has already been stored. However, an attacker may abuse the information to launch a brute-force attack by trying all possible variants of the same file. Mulazzani et al. [39] show how to carry out this attack against mainstream cloud storage provider (i.e., Dropbox). Furthermore, Halevi et al. [23] argued that an attacker can obtain the ownership of a file that he actually does not own by providing the hash of file. The main reason is that the CSP determines whether a client owns a specific file using a small piece of information about the file (i.e., hash value). Thus, anyone who possess the short hash value for a specific file can be allowed to access the entire content of file.

To protect against such attack, Halevi et al. [23] introduced the concept of *proof of ownership* (PoW), which can be used to ensure data privacy and confidentiality in case of client-side deduplication. Namely, a user can efficiently prove to the cloud storage server that he indeed owns a file without uploading it. Three concrete PoW constructions have been presented—all based on a Merkle hash tree (MHT) built from the content of a data file.

Specifically, a challenge/response protocol is run between server and client. Each data file is denoted as a MHT (the leaf nodes constitute the data file), and the server first asks for a random subset of the MHT leaf nodes from the client. If the client does not possess the whole file, it cannot generate a valid proof with overwhelming probability. Using a PoW, the cheating attacks can be prevented. That is, a user that only knows only the hash signature of a file cannot convince the cloud server that he owns that file. Di Pietro and Sorniotti [18] proposed an efficient PoW scheme, in which each challenge is a seed for a pseudo-random generator and the response is the set of values in the file at bit positions derived by the generator from the seed. Every time a file is uploaded to the server, the latter computes a set of challenges for that file and stores them for a later check. Alís et al. [1] proposed a PoW scheme based on a Bloom filter, which is efficient at both the server and the client side.

3.3 Deduplication Efficiency

Recent approaches to secure deduplication have focused on security enhancements and efficiency. [2, 13, 25, 28–32, 51, 53, 60, 61]. Among those works, most are focused on security enhancement and efficiency improvement. Stanek et al. [51] proposed a novel deduplication encryption scheme that can provide different security levels for data files according their *popularity* that refers to how frequently the file is shared among users. Their approach can achieve a fine-grained trade-off between the storage efficiency and data security for the outsourced data. Armknecht et al. [2] designed a novel verifiable deduplication storage system, namely ClearBox, which ensures that the client can check the deduplication pattern of his own encrypted data, i.e., whether his files are deduplicated or not. Li et al. [31] and Hur et al. [25] have investigated the key update and user revocation problems, respectively.

Li et al. [28] have proposed DeKey [29], an efficient and reliable key management scheme for block-level deduplication. In DeKey, each client distributes the convergent key shares across multiple servers based on the ramp secret sharing scheme. Zhou et al. [61] proposed a more fine-grained key management scheme called SecDup, which mitigates the key generation overhead by exploiting hybrid deduplication policies. Li et al. [30] proposed a fine-grained deduplication mechanism based on user privileges. A client can perform a duplication check only for the files marked with matching privileges. Li et al. [28] designed a distributed reliable deduplication scheme, which can achieve data reliability and secure deduplication simultaneously by dispersing the data shares across multiple cloud servers. Chen et al. [13] proposed a novel storage-efficient deduplication scheme, called block-level message-locked encryption (BL-MLE), in which the block keys are encapsulated into the block tag to reduce metadata storage space.

4 Conclusion and Future Work

Secure data outsourcing is an important research topic in cloud computing. Even though secure data outsourcing has been widely investigated, more research work is needed. Relevant research directions include the following:

- *Publicly Verifiable ODB* The existing ODB schemes just support private verifiability. That is, as only the data owner can check the validity of his own data because only the data owner knows the secret key. The data owner must be involved in every verification[1]. Thus, how to design a publicly verifiable ODB scheme is an interesting problem.
- *Privacy-preserving VDB* The traditional VDB schemes do not consider the privacy of users. Specifically, information about update patterns (i.e., the updated data items and the update frequency) is leaked to the CSP. A valuable research direction is how to construct a construct privacy-preserving VDB scheme.
- *User-Revokable deduplication* Although the traceability of malicious users can be achieved in secure data deduplication, the problem of user revocation still needs to be addressed in multi-user scenarios. Thus, one valuable research topic is the development of data deduplication mechanism supporting user revocation.

Acknowledgments We are grateful to the anonymous reviewers for their valuable comments and suggestions. This work was supported by the National Natural Science Foundation of China (No. 61572382), China 111 Project (No. B16037), Doctoral Fund of Ministry of Education of China (No. 20130203110004).

References

1. Alís JB, Di Pietro R, Orfila A, Sorniotti A (2014) A tunable proof of ownership scheme for deduplication using bloom filters. In: IEEE Conference on Communications and Network Security, CNS'14, pp 481–489

2. Armknecht F, Bohli J, Karame GO, Youssef F (2015) Transparent data deduplication in the cloud. In: Proceedings of the 22nd ACM SIGSAC Conference on Computer and Communications Security, CCS'15, pp 886–900

3. Ateniese G, Burns RC, Curtmola R, Herring J, Kissner L, Peterson ZNJ, Song DX (2007) Provable data possession at untrusted stores. In: Proceedings of the 2007 ACM Conference on Computer and Communications Security, CCS'07, pp 598–609

4. Bellare M, Keelveedhi S (2015) Interactive message-locked encryption and secure deduplication. In: Proceedings of the 18th IACR International Conference on Practice and Theory in Public-Key Cryptography-PKC 2015, LNCS, vol 9020. Springer, pp 516–538

5. Bellare M, Keelveedhi S, Ristenpart T (2013a) Dupless: Server-aided encryption for deduplicated storage. In: Proceedings of the 22th USENIX Security Symposium, pp 179–194

6. Bellare M, Keelveedhi S, Ristenpart T (2013b) Message-locked encryption and secure deduplication. In: Proceedings of the 32nd Annual International Conference on the Theory and Applications of Cryptographic Techniques, Advances in Cryptology-EUROCRYPT'13, LNCS, vol 7881. Springer, pp 296–312

7. Benabbas S, Gennaro R, Vahlis Y (2011) Verifiable delegation of computation over large datasets. In: Proceedings of the 31st Annual Cryptology Conference on Advances in Cryptology, CRYPTO'11, Springer, pp 111–131

8. Bertino E, Carminati B, Ferrari E, Thuraisingham BM, Gupta A (2004) Selective and authentic third-party distribution of XML documents. IEEE Trans Knowl Data Eng 16(10):1263–1278

9. Buonanno E, Katz J, Yung M (2001) Incremental unforgeable encryption. In: Fast Software Encryption, 8th International Workshop, FSE 2001 Yokohama, Japan, April 2–4, 2001, Revised Papers, Springer, pp 109–124

10. Camenisch J, Kohlweiss M, Soriente C (2009) An accumulator based on bilinear maps and efficient revocation for anonymous credentials. In: Proceedings of the 12th International Conference on Practice and Theory in Public Key Cryptography, PKC'09, Springer, pp 481–500

11. Camenisch J, Lysyanskaya A (2002) Dynamic accumulators and application to efficient revocation of anonymous credentials. In: Proceedings of the 22nd Annual International Cryptology Conference on Advances in Cryptology, CRYPTO'02, Springer, pp 61–76

12. Catalano D, Fiore D (2013) Vector commitments and their applications. In: Proceedings of 16th International Conference on Practice and Theory in Public-Key Cryptography, PKC'13, Springer, pp 55–72

13. Chen R, Mu Y, Yang G, Guo F (2015) BL-MLE: block-level message-locked encryption for secure large file deduplication. IEEE Trans Inf Forensics Secur 10(12):2643–2652

14. Chen X, Li J, Huang X, Ma J, Lou W (2015) New publicly verifiable databases with efficient updates. IEEE Trans Dependable Secure Comput 12(5):546–556

15. Chen X, Li J, Weng J, Ma J, Lou W (2016) Verifiable computation over large database with incremental updates. IEEE Trans Comput. doi:10.1109/TC.2015.2512870

16. Devanbu PT, Gertz M, Martel CU, Stubblebine SG (2000) Authentic third-party data publication. In: Proceeddings of the IFIP TC11/ WG11.3 Fourteenth Annual Working Conference on Database Security, pp 101–112

17. Devanbu PT, Gertz M, Martel CU, Stubblebine SG (2003) Authentic data publication over the internet. J Comput Secur 11(3):291–314

18. Di Pietro R, Sorniotti A (2012) Boosting efficiency and security in proof of ownership for deduplication. In: Proceedings of the 7th ACM Symposium on Information, Compuer and Communications Security, ASIACCS'12, pp 81–82

---

[1] Here, we do not distinguish between the data owner and the authorized user because they are shared the secret key for verification.

19. Douceur JR, Adya A, Bolosky WJ, Simon D, Theimer M (2002) Reclaiming space from duplicate files in a serverless distributed file system. In: Proceedings of The 22nd International Conference on Distributed Computing Systems, ICDCS'02, pp 617–624

20. Duan Y (2014) Distributed key generation for encrypted deduplication: Achieving the strongest privacy. In: Proceedings of the 6th edition of the ACM Workshop on Cloud Computing Security, CCSW'14, pp 57–68

21. Goldwasser S, Micali S (1984) Probabilistic encryption. J Comput Syst Sci 28(2):270–299

22. Hacigümüs H, Mehrotra S, Iyer BR (2002) Providing database as a service. In: Proceedings of the 18th International Conference on Data Engineering, San Jose, CA, USA, February 26–March 1, 2002, pp 29–38

23. Halevi S, Harnik D, Pinkas B, Shulman-Peleg A (2011) Proofs of ownership in remote storage systems. In: Proceedings of the 18th ACM Conference on Computer and Communications Security, CCS'11, pp 491–500

24. Harnik D, Pinkas B, Shulman-Peleg A (2010) Side channels in cloud services: deduplication in cloud storage. IEEE Secur Priv 8(6):40–47

25. Hur J, Koo D, Shin Y, Kang K (2016) Secure data deduplication with dynamic ownership management in cloud storage. IEEE Trans Knowl Data Eng. doi:10.1109/TKDE.2016.2580139

26. Juels A, Kaliski Jr BS (2007) Pors: proofs of retrievability for large files. In: Proceedings of the 2007 ACM Conference on Computer and Communications Security, CCS 2007, Alexandria, VA, USA, October 28–31, 2007, pp 584–597

27. Li F, Hadjieleftheriou M, Kollios G, Reyzin L (2006) Dynamic authenticated index structures for outsourced databases. In: Proceedings of the ACM SIGMOD International Conference on Management of Data, SIGMOD'06, pp 121–132

28. Li J, Chen X, Huang X, Tang S, Xiang Y, Hassan MM, Alelaiwi A (2015) Secure distributed deduplication systems with improved reliability. IEEE Trans Comput 64(12):3569–3579

29. Li J, Chen X, Li M, Li J, Lee PPC, Lou W (2014) Secure deduplication with efficient and reliable convergent key management. IEEE Trans Parallel Distrib Syst 25(6):1615–1625

30. Li J, Li YK, Chen X, Lee PPC, Lou W (2015) A hybrid cloud approach for secure authorized deduplication. IEEE Trans Parallel Distrib Syst 26(5):1206–1216

31. Li J, Qin C, Lee PP (2016) Rekeying for encrypted deduplication storage. In: Proceedings of the 46th IEEE/IFIP International Conference on Dependable Systems and Networks, DSN'16

32. Li M, Qin C, Li J, Lee PPC (2016) Cdstore: toward reliable, secure, and cost-efficient cloud storage via convergent dispersal. IEEE Internet Comput 20(3):45–53

33. Liu J, Asokan N, Pinkas B (2015) Secure deduplication of encrypted data without additional independent servers. In: Proceedings of the 22nd ACM SIGSAC Conference on Computer and Communications Security, Denver, CO, USA, October 12–16, 2015, pp 874–885

34. Ma D, Deng RH, Pang H, Zhou J (2005) Authenticating query results in data publishing. In: Proceedings of the 7th International Conference on Information and Communications Security, Springer, ICICS'05, pp 376–388

35. Martel CU, Nuckolls G, Devanbu PT, Gertz M, Kwong A, Stubblebine SG (2004) A general model for authenticated data structures. Algorithmica 39(1):21–41

36. Merkle RC (1980) Protocols for public key cryptosystems. In: Proceedings of the 1980 IEEE Symposium on Security and Privacy, S&P'1980, pp 122–134

37. Miao M, Wang J, Ma J (2015) New publicly verifiable databases supporting insertion operation. In: Proceedings of the 18th International Conference on Network-Based Information Systems, NBis'15, pp 640–642

38. Mouratidis K, Sacharidis D, Pang H (2009) Partially materialized digest scheme: an efficient verification method for outsourced databases. VLDB J 18(1):363–381

39. Mulazzani M, Schrittwieser S, Leithner M, Huber M, Weippl ER (2011) Dark clouds on the horizon: Using cloud storage as attack vector and online slack space. In: Proceedings of the 20th USENIX Security Symposium

40. Mykletun E, Narasimha M, Tsudik G (2004a) Authentication and integrity in outsourced databases. In: Proceedings of the Network and Distributed System Security Symposium, NDSS'04, The Internet Society

41. Mykletun E, Narasimha M, Tsudik G (2004b) Signature bouquets: immutability for aggregated/condensed signatures. In: Proceedings of the 9th European Symposium on Research Computer Security, ESORICS'04, Springer, pp 160–176

42. Naor M, Nissim K (2000) Certificate revocation and certificate update. IEEE J Sel Areas Commun 18(4):561–570

43. Narasimha M, Tsudik G (2005) DSAC: integrity for outsourced databases with signature aggregation and chaining. In: Proceedings of the 2005 ACM International Conference on Information and Knowledge Management, CIKM'05, pp 235–236

44. Nguyen L (2005) Accumulators from bilinear pairings and applications. In: Proceedings of The Cryptographers' Track at the RSA Conference, CT-RSA'05, Springer, pp 275–292

45. Nuckolls G (2005) Verified query results from hybrid authentication trees. In: Proceedings of the 19th Annual IFIP WG 11.3 Conference on Data and Applications Security and Privacy, DBSec'05, Springer, pp 84–98

46. Pang H, Jain A, Ramamritham K, Tan K (2005) Verifying completeness of relational query results in data publishing. In: Proceedings of the ACM SIGMOD International Conference on Management of Data, SIGMOD'05, pp 407–418

47. Pang H, Tan K (2004) Authenticating query results in edge computing. In: Proceedings of the 20th International Conference on Data Engineering, ICDE'04, pp 560–571

48. Pang H, Zhang J, Mouratidis K (2009) Scalable verification for outsourced dynamic databases. PVLDB 2(1):802–813

49. Papamanthou C, Tamassia R (2007) Time and space efficient algorithms for two-party authenticated data structures. In: Proceedings of the 9th International Conference on Information and Communications Security, ICICS'07, Springer, pp 1–15

50. Sion R (2005) Query execution assurance for outsourced databases. In: Proceedings of the 31st International Conference on Very Large Data Bases, VLDB'05, pp 601–612

51. Stanek J, Sorniotti A, Androulaki E, Kencl L (2014) A secure data deduplication scheme for cloud storage. In: Proceedings of the 18th International Conference Financial Cryptography and Data Security, FC'14, Springer, pp 99–118

52. Tamassia R, Triandopoulos N (2010) Certification and authentication of data structures. In: Proceedings of the 4th Alberto Mendelzon International Workshop on Foundations of Data Management

53. Tang H, Cui Y, Guan C, Wu J, Weng J, Ren K (2016) Enabling ciphertext deduplication for secure cloud storage and access control. In: Proceedings of the 11th ACM on Asia Conference on Computer and Communications Security, AsiaCCS'16, pp 59–70

54. Turner V, Gantz J, Reinsel D, Minton S (2014) The digital universe of opportunities: rich data and the increasing value of the internet of things. IDC White Paper, April 2014

55. Wang J, Chen X, Huang X, You I, Xiang Y (2015) Verifiable auditing for outsourced database in cloud computing. IEEE Trans Comput 64(11):3293–3303

56. Wang J, Chen X, Li J, Kluczniak K, Kutylowski M (2015) A new secure data deduplication approach supporting user traceability. In: 10th International Conference on Broadband and Wireless Computing, Communication and Applications, BWCCA'15, pp 120–124

57. Xie M, Wang H, Yin J, Meng X (2007) Integrity auditing of outsourced data. In: Proceedings of the 33rd International Conference on Very Large Data Bases, VLDB'07, pp 782–793

58. Xu J, Chang E, Zhou J (2013) Weak leakage-resilient client-side deduplication of encrypted data in cloud storage. In: 8th ACM Symposium on Information, Computer and Communications Security, ASIA CCS '13, pp 195–206

59. Yuan J, Yu S (2013) Flexible and publicly verifiable aggregation query for outsourced databases in cloud. In: IEEE Conference on Communications and Network Security, CNS'13, pp 520–524

60. Zheng Y, Yuan X, Wang X, Jiang J, Wang C, Gui X (2015) Enabling encrypted cloud media center with secure deduplica-tion. In: Proceedings of the 10th ACM Symposium on Information, Computer and Communications Security, ASIA CCS '15, Singapore, April 14–17, 2015, pp 63–72

61. Zhou Y, Feng D, Xia W, Fu M, Huang F, Zhang Y, Li C (2015) Secdep: a user-aware efficient fine-grained secure deduplication scheme with multi-level key management. In: IEEE 31st Symposium on Mass Storage Systems and Technologies, MSST'15, pp 1–14

Formal Modelling of Data Integration Systems Security Policies

Fatimah Akeel[1,2] · Asieh Salehi Fathabadi[1] · Federica Paci[1] · Andrew Gravell[1] ·
Gary Wills[1]

Abstract Data Integration Systems (DIS) are concerned
with integrating data from multiple data sources to resolve
user queries. Typically, organisations providing data
sources specify security policies that impose stringent
requirements on the collection, processing, and disclosure
of personal and sensitive data. If the security policies were
not correctly enforced by the integration component of
DIS, the data is exposed to data leakage threats, e.g.
unauthorised disclosure or secondary use of the data.
SecureDIS is a framework that helps system designers to
mitigate data leakage threats during the early phases of DIS
development. SecureDIS provides designers with a set of
informal guidelines written in natural language to specify
and enforce security policies that capture confidentiality,
privacy, and trust properties. In this paper, we apply a
formal approach to model a DIS with the SecureDIS
security policies and verify the correctness and consistency
of the model. The model can be used as a basis to perform
security policies analysis or automatically generate a Java
code to enforce those policies within DIS.

✉ Fatimah Akeel
  fya1g12@ecs.soton.ac.uk

  Asieh Salehi Fathabadi
  asf08r@ecs.soton.ac.uk

  Federica Paci
  f.m.paci@ecs.soton.ac.uk

  Andrew Gravell
  amg@ecs.soton.ac.uk

  Gary Wills
  gbw@ecs.soton.ac.uk

[1] University of Southampton, Southampton, UK

[2] King Saud University, Riyadh, Saudi Arabia

Keywords Security policy · Event-B · Formal method ·
Privacy · Trust · Confidentiality · RBAC · Trust model ·
Access control · Modelling

1 Introduction

With the advent of cloud computing and big data analysis,
Data Integration Systems (DIS) regained popularity. DIS
retrieve data from multiple sources to resolve consumer
queries [19]. The main architecture of a DIS consists of a
mediator [22] that provides an interface between *data
consumers* and a set of *data sources*. Data consumers place
queries that are resolved by the mediator by integrating
data from different data sources.

Organisations providing data sources specify the
security policies that impose stringent requirements on the
collection, processing, and disclosure of personal and
sensitive data. Integrating and enforcing these policies is
the responsibility of the mediator during the execution of
a query placed by a data consumer. However, if the
mediator does not correctly enforce the security policies,
this can result in serious data leakage and/or privacy
violations leading to significant legal and financial
consequences.

Data leakage can occur in a DIS by violating the *confidentiality* of data provided by data sources. For example,
the queries executed by the mediator expose data to consumers that were not allowed to access that data according
to the security policies of the data sources. Moreover, data
leakage can occur by violating the *privacy* of the data when
a query discloses the data to a consumer that has a purpose
different from the data sources allowed purposes. However,
even when the mediator enforces security policies on the
execution of a query that discloses data only to authorised

consumers and only if the purpose of the query matches the purpose for which the data has been collected, data leakage threats can still materialise in a DIS.

In fact, once the data has been disclosed to data consumers, it is possible that the consumer does not process the data according to the data sources' security policies. The consumer may share the data with unauthorised parties or use the data for fraudulent purposes.

Therefore, to mitigate data leakage threats in DIS, it is important to enforce security policies that not only specify who is entitled to access the data and for which purposes, but also take into account the risks of disclosing this data to data consumers. The risks of consumers not behaving according to a security policy are usually quantified by the degree of *trust* [23] placed into the consumer.

SecureDIS [4] is a novel framework to design DIS resilient to data leakage threats. In order to mitigate data leakage threats, SecureDIS argues that it is very important to enforce security policies that satisfy Confidentiality, Privacy, and Trust (CPT) properties. In particular, SecureDIS helps system designers in considering data leakage threats into the early design phases of DIS by mapping data leakage threats to the different components of a DIS architecture [5] and by providing a set of *informal* guidelines, written in natural language, to implement security policies that mitigate those risks.

In this paper, we provide a *formal* approach to model SecureDIS security policies enforced on the execution of a query. The approach consists of modelling the DIS and the SecureDIS security policies, and verifying the consistency and correctness of the model using Event-B formal method [1] supported by Rodin toolset [2]. The generated model can help designers to analyse the policies or to automatically generate a Java code to enforce the policies within DIS.

The rest of the paper is organised as follows: Section 2 provides an overview on the SecureDIS framework and the requirements to specify and enforce security policies that mitigate data leakage threats. Section 3 explains the modelling of the security policies in Event-B. Section 4 discusses the formal verification of the model. Section 5 reviews the related work, while Section 6 concludes and discusses future research directions.

2 An Overview of the SecureDIS Framework

SecureDIS [4] is a design framework that assists system designers in building DIS resilient to data leakage threats. The framework consists of three main components: (a) a reference architecture of the DIS; (b) a list of data leakage threats mapped to DIS architectural components; and (c) a set of guidelines to mitigate data leakage threats. The components are described as follows:

(a) *The reference architecture* it consists of the following components, as shown in Fig. 1:

1. *Data and data sources* is the core component of the DIS representing the data sources integrated, through their data items, to answer consumers' queries.
2. *The integration approach* is the approach or method used to integrate the data.
3. *The integration location* is the location where the integration process takes place to answer data consumers' queries.
4. *Security policies* combine the security policies from different data sources. It is enforced by the integration location during the execution of the queries.
5. *Data consumers* represent the client side of the system, where data consumers request data by queries and where the results are returned to consumers.

(b) *The data leakage threats* SecureDIS considers different types of data leakage threats, such as inference attacks, unauthorised access, secondary use of information, and non-compliance to policies [5]. Each threat is mapped to one or more of the architectural components of the DIS to understand its consequences and the ways to mitigate it. For example, unauthorised disclosure of sensitive data within the integration location to an entity either inside or outside the DIS is caused by the lack of employing data protection techniques.

(c) *The SecureDIS guidelines* Each component of the DIS architecture is associated with a set of data leakage mitigation guidelines. These guidelines represent the activities proposed to system designers, such as the use of security policies, encryption, and logging. Each guideline covers one or more of the CPT properties and targets one or more data leakage threats. For example, SecureDIS suggests logging and analysing consumers' queries at the data consumers component in order to identify possible secondary use threats.

2.1 SecureDIS Guidelines and Requirements for Security Policies

In this work, we focus on the SecureDIS guidelines related to the specification and enforcement of security policies achieved at the integration location. SecureDIS argues that in order to mitigate data leakage threats, it is crucial for security policies to include the following CPT properties:

Fig. 1 SecureDIS architecture

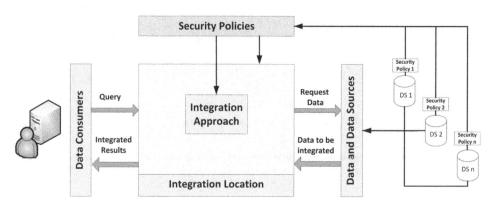

Confidentiality is defined as limiting access to authorised entities [17]. Data leakage threats to confidentiality materialise when the integration location returns data items to a consumer who was not allowed to access those items based on the data sources' security policies. To avoid this threat is important to implement a Role-Based Access Control (RBAC) policy and configure it so that each consumer can access only the pieces of data necessary to answer the query [21].

Privacy is the right of the individual to decide what information about himself/herself should be communicated to others and under what circumstances [27]. Data leakage threats to privacy are caused by: disclosing data for purposes different from the one for which the data has been collected [13], by revealing Personally Identifiable Information (PII) intentionally or unintentionally, or by exposing sensitive information protected by data protection laws and regulations. Therefore, in order to prevent data leakage threats to privacy, the security policy should include the following two dimensions:

– *Purpose* determines the reasons for data to be collected or used. The integration location should only grant the execution of a query if the purpose of the query specified by the data consumer matches one of the purposes for which the data items have been collected [13].
– *Data sensitivity* quantifies who should have access to data items and how much harm would be done if the data was disclosed. In order to protect the disclosure of sensitive data items, a security policy similar to the one of the Bell–LaPadula mandatory access control model [12] should be enforced by the data integration location. The security policy should restrict access to data items returned by a query based on the sensitivity of the data items (represented by a label) and the authorisation (represented by security level) of consumers to access data items of such sensitivity. Therefore, the integration location should only grant the execution of a query if the security level assigned to the data consumer is higher or equal to the sensitivity label assigned to data items returned by that query.

Trust is defined as the belief that an entity will behave in a predictable manner by following a security policy [24]. Therefore, trust is used to quantify the risk of data leakage threats that materialise after the execution of queries is granted to data consumers. Once the data is disclosed to data consumers, they could misuse the data by sharing it with unauthorised parties or use it for purposes other than the data provider's intended purposes. Therefore, the security policy should grant the execution of a query only if the trust level of the data consumer is equal or higher to the one specified by the data sources' security policies.

The guidelines above are transformed into specific system requirements shown in Table 1, where the property column indicates the CPT property covered by the requirement. These requirements are used to model the security policies of the DIS.

3 Formal Modelling of Security Policies in Event-B

This section starts by introducing the Event-B formal method, followed by the process of modelling SecureDIS security policies in Event-B.

3.1 Overview of the Event-B Formal Method

Formal methods have been widely used to specify systems rigorously and to ensure the specification is correct and consistent. In the area of computer security, formal methods provide a structured approach for modelling systems using mathematical notations [7] that capture the security policies, system properties, and underlying assumptions. We propose using the Event-B formalism to capture security policies of DIS.

Event-B is a formal method extended from B-Method [1]. It is a state-based method that uses set theory as a main distinctive attribute [6] to model systems for specification and verification purposes. A system can be modelled gradually to reflect its complexity by the use of abstraction

Table 1 System requirements details

Req. no.	System requirement	Property	Type
1	Each data consumer must be assigned to a role to access data sources items	C	Specification
2	Each data source specifies which roles are allowed to access the sources data items	C	Specification
3	A data consumer is granted access to data items returned by a query if the assigned role is an allowed role	C	Enforcement
4	Each data consumer specifies a purpose to access data items	P	Specification
5	Each data item is associated with a purpose for which it was collected	P	Specification
6	A data consumer is granted access to data items returned by a query, if the purpose of the query matches the purpose for which the data items were collected	P	Enforcement
7	Each data item is classified based on its sensitivity	P	Specification
8	Each data consumer is assigned to a security level that specifies the authorisation to access data of a certain sensitivity	P	Enforcement
9	A data consumer is granted access to data items returned by a query, if the security level of the consumer is equal to the sensitivity level of the data items	P	Enforcement
10	Each data consumer is assigned to a trust level	T	Specification
11	Data sources determine the acceptable data consumers trust levels	T	Specification
12	A data consumer is granted access to data items returned by a query, if the trust level of the consumer matches the accepted trust level of data items	T	Enforcement

and refinement techniques. Event-B uses mathematical proofs to ensure the correctness of each level and the consistency between refinement levels [6].

An Event-B model consists of two main components: CONTEXT and MACHINE. The CONTEXT includes the static part of the model that defines SETS, CONSTANTS, and AXIOMS to add constraints on the sets. The MACHINE contains the dynamic part of the model that includes VARIABLES, INVARIANTS, and EVENTS. The VARIABLES specify the states of the system and can be modified by guarded EVENTS. The INVARIANTS specify the constraints on variables, which need to be proved true at any state of the system. The verification of the model demonstrates consistency by ensuring the correctness among all refinements.

The integrated toolsets used to model Event-B is Rodin [2]. The verification process achieved by Rodin includes: (1) model checking: by ProB [20] model checker integrated in Rodin and (2) theorem proving: by generating and proving proof obligations.

3.2 Modelling Security Policies

The security policies modelled in this case study are derived from the aforementioned system requirements in Table 1 that are focused on CPT properties. A security policy consists of the following basic components: a subject, permission(s), and an object [8], and targets a specific property.

The security policies that satisfy the requirements in Table 1 are modelled through Event-B refinements. Three levels of refinements are proposed (see Fig. 2), where each level is represented by a CONTEXT, namely C0, C1, and C2:

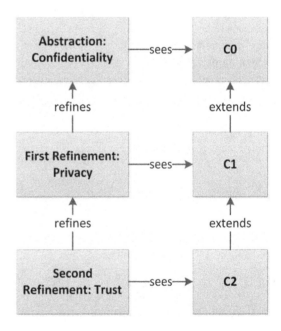

Fig. 2 Security policy refinements

1. *System abstraction* it captures the process of data consumers querying the data provided by different data sources in addition to the security policy that grants the execution of the query. The policy grants the execution only if the consumer is assigned to a specific role that provides the permission to execute the query.
2. *The first refinement* it extends the security policy with the purpose for which data items can be accessed in addition to the data sensitivity.
3. *The second refinement* it extends the security policy with the trust levels that data sources should place into data consumers for granting them the query execution.

3.2.1 System Abstraction: Modelling Confidentiality

The first step is to model the data consumer queries to different data sources and the RBAC policy governing query execution granted to consumers. The system abstraction includes four main sets: *DATA_CONSUMER*, the set of data consumers; *CONSUMER_ROLE*, the set of roles assigned to consumers; *DATA_ITEM*, the set of data items associated with data sources and also returned by queries; and *DATA_SOURCE*, the set of data sources providing the data items to answer data consumers queries.

The system abstraction also includes the main VARI-ABLES and EVENTS to capture the DIS environment, see Fig. 3. The events are summarised as follows:

– **AddDataSources** to add data sources to the model.
– **AddDataItemsToSources** to create data items and associate them to data sources.
– **AddDataConsumers** to add data consumers to the model.
– **AddRoles** to add consumers's roles to the model.
– **AssignRolesToConsumers** to assign consumer roles to data consumers.
– **AddConsumersQueries** to create consumer queries containing data items.

The variable *belong_to* is defined to associate data items with their data sources, where multiple data items belong to multiple data sources. The invariant that ensures this relation is defined as follows:

inv1 : $belong\_to \in \mathbb{P}1(DATA\_ITEM) \leftrightarrow sources$

Data consumers can access the data items coming from data sources by creating a *query*. The variable *query* is defined as the relationship between consumers and data items. The following invariant shows that multiple consumers can query multiple data items:

inv2 : $query \in consumers \leftrightarrow \mathbb{P}1(DATA\_ITEM)$

However, the *query* has one main restriction that is when a consumer (*c*) requests a set of data items (*items*), these items need to belong to existing data sources (*s*). This restriction is enforced by the following invariant:

inv3 : $\forall c, items.c \mapsto items \in query$
$$\Rightarrow (\exists s.belong\_to\big[\{items\}\big] = s)$$

The *query* is created in the **AddConsumersQueries** event shown below. The event contains a list of parameters (ANY), a collection of guards (WHERE), and collection of actions (THEN). An event can execute its action(s) only when its guard(s) are true. In this case, the event needs to essentially check whether data items map to sources in **grd4** to satisfy **inv3**.

Event *AddConsumersQueries*
ANY
consumer, data_items, source
WHERE
grd1 : *consumer* $\in$ *consumers*
grd2 : $(data\_items \in \mathbb{P}1(DATA\_ITEM))\wedge$ $(data\_items \neq \emptyset)$
grd3 : $(source \in sources)$
grd4 : $data\_items \mapsto source \in belong\_to$
THEN
act1 : $query := query \cup$ $\{consumer \mapsto data\_items\}$
END

To specify the security policy that captures the confidentiality property, we model the following components:

– The *assigned* invariant to denote that a data consumer can be assigned to more than one role, which fulfils sys. req. 1, and that a role can be assigned to one or more consumers, as follows:

inv4 : $assigned \in consumers \leftrightarrow roles$

– The *allowed* invariant to indicate the roles allowed to access the data items. Also, *allowed* ensures that data items are actually coming from existing data sources (sys. req. 2). Both these aspects are modelled as follows:

inv5 : $allowed \in roles \leftrightarrow \mathbb{P}1(DATA\_ITEM)$
inv6 : $\forall role, items.role \mapsto items \in allowed \Rightarrow$ $(\exists source.items \mapsto source \in belong\_to)$

– The event **AddAuthorisation** to add the RBAC policy to the system by updating the variable *allowed*. To add

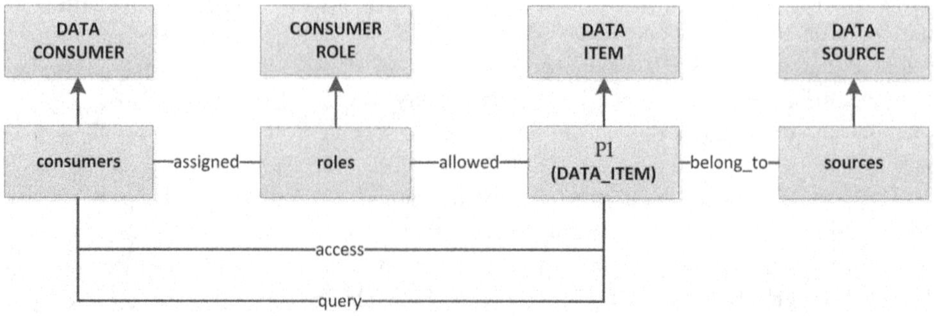

Fig. 3 System abstraction: modelling data query and confidentiality

the pair of a data item (i) and a role (r) to the *allowed* access control list, the guard **grd3** checks whether the data item is associated with existing data sources, as follows:

Event *AddAuthorisation*
    ANY
       r, i, s
    WHERE
       grd1 : $i \in \mathbb{P}1(DATA\_ITEM)$
       grd2 : $(s \in sources) \wedge (sources \neq \emptyset)$
       grd3 : $i \mapsto s \in belong\_to$
       grd4 : $(r \in roles) \wedge (roles \notin \emptyset)$
       grd5 : $r \mapsto i \notin allowed$
    THEN
       act1 : $allowed := allowed \cup \{r \mapsto i\}$
    END

To model the enforcement of the security policy specified earlier, we include the following:

– **inv7** to model the actual access of consumers to data items and **inv8** to ensure the accessed items are returned by a query:

inv7 : $access \in consumers \leftrightarrow \mathbb{P}1(DATA\_ITEM)$

inv8 : $\forall c, items.c \mapsto items \in access$
       $\Rightarrow (c \mapsto items \in query)$

– The ***AccessData*** event checks whether the consumer is assigned to a role (**grd3**), and the assigned role is entitled to execute the query (**grd4**), to fulfil sys. req. 3. It also ensures the data items accessed by the consumer are returned as result of a query by the same consumer (**grd2**). The event is modelled as follows:

Event *AccessData*
    ANY
  $consumer, data\_items,$
    $consumer\_roles$
    WHERE
      grd1 : $consumer \in consumers$
      grd2 : $data\_items \in query[\{consumer\}]$
      grd3 : $(consumer\_roles \subseteq roles) \wedge$
      $(assigned[\{consumer\}] = consumer\_roles)$
      grd4 : $\exists role.(roles \in consumer\_roles) \wedge$
      $(role \mapsto data\_items \in allowed)$
      grd5 : $(consumer \mapsto data\_items) \notin access$
    THEN
      act1 : $access := access \cup \{consumer \mapsto data\_items\}$
    END

3.2.2 First Refinement: Modelling Privacy

The system abstraction in Sect. 3.2.1 models who can have access to the data items returned by a query. This refinement extends the previous level by adding the purpose and data sensitivity privacy dimensions to the security policy as discussed in Sect. 2.1.

To model the *purpose*, we have introduced the following components:

– A set *DATA_USE_PURPOSE* is defined in the context (C1) to include the possible data use purposes assigned to data consumers or data items:

axm1 : $partition(DATA\_USE\_PURPOSE, \{research\},$
      $\{commercial\}, \{personal\}, \{public\})$

– The variable *item_purpose* is defined to represent the relationship between the $\mathbb{P}1$ (*DATA_ITEM*) and *DATA_USE_PURPOSE*:

inv9 : $item\_purpose \in \mathbb{P}1(DATA\_ITEM)$
      $\leftrightarrow DATA\_USE\_PURPOSE$

– The variable *query_purpose* is defined to represent the relationship between the *consumers* and *DATA_USE_ PURPOSE*:

inv10 : $query\_purpose \in consumers$
      $\rightarrow DATA\_USE\_PURPOSE$

– A new event, ***AddItemsPurposes***, to assign several purposes to data items (sys. req. 5). The guards and actions of the event ***AddItemsPurposes*** are as follows:

grd1 : $purpose \in DATA\_USE\_PURPOSE$

grd2 : $i \in \mathbb{P}1(DATA\_ITEM)$

act1 : $item\_purpose := item\_purpose \cup \{i \mapsto purpose\}$

– The event ***AddConsumersQueries*** is refined to assign a purpose to each consumer request to query the system (sys. req. 4) by adding the following:

grd1 : $purpose \in DATA\_USE\_PURPOSE$

grd2 : $c \in consumers$

act1 : $query\_purpose := query\_purpose \cup \{c \mapsto purpose\}$

To model the *data classification*, we include the following:

• A set named *CLASSIFICATION* is defined in the context(C1) to contain the possible levels that can be assigned to data items and data consumers. The set includes the following labels:

- *Regulated* data items that are protected by data protection regulations. For example, the items that contain the PII, such as names, SSN, and credit card numbers. If these items were disclosed, harm is caused to the reputation of the data sources and may lead to financial losses.
- *Confidential* data items that include sensitive information that when disclosed, it can result in a medium level of harm and financial losses.
- *Public* data items that can be disclosed to the general public that when disclosed, it results in a low risk to privacy and reputation.

  axm2 : $partition(CLASSIFICATION, \{Regulated\},$
  $\{Confidential\}, \{Public\})$

- A variable *classified* is defined to link each data item with a *CLASSIFICATION* (sys. req. 7) as follows:

  inv11 : $classified \in \mathbb{P}1(DATA\_ITEM)$
  $\twoheadrightarrow CLASSIFICATION$

- The event ***AddDataItemsToSource*** is refined to classify each data item by updating the variable *classified* as follows:

  grd1 : $i \in \mathbb{P}1(DATA\_ITEM)$
  grd2 : $j \in CLASSIFICATION$
  grd3 : $i \notin dom(classified)$
  act1 : $classified := classified \cup \{i \mapsto j\}$

- A variable *security_clearance* to associate a consumer with the security clearance. It is defined as follows:

  inv12 : $security\_clearance \in consumers$
  $\rightarrow CLASSIFICATION$

- The event ***AddDataConsumers*** is refined to assign each new data consumer an appropriate security clearance (sys. req. 8):

  grd1 : $sc \in CLASSIFICATION$
  grd2 : $c \in consumers$
  grd3 : $c \mapsto sc \notin security\_clearance$
  act1 : $security\_clearance :$
  $= security\_clearance \cup \{c \mapsto sc\}$

To enforce the extended security policy, we refined the *AccessData* event by including the following guards:

- A guard to enforce accessing data when the data consumer's purpose, during query creation, matches one of the data item purposes (sys. req. 6):

  grd6 : $item\_purpose[\{data\_items\}]$
  $= query\_purpose[\{consumer\}]$

- A guard to ensure that the classification of the data items requested for access matches the consumer's security clearance (sys. req. 9):

  grd7 : $security\_clearance[\{consumer\}]$
  $= classified[\{data\_items\}]$

3.2.3 Second Refinement: Modelling Trust

The second refinement extends the first to capture the trust property. Trust is introduced into the security policy to minimise threats that are related to secondary disclosure of information caused by data consumers abuse of privileges. Therefore, in this refinement we introduce the trust model proposed in [3]. This trust model labels an entity with any of the following levels: very good, good, neutral, bad, and very bad, based on calculations conducted on that entity to assess its risks. This trust model is included in the second refinement by adding the following components:

- A set *TRUST_LEVEL* containing all possible trust levels in the trust model:

  axm3 : $partition(TRUST\_LEVEL, \{very\_good\},$
  $\{good\}, \{neutral\}, \{bad\}, \{very\_bad\})$

- A variable *consumer_tlevel* to associate each data consumer with its trust level:

  inv13 :
  $consumer\_tlevel \in consumers \rightarrow TRUST\_LEVEL$

- A variable *item_tlevel* to associate data items with their acceptable trust levels:

  inv14 :
  $item\_tlevel \in \mathbb{P}1(DATA\_ITEM) \leftrightarrow TRUST\_LEVEL$

- The event ***AddConsumers*** is refined to associate a data consumer with its trust level during the addition of the consumer to the system (sys. req. 10):

  grd5 : $c \in consumers$
  grd6 : $t \in TRUST\_LEVEL$
  act3 : $consumer\_tlevel = consumer\_tlevel \cup \{c \mapsto t\}$

- The event ***AddDataItemsToSources*** is refined to associate data items with acceptable trust levels (sys. 487 req. 11):

grd5 : $i \in \mathbb{P}1(DATA\_ITEM)$

grd6 : $t \in TRUST\_LEVEL$

act3 : $item\_tlevel = item\_tlevel \cup \{i \mapsto t\}$

To enforce the security policy related to the trust property, we refined the **AccessData** event to check whether the consumer's trust level matches the expected trust level associated with the data items returned by a query (sys. req. 12). The following guard is included:

grd8 : $item\_tlevel[\{data\_items\}]$
$\qquad = consumer\_tlevel[\{consumer\}]$

4 Formal Verification of the Model

The Rodin toolset provides an environment for both modelling and proving by theorem proving and model checking. In addition to formal modelling, we also prove that the proposed Event-B model is correct and consistent. Table 2 presents an overview of the proof efforts provided by Rodin. These statistics measure the proof obligations (PO) generated and discharged by the Rodin prover and the POs that are interactively proved. The complete development of the DIS security policies results in 38 POs, in which (100 %) are proved automatically by Rodin. The number of POs in the system abstraction that captures the confidentiality property is larger than other refinements. This is due to establishing the main components of the security policies (the subject, the permission(s), and the object), and therefore many invariants are introduced in that layer to guarantee the correctness of these components.

4.1 Theorem Proving

There are different POs generated by Rodin during the development of a system [14]. As an example of a PO, we demonstrate an "Invariant Preservation" PO here. The INV PO ensures that each invariant is preserved by each event. To prove that inv 6 , below, is preserved by *AddAuthorisation* event, "AddAuthorisation/inv6/INV" PO is generated and proved by Rodin.

inv6 : $\forall role, items.role \mapsto items \in allowed \Rightarrow$
$\qquad (\exists source.items \mapsto source \in belong\_to)$

Table 2 The statistics of the model

Element name	Total	Auto	Manual
Model	38	38	0
Confidentiality	25	25	0
Privacy	9	9	0
Trust	4	4	0

To prove this PO, guard **grd3** below is added to the *AddAuthorisation* event to ensure that each role is linked to a data item that actually belongs to a data source.

grd3 : $i \mapsto s \in belong\_to$

4.2 Model Checking

ProB is an animator and model checker for Event-B. ProB allows fully automatic exploration of Event-B models and can be used to systematically check a specification for a range of errors. We analysed our model using ProB to ensure that the model is deadlock free. For each new event added in the refinements, we have verified that it would not introduce a deadlock using ProB.

5 Related Work

The work presented in this paper is related to two main areas of research: security and privacy engineering and formal analysis of security policies.

5.1 Security and Privacy Engineering

This area of research focuses on considering security and privacy threats in the early phases of the software development lifecycle. Two of the popular techniques that help system designers in identifying security and privacy threats are Microsoft's STRIDE [25] and LINDDUN [9]. STRIDE provides a taxonomy of the type of threats. It is the acronym of: Spoofing, Tampering, Repudiation, Information Disclosure, Denial of Service, and Elevation of Privilege. Each of these categories of threats negates a security property, namely confidentiality, integrity, availability, authentication, authorisation, and non-repudiation. STRIDE guides the system designers on the identification of security threats through a systematic process. First, a model of the system is created and the system components are mapped to the six threat categories. Then, a catalogue of threat tree patterns is used to identify specific instances of threat categories, where the level of risk of each threat is determined. Finally, the risk of the threat is reduced or eliminated by introducing proper countermeasures and defences.

LINDDUN follows a process similar to STRIDE to help system designers in identifying privacy rather than security threats. Similar to STRIDE, LINDDUN provides a taxonomy of privacy threats that violate specific privacy properties. It includes an extensive catalogue of specific threats. For each category of threats, a list of privacy-enhancing technologies that mitigate privacy threats are provided.

Similar to STRIDE and LINDDUN, SecureDIS framework aims to help designer in identifying threats early in the software development lifecycle. However, SecureDIS focuses only on a specific category of threats, namely data leakage threats, and a specific type of systems, namely DIS.

5.2 Formal Analysis of Security Policies

This area of research focuses on automated methods and tools to detect and correct errors in policy specifications before they are deployed. Several approaches have been proposed to analyse security policies, which mainly differ in the formalism and tools used to model and analyse the policies. These approaches pursue different techniques, ranging from SMT formulae to Multi-Terminal Binary Decision Diagrams (MTBDD) and different kinds of logics.

Margrave [11] uses MTBDDs as the underlying representation of XACML policies. It supports two main types of policy analysis: policy querying, which analyses access requests evaluated to a certain decision, and change-impact analysis, which is used to compare policies. However, BDD-based approaches allow the analysis of policies only against a limited range of properties.

Alternative approaches encode policies and properties as propositional formulas and analyse them using SAT solvers [16]. However, SAT solvers cannot handle Boolean variables and therefore are limited in the type of access control policies that can be modelled and analysed.

Other formalisms have also been used for the analysis of access control policies. Description logic (DL) [18] is used to formalise access control policies and employs off-the-shelf DL reasoners for policy analysis. The use of DL reasoners allows modelling more expressive access control policies, but it suffers from scalability issues.

Answer Set Programming (ASP) [10] has also being used to model and analyse access control policies, but it also has some limitations. ASP does not support quantifiers and does not easily allow the expression of constraints, such as Linear Arithmetic.

More recent approaches to policy analysis are based on SMT [26]. The use of SMT does not only enable wider coverage of access control policies compared to the analysis tools mentioned above but also improves the performance.

Similar to our work, other works have applied Event-B to model and analyse access control policies [6, 15]. One of the main advantages of using Event-B to model and analyse security policies is that it is possible to model not only the access control policies but also the system where the policies are going to be deployed. Another advantage is the expressiveness of the Event-B formalism that allows modelling fine-grained policies. Last, but not least, the

Rodin tool that supports the Event-B formalism allows Java code generation from the formal model of the system and its policies.

6 Conclusion and Future Work

SecureDIS is a framework that helps system designers to mitigate data leakage threats during the early phases of the DIS development. SecureDIS provides designers with a set of *informal* guidelines written in natural language to specify and enforce security policies that capture Confidentiality, Privacy, and Trust (CPT) properties.

In this paper, we applied a *formal* approach to model the SecureDIS system and its security policies and verify the correctness and consistency of the model. We used Event-B formal method to formalise the requirements on the specific policy elements that satisfy the CPT properties. These elements were gradually built throughout the model by utilising Event-B abstraction and refinements.

Modelling security policies that capture the SecureDIS main properties is useful to demonstrate how access to data can be controlled by several conditions, as explained in Sect. 3: the allowed role specified as invariant 5 and 6, the allowed purpose specified as guard 6 of the AccessData Event, and the allowed trust level specified as guard 7 of the AccessData Event. This helps in mitigating the threats of data leakage by minimising data exposure due to the incorrect specification of the security policies, such as unauthorised access, non-compliance to security policy, and the misuse of data by authorised consumers.

We are planning to extend this work in several directions. A first direction is to model an instance of a real DIS along with its security policies and check the correctness of those policies before deployment. Another direction is to use the correct model of the security policies to automatically generate the code for their enforcement using the Rodin tool.

Acknowledgments The work reported in this paper is funded by King Saud University, Riyadh, Saudi Arabia.

References

1. Abrial JR (2010) Modeling in Event-B: system and software engineering. Cambridge University Press, Cambridge
2. Abrial JR, Butler M, Hallerstede S, Voisin L (2006) An open extensible tool environment for Event-B. Formal methods and software engineering. Lect Notes Comput Sci 4260:588–605
3. Agudo I, Fernandez-Gago C, Lopez J (2010) A scale based trust model for multi-context environments. Comput Math Appl 60(2):209–216
4. Akeel F, Wills G, Gravell A (2013) SecureDIS: a framework for secure data integration systems. In: The 8th international conference for internet technology and secured transactions, pp 588–593

5. Akeel FY, Wills GB, Gravell AM (2014) Exposing data leakage in Data Integration Systems. In: 9th International conference for internet technology and secured transactions, ICITST 2014, pp 420–425

6. Butler M (2013) Mastering system analysis and design through abstraction and refinement. In: Broy M, Peled D, Kalus G (eds) Engineering dependable software systems. IOS Press, pp 49–78

7. Butler MJ, Leuschel M, Presti SL, Turner P (2004) The use of formal methods in the analysis of trust (position paper). Trust Manag Lect Notes Comput Sci 2995:333–339

8. Crampton J, Huth M (2010) Towards an access-control framework for countering insider threats. Adv Inf Secur 49:173–195

9. Deng M, Wuyts K, Scandariato R, Preneel B, Joosen W (2011) A privacy threat analysis framework: supporting the elicitation and fulfillment of privacy requirements. Requir Eng 16(1):3–32

10. Ramli CDPK, Nielson HR, Nielson F (2013) XACML 3.0 in Answer Set Programming. In: Logic-based program synthesis and transformation. Springer, Berlin, pp 89–105

11. Fisler K, Krishnamurthi S, Meyerovich LA, Tschantz MC (2005) Verification and change-impact analysis of access-control policies. In: Proceedings of the 27th international conference on software engineering, pp 196–205

12. Gollmann D (1999) Computer security. Wiley, New York

13. Guarda P, Zannone N (2009) Towards the development of privacy-aware systems. Inf Softw Technol 51(2):337–350

14. Hallerstede S (2011) On the purpose of Event-B proof obligations. Form Asp Comput 23(1):133–150

15. Hoang TS, Basin D, Abrial JR (2009) Specifying access control in Event-B. Technical report, vol 624

16. Hughes G, Bultan T (2008) Automated verification of access control policies using a SAT solver. Int J Softw Tools Technol Transf 10(6):503–520

17. ISO: ISO/IEC27000 (2014) Information technology: security techniques: information security management systems: overview and vocabulary

18. Kolovski V, Hendler J, Parsia B (2007) Analyzing web access control policies. In: Proceedings of the 16th international conference on World Wide Web—WWW '07, p 677

19. Lenzerini M (2002) Data integration: a theoretical perspective. In: Proceedings of the 21st ACM SIGMOD-SIGACT-SIGART symposium on principles of database systems. Madison, Wisconsin, USA, pp 233–246

20. Leuschel M, Butler M (2003) The ProB animator and model checker for B - A tool description. Int Symp Form Methods Eur 2805:855–874

21. McCallister E, Grance T, Scarfone K (2010) Guide to protect the confidentiality of personal identifiable information (PII). NIST Special Publication (800-122), p 59

22. Nachouki G, Quafafou M (2011) MashUp web data sources and services based on semantic queries. Inf Syst 36(2):151–173

23. Paci F, Fernandez-Gago C, Moyano F (2013) Detecting insider threats: a trust-aware framework. In: 2013 Eighth international conference on availability, reliability and security (ARES), pp 121–130

24. Ross R, Oren JC, Mcevilley M (2014) Systems security engineering an integrated approach to building trustworthy resilient systems. NIST Special Publication (800-160), p 121

25. Torr P (2005) Demystifying the threat modeling process. IEEE Secur Priv 3(5):66–70

26. Turkmen F, Den Hartog J, Ranise S, Zannone N (2015) Analysis of XACML policies with SMT. Lecture notes in computer science (including subseries lecture notes in artificial intelligence and lecture notes in bioinformatics), vol 9036, pp 115–134

27. Westin A (1970) Privacy and freedom. Bodley Head, London

Efficient Breadth-First Search on Massively Parallel and Distributed-Memory Machines

Koji Ueno[1] · Toyotaro Suzumura[2] · Naoya Maruyama[3] ·
Katsuki Fujisawa[4] · Satoshi Matsuoka[5]

Abstract There are many large-scale graphs in real world such as Web graphs and social graphs. The interest in large-scale graph analysis is growing in recent years. Breadth-First Search (BFS) is one of the most fundamental graph algorithms used as a component of many graph algorithms. Our new method for distributed parallel BFS can compute BFS for one trillion vertices graph within half a second, using large supercomputers such as the K-Computer. By the use of our proposed algorithm, the K-Computer was ranked 1st in Graph500 using all the 82,944 nodes available on June and November 2015 and June 2016 38,621.4 GTEPS. Based on the hybrid BFS algorithm by Beamer (Proceedings of the 2013 IEEE 27th International Symposium on Parallel and Distributed Processing Workshops and PhD Forum, IPDPSW '13, IEEE Computer Society, Washington, 2013), we devise sets of optimizations for scaling to extreme number of nodes, including a new efficient graph data structure and several optimization techniques such as vertex reordering and load balancing. Our performance evaluation on K-Computer shows that our new BFS is 3.19 times faster on 30,720 nodes than the base version using the previously known best techniques.

Keywords Distributed-memory · Breadth-First Search · Graph500

1 Introduction

Graphs have quickly become one of the most important data structures in modern IT, such as in social media where the massive number of users is modeled as vertices and their social connections as edges, and collectively analyzed to implement various advanced services. Another example is to model biophysical structures and phenomena, such as brain's synaptic connections, or interaction network between proteins and enzymes, thereby being able to diagnose diseases in the future. The common properties among such modern applications of graphs are their massive size and complexity, reaching up to billions of edges and trillions of vertices, resulting in not only tremendous storage requirements but also compute power to conduct their analysis.

With such high interest in analytics of large graphs, a new benchmark called the Graph500 [8, 11] was proposed in 2010. Since the predominant use of supercomputers had been for numerical computing, most of the HPC benchmarks such as the Top500 Linpack had been compute centric. The Graph500 benchmark instead measures the data analytics performance of supercomputers, in particular those for graphs, with the metric called traversed edges per second or TEPS. More specifically, the benchmark measures the performance of Breadth-First Search (BFS), which is utilized as a kernel for important and more complex algorithms such as connected components analysis and centrality analysis. Also, the target graph used in the benchmark is a scale-free, small-diameter graph called the Kronecker graph, which is known to model realistic

✉ Koji Ueno
  kojiueno5@gmail.com

[1] Tokyo Institute of Technology, Tokyo, Japan

[2] IBM T.J. Watson Research Center, Westchester County, NY, USA

[3] RIKEN, Kobe, Japan

[4] Kyushu University, Fukuoka, Japan

[5] Tokyo Institute of Technology/AIST, Tokyo, Japan

graphs arising out of practical applications, such as Web and social networks, as well as those that arise from life science applications. As such, attaining high performance on the Graph500 represents the important abilities of a machine to process real-life, large-scale graphs arising from big-data applications.

We have conducted a series of work [11–13] to accelerate BFS in a distributed-memory environment. Our new work extends the data structures and algorithm called hybrid BFS [2] that is known to be effective small-diameter graphs, so that it scales to top-tier supercomputers with tens of thousands of nodes with million-scale CPU cores with multi-gigabyte/s interconnect. In particular, we apply our algorithm to the Riken's K-Computer [15] with 82,944 compute nodes and 663,552 CPU cores, once the fastest supercomputer in the world on the Top500 in 2011 with over 10 Petaflops. The result obtained is currently No. 1 on the Graph500 for two consecutive editions in 2016, with significant TEPS performance advantage compared to the result obtained on the Sequoia supercomputer hosted by Lawrence Livermore National Laboratory in the USA, which is a machine with twice the size and performance compared to the K-Computer, with over 20 Petaflops and embodying approximately 1.6 million cores. This demonstrates that top supercomputers compete for the top ranks on the Graph500, but the Top500 ranking does not necessarily directly translate in this regard; rather architectural properties other than the amount of FPUs, as well as algorithmic advances, play a major role in attaining top performance, indicating the importance of codesign of future top-level machines including those for exascale, with graph-centric applications in mind .

In fact, the top ranks of the Graph500 has been historically dominated by large-scale supercomputers to date, with other competing infrastructures such as Clouds being notably missing; performance measurements of the various work including ours reveal that this is fundamental, in that interconnect performance plays a significant role in the overall performance of large-scale BFS, and this is one of the biggest differentiators between supercomputers and Clouds.

2 Background: Hybrid BFS

2.1 The Base Hybrid BFS Algorithm

We first describe the background BFS algorithms, including hybrid algorithm as proposed in [2]. Figure 1 shows the standard sequential textbook BFS algorithm. Starting from the source vertex, the algorithm conducts the search by effectively expanding the *"frontier"* set of vertices in a

```
 1: function BREADTH-FIRST-SEARCH(vertices, source)
 2:     frontier ← {source}
 3:     next ← {}
 4:     parents ← [−1, −1, · · · , −1]
 5:     while frontier ≠ {} do
 6:         top-down-step (vertices, frontier, next, parents)
 7:         frontier ← next
 8:         next ← {}
 9:     end while
10:     return parents
11: end function
12: function TOP-DOWN-STEP(vertices, frontier, next, parents)
13:     for v ∈ frontier do
14:         for n ∈ neighbors[v] do
15:             if parents[n] = -1 then
16:                 parents[n] ← v
17:                 next ← next ∪ {n}
18:             end if
19:         end for
20:     end for
21: end function
```

Fig. 1 Top-down BFS

breadth-first manner from the root. We refer to this search direction as *"top-down."*

A contrasting approach is *"bottom-up"* BFS as shown in Fig. 2. This approach is to start from the vertices that have not been visited and iterate with each step investigating whether a frontier node is included in its direct neighbor. If it is, then the node is added to the frontier of visited nodes for the next iteration. In general, this *"bottom-up"* approach is more advantageous over top-down when the frontier is large, as it will quickly identify and mark many nodes as visited. On the other hand, top-down is advantageous when the frontier is small, as bottom-up will result in wasteful scanning of many unvisited vertices and their edges without much benefit.

For a large but small-diameter graphs such as the Kronecker graph used in the Graph500, the *hybrid BFS algorithm* [2] (Fig. 3) that heuristically minimizes the number of edges to be scanned by switching between top-down and bottom-up, has been identified as very effective in significantly increasing the performance of BFS.

```
 1: function BOTTOM-UP-STEP(vertices, frontier, next, parents)
 2:     for v ∈ vertices do
 3:         if parents[v] = -1 then
 4:             for n ∈ neighbors[v] do
 5:                 if n ∈ frontier then
 6:                     parents[v] ← n
 7:                     next ← next ∪ {v}
 8:                     break
 9:                 end if
10:             end for
11:         end if
12:     end for
13: end function
```

Fig. 2 A step in bottom-up BFS

```
1: function HYBRID-BFS(vertices, source)
2:     frontier ← {source}
3:     next ← {}
4:     parents ← [-1,-1,···,-1]
5:     while frontier ≠ {} do
6:         if next-direction() = top-down then
7:             top-down-step (vertices, frontier, next, parents)
8:         else
9:             bottom-up-step (vertices, frontier, next, parents)
10:        end if
11:        frontier ← next
12:        next ← {}
13:    end while
14:    return parents
15: end function
```

Fig. 3 Hybrid BFS

2.2 Parallel and Distributed BFS Algorithm

In order to parallelize the BFS algorithm over distributed-memory machines, it is necessary to spatially partition the graphs. A proposal by Beamer et. al. [3] conducts 2-D partitioning of the adjacency matrix of the graph in two dimensions, as shown in Fig. 4, where adjacency matrix A is partitioned into $R \times C$ submatrices.

Each of the submatrices is assigned to a compute node; the compute nodes themselves are virtually arranged into a $R \times C$ mesh, being assigned a 2-D index $P(i, j)$. Figures 5 and 6 illustrate the top-down and bottom-up parallel-distributed algorithms with such a partitioning scheme. In the figures, $P(\,:\,, j)$ means all the processors in j-th column of 2-D processor mesh, and $P(i,\,:\,)$ means all the processors in i-th row of 2-D processor mesh. Line 8 of Fig. 5 performs the allgatherv communication operation among all the processors in j-th column, and line 15 performs the alltoallv communication operation among all the processors in i-th row.

In Figs. 5 and 6, f, n, and π correspond to frontier, next, and parent in the base sequential algorithms, respectively. Allgatherv() and alltoallv() are standard MPI collectives. Beamer [3]'s proposal encodes f, c, n, w as 1 bit per vertex for optimization. Parallel-distributed hybrid BFS is similar to the sequential algorithm in Fig. 4, heuristically switching between top-down and bottom-up per each iteration step, being essentially a hybrid of algorithms in Figs. 5 and 6.

In parallel 2-D bottom-up BFS algorithm in Fig. 6, each search step is broken down into C substeps assuming that

$$A = \begin{pmatrix} A_{1,1} & \cdots & A_{1,C} \\ \vdots & \ddots & \vdots \\ A_{R,1} & \cdots & A_{R,C} \end{pmatrix}$$

Fig. 4 $R \times C$ partitioning of adjacency matrix A

```
1: function PARALLEL-2D-TOP-DOWN(A, source)
2:     f ← {source}
3:     n ← {}
4:     π ← [-1, -1, ···, -1]
5:     for all compute nodes P(i, j) in parallel do
6:         while f ≠ {} do
7:             transpose-vector(f_{i,j})
8:             f_i = allgatherv(f_{i,j}, P(:, j))
9:             t_{i,j} ← {}
10:            for u ∈ f_i do
11:                for v ∈ A_{i,j}(:, u) do
12:                    t_{i,j} ← t_{i,j} ∪ {(u, v)}
13:                end for
14:            end for
15:            w_{i,j} ← alltoallv(t_{i,j}, P(i, :))
16:            for (u, v) ∈ w_{i,j} do
17:                if π_{i,j}(v) = -1 then
18:                    π_{i,j}(v) ← u
19:                    n_{i,j} ← n_{i,j} ∪ v
20:                end if
21:            end for
22:            f ← n
23:            n ← {}
24:        end while
25:    end for
26:    return π
27: end function
```

Fig. 5 Parallel-distributed 2-D top-down algorithm

an adjacency matrix is partitioned into $R \times C$ submatrices in a two-dimensional, and during each substep, a given vertex's edges will be examined by only one processor. During each substep, a processor processes $1/C$ of the assigned vertices in the processor row. After each substep, it passes on the responsibility for those vertices to the processor to its right and accepts new vertices from the processor to its left. This pairwise communication sends which vertices have been completed (called found parents), so that the next processor will have the knowledge to skip examining over them. This has the effect of the processor responsible for processing a vertex rotating right along the row for each substep. When a vertex finds a valid parent to become visited, its index along with its discovered parent is queued up and sent to the processor responsible for the corresponding segment of the parent array to update it. Each step of the algorithm in Fig. 6 has four major operations [3];

Frontier Gather (per step) (lines 8–9)

Each processor is given the segment of the frontier corresponding to their assigned submatrix.

Local discovery (per substep) (lines 11–20)

Search for parents with the information available locally.

Parent Updates (per substep) (lines 21–25)

Send updates of children that found parents and process updates for own segment of parents.

Fig. 6 Parallel-distributed 2-D bottom-up algorithm

```
1: function PARALLEL-2D-BOTTOM-UP(A, source)
2:     f ← {source}                                          ▷ bitmap for frontier
3:     c ← {source}                                          ▷ bitmap for completed
4:     n ← {}
5:     π ← [−1, −1, · · · , −1]
6:     for all compute nodes P(i, j) in parallel do
7:         while f ≠ {} do
8:             transpose-vector(f_{i,j})
9:             f_i = allgatherv(f_{i,j}, P(:, j))
10:            for s in 0 . . . C − 1 do                      ▷ C sub-steps
11:                t_{i,j} ← {}
12:                for u ∈ c_{i,j} do
13:                    for v ∈ A_{i,j}(u, :) do
14:                        if v ∈ f_i then
15:                            t_{i,j} ← t_{i,j} ∪ {(v, u)}
16:                            c_{i,j} ← c_{i,j} \u
17:                            break
18:                        end if
19:                    end for
20:                end for
21:                w_{i,j} ← sendrecv(t_{i,j}, P(i, j + s), P(i, j − s))
22:                for (v, u) ∈ w_{i,j} do
23:                    π_{i,j}(v) ← u
24:                    n_{i,j} ← n_{i,j} ∪ v
25:                end for
26:                c_{i,j} ← sendrecv(c_{i,j}, P(i, j + 1), P(i, j − 1))
27:            end for
28:            f ← n
29:            b ← {}
30:        end while
31:    end for
32:    return π
33: end function
```

Rotate Completed (per substep) (line 26)

Send completed to the right neighbor and receive completed for the next substep from the left neighbor.

3 Problems of Hybrid BFS in Extreme-Scale Supercomputers

Although the algorithm in Sect. 2 would work efficiently on a small-scale machine, for extremely large, up to and beyond million-core scale supercomputers toward exascale, various problems would manifest themselves which severely limit the performance and scalability of BFS. We describe the problems in Sect. 3 and present our solutions in Sect. 4.

3.1 Problems with the Data Structure of the Adjacency Matrix

The data structure describing the adjacency matrix is of significant importance as it directly affects the computational complexity of graph traversal. For small machines, the typical strategy is to employ the Compressed Sparse Row (CSR) format, commonly employed in numerical computing to express sparse matrices. However, we first show that direct use of CSR is impractical due to its memory requirements on a large machine; we then show that the existing proposed solutions, DCSR [4] and Coarse index + Skip list [6] that intend to reduce the footprint at the cost of increased computational complexity, are still insufficient for large graphs with significant computational requirement.

3.1.1 Compressed Sparse Row (CSR)

CSR utilizes two arrays, *dst* that holds the destination vertex ID of the edges in the graph and *row-starts* that describes the offset index of the edges of each vertex in the *dst* array. Given a graph with V vertices and E edges, the size of $dst = E$ and $row\text{-}starts = V$, respectively, so the required memory would be as follows in a sequential implementation:

$$V + E \tag{1}$$

For parallel-distributed implementation with $R \times C$ partitioning, if we assume that the edges and vertices are distributed evenly, since the number of rows in the distributed submatrices is V / R, the required memory per node is:

$$\frac{V}{R} + \frac{E}{RC} \tag{2}$$

By denoting the average vertices per node as V' and the average degree of the graph as $\hat{d}$, the following equation holds:

$$V' = \frac{V}{RC}, E = V\hat{d} \tag{3}$$

(2) can then be expressed as follows:

$$V'C + V'\hat{d} \tag{4}$$

This indicates that, for large machines, as C gets larger, the memory requirement per node increases, as the memory requirement of row-starts is $V'C$. In fact, for very large graphs on machines with thousands of nodes, row-starts can become significantly larger than *dst*, making its straightforward implementation impractical.

There is a set of work that proposes to compress row-starts, such as DCSR [4] and *Coarse index + Skip list* [6], but they involve non-negligible performance overhead as we describe below:

3.1.2 DCSR

DCSR [4] was proposed to improve the efficiency of matrix-matrix multiplication in a distributed-memory environment. The key idea is to eliminate the row-starts value for rows that has no nonzero values, thereby compressing row-starts. Instead, two supplemental data structures called the JC and AUX arrays are employed to calculate the appropriate offset in the *dst* array. The drawback is that one needs to iterate in order to navigate over the JC array from the AUX array, resulting in significant overhead for repeated access of sparse structures, which is a common operation for BFS.

3.1.3 Coarse Index + Skip List

Another proposal [6] was made in order to efficiently implement Breadth-First Search for 1-D partioning in a distributed-memory environment. Sixty-four rows of non-zero elements are batched into a *skip list*, and by having the row-starts hold the pointer to the *skip list*, this method compresses the overall size of the row-starts to be 1/64th the original size. Since each skip list embodies 64 rows of data, we can traverse all 64 rows contiguously, making algorithms with batched row access efficient in addition to data compression. However, for sparse accesses, on average one would have to traverse and skip over 31 elements to access the designated matrix element, potentially introducing significant overhead.

3.1.4 Other Sparse Matrix Formats

There are other known sparse matrix formats that do not utilize row-starts [9], significantly saving memory; however, although such formats would be useful for algorithms that systematically iterate over all elements of a matrix, they perform badly for BFS where individual accesses to the edges of a given vertex need to be efficient.

3.2 Problems with Communication Overhead

Hybrid BFS with 2-D partitioning scales for small number of nodes, but its scalability is known to quickly saturate when the number of nodes scales beyond thousands [3].

In particular, for distributed hybrid BFS over small-diameter large graph such as the Graph500 Kronecker graph, it has been reported that bottom-up search involves significant longer execution time compared to top-down [3, 14]. Table 1 shows the communication cost of bottom-up search when f, c, n, w are implemented as bitmaps as proposed in [3]. Each operation corresponds to the program in the following fashion: Transpose is line 8 of Fig. 6, Frontier Gather is line 9, Parent Update is line 21, and Rotate Completed is line 26, respectively.

As we can see in Table 1, the communication cost of Frontier Gather and Rotate Completed is proportional to R and C in the submatrix portioning—being one of the primary sources overhead when number of nodes are in the thousands or more. Moreover, lines 21 and 26 involve synchronous communication with other nodes, and the number of communication is proportional to C, again becoming significant overhead. Finally, it is very difficult to achieve perfect load balancing, as a small number of vertices tend to involve number of edges that could be orders of magnitude larger than the average; this could result in sever load imbalance in simple algorithms that assume even distribution of vertices and edges.

Such difficulties have been the primary reasons why one could not obtain near linear speedups, even in weak scaling, as the number of compute nodes the associated graph sizes increased to thousands or more on a very large machine. We next introduce our extremely scalable hybrid BFS that alleviates these problems, to achieve utmost scalability for Graph500 execution on the K-Computer.

4 Our Extremely Scalable Hybrid BFS

The problems associated with previous algorithms are largely storage and communication overheads of extremely large graphs scaling to be analyzed over thousands of

Table 1 Communication cost of bottom-up search [3]

Operation	Comm type	Comm complexity per step	Data transfer per each search (64 bit word)
Transpose	P2P	$O(1)$	$s_b V/64$
Frontier Gather	Allgather	$O(1)$	$s_b VR/64$
Parent Updates	P2P	$O(C)$	$2V$
Rotate Completed	P2P	$O(C)$	$s_b VC/64$

nodes or more. These are fundamental to the fact that we are handling irregular, large-scale "big" data structures and not floating point numerical values. In order to alleviate the problems, we propose several solutions that are unique to graph algorithms

4.1 Bitmap-Based Sparse Matrix Representation

First, our proposed bitmap-based sparse matrix representation allows extremely compact representation of the adjacency matrix, while still being very efficient in retrieving the edges between given vertices. We compress the CSR row-starts data structure by only holding the starting position of the sequence of edges for vertices that has one or more edges and then having an additional bitmap to identify whether a given vertex has more than one edge or not, one bit per vertex.

In our bitmap-based representation, since the sequence of edges is held in row-starts in the same manner as CSR, the main point of the algorithm is to how to identify the starting index of the edges given a vertex efficiently, as shown in Fig. 7. Here, B is number of bits in a word (typically 64), "≪" and "&" are the bit-shift and bitwise operators, and mod is the modulo operator. Given a vertex v, the index position of v in the row-starts corresponds to the number of vertices with nonzero edges from the vertex zero, which is equivalent to the number of bits that are 1 leading up to the v'th position in the bitmap. We further optimize this calculation by counting the summation of the number of 1 bits on a word-by-word basis and store it in the

offset array. This effectively allows constant calculation of the number of nonzero bits for v by looking at the offset value and the number of bits that are one leading up to the v's position in that particular word.

Table 2 shows a comparative example of bitmap-based sparse matrix representation with 8 vertices and 4 edges. As we observe, much of the repetitive waste resulting from relatively small number of edges compared to vertices arising in CSR is minimized. Table 3 shows the actual savings we achieve over CSR in a real setting in a Graph500 benchmark. Here, we partition a graph with 16 billion vertices and 256 billion edges into $64 \times 32 = 2048$ nodes in 2-D. Here, we achieve similar level of compression as previous work such as DCSR and Coarse index + Skip list, achieving nearly 60% reduction in space. As we see later, this compression is achieved with minimal execution overhead, in contrast to the previous proposals.

4.2 Reordering of the Vertex IDs

Another associated problem with BFS is the randomness of memory accesses of graph data, in contrast to traditional numerical computing using CSR such as the Conjugate Gradient method, where the access to the row elements of a matrix can become contiguous. Here, we attempt to exploit similar locality properties.

The basic idea is as follows: As described in Sect. 2.2, much of the information regarding hybrid BFS is held in bitmaps that represent the vertices, each bit corresponding to a vertex. When we execute BFS over a graph, higher-

Fig. 7 Bitmap-based sparse matrix: algorithms to calculate the offset and identify the start and end indices of a row of edges given a vertex

```
1: function MAKE-OFFSET(offset, bitmap)
2:     i ← 0
3:     offset[0] ← 0
4:     for each word w of bitmap do
5:         offset[i + 1] ← offset[i] + popcount(w)
6:         i ← i + 1
7:     end for
8: end function
9: function ROW-START-END(offset, bitmap, row-starts, v)
10:     w ← v/B
11:     b ← (1 ≪ (v mod B))
12:     if (bitmap[w] & b) ≠ 0 then
13:         p ← offset[w] + popcount(bitmap[w] & (b − 1))
14:         return (row-starts[p], row-starts[p + 1])
15:     end if
16:     return (0, 0)                          ▷ Vertex v has no edge
17: end function
```

Table 2 Examples of bitmap-based sparse matrix representation

Edges list		SRC	0 0 6 7
		DST	4 5 3 1
CSR		Row-starts	0 2 2 2 2 2 2 3 4
		DST	4 5 3 1
Bitmap-based sparse matrix representation		Offset	0 1 3
		Bitmap	1 0 0 0 0 0 1 1
		Row-starts	0 2 3 4
		DST	4 5 3 1
DCSR		AUX	0 1 1 3
		JC	0 6 7
		Row-starts	0 2 3 4
		DST	4 5 3 1

Table 3 Theoretical order and the actual per-node measured memory consumptions of bitmap-based CSR compared to previous proposals

Data structure	CSR		Bitmap-based CSR	
	Order	Actual	Order	Actual
Offset	–	–	$V'C/64$	32 MB
Bitmap	–	–	$V'C/64$	32 MB
Row-starts	$V'C$	2048 MB	$V'p$	190 MB
DST	$V'\hat{d}$	1020 MB	$V'\hat{d}$	1020 MB
Total	$V'(C+\hat{d})$	3068 MB	$V'(C/32+p+\hat{d})$	1274 MB
Data structure	DCSR		Coarse index + Skip list	
	Order	Actual	Order	Actual
AUX	$V'p$	190 MB	–	–
JC	$V'p$	190 MB	–	–
Row-starts	$V'p$	190 MB	$V'C/64$	32 MB
DST or skip list	$V'\hat{d}$	1020 MB	$V'\hat{d}+V'p$	1210 MB
Total	$V'(3p+\hat{d})$	1590 MB	$V'(C/64+p+\hat{d})$	1242 MB

We partition a Graph500 graph with 16 billion vertices and 256 billion edges into $64 \times 32 = 2048$ Nodes

degree vertices are typically accessed more often; as such, by clustering access to such vertices by reordering them according to their degrees (i.e., # of edges), we can expect to achieve higher locality. This is similar to switching rows in a matrix in a sparse numerical algorithm to achieve higher locality. In [12], they proposed such reordering for top-down BFS, where they only utilize the reordered vertices where needed, while maintaining the original BFS tree with original vertex IDs for overall efficiency. Unfortunately, this method cannot be used for hybrid BFS; instead, we propose the following algorithm.

Reordered IDs of the vertices are computed by sorting them top-down according to their degrees on a per-node basis and then reassigning the new IDs according to their order. We do not conduct any inter-node reordering. A subadjacency matrix on each node stores reordered IDs of the vertices. The mapping information between original vertex ID and its reordered vertex ID is maintained by an owner node where the vertex is located. When constructing an adjacency matrix of the graph, the original vertex ID is converted to the reordered ID by (a) firstly performing all-to-all communication once over all the nodes in a row of processor grid in 2-D partitioning to compute the degree information of each vertex, and then (b) secondly computing the reordered IDs by sorting all the vertices according to their degrees and then (c) thirdly performing all-to-all communication again over all the nodes in a column and a row of processor grid in order to convert the vertex IDs in the subadjacency matrix on each node to the reordered IDs.

The drawback with this scheme requires expensive all-to-all communication multiple times: Since the resulting BFS tree had the reordered IDs for the vertices, we must reassign their original IDs. However, if we are to conduct

Table 4 Adding the original IDs for both the source and the destination

Offset	0 1 3	
Bitmap	1 0 0 0 0 0 1 1	
SRC(Orig)	2 0 1	
Row-starts	0 2 3 4	
DST	2 3 0 1	
DST(Orig)	4 5 3 1	

such reassignment at the very end, the information must be exchanged among all the nodes using a very expensive all-to-all communication for large machines again, since the only node that has the original ID info of each vertex is the node that owns it. In fact, we show in Sect. 6 that all-to-all is a significant impediment in our benchmarks.

The solution to this problem is to add two arrays SRC(Orig) and DST(Orig) as shown in Table 4. Both arrays hold the original indices of the reordered vertices. When the algorithm writes to the resulting BFS tree, the original ID is referenced from either of the arrays instead of the reordered ID, avoiding all-to-all communication. Also, a favorable by-product of vertex reordering is removal of vertices with no edges, allowing further compaction of the data structure, since such vertices will never show up in the resulting BFS tree.

4.3 Optimizing Inter-Node Communications for Bottom-Up BFS

The original bottom-up BFS algorithm shown in Fig. 6 conducts communication per each substep, C times per each iteration assuming that we have 2-D partitioning of $R \times C$ for an adjacency matrix). For large systems, such frequent communication presents significant overhead and thus subject to the following optimizations:

4.3.1 Optimizing Parent Updates Communication

Firstly, we cluster the Parent Updates communication. The sendrecv() communication for line 21 in Fig. 6 sends a request called *"Parent Updates"* to update the BFS tree located at the owner node with the vertices that found a parent in the BFS tree, but such a request can be sent at any time, even after other processing is finished. As such we cluster the Parent Updates as Alltoallv() communication as shown in Fig. 8.

4.3.2 Overlapping Computation and Communication in Rotate Completed Operation

We also attempt to overlap computation in lines 12–20 (Fig. 8) and communication in line 21 in *"Rotate Completed"* operation mentioned in Sect. 2. If the substeps are

set to C steps as the original method, we would not be able to overlap the computation and communication since the computational result depends on the result in a previous substep. Thus, we increase this substep from C to multiple substeps such as 2C, 4C. For the K-Computer described in Sect. 5, we increase this to 4C. If the substeps is set to 4C, the computational result depends on the one in 4 substeps before, and we can perform parallel execution by overlapping computation and communication for 4 substeps. In this case, when the computation is performed for 2 substeps, the communication for other 2 substeps are simultaneously executed. The communication is accelerated by allocating these 2 substeps to 2 different communication channels in the 6-D torus network of the K-Computer that supports multiple channel communication using rDMA.

4.4 Reducing Communication with Better Partitioning

We further reduce communication via better partitioning of the graph. The original simple 2-D partitioning by Beamer [3] requires transpose-vector communication per each step. Yoo [16] improves on this by employing block-cyclic distribution, eliminating the need for transpose vector at the cost of added code complexity. We adapt Yoo's method so that it becomes applicable to hybrid BFS (Fig. 9; Table 5).

4.5 Load Balancing the Top-Down Algorithm

We resolve the following load-balancing problem for the top-down algorithm. As shown in Fig. 5 lines 10–14, we need to create $t_{i,j}$ from the edges of each vertex in the frontier; this is implemented so that the each vertex pair of the edges is placed in a temporary buffer and then copied to the communication buffer just prior to alltoallv(). Here, as we see in Fig. 10, thread parallelism is utilized so that each thread gets assigned equal number of frontier vertices. However, since the distribution of edges per each vertex is quite uneven, this will cause significant load imbalance among the threads.

A solution to this problem is shown in Fig. 11, where we conduct partitioning and thread assignment per destination nodes. We first extract the range of edges and copy the edges directly without copying into a temporary buffer. In the figure, owner(v) is a function that returns the owner node of vertex v and edge-range($A_{i,j}(:, u), k$) returns the range in edge list $A_{i,j}(:, u)$ for a given owner node k using binary search, as the edge list is sorted in destination ID order. One caveat, however, is when the vertex has only a small number of edges; in such a case, the edge-range data $r_{i,j,k}$ could become larger and thus inefficient. We alleviate

Fig. 8 Bottom-up BFS with optimized inter-node communication

```
 1: function PARALLEL-2D-BOTTOM-UP-OPT(A, source)
 2:     f ← {source}                                          ▷ bitmap for frontiers
 3:     c ← {source}                                          ▷ bitmap for completed
 4:     n ← {}
 5:     π ← [−1, −1, · · · , −1]
 6:     for all compute nodes P(i, j) in parallel do
 7:         while f ≠ {} do
 8:             transpose-vector(f_{i,j})
 9:             f_i =allgatherv(f_{i,j}, P(:, j))
10:             for s in 0 . . . C − 1 do
11:                 t_{i,j} ← {}
12:                 for u ∈ c_{i,j} do
13:                     for v ∈ A_{i,j}(u, :) do
14:                         if v ∈ f_i then
15:                             t_{i,j} ← t_{i,j} ∪ {(v, u)}
16:                             c_{i,j} ← c_{i,j}\u
17:                             break
18:                         end if
19:                     end for
20:                 end for
21:                 c_{i,j} ←sendrecv(c_{i,j}, P(i, j + 1), P(i, j − 1))
22:             end for
23:             w_{i,j} ←alltoallv(t_{i,j}, P(i, :))
24:             for (v, u) ∈ w_{i,j} do
25:                 π_{i,j}(v) ← u
26:                 n_{i,j} ← n_{i,j} ∪ v
27:             end for
28:             f ← n
29:             n ← {}
30:         end while
31:     end for
32:     return π
33: end function
```

$$\begin{bmatrix}
A_{1,1}^{(1)} & A_{1,2}^{(1)} & \cdots & A_{1,C}^{(1)} \\
A_{2,1}^{(1)} & A_{2,2}^{(1)} & \cdots & A_{2,C}^{(1)} \\
\vdots & \vdots & \ddots & \vdots \\
A_{R,1}^{(1)} & A_{R,2}^{(1)} & \cdots & A_{R,C}^{(1)} \\
A_{1,1}^{(2)} & A_{1,2}^{(2)} & \cdots & A_{1,C}^{(2)} \\
A_{2,1}^{(2)} & A_{2,2}^{(2)} & \cdots & A_{2,C}^{(2)} \\
\vdots & \vdots & \ddots & \vdots \\
A_{R,1}^{(2)} & A_{R,2}^{(2)} & \cdots & A_{R,C}^{(2)} \\
 & & & \\
A_{1,1}^{(C)} & A_{1,2}^{(C)} & \cdots & A_{1,C}^{(C)} \\
A_{2,1}^{(C)} & A_{2,2}^{(C)} & \cdots & A_{2,C}^{(C)} \\
\vdots & \vdots & \ddots & \vdots \\
A_{R,1}^{(C)} & A_{R,2}^{(C)} & \cdots & A_{R,C}^{(C)}
\end{bmatrix}$$

```
 1: function TOP-DOWN-SENDER-NAIVE(A_{i,j}, f_i)
 2:     for u ∈ f_i in parallel do
 3:         for v ∈ A_{i,j}(:, u) do
 4:             k ← owner(v)
 5:             t_{i,j,k} ← t_{i,j,k} ∪ {(u, v)}
 6:         end for
 7:     end for
 8: end function
```

Fig. 10 Simple thread parallelism for top-down BFS

this problem by using a hybrid method depending on the number of edges, where we switch between the simple copy method and the range method according to the number of edges.

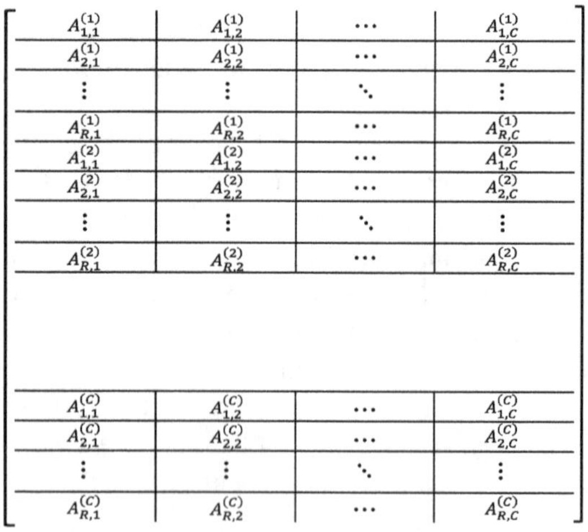

Fig. 9 Block-cyclic 2-D distribution proposed by Yoo [16]

Table 5 Bitmap-based CSR data communication volume (difference from Table 1 is in italics)

Operation	Comm type	Comm complexity per step	Data transfer per each search (64 bit word)
Frontier Gather	Allgather	$O(1)$	$s_b VR/64$
Parent Updates	*Alltoall*	*$O(1)$*	*2V*
Rotate Completed	P2P	$O(C)$	$s_b VC/64$

```
 1: function TOP-DOWN-SENDER-LOAD-BALANCED(A_{i,j}, f_i)
 2:     for u ∈ f_i in parallel do
 3:         for k ∈ P(i, :) do
 4:             (v_0, v_1) ← edge-range(A_{i,j}(:, u), k)
 5:             r_{i,j,k} ← r_{i,j,k} ∪ {(u, v_0, v_1)}
 6:         end for
 7:     end for
 8:     for k ∈ P(i, :) in parallel do
 9:         for (u, v_0, v_1) ∈ r_{i,j,k} do
10:             for v ∈ A_{i,j}(v_0 : v_1, u) do
11:                 t_{i,j,k} ← t_{i,j,k} ∪ {(u, v)}
12:             end for
13:         end for
14:     end for
15: end function
```

Fig. 11 Load-balanced thread parallelism for top-down BFS

5 Machine Architecture-Specific Communication Optimizations for the K-Computer

The optimizations we have proposed so far are applicable to any large supercomputer that supports MPI+OpenMP hybrid parallelism. We now present further optimizations specific to the K-Computer, exploiting its unique architectural capabilities. In particular, the node-to-node interconnect employed in the K-Computer is a proprietary *"Tofu"* network that implements a six-dimensional torus topology, with high injection bandwidth and multi-directional DMA to achieve extremely high performance in communication-intensive HPC applications. We exploit the features of the Tofu network to achieve high performance on BFS as well.

5.1 Mapping to the Six-Dimensional Torus *"Tofu"* Network

Since our bitmap-based hybrid BFS employs two-dimensional $R \times C$ partitioning, there is a choice of how to map this onto the six-dimensional Tofu network, whose dimensions are named *"x, y, z, a, b, c."* One obvious choice is to assign three dimensions to each R and C (say $R = x, y, z$ and $C = a, b, c$), allowing physically proximal communications for adjacent nodes in the $R \times C$ partitioning. Another interesting option is to assign $R = y, z$ and $C = x, a, b, c$, where we achieve square 288×288

```
 1: function SENDRECV-COMPLETED(c_{i,j}, s)
 2:     route ← s mod 2
 3:     if route = 0 then
 4:         c_{i,j} ← sendrecv(c_{i,j}, P(i, j + 1), P(i, j − 1))
 5:     else
 6:         c_{i,j} ← sendrecv(c_{i,j}, P(i, j − 1), P(i, j + 1))
 7:     end if
 8: end function
```

Fig. 12 Bidirectional communication in bottom-up BFS

partitioning when we use the entire K-Computer. We test both cases in the benchmark for comparison.

5.2 Bidirectional Simultaneous Communication for Bottom-Up BFS

Each node on the K-Computer has six 5 Gigabyte/s bidirectional links to comprise a six-dimensional torus and allows simultaneous DMA to four of the six links. Blue-Gene/Q has a similar mechanism. By exploiting such simultaneous communication capabilities over multiple links, we can significantly speed up the communication for bottom-up BFS. In particular, we have optimized Rotate Completed communication by communicating simultaneously to both directions, as shown in Fig. 12. Here, $c_{i,j}$ is the data to be communicated, and s is the number of steps up to 2C or 4C steps. We case-analyze s to even/odd to communicate to different directions simultaneously.

One thing to note is that, despite these K-Computer-specific optimizations, we still solely use the vendor MPI for communication and do not employ any machine-specific low-level communication primitives that are non-portable.

6 Performance Evaluation

We now present the results of the Graph500 benchmark using our hybrid BFS on the entire K-Computer. The Graph500 benchmark measures the performance of each machine by the (traversed edges per second (TEPS) value of the BFS algorithm on a synthetically generated Kronecker graphs, with parameters A=0.57, B=0.19, C=0.19, D=0.05. The size of the graph is expressed by the scale parameter where the #vertices $= 2^{Scale}$, and the #edges $= $ #vertices $\times 16$.

The K-Computer is located at the Riken AICS facility in Japan, with each node embodying a 8-core Fujitsu SPARC64 VIIIfx processor and 16 GB of memory. The Tofu network composes a six-dimensional torus as mentioned, with each link being bidirectional 5GB/s. The total number of nodes is 82,944, or embodying 663,552 CPU cores and approximately 1.3 Petabytes of memory.

6.1 Effectiveness of the Proposed Methods

We measure the effectiveness of the proposed methods using up to 15,360 nodes of the K-Computer. We increased the number of nodes in the increments of 60, with minimum being Scale 29 (approximately 537 million vertices and 8.59 billion edges), up to Scale 37. We picked a random vertex as the root of BFS and executed each

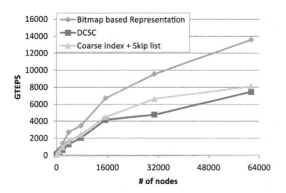

Fig. 13 Evaluation of bitmap-based sparse matrix representation compared to previously proposed methods (K-Computer, weak scaling)

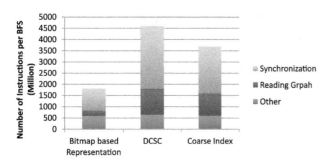

Fig. 14 Performance breakdown—# of instructions per step (Scale 33 graph on 1008 nodes)

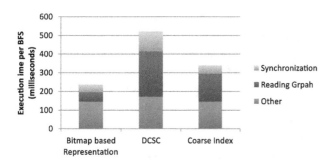

Fig. 15 Performance breakdown—execution time per step (Scale 33 graph on 1008 nodes)

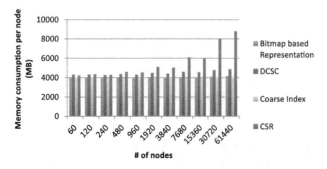

Fig. 16 Memory consumption per node on BFS execution

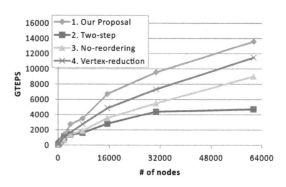

Fig. 17 Reordering of vertex IDs and comparisons to other proposed methods

benchmark 300 times. The reported value is the median of the 300 runs.

We first compared our bitmap-based sparse matrix representation to previous approaches, namely DCSR [4] and Coarse index + Skip list [6]. Figure 13 shows the weak scaling result of the execution performance in GTEPS, and Figs. 14, 15, and 16 shows various execution metrics—#instructions, time, and memory consumed. The processing of *"Reading Graph"* in Figs. 14 and 15 corresponds to lines 10–14 of Fig. 5 and lines 12–20 of Fig. 6. *"Synchronization"* is the inter-thread barrier synchronization over all computation. Since the barrier is implemented with *"spin wait,"* the number of executed instructions for this barrier is large compared with others.

Our proposed method excels in all aspects in comparison with others in performance, while being modest in memory consumption. In particular, for graph reading and manipulation, our proposed method is 5.5 times faster than DCSR and 3.0 times faster than Coarse index + Skip list, while the memory consumption is largely equivalent.

Figure 17 shows the effectiveness of reordering of vertex ID. We compare the four methodological variations, namely (1) our proposed method, (2) reorder but reassign the original ID at the very end using alltoall(), (3) no vertex reordering, and (4) no vertex reordering but pre-eliminate the vertices with no edges. The last method (4) was introduced to assess the effectiveness of our approach more purely with respect to locality improvement, as (1) embodies the effect of both locality improvement and zero-edge vertex elimination. Figure 17 shows that method (2) involves significant overhead in alltoall() communication for large systems, even trailing the non-reordered case. Method (4) shows good speedup over (3), and this is due to the fact that the Graph500 graphs generated at large scale contain many vertices with zero edges—for example, for 15,360 nodes at Scale 37, more than half the vertices have zero edges. Finally, our method (1) improves upon (4), indicating that vertex reordering has notable merit in improving the locality.

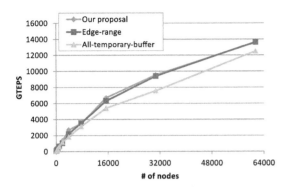

Fig. 18 Effects of hybrid load balancing on top-down BFS

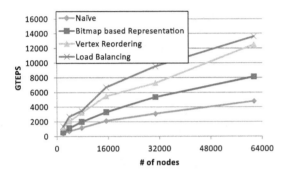

Fig. 19 Cumulative effect of all the proposed optimizations

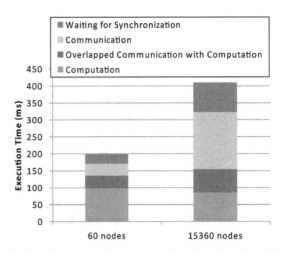

Fig. 21 Breakdown of performance numbers, 60 nodes versus 15,360

presented, we achieve 3.19 times speedup over the original version.

Figure 20 shows the per-node performance of weak scaling our proposed algorithm, where it slowly degrades as we scale the problem. Figure 21 shows the breakdown of time spent per each BFS for 60 and 15,360 nodes, exhibiting that the slowdown is largely due to increase in communication, despite various communication optimizations. This demonstrates that, even with an interconnect as fast as the K-Computer, network is still the bottleneck for large graphs, and as such, further hardware and algorithmic improvements are desirable for future extreme graph processing.

6.2 Using the Entire K-Computer

By using the entire K-Computer, we were able to obtain 38,621.4 GTEPS using 82,944 nodes and 663,552 cores with a Scale 40 problem in June 2015. This bested the previous record of 23,751 GTEPS recorded by LLNL's Sequoia BlueGene/Q supercomputer, with 98,304 nodes and 1,572,864 cores with a Scale 41 problem.

In the Tofu network of the K-Computer, a position in a six-dimensional mesh/torus network is given by six-dimensional coordinates, x, y, z, a, b, c. The x- and y-axes are coordinate axes that connect racks, and the length of the

Next, we investigate the effects of load balancing in top-down BFS. Figure 18 shows the results, where *"edge-range"* is using the algorithm in Fig. 13, whereas *"all-temporary-buffer"* is using the algorithm in Fig. 10, and *"Our proposal"* is the hybrid of the both. In the hybrid algorithm, the longer edge list is processed with the algorithm Fig. 13 and the shorter edge list is processed with the algorithm Fig. 10. We set the threshold for the length of the edge list to 1000. At some node sizes, the performance of *"Edge-range"* is almost identical to our proposed hybrid method. But this hybrid method performs best of those three methods.

Figure 19 shows the cumulative effect of all the optimization. The naive version uses DCSR without vertex reordering, and load-balanced using the algorithm in Fig. 10. By applying all the optimizations we have

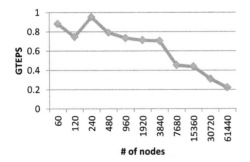

Fig. 20 Per-node execution performance in weak scaling

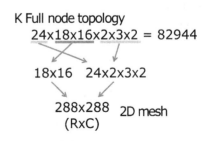

Fig. 22 Coordinates of K-Computer

x- and y-axes corresponds to the scale of the system. The z- and b-axes connect system boards, and the a- and c-axes are coordinate axes with a length of 2 that connect processors on each system board [1, 15]. For 2-D partitioning of a graph, $yz \times xabc$ is used instead of $xyz - abc$ and then we can obtain 288×288 for balanced 2-D mesh. The value for each coordinate is shown in Fig. 22 to fully leverage the full nodes of the K-Computer and balance the value of R and C in 2-D partitioning.

By all means, it is not clear whether we have hit the ultimate limit of the machine, i.e., whether or not we can tune the efficiency any further just by algorithmic changes. We know that BFS algorithm used for Sequoia is quite different from our proposed one, and it would be interesting to compare the algorithms vs. machines effect by cross-execution of the two (our algorithm on Sequoia and LLNL's algorithm on the K-Computer) and conducting a detailed analysis of both to investigate further optimization opportunities.

7 Related Work

As we mentioned, Yoo [16] proposed an effective method for 2-D graph partitioning for BFS in a large-scale distributed-memory computing environment; the base algorithm itself was a simple top-down BFS and was evaluated on a large-scale environment 32,768 node BlueGene/L.

Buluc et al. [5] conducted extensive performance studies of partitioning schemes for BFS on large-scale machines at LNBL, Hopper (6,392 nodes) and Franklin (9,660 nodes), comparing 1-D and 2-D partitioning strategies. Satish et al. [10] proposed an efficient BFS algorithm on commodity supercomputing clusters consisting of Intel CPU and the Infiniband Network. Checconi et al. [7] proposed an efficient parallel-distributed BFS on BlueGene using a communication method called *"wave"* that proceeds independently along the rows of the virtual processor grids. All the efforts here, however, use a top-down approach only as the underlying algorithm and are fundamentally at a disadvantage for graphs such as the Graph500 Kronecker graph whose diameter is relatively small compared to its size, as many real-world graphs are.

Hybrid BFS by Beamer [2] is the seminal work that solves this problem, on which our work is based. Efficient parallelization in a distributed-memory environment on a supercomputer is much more difficult and includes the early work by Beamer [3] and the work by Checconi [6] which uses a 1-D partitioning approach. The latter is very different to ours, not only in the difference in partitioning being 1-D compared to our 2-D, but also in taking advantage of the simplicity in ingeniously replicating the vertices with large number of edges among all the nodes,

achieving very good overall load balancing. Performance evaluation on BlueGene/Q 65536 nodes has achieved 16,599 GTEPS, and it would be interesting to consider utilizing some of the strategies in our work.

8 Conclusion

For many graphs we see in the real world, with relatively small diameter compared to its size, hybrid BFS is known to be very efficient. The problem has been that, although various algorithms have been proposed to parallelize the algorithm in a distributed-memory environment, such as the work by Beamer [3] using 2-D partitioning, the algorithms failed to scale or be efficient for modern machines with tens of thousands of nodes and million-scale cores, due to the increase in memory and communication requirements overwhelming even the best machines. Our proposed hybrid BFS algorithm overcomes such problems by combination of various new techniques, such as bitmap-based sparse matrix representation, reordering of vertex ID, as well as new methods for communication optimization and load balancing. Detailed performance on the K-Computer revealed the effectiveness of each of our approach, with the combined effect of all achieving over $3 \times$ speedup over previous approaches, and scaling to the entire 82,944 nodes of the machine effectively. The resulting performance of 38,621.4 GTEPS allowed the K-Computer to be ranked No. 1 on the Graph500 in June 2015 by a significant margin, and it has retained this rank to this date as of June 2016. We hope to further advance the optimizations to other graph algorithms, such as SSSP, on large-scale machines.

Acknowledgements This research was supported by the Japan Science and Technology Agency's CREST project titled "Development of System Software Technologies for post-Peta Scale High Performance Computing."

References

1. Ajima Y, Takagi Y, Inoue T, Hiramoto S, Shimizu T (2011) The tofu interconnect. In: 2011 IEEE 19th Annual Symposium on High Performance Interconnects, pp 87–94. doi:10.1109/HOTI. 2011.21
2. Beamer S, Asanović K, Patterson D (2012) Direction-optimizing breadth-first search. In: Proceedings of the International Conference on High Performance Computing, Networking, Storage and Analysis, SC '12, pp 12:1–12:10. IEEE Computer Society Press, Los Alamitos, CA, USA. http://dl.acm.org/citation.cfm?id= 2388996.2389013
3. Beamer S, Buluc A, Asanovic K, Patterson D (2013) Distributed-memory breadth-first search revisited: Enabling bottom-up search. In: Proceedings of the 2013 IEEE 27th International Symposium on Parallel and Distributed Processing Workshops

and PhD Forum, IPDPSW '13, pp 1618–1627. IEEE Computer Society, Washington, DC, USA. doi:10.1109/IPDPSW.2013.159

4. Buluc A, Gilbert JR (2008) On the representation and multiplication of hypersparse matrices. In: IEEE International Symposium on Parallel and Distributed Processing, 2008. IPDPS 2008, pp 1–11. doi:10.1109/IPDPS.2008.4536313

5. Buluç A, Madduri K (2011) Parallel breadth-first search on distributed-memory systems. In: Proceedings of 2011 International Conference for High Performance Computing, Networking, Storage and Analysis, SC '11, pp 65:1–65:12. ACM, New York, NY, USA. doi:10.1145/2063384.2063471

6. Checconi F, Petrini F (2014) Traversing trillions of edges in real time: graph exploration on large-scale parallel machines. In: 2014 IEEE 28th International Parallel and Distributed Processing Symposium, pp 425–434. doi:10.1109/IPDPS.2014.52

7. Checconi F, Petrini F, Willcock J, Lumsdaine A, Choudhury AR, Sabharwal Y (2012) Breaking the speed and scalability barriers for graph exploration on distributed-memory machines. In: Proceedings of the International Conference on High Performance Computing, Networking, Storage and Analysis, SC '12, pp 13:1–13:12. IEEE Computer Society Press, Los Alamitos, CA, USA. http://dl.acm.org/citation.cfm?id=2388996.2389014

8. Graph500: http://www.graph500.org/

9. Montagne E, Ekambaram A (2004) An optimal storage format for sparse matrices. Inf Process Lett 90(2):87–92. doi:10.1016/j.ipl.2004.01.014

10. Satish N, Kim C, Chhugani J, Dubey P (2012) Large-scale energy-efficient graph traversal: a path to efficient data-intensive supercomputing. In: 2012 International Conference for High Performance Computing, Networking, Storage and Analysis (SC), pp 1–11. doi:10.1109/SC.2012.70

11. Suzumura T, Ueno K, Sato H, Fujisawa K, Matsuoka S (2011) Performance characteristics of graph500 on large-scale distributed environment. In: Proceedings of the 2011 IEEE International Symposium on Workload Characterization, IISWC '11, pp 149–158. IEEE Computer Society, Washington, DC, USA. doi:10.1109/IISWC.2011.6114175

12. Ueno K, Suzumura T (2012) Highly scalable graph search for the graph500 benchmark. In: Proceedings of the 21st International Symposium on High-Performance Parallel and Distributed Computing, HPDC '12, pp 149–160. ACM, New York, NY, USA. doi:10.1145/2287076.2287104

13. Ueno K, Suzumura T (2013) Parallel distributed breadth first search on GPU. In: 20th Annual International Conference on High Performance Computing, pp 314–323. doi:10.1109/HiPC.2013.6799136

14. Yasui Y, Fujisawa K (2014) Fast and energy-efficient Breadth-First Search on a single NUMA system. Springer International Publishing, Cham. doi:10.1007/978-3-319-07518-1_23

15. Yokokawa M, Shoji F, Uno A, Kurokawa M, Watanabe T (2011) The k computer: Japanese next-generation supercomputer development project. In: Proceedings of the 17th IEEE/ACM International Symposium on Low-power Electronics and Design, ISLPED '11, pp 371–372. IEEE Press, Piscataway, NJ, USA. http://dl.acm.org/citation.cfm?id=2016802.2016889

16. Yoo A, Chow E, Henderson K, McLendon W, Hendrickson B, Catalyurek U (2005) A scalable distributed parallel breadth-first search algorithm on bluegene/l. In: Proceedings of the 2005 ACM/IEEE conference on Supercomputing, SC '05, pp 25. IEEE Computer Society, Washington, DC, USA. doi:10.1109/SC.2005.4

Efficient Maximal Clique Enumeration Over Graph Data

Boyi Hou[1] · Zhuo Wang[1] · Qun Chen[1] · Bo Suo[1] · Chao Fang[1] · Zhanhuai Li[1] ·
Zachary G. Ives[2]

Abstract In a wide variety of emerging data-intensive
applications, such as social network analysis, Web document
clustering, entity resolution, and detection of consistently co-
expressed genes in systems biology, the detection of *dense
subgraphs* (cliques) is an essential component. Unfortunately, this problem is NP-Complete and thus computationally intensive at scale—hence there is a need for efficient
processing, as well as the techniques for distributing the
computation across multiple machines such that the computation, which is too time-consuming on a single machine,
can be efficiently performed on a machine cluster given that
it is large enough. In this paper, we propose a new algorithm
(called GP) for maximal clique enumeration. It identifies
cliques by the operation of binary graph partitioning, which
iteratively divides a graph until each task is sufficiently small
to be processed in parallel. Given a connected graph
$G = (V, E)$, the GP algorithm has a space complexity of
$O(|E|)$ and a time complexity of $O(|E|\mu(G))$, where $\mu(G)$
represents the number of different cliques existing in G. We
also present a hybrid algorithm, which can effectively
leverage the advantages of both the GP algorithm and the
classical Bron-and-Kerbosch (BK) algorithm. Then, we
develop corresponding parallel solutions based on the GP
and hybrid algorithms. Finally, we evaluate the performance
of the proposed solutions on real and synthetic graph data.
Our extensive experiments show that in both centralized and
parallel setting, our proposed GP and hybrid approaches
achieve considerably better performance than the state-of-
the-art BK approach. Our parallel solutions are implemented
and evaluated on MapReduce, a popular shared-nothing
parallel framework, but can easily generalize to other shared-
nothing or shared-memory parallel frameworks.

Keywords Maximal clique enumeration · Parallel graph
processing · Iterative graph partitioning · MapReduce

✉ Qun Chen
chenbenben@nwpu.edu.cn

Boyi Hou
byhou.mail@nwpu.edu.cn

Zhuo Wang
wzhuo918@mail.nwpu.edu.cn

Bo Suo
caitou@mail.nwpu.edu.cn

Chao Fang
cfang.mail@nwpu.edu.cn

Zhanhuai Li
lizhh@nwpu.edu.cn

Zachary G. Ives
zives@cis.upenn.edu

[1] School of Computer Science, Northwestern Polytechnical
University, Xi'an, China

[2] Department of Computer and Information Systems,
University of Pennsylvania, Philadelphia, PA, USA

1 Introduction

A variety of emerging applications are focused on computations over data modeled as a graph: examples include
finding groups of actors or communities in social networks
[18, 22], Web mining [19], entity resolution [26], graph
mining [37, 41], and detection of consistently co-expressed
gene groups in systems biology [27]. For the problems just
cited, as well as a number of others, a critical component of
the analysis is the detection of cliques (fully connected
components) in the structure of the network graph.

Maximal clique enumeration is NP-Complete. Hence, a
great deal of effort has been spent on efficient search

algorithms [1, 4, 6, 14, 33, 34]. Most of existing algorithms for maximal clique enumeration are based on the classical BK algorithm proposed by Bron and Kerbosch [4], which uses a backtracking technique to explore search space and limits the size of its search space by remembering the search paths it has already visited. A variant [34] of the BK algorithm also provides a worst-case optimal solution. In practice, the BK algorithm has been widely reported as being faster than its alternatives [5, 15].

Data-intensive applications usually require clique detection to be operated over large graphs. We observe that the existing algorithms were optimized for centralized implementation, but not for parallel implementation. Their performance has not been adequately evaluated on real big graphs either, especially the natural graphs with the skewed power-law degree distributions commonly found in real world. In fact, as we show in experimental evaluation of Sect. 5, their performance is quite sensitive to particular graph characteristics. We also note that there have been a variety of proposals that divide the graph into smaller subcomponents and exploit parallelism to improve performance [10, 23, 32, 38, 40]. They have been empirically shown to speed computation in massive networks. However, built on the BK algorithm, their performance may be limited by the efficiency of *BK* search and how evenly a graph is partitioned.

In this paper, we present a new approach for maximal clique enumeration. Versus prior work in this area, its key insight is to exploit iterative binary decomposition during the computation. It iteratively divides a graph until each task is sufficiently small to be processed in parallel. As a result, a computation, which may be too time-consuming on a single machine, can be effectively parallelized across a cluster. In this paper, we choose MapReduce for parallel evaluation due to the maturity and wide availability of its implementations. However, the implementation can easily generalize to other shared-nothing or shared-memory parallel architectures. The major contributions of this paper are summarized as follows:

1. We present a novel algorithm (GP) for maximal clique enumeration based on iterative binary graph partitioning. Given a connected graph $G = (V, E)$, it has the space complexity of $O(|E|)$ and the time complexity of $O(|E|\mu(G))$, where $\mu(G)$ represents the number of different cliques existing in G.

2. We propose a hybrid algorithm for maximal clique enumeration, which can effectively leverage the advantages of both GP and BK algorithms.

3. We develop parallel solutions to maximal clique enumeration based on the GP and hybrid algorithms and implement them on MapReduce. By using binary graph partitioning to divide the tasks, the proposed

solutions can effectively parallelize maximal clique computation with improved load balancing.

4. We experimentally evaluate the performance of our proposed solutions over a wide variety of graph data available in open source. Our extensive experiments show that in both centralized and parallel settings, our proposed GP approach achieves considerably better performance than the state-of-the-art BK approach and the hybrid approach performs better than both of them.

Note that this paper is an extension of our preliminary work published in [7]. The major new contribution of this extended work is the hybrid approach that can achieve better performance than both BK and GP. The rest of this paper is organized as follows: Sect. 2 provides the background information and briefly describes the existing techniques. Section 3 presents the GP and hybrid algorithms. Section 4 presents our parallel solutions and their MapReduce implementation. Section 5 empirically evaluates the performance of the proposed solutions. Section 6 discusses related work. Finally, Sect. 7 concludes this paper.

2 Preliminaries

2.1 Definition: Clique and Maximal Clique

A clique is a subgraph in which every pair of vertices is connected by an edge. The definition of a *maximal* clique is as follows:

Definition 1 A maximal clique in a graph G is a clique not contained by any other clique in G.

The problem of maximal clique enumeration refers to identifying all the maximal cliques in a given graph G. Since each connected component in G can be processed independently, we assume that G is a connected graph in this paper.

2.2 Background: MapReduce

The MapReduce model processes distributed data across many nodes via three basic phases. In the Map phase, it takes an input and produces a list of intermediate key/value pairs without communication between nodes. Next, the Shuffle phase repartitions these intermediate pairs according to their keys across nodes. Finally, the Reduce phase aggregates the intermediate pairs it receives to produce final results. This process can be repeated by invoking an arbitrary number of additional Map-Shuffle–Reduce cycles as necessary.

In this paper, we use Hadoop for parallel evaluation and develop corresponding MapReduce solutions, in which graph partitioning is programmed in the Reduce phase.

2.3 Classical Sequential Algorithms

Algorithm 1: enumerateBK(anchor,cand,not)

---

1 **if** $(cand = \emptyset)$ **then**
2   **if** $(not = \emptyset)$ **then**
3 | Output anchor;
4 **else**
5   $fix\_v \leftarrow$ the vertex in cand that is connected to the greatest number of other vertices in cand;
6   $cur\_v \leftarrow fix\_v$;
7   **while** $(cur\_v \neq NULL)$ **do**
8   n_not$\leftarrow$ all the vertices in not that are connected to cur_v;
9   n_cand$\leftarrow$ all the vertices in cand that are connected to cur_v;
10   n_anchor$\leftarrow$sub + $\{cur\_v\}$;
11   enumerateBK(n_anchor,n_cand,n_not);
12   not$\leftarrow$not+ $\{cur\_v\}$;
13   cand$\leftarrow$cand - $\{cur\_v\}$;
14   **if** (there is a vertex v in cand that is not connected to fix_v) **then**
15 | $cur\_v \leftarrow v$;
16   **else**
17 | $cur\_v \leftarrow NULL$;

For maximal clique enumeration, the BK algorithm [4] has been widely reported as being faster in practice than its alternatives [15, 32]. It is in essence a depth-first search, augmented with pruning tricks. Given a current vertex v and a set of candidate vertices S, it iteratively chooses a vertex u in S such that $N(u)$ has the biggest intersection set with S, in which $N(u)$ represents the set of u's neighboring vertices in S. When the candidate set S becomes empty, the algorithm outputs corresponding cliques and backtracks. It recursively traverses a search tree, performing the operations of vertex selection, set update, clique generation and backtracking.

The BK algorithm can be sketched by Algorithm 1. It uses three vertex sets to represent a search subtree: the set anchor records the list of vertices in the current search path, the set cand records the list of candidate vertices that are not in anchor but connected to every vertex in anchor, and the set not records the list of vertices that are connected to every vertex in anchor but could not produce new maximal cliques if combined with the vertices in the anchor set.

2.4 Existing Parallel Solutions

In this subsection, we describe the idea behind the typical parallel approach [23, 32, 38] for maximal clique enumeration based on MapReduce. It enumerates maximal cliques for different vertices in a graph in parallel.

Given a graph G and a vertex v in G, the maximal cliques of the vertex v refer to the maximal cliques containing v in G. Note that a vertex v's maximal cliques are

the induced subgraphs consisting of v and its neighboring vertices in G. The parallel search consists of two steps. In the first one, the parallel approach retrieves each vertex's neighboring information relevant to its clique computation. In the second step, it searches for each vertex's maximal cliques in parallel. For the computation on an individual vertex, it simply adopts the classical sequential algorithms (e.g., the BK algorithm).

In the typical approach, enumerating the maximal cliques of a vertex is supposed to be performed on a single machine. In case that the computation on an individual vertex is extremely time-consuming due to the large number of maximal cliques, it may become a parallel performance bottleneck. The method proposed in [32] can parallelize maximal clique enumeration on an individual vertex. It uses candidate path data structures to record the search progress such that any search subtree can be traversed independently. It achieves better load balancing by allowing a computing node to steal some tasks from others when becoming almost idle. The proposed load balancing technique was implemented by MPI, but can easily generalize to other shared-nothing parallel frameworks such as MapReduce. However, as we will show in Sect. 5, its parallel performance depends on the performance of the *BK* algorithm, and may be limited by size unevenness among search subtrees.

3 Sequential Algorithms

3.1 Idea: Graph Partitioning

We illustrate the idea behind the new sequential algorithms by an example. As shown in Fig. 1a, the graph G consists of the vertices, $\{v_1, v_2, v_3, v_4, v_5\}$. We randomly choose a vertex in G (e.g., v_1) as the partitioning anchor and partition G into two subgraphs G_1^+ and G_1^-. G_1^+ denotes the induced subgraph consisting of v_1 and its neighboring vertices in G, $\{v_1, v_2, v_3\}$. G_1^- denotes the induced subgraph of G consisting of all the vertices not in G_1^+, $\{v_4, v_5\}$, and their neighboring vertices in G, $\{v_2, v_3\}$. The subgraphs G_1^+ and G_1^- are shown in Fig. 1b, c, respectively. We observe that any maximal clique of G is an induced subgraph of either G_1^+ or G_1^-.

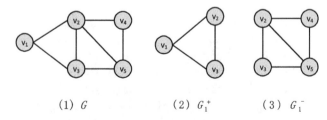

(1) G (2) G_1^+ (3) G_1^-

Fig. 1 A graph partitioning example

Generally, we have the following theorem:

Theorem 1 *Given a graph G, we partition G into two subgraphs, G_v^+ and G_v^-, in which v denotes a partitioning anchor, G_v^+ denotes the induced subgraph consisting of vertex v and its neighboring vertices in G, and G_v^- denotes the induced subgraph consisting of all the vertices not in G_v^+ and their neighboring vertices in G. Then, any maximal clique of G is an induced subgraph of either G_v^+ or G_v^-.*

Proof If a maximal clique contains the vertex v, it should be an induced subgraph of G_v^+. Otherwise, it should contain at least one vertex not in G_v^+. Suppose that it is the vertex u. As a result, the maximal clique is an induced subgraph of G_u, which consists of vertex u and its neighboring vertices. According to the definition of G_v^-, G_u is obviously an induced subgraph of G_v^-. Therefore, the maximal clique is an induced subgraph of G_v^-. □

According to Theorem 1, maximal clique detection in G can be performed by searching for the maximal cliques in G_v^+ and G_v^- independently. The partitioning operation can be iteratively invoked until all the resulting subgraphs become cliques. Obviously, all the maximal cliques in G are contained in the set of the resulting cliques. Unfortunately, a resulting clique generated by the above process cannot be guaranteed to be maximal. Therefore, enumeration algorithms should filter out the non-maximal cliques among them.

3.2 GP Algorithm

Algorithm 2: enumerateGP(anchor,cand,not)
---
1 **if** *(G(cand) is a clique)* **then**
2   Output the clique G(anchor ∪ cand);
3 **else**
4   **while** *(G(cand) is NOT a clique)* **do**
5   Choose a vertex v with the smallest degree in G(cand);
6   anchor$^+$ ← anchor ∪ {v};
7   cand$^+$ ← cand ∩ N(v);
8   not$^+$ ← not ∩ N(v);
9   **if** *($\nexists u \in$ not$^+$:u is connected to all the vertices in cand$^+$)* **then**
10   enumerateGP(anchor$^+$,cand$^+$,not$^+$);
11   cand ← cand − {v};
12   not ← not ∪ {v};
13   **if** *($\nexists u \in$ not:u is connected to all the vertices in cand)* **then**
14   Output the clique G(anchor ∪ cand);

The algorithm iteratively partitions a graph until it becomes cliques. To reduce search space, it always chooses the vertex v with the smallest degree in a graph as the partitioning anchor. It can be observed that this strategy would usually result in a relatively small graph and a larger one. Generally, the small graph would be partitioned into cliques after only a few iterations, while the size of the larger one could be effectively reduced. Unlike the BK algorithm, which recursively extracts the induced subgraph consisting of the vertex with the largest degree and its neighbors, our approach instead recursively performs binary partitioning by choosing the partitioning anchor with the smallest degree.

The algorithm is sketched in Algorithm 2. Similar to the BK algorithm as shown in Algorithm 1, it employs three sets of vertices (anchor, cand and not) to record the partitioning progress and prune the subtrees that cannot generate maximal cliques. The recursive function first checks whether the resulting subgraph is a clique (Line 1). If yes, it simply outputs the subgraph. Otherwise, it chooses a partitioning anchor v with the smallest degree in cand and partitions G(cand) into G(cand$^+$) and G(cand$^-$). G(cand$^+$) consists of v and its neighboring vertices in G(cand) (Lines 6–8). G(cand$^-$) consists of all the vertices in G(cand) except v (Lines 11–12). The algorithm recursively processes the subgraph G(cand$^+$) (Lines 9–10). Note that before the recursive function is invoked, the algorithm prunes the search space by inspecting whether there exists a vertex in the not$^+$ set that is connected to all the vertices in the cand$^+$ set (Line 9). Updating G(cand) with G(cand$^-$) (Lines 11–12), it then iteratively invokes the partition operation to search for the maximal cliques in G(cand$^-$) until G(cand$^-$) becomes a clique (Lines 4–12). After G(cand$^-$) becomes a clique, the algorithm checks whether it is maximal (Lines 13–14).

Given an input graph $G = (V, E)$, the algorithm can be set in motion by setting anchor $= \emptyset$, not $= \emptyset$ and cand $= V$. Suppose that we are running Algorithm 2 on the example graph as shown in Fig. 1. Originally, anchor $= \emptyset$, not $= \emptyset$ and cand $= \{v_1, v_2, v_3, v_4, v_5\}$. The vertex v_1 has the smallest degree of 2, is thus chosen as the partitioning anchor. G is then partitioned into G_1^+ and G_1^-. G_1^+ consists of v_1 and its neighboring vertices, $\{v_1, v_2, v_3\}$. G_1^- consists of the vertices, $\{v_2, v_3, v_4, v_5\}$. For G_1^+, anchor $= \{v_1\}$, not$=\emptyset$ and cand$=\{v_2, v_3\}$. For G_1^-, anchor$=\emptyset$, not$=\{v_1\}$ and cand$=\{v_2, v_3, v_4, v_5\}$. It can be observed that G_1^- is not a clique and v_3 has the smallest degree of 2 in G_1^-. G_1^- would then be partitioned into two subgraphs consisting of $\{v_2, v_3, v_5\}$ and $\{v_2, v_4, v_5\}$, respectively, which are both clique. Therefore, the maximal cliques of G can be computed with two partitioning operations.

In practical implementation, the algorithm iteratively partitions an input graph in a depth-first manner. After partitioning G into G(cand$^-$) and G(cand$^+$), it always processes the G(cand$^-$) subgraph before G(cand$^+$), and pushes the resulting G(cand$^+$) into a stack for later processing. Whenever a G(cand$^-$) subgraph becomes a clique, it pops a $G(\text{cand}^+)$ subgraph from the stack and repeats the iterative partitioning operation.

We have Theorems 2 and 3, whose proofs are presented in "Appendices 1 and 2", respectively. Note that in Theorem 3, *different cliques* include both maximal and non-maximal cliques.

Theorem 2 *Algorithm 2 exactly returns all the maximal cliques in G.*

Theorem 3 *Given a connected graph $G = (V, E)$, Algorithm 2 has the space complexity of $O(|E|)$ and the time complexity of $O(|E|\mu(G))$, in which $\mu(G)$ represents the number of different cliques in G.*

3.3 Hybrid Algorithm

Algorithm 3: enumerateHybrid(anchor,cand,not)
---

1   **if** *(G(cand) is a clique)* **then**
2   Output the clique G(anchor ∪ cand);
3   **else**
4   **while** *(G(cand) is NOT a clique)* **do**
5   **if** *(the largest vertex degree of G(cand) exceeds θ)* **then**
6             $v \leftarrow$ the vertex with the largest degree in $G(\text{cand})$;
7   *cur_v=v*;
8   **while** *cur_v ≠ NULL* **do**
9   n_anchor=anchor ∪ {*cur_v*};
10   n_not=not ∩ $N(cur\_v)$;
11   n_cand=cand ∩ $N(cur\_v)$;
12   **if** *(∄u ∈ n_not:u is connected to all the vertices in n_cand)* **then**
13   enumerateHybrid(n_anchor,n_cand, n_not);
14   not=not∪{*cur_v*};
15   cand=cand − {*cur_v*};
16   **if** *(there is a vertex u in cand that is not connected to v)* **then**
17   *cur_v=u*;
18   **else**
19   *cur_v=NULL*
20   return; // terminate this function;
21   **else**
22   Choose a vertex v with the smallest degree in $G(\text{cand})$;
23   anchor$^+$ ← anchor ∪ {v};
24   cand$^+$ ← cand ∩ $N(v)$;
25   not$^+$ ← not ∩ $N(v)$;
26   **if** *(∄u ∈ not$^+$:u is connected to all the vertices in cand$^+$)* **then**
27   enumerateHybrid(anchor$^+$,cand$^+$,not$^+$)
                 cand ← cand − {v};
28   not ← not ∪ {v};
29   **if** *(∄u ∈ not:u is connected to all the vertices in cand)* **then**
30   Output the clique G(anchor ∪ cand);

We observe that the performance of Algorithm 2 largely depends on the number of the generated $G(\text{cand}^+)$

subgraphs, on which the partition operation is iteratively executed. To reduce the number of invoked partition operations, the hybrid algorithm considers multi-way partitioning as well as binary partitioning. The operation of multi-way partitioning selects a vertex v with the largest degree in $G(\text{cand})$, and partitions $G(\text{cand})$ into $\{G_v(\text{cand}), G_{u_1}(\text{cand}), \ldots, G_{u_k}(\text{cand})\}$, in which $\{u_1, \ldots, u_k\}$ represent the set of vertices *not* connected to v in $G(\text{cand})$ and $G_v(\text{cand})$ denotes the induced subgraph consisting of the vertex v and all its neighbors in $G(\text{cand})$. It is worthy to point out that the multi-way partition operation is essentially the core search operation used by the classical BK algorithm. As proved in the BK algorithm, it can be shown that all the maximal cliques in $G(\text{cand})$ can be searched in the induced subgraphs of $\{G_v(\text{cand}), G_{u_1}(\text{cand}), \ldots, G_{u_k}(\text{cand})\}$ independently. Since this algorithm uses both binary and multi-way partitioning operations, which are the key characteristics of the GP and BK algorithms, respectively, it is called *Hybrid*.

The hybrid algorithm invokes the operation of multi-way partitioning if and only if the largest vertex degree of $G(\text{cand})$ is large enough. We define the largeness of a vertex degree in a graph by $p = \frac{d}{n}$, in which n represents the total number of vertices in the graph and d represents a vertex degree. Specifically, if the largest degree of the vertices in $G(\text{cand})$, compared with the total number vertices in the graph, exceeds a predefined threshold θ (e.g., $\theta = 0.8$), the hybrid algorithm would execute the multi-way partitioning operation; otherwise, it would execute the binary partitioning operation. As shown in Sect. 5.3, the value of the threshold θ has only marginal influence on the performance of the hybrid algorithm if it is set between 0.6 and 0.8. We suggest that it is set to be 0.8 in practical implementation.

The hybrid algorithm is sketched in Algorithm 3. Lines 5–19 specify the multi-way partitioning operation and Lines 22–28 specify the binary partitioning operation. The operation of multi-way partitioning is similar to the core search operation used by the *BK* algorithm. The difference is that it uses the not set to filter out unnecessary search subtrees (Line 12). Once $G(\text{cand})$ meets the condition specified at Line 5, it is partitioned into multiple subgraphs, each of which invokes a new recursive function (Line 13). After that, the current function terminates its execution (Line 20). Otherwise, $G(\text{cand})$ is partitioned into $G(\text{cand}^+)$ and $G(\text{cand}^-)$. A new recursive function is invoked to process $G(\text{cand}^+)$ (Line 27). The subgraph $G(\text{cand}^-)$ is instead iteratively partitioned until it becomes clique (Line 4 and Lines 29–30).

Based on the correctness proofs of the *BK* and *GP* algorithms, it can be easily shown that Algorithm 3 exactly returns all the maximal cliques in G. On the space and time complexity of Algorithm 3, we have Theorem 4, whose proof is presented in "Appendix 3".

Theorem 4   *Given a connected graph $G = (V, E)$, Algorithm 3 has the space complexity of $O(|E|)$ and the time complexity of $O(|E|\mu(G))$, in which $\mu(G)$ represents the number of different cliques in G.*

3.4 Notes on Implementation

The program reads a graph G into memory, and then iteratively computes the maximal cliques of every vertex in G. We store the vertices in the original graph G in an array and their adjacency lists as hash sets. Similarly, all the cand sets are maintained by hash sets. As a result, the intersection of two vertex sets can be performed by hash look-ups. Clique verification is achieved by checking vertex degrees.

For the Hybrid algorithm, vertex degrees in each subgraph resulting from a multi-way BK partitioning operation are computed by intersecting two adjacency sets. For the GP algorithm, the degree of a vertex v_i in cand$^+$ of G_v^+ is computed by intersecting the adjacency set of v_i with the cand$^+$ set. For the vertices in the cand$^-$ set of G_v^-, only those connected to v needs to decrease their degrees by 1. Selecting a partitioning anchor with the minimal degree in cand however requires $O(|\text{cand}|)$ time because it has to sequentially scan all the vertices in the hash set. To enable more efficient anchor selection, we also maintain a degree map, in which the vertex degrees of cand are stored as a sorted linked list and each entry in the degree list has a corresponding vertex list consisting of all the vertices with the specified degree. The degree map of the G_v^- subgraph is inherited from that of its parent with corresponding updates while the degree map of G_v^+ is constructed from scratch. With the degree map, selecting a partitioning anchor in cand only involves picking up a vertex in the vertex list of the first entry in the degree list. It takes only constant time.

4 Parallel Solutions

4.1 General Procedure

The parallel solution consists of two steps. In the first step, for every vertex v in the graph G, it retrieves an induced subgraph of G whose vertices are relevant to the computation of v's maximal cliques. In the second step, it

performs iterative graph partitioning on every vertex. Both subgraph retrieval and clique computation on individual vertices are distributed across multiple computing nodes.

We observe that the computational workload on the vertices may be unbalanced: the computation on a vertex may be more expensive than on another because it has a larger search space. In case that the computation on a vertex is too time-consuming, it becomes a parallel performance bottleneck. A good property of the GP approach is that it enables easy and effective load balancing. Since GP iteratively partitions a large G_v into a series of small graphs, whose computations are independent, the computation on a vertex can be easily parallelized. In practice, recursive function usually takes only a few iterations (no more than 3–4 iterations in our experiments in Sect. 5.2) to transform a big G_v into many sufficiently small subgraphs. With sufficiently small tasks, effective load balancing can be achieved by sending some tasks on a computing node with heavy workload to another with lighter workload.

To achieve workload balance, the procedure iteratively invokes the Compute–Shuffle cycle. In the Compute phase, every computing node performs the partitioning operation on the subgraphs it has received; in the Shuffle phase, all the intermediate subgraphs on the nodes are reshuffled so that every node receives roughly the same number of them. The workload limit of each Compute phase can be quantified by the consumed CPU time.

In general, the parallel procedure consists of the following two steps:

1. *Subgraph retrieval* For every vertex v in the graph G, retrieve the induced graph G_v consisting of v and its neighboring vertices in G;
2. *Iterative computation*

   - *Compute phase* For each computing node, sequentially compute the maximal cliques of its assigned subgraphs by the GP or hybrid algorithm;
   - *Shuffle phase* Evenly reshuffle all the intermediate subgraphs across the nodes;

4.2 MapReduce Solutions

This subsection describes the MapReduce solutions based on the GP and hybrid sequential algorithms. Based on the observation that non-trivial cliques consist of triangles, we uses the technique of triangle enumeration proposed in [12], which is more efficient than 2-hop retrieval, to implement the process of subgraph retrieval.

Algorithm 4: The Computation at Reducer based on the GP Algorithm

---

Input: A queue of unfinished subgraphs Q;
1 **while** *(Q is not empty) and (workload limit has not been reached)* **do**
2   Dequeue a subgraph G_u from Q;
3   **while** *(G_u is not a clique)* **do**
4   Choose the vertex w with the minimal degree in G_u as the anchor;
5   Partition G_u into G_w^+ and G_w^-;
6   **if** $|cand(G_w^+)| \le k$ **then**
7   **if** *(workload limit has been reached)* **then**
8                  $Enqueue(G_w^+, Q)$;
9   **else**
10   Process G_w^+ using Algorithm 2 to the end;
11   **else**
12              $Enqueue(G_w^+, Q)$;
13          $G_u = G_w^-$;
14   **if** *(G_u can not be pruned)* **then**
15   Output G_u;

Algorithm 5: The Function of $Enqueue(G, Q)$

---

1 **if** G can not be pruned **then**
2   **if** G is a clique **then**
3   Output G;
4   **else**
5   Enqueue G into Q;

Algorithm 6: The Computation at Reducer based on the Hybrid Algorithm

---

Input: A queue of unfinished subgraphs Q;
1 **while** *(Q is not empty) and (workload limit has not been reached)* **do**
2   Dequeue a subgraph G_u from Q;
3   **while** *(G_u is not a clique)* **do**
4   **if** *(the largest degree of the vertices in G_u exceeds θ)* **then**
5              $w \leftarrow$ the vertex with the largest degree in G_u;
6   Partition G_u into G_v and $\{G_{w_1}, \ldots, G_{w_h}\}$;
7   **for** $(1 \le i \le h)$ **do**
8   **if** $|G_{w_i}| \le k$ **then**
9   **if** *(workload limit has been reached)* **then**
10                          $Enqueue(G_{w_i}, Q)$;
11   **else**
12   Process G_{w_i} using Algorithm 3 to the end;
13   **else**
14                      $Enqueue(G_{w_i}, Q)$;
15   **if** *(G_v can not be pruned)* **then**
16                  $G_u = G_v$;
17   **else**
18   Choose the vertex v with the minimal degree in G_u as the anchor;
19   Partition G_u into G_v^+ and G_v^-;
20   **if** $|cand(G_v^+)| \le k$ **then**
21   **if** *(workload limit has been reached)* **then**
22                      $Enqueue(G_v^+, Q)$;
23   **else**
24   Process G_v^+ using Algorithm 3 to the end;
25   **else**
26                  $Enqueue(G_v^+, Q)$;
27              $G_u = G_v^-$;
28   **if** *(G_u can not be pruned)* **then**
29   Output G_u;

The program of iterative computation consists of a series of MapReduce cycles. In the Map phase, the mappers reads the unfinished subgraphs and randomly map them to reducers such that each reducer receives roughly the same number of subgraphs. In the Reduce phase, the reducers enumerate the maximal cliques of their assigned subgraphs by sequential algorithms. The MapReduce cycle is iteratively invoked until no unfinished subgraph is left.

The computation at a reducer based on the GP algorithm is sketched in Algorithm 4. Maintaining the subgraphs by a queue Q, it iteratively dequeues a subgraph G_u from the queue for graph partitioning. If the resulting G_w^+ has a small size, which means that its maximal clique computation can be finished in short time, it is iteratively partitioned to the end (Lines 7–10). Otherwise, it is temporarily enqueued into Q if it is not a clique (Line 12). It then iteratively partitions G_w^- in the same manner as G_u (Line 13). The operations of subgraph dequeue and graph partitioning are iteratively performed until the queue becomes empty or a predefined workload limit is reached.

The computation at a reducer based on the Hybrid algorithm, as sketched in Algorithm 6, is similar. If the largest vertex degree of a dequeued subgraph G_u exceeds the threshold of θ, it executes the operation of multi-way partitioning (Lines 5–16); otherwise, it executes the operation of binary partitioning (Lines 18–27). To ensure that G_u can be divided into many small subgraphs in a single reduce phase, the algorithm iteratively processes G_v resulting from the multi-way partitioning operation until it becomes a clique (Line 3) or it can be pruned (Lines 15–16).

5 Experimental Evaluation

This section empirically evaluates the performance of our proposed approaches by a comparative study. Since the BK algorithm has been widely reported to be faster than its alternatives, we compare our approach with the state-of-the-art implementation of the BK algorithm [28]. The typical parallel approach based on BK confines the computation on a vertex to a computing node. We enhance the parallel BK approach with the dynamic load balancing proposed in [32]. It was originally implemented by MPI in [32]. We have instead implemented a MapReduce version. Each reducer is set to have a predefined workload limit. After every reducer reaches its workload limit, the unfinished subgraphs are evenly redistributed across computing nodes. All our implementations have been made open source. They can be downloaded at [16].

Our experiments are conducted on both real and synthetic graph datasets. The evaluation on real datasets can show the efficiency of the proposed algorithms in real applications, while the evaluation on synthetic datasets can easily demonstrate their sensitivity to varying graph characteristics. Two synthetic datasets are generated by the SSCA#2 generator [2] and the power-law generator R-MAT [3] respectively. A SSCA#2 graph is directed, and made up of random-sized cliques, with a hierarchical inter-clique distribution of edges based on a distance metric. We vary the values of the *TotVertices* and *MaxCliqueSize* parameters, which specify the number of vertices and the size of the maximum clique respectively. The R-MAT generator applies the Recursive Matrix (R-MAT) graph model to produce the graphs with power-law degree distributions and small-world characteristics, which are common in many real life graphs. We vary two parameter

values, the number of vertices and the number of edges. The real graphs, which are selected from [29], are in various domains including communication networks, social networks, web graphs and protein networks. The details of test datasets are summarized in Table 1.

For the hybrid algorithm, we set the largest degree threshold θ in Algorithm 3 to 0.8 in the comparative study of Sects. 5.1 and 5.2. Our evaluation in Sect. 5.3 shows that if set between 0.0 and 0.8, the value of the threshold θ has only marginal influence on the performance of the hybrid algorithm.

Sequential algorithms are evaluated on a desktop with memory size of 16G and 6 Intel Core i7 CPU with the frequency of 3.3GHz. Parallel evaluation are conducted on a 13-machine cluster. Each machine runs the Ubuntu Linux (version 10.04) and has memory size of 16G, disk storage of 160G and 16 Intel Xeon E5502 CPUs with the frequency of 1.87GHz. The parallel solutions based on MapReduce are implemented on Hadoop (version 0.20.2) [17]. Each experiment is run three times and its running time averaged. We observe that time difference between different runnings does not exceed 10% of the total consumed time.

5.1 Evaluation of Sequential Algorithms

In this subsection, we evaluate the performance of the sequential algorithms on both real and synthetic graphs. Performance is evaluated on the metric of runtime.

5.1.1 On Real Datasets

The evaluation results on the real graphs are presented in Table 2. Note that running the Twitter dataset is beyond

Table 1 Details of the real and synthetic graph datasets

Dataset	Data description	Number of vertexes	Number of edges
EuAll	Email network from a EU Research Institution	265,214	364,481
WebGoogle	Web graph from Google	875,713	4,322,051
BerkStan	Web graph of Berkeley and Stanford	685,230	7,600,595
WikiComm	Wikipedia communication network	1,928,669	3,494,674
Pokec	Pokec online social network	1,632,803	30,622,564
Protein-1	A protein network	5816	313,628
Protein-2	A protein network	8176	457,991
WikiTalk	A social network	2,394,385	4,659,565
Skitter	Autonomous systems graphs	1,696,415	11,095,298
Twitter	Social circles from Twitter	11,316,811	85,331,846
R-MAT	Synthetic graphs with power-law degree distributions and small-world characteristics	Two parameters used: the number of vertices and the ratio of edges to vertices	
SSCA#2	Synthetic graphs with a hierarchical inter-clique distribution of edges based on a distance metric	Two parameters used: the number of vertices and the size of maximum clique	

Table 2 Evaluation of sequential algorithms on real graphs

Runtime(s)	EuAll	WebGoogle	BerkStan	WikiComm	Pokec	Protein-1	Protein-2	WikiTalk	Skitter
BK	1.56	8.94	28.79	388.70	**55.73**	115.76	216.53	9247.08	1720.48
GP	1.00	**8.78**	**17.57**	42.41	105.86	221.16	660.73	898.01	686.79
Hybrid	**0.97**	9.04	32.35	**35.19**	103.05	**103.06**	**154.27**	**554.64**	**359.26**

The bold values represent the minimal runtime consumed by the three approaches

the capability of a single machine. Therefore, they will be used later for parallel evaluation.

It can be observed that GP achieves overall better performance than BK. On some datasets (e.g., WikiComm and WikiTalk), GP runs roughly 10 times faster than BK. On the datasets where GP performs worse than BK (e.g., Berkstan and Protein-1), their performance difference is much smaller. It can also be clearly observed that the hybrid algorithm achieves the best performance among them. On most test datasets, Hybrid consumes the least runtime. It is worthy to point out that the outperformance margins achieved by Hybrid are considerable on many test datasets. For instance, on the Skitter dataset, GP takes around 40% of the runtime consumed by BK and Hybrid further cuts runtime by around 50%.

Our experiment show that the BK algorithm is very sensitive to particular graph characteristics. Its performance is usually very volatile. In comparison, GP's performance is more stable. The Hybrid algorithm achieves the best and most stable performance by effectively leveraging the advantages of the BK and GP algorithms.

5.1.2 On Synthetic Datasets

On synthetic datasets, we aim to investigate the comparative performance of different algorithms and how their performance varies with graph characteristics. On R-MAT graphs, the number of vertices is set to be 5000 and the edge-to-vertex ratio varies from 40 to 140. On SSCA graphs, the number of vertices is set to be 2^{20} and the size of the maximum clique varies from 100 to 200.

The evaluation results are presented in Fig. 2. On R-MAT, GP performs better than BK and Hybrid performs better than GP. On SSCA, Hybrid and GP achieve similar performance and both of them perform better than BK. It is interesting to note that the outperformance margins of GP and Hybrid over BK steadily increase with graph density. Similar to what were observed in the evaluation on real graphs, our results on synthetic datasets demonstrate that compared with GP and Hybrid, BK is much more sensitive to particular graph characteristics (e.g., graph density and sizes of maximal cliques).

5.2 Evaluation of Parallel Solutions

In this subsection, we evaluate the performance of different approaches, comparing GP and Hybrid against BK, on the Twitter dataset. Since all the parallel solutions use the same method of subgraph retrieval, we exclude its cost from performance evaluation in our study. We specify the parameter k in Algorithms 4 and 6 by the number of vertices contained by a graph. It is set to be 80. The maximal execution time per reduce phase is set to be 300 s. The workload limit of reduce phase is similarly set for the BK approach.

On the synthetic RMAT and SSCA graphs, the parallel performance of different approaches is similar to what are observed in sequential evaluation. Their detailed evaluation results are thus omitted here. We present the evaluation results on the largest real graph, Twitter. Note that processing the entire Twitter graph takes too long even on our machine cluster. We therefore generate 5 random test tasks,

Fig. 2 Evaluation of sequential algorithms on R-MAT and SSCA datasets

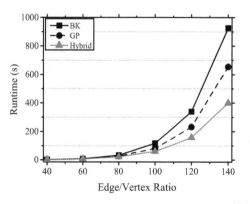

(a) R-MAT Graphs   **(b)** SSCA Graphs

Table 3 Parallel evaluation based on Hadoop on Twitter

	MapReduce cycles			Runtime (s)		
	BK	GP	Hybrid	BK	GP	Hybrid
D_T^1	3	2	2	775	441	**423**
D_T^2	3	3	3	944	917	**728**
D_T^3	4	3	2	1278	707	**486**
D_T^4	16	3	3	5455	**711**	772
D_T^5	18	4	3	5760	1111	**1054**

The bold values represent the minimal runtime consumed by the three approaches

denoted by $D_T^1, \ldots, D_T^5$, by choosing some vertices with large degrees in the graph for evaluation purpose. The maximal cliques of the chosen vertices are computed over the entire graph. The maximal vertex degree in the Twitter graph is more than one million. We randomly choose 5 vertices with degrees of more than 500,000 for each test task.

The comparative results on Twitter are presented in Table 3. Similar to what were observed in sequential evaluation, the performance of BK is very volatile. On some test tasks (e.g., D_T^2), the performance of BK is similar to that of GP. On other test tasks (e.g., D_T^4 and D_T^5), it performs significantly worse than GP. GP achieves overall better performance than BK. It can also be observed that Hybrid performs better than both BK and GP. On some test tasks (e.g., D_T^2 and D_T^3), its outperformance margins over GP are considerable.

5.3 Hybrid: Varying the Threshold θ

Our experiment evaluates the performance variation of the hybrid algorithm with the value of θ. We set the value of θ to be 0.6, 0.7 and 0.8. The detailed results on some of the real graphs listed in Table 1 are presented in Table 4. The results on other datasets are similar, thus omitted here. It can be observed that in the range of [0.6,0.8], the value of θ can only marginally influence the performance of the hybrid algorithm. This observation bodes well for the efficacy of the hybrid algorithm in real applications.

6 Related Work

Maximal clique enumeration have been studied extensively in the literature [4, 8–10, 25, 33, 34]. Due to its NP-Completeness, existing work focused on efficient search. Most of the proposed approaches were based on the classical BK algorithm [4], which has been widely reported as being faster than its alternatives [5, 15]. Authors of [10] proposed an efficient algorithm, which was also based on BK search, for maximal clique enumeration with limited

Table 4 Influence of the parameter θ on hybrid

Runtime(s)	EuAll	WebGoogle	Berkstan	WikiComm	Pokec
$p = 0.8$	0.97	9.04	32.35	35.19	103.05
$p = 0.7$	0.97	9.14	32.95	34.48	105.48
$p = 0.6$	0.99	9.24	32.65	35.98	103.85

memory. Authors of [8, 9] proposed to speed up clique detection by indexing the core structures of a special type of graph called H*-graph. Instead of BK, another approach [11, 24, 36] uses the strategy of *reverse search*. The key feature of this approach is that it is possible to define an upper bound on their runtime as a polynomial with respect to the number of maximal cliques in a graph. Note that focusing on centralized search, the efficient implementations of existing algorithms usually rely on global state and cannot be easily parallelized. There are also some work [30, 31] studying the closely related problem of detecting maximum clique. The algorithms they used are, however, variants of the BK algorithm.

Due to the increasing popularity of the MapReduce framework, the solutions have been proposed to parallelize maximal clique detection on MapReduce [13, 23, 38]. They proposed to distribute the vertices across workers and compute every vertex's maximal cliques in parallel. On the core algorithm for efficient search, they, however, used the BK algorithm or its variants. Authors of [39] proposed a fault-tolerant parallel solution for maximum clique detection based on MapReduce. It also used the BK algorithm for efficient search. A parallel solution for maximal clique enumeration based on MPI has been proposed in [32]. It proposed a dynamic load balancing technique that enabled an idle worker to "steal" workload from another busy worker. As we showed in Sect. 5.2, limited by the efficiency of BK search, its performance was still quite sensitive to graph characteristics.

Orthogonal to our work, many works extended the definition of clique to other dense subgraph structures (e.g., maximal cliques in an uncertain graph [42], cross-graph quasi-cliques [21], k-truss [20], and densest-subgraph [35]), and studied their applications. The existing algorithms for these problem are centralized. The search process of these dense structures is usually NP-Complete, thus computationally expensive over massive real graphs. However, efficient parallelization of their search processes over a machine cluster remains an open question.

7 Conclusion

In this paper, we propose a novel approach based on binary graph partitioning for maximal clique enumeration over graph data. Compared with the state-of-the-art BK approach, it can effectively divide a graph into many small tasks with less iterations. We also present a hybrid approach that can effectively leverage the advantages of both BK and GP approaches. We develop efficient sequential algorithms as well as corresponding parallel solutions. Finally, our extensive experiments on real and synthetic graph data demonstrate the performance advantage of our proposed solutions over the state-of-the-art ones.

Appendix 1: Proof of Theorem 2

Proof Firstly, if without the pruning operations specified in Lines 9 and 13 of Algorithm 2, all the maximal cliques in G are contained in the set of cliques returned by Algorithm 2.

Secondly, if there exists a vertex in the current not set that is connected to all the vertices in the current cand set, the recursive function cannot generate any new maximal clique. Consider a clique C_i in the graph $G(\text{anchor} \cup \text{cand})$. Suppose that the vertex u in the not set is connected to all the vertices in the cand set. Note that Algorithm 2 ensures that every vertex in not is connected to all the vertices in the anchor set. As a result, u is connected to all the vertices of C_i. Therefore, the clique C is not maximal.

Finally, any clique returned by Algorithm 2 is maximal. Assume that it returns two cliques, C_1 and C_2, and C_1 is contained by C_2. Suppose that C_1 consists of k vertices, $\{v_1, v_2, \ldots, v_k\}$, and C_2 has an additional vertex u. Also suppose that C_1 is generated by combining the anchor_1 set and the cand_1 set. Since the vertex u is not in anchor_1 but connected to all the vertices in anchor_1, its exclusion from cand_1 should be a result of a previous graph partitioning operation with u as the partitioning anchor. Therefore, the vertex u should be included in the not set of the corresponding partitioned graph $G(\text{anchor}^- \cup \text{cand}^-)$, whose recursive partitioning later generates the clique C_1. Since u is connected to all the vertices in anchor_1, Algorithm 2 ensures that it is in the not set of the partitioned graph $G(\text{anchor}_1 \cup \text{cand}_1)$. With u being connected to all the vertices in cand_1, Algorithm 2 should have filtered C_1 out. Contradiction. $\square$

Appendix 2: Proof of Theorem 3

Proof We first analyze its space complexity. It iteratively partitions the $G(\text{cand}^-)$ branch until $G(\text{cand}^-)$ becomes a clique. Besides the $G(\text{cand}^-)$ graph, it also has to store the resulting $G(\text{cand}^+)$ subgraphs in a stack S. Each $G(\text{cand}^+)$ results from a partitioning operation with a vertex v_i as anchor. Note that the first-in-last-out operation order of stack ensures that each $G(\text{cand}^+)$ subgraph in the stack S has a distinct partitioning anchor. Since each vertex in the anchor^+, cand^+ and not^+ sets of $G(\text{cand}^+)$ (except the vertex v_i itself) should be connected to v_i, the required space to store $G(\text{cand}^+)$ is bound by $O(|E_i|)$, in which E_i represents the set of edges with v_i as one of its end points. As a result, the required space to store all $G(\text{cand}^+)$ branches is bound by $O(|E|)$. It follows that the space complexity of Algorithm 2 is $O(|E|)$.

Secondly, we analyze its time complexity. Consider a variant of Algorithm 2 without the pruning operation specified on Line 9. Obviously, its time complexity is an upper bound on the time complexity of Algorithm 2. The traversal tree generated by the recursive function without pruning is a binary tree, in which each internal node has exactly two children. Since the cliques generated by the $G(\text{cand}^+)$ branch are guaranteed to be different from those generated by the $G(\text{cand}^-)$ branch, each leaf node corresponds to a different clique (maximal or non-maximal). Therefore, the size of the binary tree is bounded by $O(\mu(G))$. Accordingly, the total number of invoked graph partitioning operations is bounded by $O(\mu(G))$. Since each invocation of graph partitioning requires $O(|E|)$ time, the time complexity of the recursive function is $O(|E|\mu(G))$. $\square$

Appendix 3: Proof of Theorem 4

Proof The space complexity analysis of Algorithm 3 is similar to that of Algorithm 2. Each subgraph recorded for later processing can be considered to correspond to a different anchor. Therefore, its required space is bounded by $O(|E|)$.

Secondly, we analyze its time complexity. Consider a variant of Algorithm 3 without the pruning operation by the not set. Obviously, its time complexity is an upper bound on the time complexity of Algorithm 3. It would generate different cliques (maximal or non-maximal). Also note that in its traversal tree, each leaf corresponds to a different clique and each internal node has at least two children. The size of its traversal tree is thus bounded by $O(\mu(G))$. Therefore, the time complexity of Algorithm 3 is bounded by $O(|E|\mu(G))$. $\square$

References

1. Akkoyunlu EA (1973) The enumeration of maximal cliques of large graphs. SIAM J Comput 2(1):1–6
2. Bader DA, Madduri K (2005) Design and implementation of the HPCS graph analysis benchmark on symmetric multiprocessors. In: In Proceedings of 12th international conference on high performance computing, pp 465–476
3. Bader DA, Madduri K (2006) Gtgraph: a synthetic graph generator suite, pp 1–4. http://www.cse.psu.edu/~madduri/software/GTgraph/
4. Bron C, Kerbosch J (1973) Algorithm 457: finding all cliques of an undirected graph. Commun ACM 16(9):575–577
5. Cazals F, Karande C (2008) A note on the problem of reporting maximal cliques. Theor Comput Sci 407(1):564–568
6. Cazals F, Karande C (2008) A note on the problem of reporting maximal cliques. Theor Comput Sci 407(1–3):564–568
7. Chen Q, Fang C, Wang Z, Suo B, Li Z, lves ZG (2016) Parallelizing maximal clique enumeration over graph data. In: DASFAA, pp 249–264
8. Cheng J, Ke Y, Fu AW-C, Yu JX, Zhu L (2011) Finding maximal cliques in massive networks. ACM Trans. Datab. Syst. 36(4):1–34
9. Cheng J, Ke Y, Fu AW, Zhu L (2010) Finding maximal cliques in massive networks by h*-graph. In: SIGMOD, pp 447–458
10. Cheng J, Zhu L, Chu YKS (2012) Fast algorithms for maximal clique enumeration with limited memory. In: KDD, pp 1240–1248
11. Chiba N, Nishizeki T (1985) Arboricity and subgraph listing algorithms. SIAM J Comput 14(1):210–223
12. Cohen J (2009) Graph twiddling in a mapreduce world. Comput Sci Eng 11(4):29–41
13. Du N, Wu B, Xu LT, Wang B, Pei X (2006) A parallel algorithm for enumerating all maximal cliques in complex network. In: ICDM workshops, pp 320–324
14. Eppstein D, Löffler M, Strash D (2010) Listing all maximal cliques in sparse graphs in near-optimal time. In: ISAAC(1), pp 403–414
15. Eppstein D, Strash D (2011) Listing all maximal cliques in large sparse real-world graphs. In: 10th International symposium on experimental algorithms, pp 364–375
16. GP Project: efficient maximal clique and k-plex detection over graph data. http://www.wowbigdata.cn/gp/clique.html
17. Hadoop: an open-source implementation of mapreduce. http://hadoop.apache.org/
18. Hanneman R (2005) Introduction to social network methods, chapter 11: cliques. http://faculty.ucr.edu/~hanneman/nettext/
19. Haraguchi M, Okubo Y (2006) A method for pinpoint clustering of web pages with pseudo-clique search. In: Jantke K, Lunzer A, Spyratos N, Tanaka Y (eds) Federation over the web, volume 3847 of lecture notes in computer science. Springer, Berlin, pp 59–78
20. Huang X, Cheng H, Qin L, Tian W, Yu JX (2014) Querying k-truss community in large and dynamic graphs. In: SIGMOD, pp 1311–1322
21. Jiang DX, Pei J (2009) Mining frequent cross-graph quasi-cliques. TKDE 2(4):1–42
22. Leskovec J, Lang KJ, Dasgupta A, Mahoney MW (2008) Statistical properties of community structure in large social and information networks. In: WWW, pp 695–704
23. Lu L, Gu Y, Grossman R (2010) dmaximalcliques: A distributed algorithm for enumerating all maximal cliques and maximal clique distribution. In: IEEE international conference on data mining workshops, pp 1320–1327
24. Makino K, Uno T (2004) New algorithms for enumerating all maximal cliques. In: SWAT, lecture notes in computer science, vol 3111, pp 260–272
25. Modani N, Dey K (2008) Large maximal cliques enumeration in sparse graphs. In: CIKM, pp 1377–1378
26. On B-W, Elmacioglu E, Lee D, Kang J, Pei J (2006) Improving grouped-entity resolution using quasi-cliques. In: ICDM, pp 1008–1015
27. Pavlopoulos GA, Secrier M, Moschopoulos CN, Soldatos TG, Kossida S, Aertes J, Schneider R, Bagos PG (2011) Using graph theory to analyze biological networks. BioData Min 4:10
28. Quick Cliques: quickly compute all maximal cliques in sparse graphs. https://github.com/darrenstrash/quick-cliques
29. Real graph datasets. http://snap.stanford.edu/data/
30. Rossi RA, Gleich DF, Gebremedhin AH, Patwary MMA (2014) Fast maximum clique algorithms for large graphs. In: WWW, pp 365–366
31. Rossi RA, Gleich DF, Gebremedhin AH (2015) Parallel maximum clique algorithms with applications to network analysis. SIAM J Sci Comput 37(5):589–616
32. Schmidt MC, Samatova NF, Thomas K, Park BH (2009) A scalable, parallel algorithm for maximal clique enumeration. J Parallel Distrib Comput 69(4):417–428
33. Stix V (2004) Finding all maximal cliques in dynamic graphs. Comput Optim Appl 2:173–186
34. Tomita E, Tanaka A, Takahashi H (2006) The worst-case time complexity for generating all maximal cliques and computational experiments. Theor Comput Sci 363(1):28–42
35. Tsourakakis C, Bonchi F, Gionis A, Gullo F, Tsiarli M (2013) Denser than the densest subgraph: Extracting optimal quasi-cliques with quality guarantees. In: KDD, pp 104–112
36. Tsukiyama S, Ide M, Shirakawa I (1977) A new algorithm for generating all the maximal independent sets. SIAM J Comput 6(3):505–517
37. Wang J, Zeng Z, Zhou L (2006) Clan: An algorithm for mining closed cliques from large dense graph databases. In: ICDE, pp 73–82
38. Wu B, Yang S, zhao H, Wang B (2009) A distributed algorithm to enumerate all maximal cliques in mapreduce. In: International conference on frontier of computer science and technology, pp 45–51
39. Xiang JG, Guo C, Aboulnaga A (2013) Scalable maximum clique computation using mapreduce. In: ICDE, pp 74–85
40. Yang S, Wang B, zhao H, Wu B (2009) Efficient dense structure mining using mapreduce. In: IEEE international conference on data mining workshops, pp 332–337
41. Zhang Y, Abu-Khzam FN, Baldwin NE, Chesler EJ, Langston MA, Samatova NF (2005) Genome-scale computational approaches to memory-intensive applications in systems biology. In: ACM/IEEE supercomputing, pp 12–12
42. Zou ZN, Li JZ, Gao H, Zhang S (2010) Finding top-k maximal cliques in an uncertain graph. In: ICDE, pp 649–652

5

Context-Aware Recommendations with Random Partition Factorization Machines

Shaoqing Wang[1,2,3] (iD) · Cuiping Li[1,2] · Kankan Zhao[1,2] · Hong Chen[1,2]

Abstract Context plays an important role in helping users to make decisions. There are hierarchical structure between contexts and aggregation characteristics within the context in real scenarios. Exist works mainly focus on exploring the explicit hierarchy between contexts, while ignoring the aggregation characteristics within the context. In this work, we explore both of them so as to improve accuracy of prediction in recommender systems. We propose a Random Partition Factorization Machines (RPFM) by adopting random decision trees to split the contexts hierarchically to better capture the local complex interplay. The intuition here is that local homogeneous contexts tend to generate similar ratings. During prediction, our method goes through from the root to the leaves and borrows from predictions at higher level when there is sparseness at lower level. Other than estimation accuracy of ratings, RPFM also reduces the over-fitting by building an ensemble model on multiple decision trees. We test RPFM over three different benchmark contextual datasets. Experimental results demonstrate that RPFM outperforms state-of-the-art context-aware recommendation methods.

Keywords Context-aware recommendations · Hierarchical information · Factorization Machines · Random decision trees

A short version of this paper appeared in the proceedings of the 17th International Conference on Web-Age Information Management (WAIM2016) [26]. Different from the conference paper, the new contents of this paper include the following. (1) We add a discussion about the relationship between the proposed RPFM and other state-of-the-art random partition based methods in Sect. 4.2. (2) We add some experiments to assess the performance of proposed RPFM with different similarity measure function in k-means method. (3) Besides, introduction, related works, preliminaries, and future work are all been extended in Sects. 1, 2, 3, and 6, respectively.

✉ Cuiping Li
licuiping@ruc.edu.cn

Shaoqing Wang
wsq@ruc.edu.cn

Kankan Zhao
zhaokankan@ruc.edu.cn

Hong Chen
chong@ruc.edu.cn

[1] Key Lab of Data Engineering and Knowledge Engineering of MOE, Beijing, China

[2] Renmin University of China, Beijing, China

[3] School of Computer Science and Technology, Shandong University of Technology, Zibo, China

1 Introduction

With the rapid development of web 2.0 and wireless communication technologies, we are going through a new era of information overload. That is, it is difficult to quickly find the available information for users. To cope with the challenge, there are two solutions: information retrieval [19] and recommender systems [12]. If users can express their requirement clearly, information retrieval is a good method to help them. For example, when will start the next game of Real Madrid football club? However, it is difficult to generate the specific demand in many cases. Such as, what the Internet is talking about right now, which movie is the most interesting recently, which book should I buy? Recommender systems can give the answers.

Recommender systems have become an important tool to help users to easily find the favorite items. In general, recommender systems can be divided into three categories: content-based recommendation, collaborative filtering and hybrid recommendation [9]. Content-based recommendation can play an important role to help users making decisions when the content can be abstracted from the items, e.g., news [4], jokes, books, reviews. However, the recommended items are very familiar to the users. Lack of novelty is the one of the weak points of content-based recommendation. The main idea of collaborative filtering approaches is to exploit information about the past behaviors of all users of the system for predicting which items the current user will most probably be interested in. Pure collaborative filtering approaches take a matrix of given user–item ratings as the only input. Though collaborative filtering approaches achieves great success, there are some shortcomings. For example, cold-start items cannot be recommended, and popular items often be recommended. Due to known limitations of either pure content-based recommender systems or collaborative filtering , it rather soon led to the development of hybrid recommendation that combine the advantages of different recommendation techniques. In this work, we focus on collaborative filtering by exploiting the hierarchal information implied to improve the performance of recommendations.

Collaborative filtering [11, 12, 23, 25] methods behind the recommender systems have been developed for many years and is still a hot research topic up to now. User's decisions (e.g., clicked, purchased, re-tweeted, commented) to the relevant items are made under the certain environments which is often referred to as *context*. The contexts which include time, location, mood, companion and so on can be collected easily in real-world applications. Comparing to conventional recommendation solely based on user–item interactions, context-aware recommendation (CAR) can significantly improve the recommendation quality.

For this purpose, a great number of context-aware recommendation methods [10, 13, 21] have been proposed. Among them, Factorization Machines (FM) [21] is currently an influential and popular one. It represents the user–item–context interactions as a linear combination of the latent factors to be inferred from the data and treats the latent factors of user, item and context equality. Despite its successful application, existing FM model is weak to utilize hierarchical information. In practice, hierarchies can capture broad contextual information at different levels and hence ought to be exploited to improve the recommendation quality. The intuition here is that local homogeneous contexts tend to generate similar ratings. For example, many men who are engaged in IT department like to browse on technology Web sites in office during the day. However, they enjoy visiting sport Web sites at home in the evening. Here, users may be arranged in a hierarchy based on gender or occupation, Web sites may be

characterized by contents, and there are natural hierarchies for time and location.

In this paper, we focus on solving the problem of exploiting the hierarchical information to improve the recommendation quality. We propose a Random Partition Factorization Machines (RPFM) by adopting random decision trees to split the contexts hierarchically to better capture the local complex interplay. More specifically, the user–item–context interactions are first partitioned to different nodes of a decision tree according to their local contexts. Then, FM model is applied to the interactions of each node to capture the tight impact of each other. During prediction, our method goes through from the root to the leaves and borrows from predictions at higher level when there is sparseness at lower level. Other than estimation accuracy of rating, RPFM also reduces the over-fitting by building an ensemble model on multiple decision trees. The main contribution of the paper is summarized as follows:

1. FM model is one of the most successful approaches for context-aware recommendation. However, there is only one set of the model parameters which can be learned from the whole training set. We propose the novel RPFM model which makes use of the intuition that similar ratings can be generated from homogeneous environments.
2. We adopt the k-means cluster method to partition the user–item–context interactions at each node of decision trees. The similarity between the latent factor vectors of FM model can be used to partition the user–item–context interactions. The subset at each node is expected to be more impacted each other.
3. We conduct experiments on three datasets and compare it with five state-of-the-art context-aware recommendations to demonstrate RPFM's performance.

The rest of the paper is organized as follows: In Sect. 2, we provide related works about context-aware and random partition-based models. In Sect. 3, we introduce the FM model. In Sect. 4, we propose the Random Partition Factorization Machines (RPFM) model which includes algorithm description and discussion with two state-of-the-art random partition-based models. In Sect. 5, we present the experimental result on three real datasets. The paper is concluded in Sect. 6, and the future research direction is outlined.

2 Related Works

The work presented in this paper is closely related to context-aware recommendation and random partition on tree structure. In the following, we introduce the related works to serve as background for our solution.

2.1 Context-Aware Recommendation

In general, there are three types of integration method [2]: (1)contextual pre-filtering method; (2) contextual post-filtering method; and (3) contextual modeling method. In contrast to the previous two methods, the contextual modeling method uses all the contextual and user–item information simultaneously to make predictions. More recent works have focused on the third method [10, 13, 24, 27].

Karatzoglou et al. [10] proposed Multiverse Recommendation model in which the different types of context are considered as additional dimensions in the representation of the data as a tensor. The factorization of this tensor leads to a compact model of the data which can be used to provide context-aware recommendations. However, for real-world scenarios its computational complexity is too high. Rendle [24] showed that Factorization Machines (FM) model can be applied to context-aware recommendation because that a wide variety of context-aware data can be transformed into prediction task using real-valued feature vectors. Nguyen et al. [16] developed a nonlinear probabilistic algorithm for context-aware recommendation using Gaussian processes which is called Gaussian Process Factorization Machines (GPFM). GPFM is applicable to both the explicit feedback setting and the implicit feedback setting. Currently, the most recent approach in terms of prediction accuracy is COT [13] model, which represented the common semantic effects of contexts as a contextual operating tensor and represents a context as a latent vector. Then, to model the semantic operation of a context combination, it generates contextual operating matrix from the contextual operating tensor and latent vectors of contexts. Thus latent vectors of users and items can be operated by the contextual operating matrices. However, its computational complexity is also too high.

2.2 Random Partition on Tree Structure

Fan et al. [5] proposed Random Decision Trees which are applicable for classification and regression to partition the rating matrix and build ensemble. Each time, according to the feature and threshold which were selected randomly, the instances at each intermediate nodes are partitioned into two parts. Zhong et al. [28] proposed Random Partition Matrix Factorization (RPMF), based on a tree structure constructed by using an efficient random partition technique, which explore low-rank approximation to the current sub-rating matrix at each node. RPMF combines the predictions at each node (non-leaf and leaf) on the decision path from root to leaves. Liu et al. [14] handled contextual information by using random decision trees to partition the original user–item–rating matrix such that the ratings with similar contexts are grouped. Matrix factorization was then

employed to predict missing ratings of users for items in the partitioned sub-matrix.

3 Preliminaries

In this section, we briefly review Factorization Machines (FM) which is closely related to our work.

The notations used in this paper are summarized in Table 1.

3.1 Factorization Machines

Factorization Machines (FM), proposed by Rendle [21], is a general predictor which can mimic classical models like biased MF [12], SVD++ [11], PITF [25] or FPMC [23]. The model equation for FM of degree $d = 2$ is defined as:

$$\hat{y}(x_i) = \omega_0 + \sum_{j=1}^{p} \omega_j x_{i,j} + \sum_{j=1}^{p} \sum_{j'=j+1}^{p} \langle <\mathbf{v}_j, \mathbf{v}_{j'}\rangle x_{i,j} x_{i,j'}, \quad (1)$$

and

$$\langle \mathbf{v}_j, \mathbf{v}_{j'} \rangle := \sum_{k=1}^{f} v_{j,k} \cdot v_{j',k}, \quad (2)$$

where the mode parameters Θ that have to be estimated are:

$$\omega_0 \in \mathbb{R}, \quad \mathbf{w} \in \mathbb{R}^p, \quad \mathbf{V} \in \mathbb{R}^{f \times p}. \quad (3)$$

A row vector $\mathbf{v_i}$ of $\mathbf{V}$ represents the ith variable with f factors. $f \in \mathbb{N}_0^+$ is the dimensionality of the factorization.

The model equation of a factorization machine in Eq. (1) can be computed in linear time $O(f * p)$ because the pairwise interaction can be reformulated:

Table 1 Definition of notations

Notation	Description
R	Training set
R_{dj}	jth training subset at dth level
n_i	Number of the context C_i
m	Number of the contextual variables
f	Dimensionality of latent factor vectors
k	Number of clusters in k-means method
fun	Similarity function in k-means method
ω_0	Global bias
ω_i	Strength of the ith variable.
$\mathbf{v_i}$	Factor vector of the ith variable
S	Structure of tree
N	Number of trees
h	Height of tree
$leastT$	Number of least support tuples at leaf node

Table 2 An example of training set of FM model

	Users			Items				Locations				Ratings
x_1	1	0	0	1	0	0	0	1	0	0	0	4
x_2	1	0	0	0	1	0	0	0	1	0	0	3
x_3	1	0	0	0	0	1	0	0	1	0	0	3
x_4	0	1	0	0	0	0	1	0	0	1	0	5
x_5	0	0	1	1	0	0	0	1	0	1	0	2
x_6	0	0	1	0	1	0	0	0	0	0	1	3

$$\sum_{j=1}^{p}\sum_{j'=j+1}^{p}\langle \mathbf{v}_j, \mathbf{v}_{j'}\rangle x_{i,j}x_{i,j'} = \frac{1}{2}\sum_{k=1}^{f}\left(\left(\sum_{j=1}^{p}v_{j,k}x_{i,j}\right)^2 - \sum_{j=1}^{p}v_{j,k}^2 x_{i,j}^2\right)$$

Table 2 shows an example of input formation of training set. Here, there are $|U| = 3$ users, $|I| = 4$ items, $|L| = 4$ locations, which are binary indicator variables.

$U = \{u_1, u_2, u_3\}$

$I = \{i_1, i_2, i_3, i_4\}$

$L = \{l_1, l_2, l_3, l_4\}$

The first tuple x_1 means that user u_1 consumed i_1 at l_1 and rated it as 4 stars. For simplicity, we only consider categorical features in the paper. Table 3 shows the model parameters learned from the training set which is shown in Table 2.

3.2 Extensions to FM

There are a lot of extensions to FM model. Freudenthaler et al. [6] presented simple and fast structured Bayesian learning for FM model. Rendle [22] scaled FM to relational data. Hong et al. [8] proposed co-FM to model user interests and predicted individual decisions in twitter. Qiang et al. [20] exploited ranking FM for microblog retrieval. Loni et al. [15] presented 'Free lunch' enhancement for collaborative filtering with FM. Oentaryo et al. [17] predicted response in mobile advertising with hierarchical importance-aware FM. Cheng et al. [3] proposed a Gradient Boosting Factorization Machine (GBFM) model to incorporate feature selection algorithm with FM into a unified framework. To the best of our knowledge, there is no extension to FM model integrated into random decision

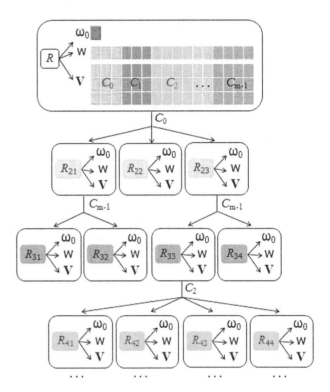

Fig. 1 Random decision trees (one tree)

trees such as to exploit the universal context-aware recommendations.

4 Random Partition Factorization Machines

The intuition is that there are similar rating behaviors among users under the same or similar contextual environments. Motivated by Zhong et al. [28], We describe the proposed Random Partition Factorization Machines (RPFM) for context-aware recommendations.

4.1 Algorithm Description

In order to efficiently take advantage of different contextual information, we adopt the idea the random decision trees algorithm.

The rational is to partition the original training set R such that the tuples generated by the similar users, items

Table 3 An example of parameters' values of FM model

	Users			Items				Locations			
w_0	1.86										
w	0.81	0.22	0.80	0.49	0.05	1.15	0.05	1.10	0.51	−0.10	0.49
V	0.03	0.06	0.03	−0.03	0.01	−0.06	0.03	−0.06	−0.08	−0.01	−0.03
	−0.03	−0.07	−0.02	0.00	0.01	0.10	0.00	0.10	0.13	−0.02	0.01
	0.03	0.03	0.02	0.01	0.01	−0.07	0.01	−0.07	−0.09	0.04	0.01
	−0.02	−0.02	−0.02	0.00	0.00	−0.07	−0.01	−0.06	−0.07	0.03	0.01

or contexts are grouped into the same node. Tuples in the same cluster are expected to be more correlated each other than those in original training set R. The main flow can be found in Fig. 1 and Algorithm 2.

To begin with, there is an input parameter S, the structure of decision trees, which can be generated by Algorithm 1 and determined by cross-validation. The parameter S includes contexts for partition at each level, numbers of clusters at each node. The maximal depth of trees can be inferred from the parameter S. For instance, if the value of

S is 'C2:4,C3:6,C1:10,C0:5', the meaning is: (1) at the root node of decision trees, the R can be divided into four groups by using k-means method according to the similarity between factor vectors of context C_2. Subsequently, the set at each node of 2nd, 3rd and 4th level of decision trees can be, respectively, divided into six, ten and five groups according to the similarity between factor vectors of context C_3, C_1 and C_0 using k-means method. (2) The maximal depth of each tree is five because there are four intermediate levels and one terminal level.

Algorithm 1 GenerateTreesStructure

Input: Depth of decsion trees: h, Numbers of Each Context: $n_0,...,n_{m-1}$
Output: Structure of Decision Trees
1: Initialize contextual information set A;
2: **for** $i=0$ to $m-1$ **do**
3:     $A(i)=C_i$;
4: **end for**
5: $j=0$;
6: **for** $i=0$ to $m-1$ **do**
7:     Select a context C_r from A randomly;
8:     Select $k \in [2, n_r]$ randomly such that the set at each node of $(i+1)$th level of decision trees will be divided into k groups;
9:     Add C_r and k to S;
10:     **if** $j >= h$ **then**
11:         break;
12:     **end if**
13:     $A = A \setminus C_r$;
14:     j++;
15: **end for**
16: **return** S;

Algorithm 2 RPFM

Input: Training Set: R, Dimensionality of Latent Factor Vectors: f, Number of Trees: N, Structure of Trees: S, Number of Least Support Instances at the Leaf Node: *leastL*, Similarity Function in k-means method: *fun*, Learning Rate: η, Regularization Values: λ
Output: Tree Ensemble with Model Parameters and Cluster Information at Each Node.
1: Get maximum depth of each tree to h according to S;
2: **for** $i = 1$ to N **do**
3:     Build tree T_i;
4:     **for** $d = 2$ to h **do**
5:         Get number of clusters to k and context for partition to C_r using S and current level d-1;
6:         Learn the parameters Θ using Eq.(1) at each node of the current level d-1;
7:         Partition R into k clusters using context C_r and matrix $\mathbf{V}$ in Θ by taking advantage of k-means method;
8:         **for** $j = 1$ to k **do**
9:             **if** the size of cluster j is less than *leastL* **then**
10:                 Let the current node as leaf node;
11:                 break;
12:             **end if**
13:         **end for**
14:         **if** $j > k$ **then**
15:             **for** $j = 1$ to k **do**
16:                 Decompose R_{dj} recursively;
17:             **end for**
18:         **end if**
19:     **end for**
20: **end for**
21: **return** $\{T_i\}_{i=1}^N$;

At each node, we learn the model parameter using FM model.

$$\frac{\lambda_2}{2}\|\mathbf{w}\|^2 + \frac{\lambda_3}{2}\|\mathbf{V}\|^2 \hat{\omega}_0, \hat{\mathbf{w}}, \hat{\mathbf{V}}$$

$$= arg \min_{\omega_0, \mathbf{w}, \mathbf{V}} \sum_{i=1}^{|R|} (y(x_i) - \hat{y}(x_i))^2 + \lambda \sum_{j=1}^{p} \|\mathbf{V}_j - \mathbf{V}_j^{pa}\|^2 \tag{4}$$

where $\| * \|$ is the Frobenius norm and $\mathbf{V}^{pa}$ is the latent factor matrix at parent node. The parameter λ controls the extent of regularization. Equation (4) can be solved using two approaches: (1) stochastic gradient descent (SGD) algorithms, which are very popular for optimizing factorization models as they are simple, work well with different loss functions. The SGD algorithm for FM has a linear computational and constant storage complexity [21]. (2) Alternating least-squares (ALS) algorithms that iteratively solves a least-squares problem per model parameter and updates each model parameter with the optimal solution [24]. Here, $\mathbf{V}$ is $f \times p$ matrix of which f is the dimensionality of factor vectors and $p = n_0 + n_1 + \dots n_{m-1}$. n_i is the number of context C_i, m is the number of contextual variables. For simplicity, we denote user set as C_0 and item set as C_1. Each of the $f \times n_i$ sub-matrix is the latent representation of context C_i, as shown in Table 3. The smaller the distance among the factor vectors of context C_i, the greater the similarity.

To partition the training set R, we extract the context and the number of clusters according to the tree structure S and current level. We group the similar latent vectors of context C by making use of the k-means method, In Table 3, suppose we get the context C_1 (i.e., Item) and number of clusters $k = 2$ according to input parameter S. Then the initial cluster central points selected randomly are i_1 and i_2. Subsequently, the generated clustering result could be $\{i_1, i_3, i_4\}$ and $\{i_2\}$. Lastly, the training set in the current node can be divided into two groups according to the clustering result of context C_1 (i.e., Item) and the value of C_1 (i.e., Item) of tuples. In other words, the current node has two children nodes. The subset of one chid node includes the tuples whose value of C_1 (i.e., Item)$\in \{i_1, i_3, i_4\}$, the remaining tuples are assigned to the other children node.

The partition process stops once one of following conditions is met: (1) the height of a tree exceeds the limitation which can be inferred from the given tree structure parameter S; (2) the number of tuples at each child node of current node is less than the number of least support tuples *leastL*.

During training, the function of each non-leaf node is to separate training set by making use of the clustering result of special context, such that the tuples in the subset have more impact each other. However, leaf nodes are responsible for prediction.

Note that in different decision trees, the training set is divided differently because that initial k cluster central points are selected randomly at each node of decision trees.

During prediction, for a given case x_i in the test set, we transfer it from root node to leaf node at each tree using the clustering information of each non-leaf node. For instance, the value of S is 'C1:2, C0:3, C2:4' and a test case $x_i = \{u_3, i_1, l_2\}$ corresponding to Table 2. Thus from the root node, the x_i would be transferred to node (e.g., R_{23}) which include i_1 at second level. Then from the node R_{23}, the x_i would be transferd to node (e.g., R_{33}) which include u_3 at third level. Subsequently, from the node R_{33}, the x_i would be transferd to node (e.g., R_{41}) which include l_2 at fourth level. At the target leaf node, the rating can be predicted by taking advantage of Eq. (1) and the parameters learned by the training subset. To the end, the predictions from all trees are combined to obtain the final prediction as shown in Eq. (5)

$$\hat{y}(x_i) = \frac{\sum_{t=1}^{N} \hat{y}_t(x_i)}{N}, \tag{5}$$

where $\hat{y}_t$ means the prediction of the tuple x_i at tth decision tree, N denotes the number of decision trees.

After partitioning the original training set, the tuples at each leaf node have the more influence on each other. So, the FM model at each leaf node can achieve high quality recommendation. By combining multiple predictions from different decision trees, all subsets in which the tuples are more correlated are comprehensively investigated, personalized and accurate context-aware recommendations can be generated.

4.2 Discussion

We discuss the relationship between the proposed RPFM and other state-of-the-art random partition-based methods.

- *Relation to RPMF* Zhong et al. [28] proposed RPMF works by applying a set of local decomposition processes on sub-rating matrices. There are some differences between RPMF and our proposed RPFM. First of all, RPMF explores a basic MF model to factorize the user–item rating matrix. However, RPFM factorizes the user–item–context interactions using FM model. Secondly, the decision trees in RPMF are binary trees created by selecting a latent factor from U, V and a splitting point randomly, while that in RPFM are irregular trees generated by k-means method where k initial cluster central points are selected randomly. Thirdly, the depth of decision trees in RPMF can be very large in theory, while that in RPFM is limited by the number of contextual variables. Finally, during prediction, for a given user–item pair, RPMF obtain a partial prediction at each node on the path from the root to leaf node on each decision tree. However, our proposed RPFM make a partial prediction only at the leaf node of each decision tree for a given user–item–context interaction tuple. So, RPMF spend more time in prediction than RPFM.

- *Relation to SoCo* Liu et al. [14] proposed SoCo to improve recommendation quality by using contexts and social network information. Here, we only pay attention to the relation between SoCo without social information and RPFM. Firstly, in SoCo contextual information c_r, used to separate data at each level of each tree, is selected randomly. Then the training data at each intermediate node are partitioned according to the value of c_r. However, the tree structure in RPFM is determined by the input parameter S and training subset is generated according to similarity of latent factor vectors of selected context c_r. Second, the prediction is made by the basic MF model in SoCo. However, our proposed RPFM makes prediction by taking advantage of FM model. It is worth mentioning that some contextual information which can improve recommendation quality may be lost in SoCo when the depth of tree is less than the number of contextual variables. For instance, the node R_{22} in Fig. 1 has no child node because the number of tuples at the node R_{22} is less than the number of least support tuples. If matrix factorization is performed, the contextual information at node R_{22} can not be taken advantage. However, our proposed RPFM can do it. Third, both the users and items cannot be used to split training set in SoCo. In other words, the number of tuples at leaf nodes in SoCo may be still enormous.

5 Experiments

In this section, we empirically investigate whether our proposed RPFM can achieve better performance compared with other state-of-the-art methods on three benchmark datasets. First we describe the datasets and settings in our experiments, then report and analyze the experiment results.

5.1 Datasets

We conduct our experiments on three datasets: the Adom. dataset [1], the Food dataset [18] as well as the Yahoo! Webscope dataset.

The Adom. dataset [1] contains 1757 ratings by 117 users for 226 movies with many contextual information. The rating scale rang from 1 (hate) to 13 (absolutely love). However, there are missing values in some tuples. After removing the tuples containing missing values, there are

Table 4 Data set statistics

Dataset	Users	Items	Context dim	Ratings	Scale
Adom.	84	192	5	1464	1–13
Food	212	20	2	6360	1–5
Yahoo!	7642	11,915	2	221,367	1–5

1464 ratings by 84 users for 192 movies in Adom. dataset. We keep 5 contextual information: withwhom, day of the week, if it was on the opening weekend, month and year seen (Table 4).

The Food dataset [18] contains 6360 ratings (1–5 stars) by 212 users for 20 menu items. We select 2 context variables. One context variable captures how hungry the user is: normal, hungry and full. The second one describes if the situation in which the user rates is virtual or real to be hungry.

The Yahoo! Webscope dataset contains 221,367 ratings (1–5 stars), for 11,915 movies by 7,642 users. There is no contextual information. However, the dataset contains user's age and gender features. Just like [24], we also follow [10] and apply their method to generate modified dataset. In other words, we modify the original Yahoo! dataset by replacing the gender feature with a new artificial feature $C \in \{0, 1\}$ that was assigned randomly to the value 1 or 0 for each rating. This feature C represents a contextual condition that can affect the rating. We randomly choose 50% items from the dataset, and for these items we randomly pick 50% of the ratings to modify. We increase (or decrease) the rating value by one if $C = 1(C = 0)$ if the rating value was not already 5 (1).

5.2 Setup and Metrics

We assess the performance of the models by conducting a fivefold cross-validation and use the most popular metrics: the mean absolute error (MAE) and root mean square error (RMSE), defined as follows:

$$\text{MAE} = \frac{\sum_{(x_i, y_i) \in \Omega_{\text{test}}} |y_i - \hat{y}(x_i)|}{|\Omega_{\text{test}}|} \quad (6)$$

$$\text{RMSE} = \sqrt{\frac{\sum_{(x_i, y_i) \in \Omega_{\text{test}}} (y_i - \hat{y}(x_i))^2}{|\Omega_{\text{test}}|}} \quad (7)$$

where Ω_{test} denotes the test set, and $|\Omega_{\text{test}}|$ denotes number of tuples in test set. The smaller the value of MAE or RMSE, the better the performance.

5.3 Performance Comparison

We first conduct some experiments to assess the performance of proposed RPFM with different similarity measure function in *k*-means method. Then we compared the performance of proposed RPFM with state-of-the-art context-aware methods.

5.3.1 What's the Better Method of Similarity Function?

The proposed RPFM algorithm takes advantage of *k*-means method to partition the training set. So the tuples in the each training subset are more impact each other. As we know, there are many metrics to measure the similarity among the tuples, for instance, Euclidean distance (*Euclid*), Cosine-based similarity (*Cosine*), correlation-based similarity (*Pearson*), adjusted Cosine-based similarity (*adjCosine*), etc. As shown in Table 5, there are some different performance under the different similarity measure function. However, the difference of performance is not significance. In the following sections, we thus report performances using Euclidean distance.

5.3.2 Comparison to Factorization-Based Context-Aware Methods

To begin with, we determine the structure of decision trees, i.e., input parameters *S*, by Algorithm 1. The parameters are 'C2:2,C6:2,C5:2,C3:3,C0:2,C4:5,C1:5', 'C3:3,C2:2, C0:5,C1:4' and 'C3:2,C2:2,C0:2,C1:2' for Adom., Food and Yahoo! dataset, respectively. Then, we select 0.01 as the values of learning rate and regularization.

Table 5 Performance comparison in terms of different similarity function

Dataset	Metric	RPFM			
		Euclid	Cosine	Pearson	adjCosine
Adom.	RMSE	2.642	**2.640**	2.643	2.649
	MAE	2.039	**2.032**	2.054	2.049
Food	RMSE	**1.022**	1.042	1.035	1.038
	MAE	**0.786**	0.814	0.800	0.813
Yahoo!	RMSE	**0.911**	0.933	0.928	0.926
	MAE	**0.617**	0.626	0.629	0.621

Bold numbers are the best performance in terms of different similarity function for each dataset

- *FM* [21] is easily applicable to a wide variety of context by specifying only the input data and achieves fast runtime both in training and prediction.
- *Multiverse* Recommendation [10] is a contextual collaborative filtering model using *N* dimensional tensor factorization. In Multiverse Recommendation, different types of context are considered as addition dimensions in the representation of the data as tensor. The factorization of this tensor leads to a compact model of the data which can be used to provide context-aware recommendations.
- *COT* [13] represents the common semantic effects of contexts as a contextual operating tensor and represents a context as a latent vector. Then, contextual operating matrix from the contextual operating tensor and latent vectors of contexts was generated so as to model the semantic operation of a context combination.

Dimensionality of latent factor vectors is one of the important parameters. Though latent factor vectors' dimensionality of various contexts can be different in Multiverse and COT. In order to compare with FM and our proposed RPFM, we just take into account the equal dimensionality of latent factor vectors of various contexts. The scale of three datasets is different, so we run models with $f \in \{2, 3, 4, 5, 6, 7\}$ over Adom. dataset, $f \in \{2, 4, 6, 8, 10, 12\}$ over Food dataset and $f \in \{5, 10, 15, 20, 25, 30\}$ over Yahoo! dataset. Figures 2 and 3 show the result of FM, Multiverse, COT and RPFM over the three real-world datasets.

We notice that in all experiment scenarios, dimensionality of latent factor vectors in RPFM is not sensitive and RPFM is more accurate than other recommendation models. These results show that in homogeneous environment which can be obtained by applying random decision trees to partition the original training set, users have similar rating behavior.

High computational complexity for both learning and prediction is one of the main disadvantages of Multiverse and COT. This make them hard to apply for larger dimensionality of latent factor vectors. In contrast to this, the computational complexity of FM and RPFM is linear.

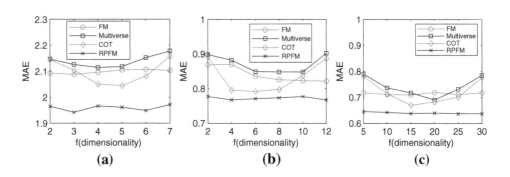

Fig. 2 MAE over three datasets with different dimensionality of latent factor vectors. **a** Adom. dataset, **b** food dataset, **c** Yahoo! dataset

Fig. 3 RMSE over three
datasets with different
dimensionality of latent factor
vectors. **a** Adom. dataset, **b** food
dataset, **c** Yahoo! dataset

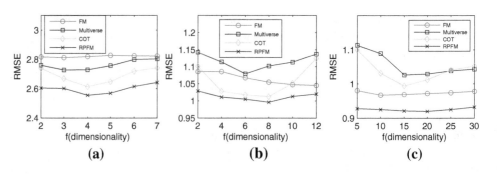

(a)   (b)   (c)

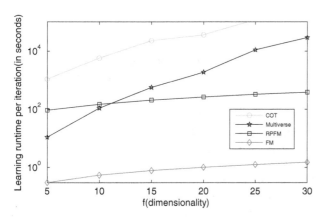

Fig. 4 Learning runtime in seconds for one iteration over the whole
training set (in log-y scale) over Yahoo! dataset with different latent
dimensions

In order to compare the runtime of various models, we do
experiment on Yahoo! dataset for one full iteration over
whole training set. Figure 4 shows that the learning runtime of RPFM is faster than that of Multiverse and COT
with increasing the dimensionality, however, slower than
that of FM which is obvious because RPFM generates an
ensemble which reduces the prediction error.

5.3.3 Comparison to Random Partition-Based Context-
Aware Methods

- *RPMF* [28] adopted a random partition approach to
  group similar users and items by taking advantage of

decision trees. The tuples at each node of decision trees
have more impact each other. Then matrix factorization
is applied at each node to predict the missing ratings.

- *SoCo* [14] explicitly handle contextual information
  which means SoCo partitions the training set based on
  the values of real contexts. SoCo incorporate social
  network information to make recommendation. There
  are not social network information in our selected
  datasets, so we just consider SoCo without social
  network information.

Both the number and depth of trees have important impact
on the decision tree-based prediction methods. Because of
space limitations, we just report the experimental result
over Food dataset.

As shown in Fig. 5, we observe that RPFM achieves the
best performance compared with RPMF and SoCo. And we
notice that MAE/RMSE decreases with increasing number
of trees, which means more trees produces higher accuracy.
However, when the number of trees increases to around 3,
improvements on prediction quality become negligible. We
thus conclude that even a small number of trees are sufficient for decision tree-based models.

The depth of trees which is one of the input parameters
in RPMF can be very large because it can select a latent
factor from *U*, *V* and a splitting point randomly at each
intermediate node during building the decision trees. Here,
we define the maximal depth of trees as five in RPFM. In
SoCo, the maximal depth of trees equals the number of
contextual variables excluding user and item. Specially, the

Fig. 5 Impact of number of
trees over Food dataset

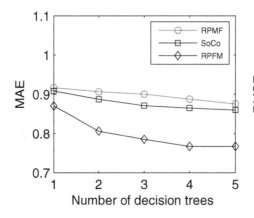
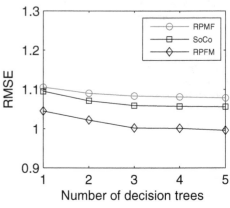

Fig. 6 Impact of depth of trees over Food dataset

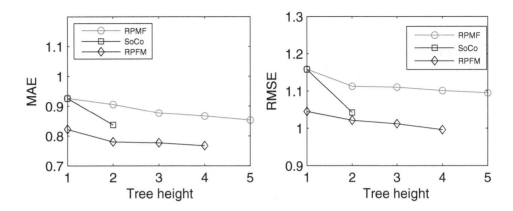

maximal depth of trees over Food dataset is two in SoCo. However, both user and item can be considered as contextual variables in RPFM. Then the maximal depth of trees over Food dataset is four in RPFM. Figure 6 shows that the deeper of trees, the better prediction quality, and RPFM outperforms RPMF and SoCo in terms of MAE and RMSE.

6 Conclusion and Future Work

In this paper, we propose Random Partition Factorization Machines (RPFM) for context-aware recommendations. RPFM adopts random decision trees to partition the original training set using k-means method. Factorization machines (FM) is then employed to learn the model parameters at each node of the trees and predict missing ratings of users for items under some specific contexts at leaf nodes of the trees. Experimental results demonstrate that RPFM outperforms state-of-the-art context-aware recommendation methods.

There are several directions for future work on RPFM. First, RPFM adopts the k-means method to partition the training set. There are many cluster methods [7] such as BIRCH, ROCK, Chameleon, DBSCAN. Some of them may be achieve better performance. Second, manipulation at each node in training phase, such as clustering, partition and learning parameters, can be parallelized. Third, there are many floating point arithmetic at leaf nodes in prediction which will spend much time. While GPU hold powerful capacity of floating point arithmetic, it can be taken advantage to accelerate the prediction.

Acknowledgements This work is supported by National Key Research&Develop Plan (No. 2016YFB1000702), National Basic Research Program of China (973) (No. 2014CB340402), National High Technology Research and Development Program of China (863) (No. 2014AA 015204) and NSFC under the Grant Nos. 61272137, 61202114, 61532021 and NSSFC (No. 12&ZD 220), and the Fundamental Research Funds for the Central Universities, and the Research Funds of Renmin University of China (15XNLQ06). It was partially done when the authors worked in SA Center for Big Data Research in RUC. This Center is funded by a Chinese National 111 Project Attracting.

References

1. Adomavicius G, Sankaranarayanan R, Sen S, Tuzhilin A (2005) Incorporating contextual information in recommender systems using a multidimensional approach. ACM Trans Inf Syst TOIS 23(1):103–145
2. Adomavicius G, Tuzhilin A (2011) Context-aware recommender systems. In: Ricci F, Rokach L, Shapira B, Kantor PB (eds) Recommender systems handbook, pp. 217–253. Springer, Berlin
3. Cheng C, Xia F, Zhang T, King I, Lyu MR (2014) Gradient boosting factorization machines. In: Proceedings of the 8th ACM conference on recommender systems. ACM, pp 265–272
4. Das AS, Datar M, Garg A, Rajaram S (2007) Google news personalization: scalable online collaborative filtering. In: Proceedings of the 16th international conference on World Wide Web. ACM, pp 271–280
5. Fan W, Wang H, Yu PS, Ma S (2003) Is random model better? On its accuracy and efficiency. In: ICDM 2003, IEEE. pp 51–58
6. Freudenthaler C, Schmidt-Thieme L, Rendle S (2011) Bayesian factorization machines
7. Han J, Kamber M, Pei J (2011) Data mining: concepts and techniques: concepts and techniques. Elsevier, Amsterdam
8. Hong L, Doumith AS, Davison BD (2013) Co-factorization machines: modeling user interests and predicting individual decisions in twitter. In: Proceedings of the sixth ACM international conference on web search and data mining. ACM, pp 557–566
9. Jannach D, Zanker M, Felfernig A, Friedrich G (2010) Recommender systems: an introduction. Cambridge University Press, Cambridge
10. Karatzoglou A, Amatriain X, Baltrunas L, Oliver N (2010) Multiverse recommendation: n-dimensional tensor factorization for context-aware collaborative filtering. In: Proceedings of the fourth ACM conference on Recommender systems. ACM, pp. 79–86
11. Koren Y (2008) Factorization meets the neighborhood: a multifaceted collaborative filtering model. In: SIGKDD2008. ACM, pp 426–434
12. Koren Y, Bell R, Volinsky C (2009) Matrix factorization techniques for recommender systems, vol 8. IEEE, New York
13. Liu Q, Wu S, Wang L (2015) Cot: contextual operating tensor for context-aware recommender systems. In: Twenty-ninth AAAI conference on artificial intelligence

14. Liu X, Aberer K (2013) Soco: a social network aided context-aware recommender system. In: Proceedings of the 22nd international conference on world wide web. International World Wide Web Conferences Steering Committee pp 781–802

15. Loni B, Said A, Larson M, Hanjalic A (2014) 'Free lunch' enhancement for collaborative filtering with factorization machines. In: Proceedings of the 8th ACM conference on recommender systems. ACM, pp 281–284

16. Nguyen TV, Karatzoglou A, Baltrunas L (2014) Gaussian process factorization machines for context-aware recommendations. In: SIGIR2014. ACM, pp. 63–72

17. Oentaryo RJ, Lim EP, Low JW, Lo D, Finegold M (2014) Predicting response in mobile advertising with hierarchical importance-aware factorization machine. In: Proceedings of the 7th ACM international conference on Web search and data mining. ACM, pp 123–132

18. Ono C, Takishima Y, Motomura Y, Asoh H (2009) Context-aware preference model based on a study of difference between real and supposed situation data. Springer, Berlin, p. 102–113

19. Page L, Brin S, Motwani R, Winograd T (1999) The PageRank citation ranking: Bringing order to the web

20. Qiang R, Liang F, Yang J (2013) Exploiting ranking factorization machines for microblog retrieval. In: Proceedings of the 22nd ACM international conference on conference on information and knowledge management. ACM, pp 1783–1788

21. Rendle S (2010) Factorization machines. In: 2010 IEEE 10th international conference on data mining (ICDM). IEEE, pp 995–1000

22. Rendle S (2013) Scaling factorization machines to relational data. In: Proceedings of the VLDB endowment, vol. 6. VLDB Endowment, pp 337–348

23. Rendle S, Freudenthaler C, Schmidt-Thieme L (2010) Factorizing personalized markov chains for next-basket recommendation. In: Proceedings of the 19th international conference on World wide web. ACM, pp 811–820

24. Rendle S, Gantner Z, Freudenthaler C, Schmidt-Thieme L (2011) Fast context-aware recommendations with factorization machines. In: SIGIR2011. ACM, pp 635–644

25. Rendle S, Schmidt-Thieme L (2010) Pairwise interaction tensor factorization for personalized tag recommendation. In: Proceedings of the third ACM international conference on web search and data mining. ACM, pp. 81–90

26. Wang S, Du C, Zhao K, Li C, Li Y, Zheng Y, Wang Z, Chen H (2016) Random partition factorization machines for context-aware recommendations. In: International conference on web-age information management. Springer, Berlin, pp 219–230

27. Yin H, Cui B, Chen L, Hu Z, Huang Z (2014) A temporal context-aware model for user behavior modeling in social media systems. In: SIGMOD 2014. ACM, pp 1543–1554

28. Zhong E, Fan W, Yang Q (2012) Contextual collaborative filtering via hierarchical matrix factorization. In: SDM. SIAM, pp 744–755

6

Big Data Reduction Methods: A Survey

Muhammad Habib ur Rehman[1] · Chee Sun Liew[1] · Assad Abbas[2] ·
Prem Prakash Jayaraman[3] · Teh Ying Wah[1] · Samee U. Khan[2]

Abstract Research on big data analytics is entering in the new phase called fast data where multiple gigabytes of data arrive in the big data systems every second. Modern big data systems collect inherently complex data streams due to the volume, velocity, value, variety, variability, and veracity in the acquired data and consequently give rise to the 6Vs of big data. The reduced and relevant data streams are perceived to be more useful than collecting raw, redundant, inconsistent, and noisy data. Another perspective for big data reduction is that the million variables big datasets cause the curse of dimensionality which requires unbounded computational resources to uncover actionable knowledge patterns. This article presents a review of methods that are used for big data reduction. It also presents a detailed taxonomic discussion of big data reduction methods including the network theory, big data compression, dimension reduction, redundancy elimination, data mining, and machine learning methods. In addition, the open research issues pertinent to the big data reduction are also highlighted.

Keywords Big data · Data compression · Data reduction · Data complexity · Dimensionality reduction

✉ Muhammad Habib ur Rehman
mhrehman@siswa.um.edu.my

[1] Faculty of Computer Science and Information Technology, University of Malaya, Kuala Lumpur, Malaysia

[2] Department of Electrical and Computer Engineering, North Dakota State University, Fargo, ND, USA

[3] Department of Computer Science and Software Engineering, Swinburne University of Technology, Melbourne, Australia

1 Introduction

Big data is the aggregation of large-scale, voluminous, and multi-format data streams originated from heterogeneous and autonomous data sources [1]. The volume is the primary characteristic of big data that is represented by the acquisition of storage spaces in large-scale data centers and storage area networks. The massive size of the big data not only causes the data heterogeneity but also results in diverse dimensionalities in the datasets. Therefore, efforts are required to reduce the volume to effectively analyze big data [2]. In addition, big data streams are needed to be processed online to avoid lateral resource consumption for storage and processing. The second key characteristic of big data is velocity. The velocity refers to the frequency of data streams, which is needed to be abridged in order to handle big data effectively. For example, solar dynamics observatory generates excess of one terabytes data per day and the analysis of such a fast big data is possible only after reduction or summarization [3]. On the other hand, big data inherits the 'curse of dimensionality.' In other words, millions of dimensions (variables, features, attributes) are required to be effectively reduced to uncover the maximum knowledge patterns [4, 5]. For example, behavior profiles of the Internet users that mainly comprise of searches, page-views, and click-stream data are sparse and high dimensional with millions of possible keywords and URLs [6]. Similarly, personal genomic high-throughput sequencing not only increases the volume and velocity of data but also adds to the high dimensionality of the data [7]. Therefore, it is imperative to reduce the high dimensions while retaining the most important and useful data.

Data reduction methods for big data vary from pure dimension reduction techniques to compression-based data reduction methods and algorithms for preprocessing, cluster-level data deduplication, redundancy elimination, and implementation of network (graph) theory concepts. Dimension reduction techniques are useful to handle the heterogeneity and massiveness of big data by reducing million variable data into manageable size [8–11]. These techniques usually work at post-data collection phases. Similarly, cluster deduplication and redundancy elimination algorithms that remove duplicated data for efficient data processing and useful knowledge discovery are primarily post-data collection methods [12–15]. Recently, the network theory concepts have also been employed for big data reduction [16–18]. The aforementioned methods first extract the semantics and linked structures from the unstructured datasets and then apply graph theory for network optimization. Conversely, some methods to reduce big data during the data collection process are also proposed in the recent literature [19–21]. In this study, we presented a detailed discussion of these data reduction methods.

This article presents a thorough literature review of methods for big data reduction. A few similar prior studies have also been conducted. However, these studies either present a generic discussion of big data reduction or discuss a specific group of relevant systems or methods. For example, the authors in [1] discussed the big data reduction to be the critical part of mining sparse, uncertain, and incomplete data. Similarly, the authors in [22, 23] argue big data reduction as the critical part of data analysis and data preprocessing. However, both of the studies lack in presenting discussion about specific systems and methods for big data reduction. The authors in [4] discussed big data reduction issue specifically by focusing on dimension reduction, whereas the authors in [24] emphasized on the data compression. However, a wide range of methods remain unexplored. Currently, there is no specific study in the literature that addresses the core issue of big data reduction. Therefore, we aim to present a detailed literature review that is specifically articulated to highlight the existing methods relevant to big data reduction. In addition, some open research issues are also presented to direct future researchers.

The main contributions of this article are:

- A thorough literature review and classification of big data reduction methods are presented.
- Recently proposed schemes for big data reduction are analyzed and synthesized.
- A detailed gap analysis for the articulation of limitations and future research challenges for data reduction in big data environments is presented.

The article is structured as follows: Sect. 2 discusses the complexity problem in big data and highlights the importance of big data reduction. The taxonomical discussion on big data reduction methods is presented in Sect. 3. The discussion on open issues and future research challenges is given in Sect. 4, and finally, the article is concluded in Sect. 5.

2 Big Data Complexity and the Need for Data Reduction

Big data systems include social media data aggregators, industrial sensor networks, scientific experimental systems, connected health, and several other application areas. The data collection from large-scale local and remote sensing devices and networks, Internet-enabled data streams, and/ or devices, systems, and networks-logs brings massively heterogeneous, multi-source, multi-format, aggregated, and continuous big data streams. Effectively handling the big data stream to store, index, and query the data sources for lateral data processing is among the key challenges being addressed by researchers [25, 26]. However, data scientists are facing data deluge issue to uncover the maximum knowledge patterns at fine-grained level for effective and personalized utilization of big data systems [3, 27]. The data deluge is due to 6Vs properties of big data, namely the volume, variety, value, velocity, veracity, and variability. The authors in [26] discussed the 6Vs as follows.

- *Volume* The data size characterizes the volume of big data. However, there is no agreed upon definition of big data which specifies the amount of data to be considered as 'big' on order to meet the definition of big data. However, a common sense is developed in research community who consider any data size as big in terms of volume which is not easily processable by underlying computing systems. For example, a large distributed system such as computing clusters- or cloud-based data centers may offer to process multiple terabytes of data but a standalone computer or resource constrained mobile devices may not offer the computational power to process even a few gigabytes of data. Therefore, the volume property of big data varies according to underlying computing systems.
- *Velocity* The velocity of big data is determined by the frequency of data streams which are entering in big data systems. The velocity is handled by big data systems in two ways. First, the whole data streams are collected in centralized systems, and then, further data processing is performed. In the second approach, the data streams are processed immediately after data collection before storing in big data systems. The second approach is more practical; however, it requires a lot of programming efforts and computational resources in order to reduce and filter the data streams before entering in big data systems.

- *Variety* Big data systems collect data stream from multiple data sources which produce data streams in multiple formats. This heterogeneity in data sources and data types impacts the variety property-related characteristics. Therefore, big data systems must be able to process multiple types of data stream in order to effectively uncover hidden knowledge patterns.

- *Veracity* The utility of big data systems increases when the data streams are collected from reliable and trustworthy sources. In addition, the data stream collection is performed with compromising the quality of data streams. The veracity property of big data relates to reliability and trustworthiness of big data systems.

- *Variability* Since all data sources in big data systems do not generate the data streams with same speed and same quality. Therefore, variability property enables to handle the relevant issues. For example, the elastic resource provisioning as per the requirements of big data systems.

- *Value* The value property of big data defines the utility, usability, and usefulness of big data systems. This property tends more toward the outcomes of data analytics and data processing processes and is directly proportional to other 5Vs in big data systems.

The well-designed big data systems must able to deal with all 6Vs effectively by creating a balance between data processing objectives and the cost of data processing (i.e., computational, financial, programming efforts) in big data systems.

Moreover, the complexity in big data systems emerges in three forms: (1) data complexity, (2) computational complexity, and (3) system complexity [28]. The data complexity arises due to multiple formats and unstructured nature of big data, which elevate the issue of multiple dimensions and the complex inter-dimensional and intra-dimensional relationships. For example, the semantic relationship between different values of the same attribute, for example, noise level in the particular areas of the city, increases the inter-dimensional complexity. Likewise, the linked relationship among different attributes (for example, age, gender, and health records) raises the intra-dimensional complexity issue. In addition, the increasing level of data complexity in any big data system is directly proportional to the increase in computational complexity where only the sophisticated algorithms and methods can address the issue. Moreover, the system-level complexity is increased due to extensive computational requirements of big data systems to handle extremely large volume, complex (mostly unstructured and semi-structured), and sparse nature of the data. The extensive literature review exhibits that the big data reduction methods and systems have potential to deal with the big data complexity at both algorithms and systems level. In addition to data complexity, the big data reduction problem is studied in various other perspectives to articulate the effects and the need of data reduction for big data analysis, management, commercialization, and personalization.

Big data analysis also known as big data mining is a tedious task involving extraneous efforts to reduce data in a manageable size to uncover maximum knowledge patterns. To make it beneficial for data analysis, a number of pre-processing techniques for summarization, sketching, anomaly detection, dimension reduction, noise removal, and outliers detection are applied to reduce, refine, and clean big data [29]. The New York Times, a leading US newspaper, reports that data scientists spend 50–80% of the time on cleaning the big datasets [30]. The terms used in the industry for the aforementioned process are 'data munging,' 'data wrangling,' or 'data janitor work.' Another issue with the large-scale high-dimensional data analysis is the over-fitting of learning models that are generated from large numbers of attributes with a few examples. These learning models fit well within the training data, but their performance with testing data significantly degrades [31].

Data management is another important aspect to discuss the big data reduction problem. The effective big data management plays a pivotal role from data acquisition to analysis and visualization. Although data acquisition from multiple sources and aggregation of relevant datasets improve the efficiency of big data systems, it increases the in-network processing and data movement at clusters and data center levels. Similarly, the indexing techniques discussed in [26] enhance the big data management; however, the techniques come across data processing overheads. Although the conversion of unstructured data to semi-structured and structured formats is useful for effective query execution, the conversion in itself is a time- and resource-consuming activity. Moreover, big data is huge in volume that is distributed in different storage facilities. Therefore, the development of learning models and uncovering global knowledge from massively distributed big data is a tedious task. Efficient storage management of reduced and relevant data enhances both the local learning and global view of the whole big data [32, 33]. Currently, visual data mining technique of selecting subspace from the entire feature spaces and subsequently finding the relevant data patterns also require effective data management techniques. Therefore, the reduction in big data at the earliest enhances the data management and data quality and therefore improves the indexing, storage, analysis, and visualization operations of big data systems.

Recently, businesses particularly the enterprises are turning into big data systems. The collection of large data streams from Web users' personal data streams (clickstreams, ambulation activities, geo-locations, and health records) and integration of those data streams with personalized services is a key challenge [34]. The collection of irrelevant data streams increases the computational burden that directly affects the operational cost of enterprises. Therefore, the collection of fine-grained, highly relevant, and reduced data streams from users is another challenge that requires serious attention while designing big data systems. Currently, user data collection by third parties without explicit consent and information about commercialization is raising the privacy issues. The participatory personal data where users collect and mine their own data and participate for further utilization and customization of services in ubiquitous environments can address the issue of fine-grained data availability for enterprises. Keeping in view the big data complexity, the need for big data reduction, and analyzing big data reduction problem in different perspective, we present a thorough literature review of the methods for big data reduction.

The core technological support for big data reduction methods is based on multilayer architecture (see Fig. 1). The data storage is enabled by large-scale data centers and networks of different computing clusters [35]. The storage infrastructures are managed by core networking services, embarrassingly parallel distributed computing frameworks, such as Hadoop map-reduce implementations and large-scale virtualization technologies [36]. In addition, cloud services for the provision of computing, networking, and storage are also enabled using different cloud-based operating systems. A recent phenomenon in cloud computing is enabling the edge-cloud services by the virtualization of core cloud services near the data sources. Recently, Cisco released a Fog cloud to enable the intercommunication between core cloud services and proximal networks of data sources [37, 38]. At the lowest layers of the big data architecture resides the multi-format data sources which include standalone mobile devices, Internet-enabled social media data streams, remotely deployed wireless sensor networks, and large-scale scientific data streams among many others. This layered architecture enables to process and manage big data at multiple levels using various computing systems with different form factors. Therefore, wide ranges of application models are designed and new systems have been developed for big data processing.

3 Big Data Reduction Methods

This section presents the data reduction methods being applied in big data systems. The methods either optimize the storage or in-network movement of data or reduce data redundancy and duplication. In addition, some of the methods only reduce the volume by compressing the

original data and some of the methods reduce the velocity of data streams at the earliest before entering in big data storage systems. Alternatively, some of the methods extract topological structures of unstructured data and reduce the overall big data using network theory approaches that are discussed as follows.

3.1 Network Theory

Network (also known as graph) theory is playing a primary role in reduction of high-dimensional unstructured big data into low-dimensional structured data [39]. However, the extraction of topological structures (networks) from big data is quite challenging due to the heterogeneity and complex data structures. The authors in [40] proposed network theory-based approach to extract the topological and dynamical network properties from big data. The topological networks are constructed by establishing and evaluating relationships (links) among different data points. The statistical node analysis of the networks is performed for optimization and big data reduction [41]. The optimized networks are represented as small-world networks, free-scale networks, and random networks and are ranked on the basis of statistical parameters, namely mean, standard deviation, and variance. Mathematically, scale-free networks are formally represented as given in Eq. 1 using the main parameter as shown in Eq. 2.

$$p_k \approx k^{-\gamma} \tag{1}$$

$$\gamma_{p_k} = -\frac{\log p_k}{\log k} \tag{2}$$

where p_k represents fraction of nodes having k degree and parameter γ having range of $2 < \gamma < 3$.

Similarly, formal representation of random networks is presented in Eq. 3 using the main parameter as shown in Eq. 4.

$$p^k \approx \frac{z^k e^{-z}}{k!} \tag{3}$$

$$\log \frac{p_k k!}{(n-1)^k} = k \cdot \log(p) + (1-n)p \tag{4}$$

where p is the probability distribution of edges between any two nodes, n shows the number of nodes and z is calculated as $z = (n-1)p$. The mathematical representation of small-world networks is performed using Eq. 5 with main parameter as shown in Eq. 6.

$$d \propto \log(n) \tag{5}$$

$$d = \alpha \log(n) \tag{6}$$

where n represents the nodes in network and d is the distance between two randomly chosen nodes in the network.

Fig. 1 Multilayer architecture for big data systems

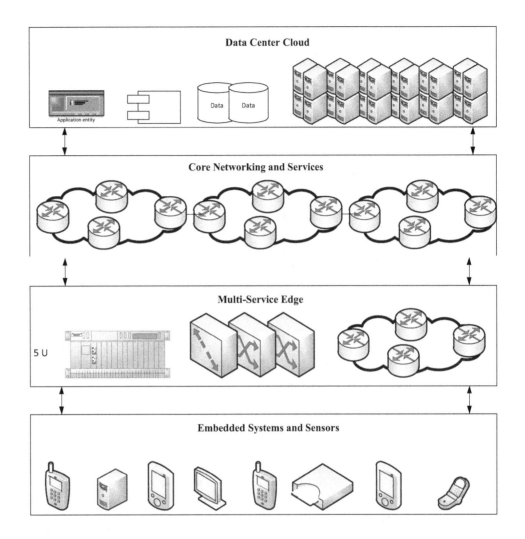

Traditionally, causality analysis is performed to establish the connection between different nodes. However, the extraction of topological networks from unstructured data is hard due to high dependency and one-way relationship on the links. The alternate to causality analysis is the assessment of influence among different nodes and establishing the connection between them on the basis of their co-occurrence. Although the technique does not ensure that nodes in the network can influence each other, the assessment of their co-occurrence could become a strong relationship parameter to link different nodes. Preferential attachment property enables influence assessment [41]. The property exhibits that newly established connections are most probably made with highly connected nodes in the topological networks. In addition, the identification of influential nodes and effective assessment of their co-occurrence can significantly reduce big data. Mathematically, the co-occurrence-based influence measure $\Delta(v_{i1}, v_{il})$ between two nodes v_{i1} and v_{il} is represented as shown in Eq. 7.

$$\Delta(v_{i1}, v_{il}) = \frac{1}{(|p(v_{i1}, v_{il})| - 1)(x - a)^n \sum_{p_i \in p(v_{i1}, v_{il})} W_{p_i}}$$
$$\times \left[\hat{L}_{(v_{i1}, v_{il})} \sum_{i \neq j=1}^{|p(v_{i1}, v_{il})|} \right.$$
$$\left. \times \left(\prod_{i=2}^{l-2} W(v_i, v_{i+1}) + \prod_{j=2}^{l-2} W(v_j, v_{j+1}) \right) \right]$$

(7)

where $W_{p_i} = \frac{w(v_{i1}, v_{i2})}{deg(v_{i1})}$ and $p(v_{i1}, v_{il})$ is the shortest path between v_{i1} and v_{il} and $0 \leq \Delta(v_{i1}, v_{il}) \leq 1$.

Aside from the influence-based assessment, similarity graph and collapsing simplicial complexes in network structures are used for topological network reduction in big datasets. Similarity graph is used to model the relationship among different datasets on the basis of their similarity matrix [17]. Further optimization of similarity graph is performed by merging every vertex with the maximal similarity clique (MSC), where a similarity clique (SC) is the collection of nodes with negligible distance. The notion is to convert a SC into MSC by adding an adjacent vertex that violates the properties of the SC. The graph is reduced when every MSC in the similarity graph is merged into a single node and the number of nodes and their edges are reduced in turn. Although the MSC is an efficient scheme to reduce topological networks, finding all of the MSCs in the similarity graph is quite challenging and computationally inefficient.

Moreover, the simplicial complexes are the multi-dimensional algebraic representations of large datasets [18]. The simplicial complex approach is applied over persistent homology, which is a method to compute topological features of large spaces at different levels of spatial resolutions. The persistent homology algorithm, as an alternate of hierarchical clustering, takes nested sequences of simplicial complexes and returns the summary of topological features at all levels. The concept of strong collapse that is keeping relevance information about all of the nodes in the simplicial complex is used to reduce the big data. The strong collapse is also useful for parallel and distributed computations, but the increasing computational complexities of maintaining relevance information of all of the nodes in complex prove to be the bottleneck. The concept of selective collapse algorithm is introduced to reduce the computational complexity of processing persistent homology. The proposed framework keeps computation traces of collapsing the complex using persistence algorithm proposed in [42]. In addition, the strong collapses are represented by forest that facilitates in easy processing of persistence across all nodes of the complex. Although the selective collapse algorithm is useful for the big data reduction, the empirical evidences are still lacking in the literature.

3.2 Compression

The reduced-size datasets are easy to handle in terms of processing and in-network data movement inside the big data storage systems. Compression-based methods are suitable candidates for data reduction in terms of size by preserving the whole data streams. Although computationally inefficient and involving decompression overhead, the methods allow to preserve the entire datasets in the original form. Numerous techniques for big data compression are proposed in the literature, including spatiotemporal compression, gzip, anamorphic stretch transform (AST), compressed sensing, parallel compression, sketching, and adaptive compression, to name a few [43–45]. Table 1 presents the summary of these methods.

Big data reduction in cloud environments is quite challenging due to multiple levels of virtualization and heterogeneity in the underlying cloud infrastructure. A spatiotemporal technique for data compression on big graph data in the cloud generates reduced datasets [45].

The technique performs online clustering of streaming data by correlating similarities in their time series to share workload in the clusters. In addition, it performs temporal compression on each network node to reduce the overall data. The proposed technique effectively meets the data processing quality and acceptable fidelity loss of the most of the application requirements. On the other hand, wireless sensor networks (WSNs) are generating large data streams at massive scales. The spatiotemporal data compression algorithm proposed in [46] ensures efficient communication, transmission, and storage of data in WSNs-based big data environment. The proposed approach not only reduces the size of transmitted data but also ensures prolonged network lifetime. The algorithm measures the correlation degree of sensed data, which determines the content of the data to be transmitted.

The authors in [44] proposed an efficient big data reduction scheme for the IP-activity dataset in social science. The techniques are based on compression method to utilize the standalone computer machines instead of large-scale distributed systems, such as Hadoop and big table. The authors used eight core processors from a 32 core AMD Opteron Processor 5356 machine of 2.3 GHZ speed and 20 GB RAM. The 9 TB of loose text files was converted into a binary format for readability in social science settings. The methodology is based on three steps for: (1) information representation, (2) parallel processing, and (3) compression and storage. Big data reduction is performed in second and third steps. First, each of the data files is processed and converted into a corresponding HDFS file; then, map-reduce approach is used to link each individual HDFS file with the corresponding geographical locations and aggregate in lateral stages. In map-phase, the files are linked, whereas in the reduce stage, all of the resultant HDFS files are converted into a single HDFS file. Finally, the gzip algorithm was used with the compression level of five over the optimal data chunk size of $100,000 \times 1$. The results exhibited a significant amount of data reduction from 9.08 TB (raw data) to 3.07 TB (HDFS converted data) and 0.50 TB (compressed data). Although the proposed approach contributed significantly, it is only useful for the given dataset. Therefore, online data analysis for big data reduction remains challenging in streaming big data environments.

The anamorphic stretch transform (AST) stretches the sharp features more strongly as compared to the coarse features of the [47]. The AST could be applied to both the analogue (for digitization) and digital signals (for compression). The technique is primarily based on self-adaptive stretch where more samples are associated with sharp features and fewer samples are associated with redundant coarse features. The strength of the AST is its ability to enhance the utility of limited samples as well as reducing the overall size of the data. The results demonstrated that

Table 1 Big data compression methods

References	Methods	Description	Strengths	Weaknesses
Yang et al. [45]	Spatiotemporal	The proposed method performs online clustering of streaming data by correlating similarities in their time series to share workload in the clusters. In addition, it performs temporal compression on each network node to reduce overall data	Performance enhancement in terms of data quality, information fidelity loss, and big data reduction	At least one time processing of whole data is performed in cloud environment which increases the operational cost
Ackermann and Angus [44]	gZip	gZip is a compression tool developed that is being used for big data reduction to improve the resource efficiency for the IP-activity dataset in social science	It provides a light weight and simple file format; therefore, it has low computational complexity	gZip compresses one file at a time; therefore, massively parallel programming models like map-reduce must be used for performance gain in terms of computation time
Jalali and Asghari [47]	AST	The AST is a novel method that is used to compress digital signal by performing selective stretching and wrapping methods. The technique is primarily based on self-adaptive stretch where more samples are associated with sharp features and less samples are associated with redundant coarse features	AST performs data compression of the signal extracted on frequency domain. The method also performs inverse transformation of the constructed signal	The method specifically works with big data involving signal processing. The generalization to other domain is a bottleneck in this research
Wang et al. [48]	Compressed sensing	Compressed sensing is a compressible and/or sparse signal that projects a high-dimensional data in low-dimensional space using random measurement matrix	The proposed scheme performs data acquisition and compression in parallel for improved performance as compared with Nyquist sampling theory-based compression methods	The probability of poor data quality and information fidelity loss increases when the analyses are performed on reduced and compressed data
Brinkmann et al. [50]	RED encoding	RED encoding used to manage massively generated voluminous electrophysiology data	RED performs best when encoding invariant signals, and it provides high compression rate with improved computational speed in lossless compression of time series signals	The performance of the RED encoding methods degrades with high variance in signals
Bi et al. [55]	Parallel compression	Parallel compression methods uses proper orthogonal decomposition method to compress data in order to effectively trace and extract useful features from the data	Balances between feature retention error and compression ratio Performs fast decompression for interactive data visualization	Due to noise, the standard deviation of error remains high in the dataset
Monreale et al. [46]	Sketching	Sketching uses count-min sketch algorithm to compress vehicular movement data and achieve compact communication	Guarantees data reduction and preserves some important characteristics of the original data	The probability of information fidelity loss is more when sketching applied with inconsistent and noisy data stream

56-fold data could be compressed using the AST equations (see Eq. 8 and Eq. 9).

$$I(\omega) = \text{AST}\{\tilde{E}(\omega)\}$$
$$= \int_{-\infty}^{+\infty} \tilde{E}(\omega)\tilde{E} * (\omega + \omega_m)e^{j[\varphi(\omega)-\varphi(\omega+\omega_m)]}d\omega \quad (8)$$

where $(\omega + \omega_m)$ and ω_m represent carrier and modulation frequencies, respectively. The $\varphi(\omega)$ is an auto-correlation function of the AST with embedded kernel that represents a frequency-dependent phase operation. The compression or expansion of time, bandwidth product is dependent on the correct selection of $\varphi(\omega)$. The structured modulation distribution function, S_M, is used to select $\varphi(\omega)$.

$$S_M(\omega_m, t) = \int_{-\infty}^{+\infty} \tilde{E}(\omega)\tilde{E} * (\omega + \omega_m)e^{j[\varphi(\omega)-\varphi(\omega+\omega_m)]}e^{j\omega t}d\omega$$
$$(9)$$

where t represents the time variable.

The storage of big data and its complete processing for anomaly detection raises the issues of privacy due to exposure of each data point. The authors proposed compressed sensing also known as compressed sampling technique for compressible and/or sparse signals that project a high-dimensional data in low-dimensional space using random measurement matrix [48]. The method is selected because compressive sensing theory enables to address the limitations of Nyquist sampling [49] theory and can perform data acquisition and compression simultaneously. This strength of the compressed sensing theory enables to detect anomalies in big data streams. Mathematically, for a signal, $x \in R^N$ compressed sensing can be represented using Eq. 10.

$$x = \sum_{i-1}^{N} \emptyset_i \theta_i \text{ or } x = \emptyset\theta \tag{10}$$

where $\emptyset$ shows the $N \times N$ orthonormal transform basis and θ is used as the expansion coefficient vector under the orthonormal basis. If $x \in R^K$ sparse signal where $K \neq 0$ in vector θ and $K < N$, the signal x can be collected with a small set of non-adaptive and linear measurements (see Eq. 11).

$$y = \Psi x = \Psi\emptyset\theta \tag{11}$$

where Ψ is a $M \times N$ random measurement matrix and $M < N$. Here, $(\emptyset, \Psi)$ represents a pair of orthobases that follow the incoherence restriction.

Compressive sensing theory is useful because low-dimensional space fully represents high-dimensional data. The results showed that the proposed algorithm produced satisfactory results with and without compressed sensing. The compression was applied by the ratio of 1:3 and 1:5, and the experiments for human detection were performed from behind the brick and gypsum walls.

The authors in [50] proposed a novel file format called multi-scale electrophysiology format (MEF) to manage massively generated electrophysiology data. The block-wise lossy compression algorithm (RED encoding) is used in addition to the cyclic redundancy check (CRC), encryption, and block index structure of the MEF. The RED encoding ensures high lossless compression rate and higher computational speed and is also able to adopt with statistical variation in the raw data, which is very important for non-stationary ECG signals. The experimental results showed that for 32 KHZ recordings with each block of 32,556 samples acquired in one second, the MEF obtained reasonably better compression rate. The authors recommend recording at least 2000 samples in each block for the maximum performance gain.

The amount of data generated in vehicular ad hoc networks is massive due to on-board monitoring of vehicles and relevant spatiotemporal data acquisition. The authors in [46] utilized sketching algorithm called count-min sketch algorithm to compress vehicular movement data and achieved compact communication. The algorithm maps frequency counters to compressed vectors using hash tables. Although the main focus of the proposed study is on privacy preservation, data reduction is also performed significantly.

The large-scale scientific simulations generate a huge amount of data that widens the gap between the I/O capacity and computation abilities of high-end computing (HEC) machines [51]. This bottleneck for data analysis raises the need for in situ analytics where simulation data are processed prior to the I/O. Although feasible, the in situ analysis of peta-scale data incurs computation overhead in the HEC machines. The authors proposed adaptive compression service for in situ analytics middle-ware to effectively utilize available bandwidth and to optimize the performance of the HEC during end-to-end data transfer. Experimental results with gyro-kinetic simulation (GKW) on 80-node 1280 core cluster machine show that the compression ratio and available computational power are two main factors to achieve the maximum compression. The authors in [43] further proposed a framework called FlexAnalytics and profiled three compression algorithms called lossy [52], bzip2 [53], and gzip [54]. The experimental results show that all three compressions are not useful for optimized data transfer with bandwidth more than 264.19 Mb/s. This bottleneck imposes the challenge of compression/decompression time reduction to cope with the I/O needs of HEC.

Although compression-based data reduction methods are feasible for big data reduction, the processing overhead of de-compression introduces latency which lowers the performance of analytics algorithms in real-time environments. Moreover, the additional computations consume more cloud resources and increase the overall operational costs of big data systems. However, the techniques enable to store big data efficiently without significantly losing the original data in both the lossy and the lossless compression-based methods.

3.3 Data Deduplication (Redundancy Elimination)

Data redundancy is the key issue for data analysis in big data environments. Three main reasons for data redundancy are: (1) addition of nodes, (2) expansion of datasets, and (3) data replication. The addition of a single virtual machine (VM) brings around 97% more redundancy, and the growth in large datasets comes with 47% redundant data points [13]. In addition, the storage mechanism for maximum data availability (also called data replication) brings 100% redundancy at the cluster level. Therefore, effective data deduplication and redundancy elimination methods can cope with the challenge of redundancy. The workload analysis shows that the $3\times$ higher throughput improves performance about 45% but in some extreme cases the performance degrades up to 161%. The energy overhead of deduplication is 7%; however, the overall energy saved by processing deduplicated data is 43%. The performance is degraded to 5%, whereas energy overhead is 6% for pure solid state drive (SSD) environments. However, in hybrid environment the system's performance is improved up to 17%.

Cluster deduplication is a generalized big data reduction scheme for disk-based cluster backup systems. The redundant data stored on multiple disks and partitions are a serious challenge for big data processing systems. The deduplication techniques allow to handle different data chunks (partitions) using hash functions to lower intra-node and inter-node communication overheads. In addition, these methods improve the storage efficiency by eliminating redundant data from multiple nodes. Large-scale cluster deduplication schemes face challenge of information-island (only server-level deduplication is possible due to the communication overhead) where data routing is the key issue. Another major challenge is disk-chunk-index-lookup (keeping duplicated chunk indexes of large datasets creates memory overheads), which degrades the performance of backup clients due to frequently random I/O for lookup and indexing.

Data deduplication schemes are based on either locality or similarity of data in the cluster. Locality-based approaches (stateful or stateless routing schemes) work on the location of duplicated data and perform optimization [14]. The major issue with the locality-based approach is the communication overhead of transferring similar data to same nodes. On the other hand, similarity-based schemes distribute the similar data to the same nodes across the cluster and reduce communication burden [56]. Although the schemes solve the problem of communication overhead, they prove ineffective for inter-node data deduplication system. To cope with challenges of communication overhead and ineffectiveness in inter-node deduplication systems, some hybrid techniques are also proposed in the recent literature. For example, SiLo [15] and Σ-Dedupe [12] used both the similarity- and locality-based techniques where SiLo addressed only the challenge of inter-node deduplication while Σ-Dedupe creates the balance between high deduplication and scalability across all of the nodes in the cluster. Although the cluster-level deduplication is effective for big data reduction, new deduplication methods are required to improve energy efficiency and resource awareness in large-scale data centers. The evaluation of Σ-Dedupe is performed in terms of efficiency analysis and normalized deduplication ratio using Eqs. 12 and 13. The duplication efficiency (DE) is measured using Eq. 12 as follows:

$$DE = \frac{L - P}{T} = \left(1 - \frac{1}{DR}\right) \times DT \qquad (12)$$

where physical and logical size of datasets are denoted by P and L, respectively, and T represents the processing time for deduplication. In addition, DT represents deduplication throughput and DR represents the deduplication ratio in the overall data. Similarly, the normalized effective deduplication ratio (NEDR) is used to measure the cluster-wide deduplication and storage imbalances collectively (see Eq. 13)

$$NEDR = \frac{CDR}{SDR} \times \frac{\alpha}{\alpha + \sigma} \qquad (13)$$

In Eq. 13, the CDR represents the cluster-level deduplication ratio and the SDR denotes single-node-level deduplication ratio. In addition, α represents the average usage of storage while σ shows the standard deviation of cluster-wide storage usage.

The massive amount of data movement in data centers increases the computational and communicational burdens. The exploitation of in-network data processing techniques can reduce the aforementioned complexities. The authors of [57] proposed an in-network data processing technique for bandwidth reduction by customizing routing algorithms, eliminating network redundancy (by caching frequent packets), and reducing on-path data. The proposed technique performs partial data reduction and significantly improved throughput for in-network query processing.

In contrast, mobile users in the same locality or with the same habits generate similar data points causing a huge amount of redundant data in participatory big data environments. In addition, the absence of spatiotemporal correlation among sensory data in mobile opportunistic networks is also a great challenge. The authors in [58] proposed a cooperative sensing and data forwarding framework for mobile opportunistic networks where sampling redundancy is eliminated to save energy consumption. The authors proposed two data forwarding protocols [epidemic routing with fusion and binary spray and wait with fusion (BSWF)] by leveraging data fusion. The essence of the research is the intelligent fusion of sensory data to eliminate redundancy. The simulation results revealed that proposed method can remove 93% of redundancy in the data as compared to non-cooperative methods.

The issue of data duplication or redundancy has been addressed by researchers in different environments at different levels (mobile, cluster, cloud, and data center). Therefore, the selection of best method depends upon the application models. For example, in mobile opportunistic networks and mobile crowd sensing environments, the data redundancy elimination methods are best suited when they are deployed in mobile devices. Similarly, for scientific and highly correlated data deduplication is best suitable when it is performed at cluster, data center, and cloud level.

3.4 Data Preprocessing

Data preprocessing is the second important phase of big data processing, and it must be preprocessed before storage at large-scale infrastructures [19]. This approach helps in big data reduction and also extracts the meta-data for further processing. The authors argue that primary approaches for data preprocessing are based on semantic analysis (using ontologies) or linked data structures (such as Google knowledge graph). However, this literature review uncovers few other techniques, such as low memory pre-filters for streaming data, URL filtration method, and map-reduce implementation of 2D peak detection methods in the big genomic data.

Low memory pre-filters are used for preprocessing genomic sequencing streaming data. The algorithm runs in a single pass and gives improved performance for error correction and lossy compression in data streams. In addition, the algorithm extracts the subsets of data streams using sketch-based techniques and applies pre-filtering algorithm for lossy compression and error correction. The algorithm first constructs the Bruijn graph, and the subsets are extracted using locus-specific graph analysis technique [59]. The massive data redundancy is handled using the k-mers median, and subsequently, digital normalization is employed as the data reduction technique. The authors argued that 95% of the data can be removed in the normal sequencing sample and the percentage reaches 98% of high-coverage single sequencing data. The results show that memory requirement for proposed algorithm is reduced from 3 TB to 300 GB of RAM.

Wearable sensors generate multi-dimensional, nonlinear, dynamic data streams with weak correlation between data points. The authors in [60] used locality-sensitive bloom filter to enhance the efficiency of instance-based learning for front-end data preprocessing near the sensing elements. The technique enables the filtration and communication of only the relevant and meaningful information to reduce computational and communication burden. The authors discussed the big healthcare data system for elderly patients and developed a prototype of the proposed solution. The architecture of the system is based upon a wearable sensor with bluetooth low energy (BLE) interface and can communicate with mobile application and/or PC to establish a personal area network (PAN). The mobile application processes the data and recognizes the state of the user. The sensor data and user states are further transmitted to a remote big data server through TCP/UDP ports. The compression algorithms are applied to incoming data streams, and resultant compressed files remain 10% of the actual data streams.

An application of big data reduction is the filtration of malicious URLs in Internet security applications. The authors in [21] proposed two feature reduction techniques that extract the lexical features and the descriptive features and then combine their results. The lexical features extract the structure of the URLs. However, the issue with lexical features is that malicious URL addresses have constantly changing behavior to abstain from malware detection software. The descriptive features are extracted to track and preserve different states of the same URL to label it as malicious. The authors selected passive-aggressive (for dense feature extraction) and confidence weighted algorithms (for sparse feature extraction) as the online learning algorithms and trained their models with extracted features [61, 62]. The prediction results of the filtration technique demonstrate around 75% data reduction with approximately 90% retention rate (inverse of data loss).

The analysis of large-scale proteomics data, which is the protein-level representation of big genomic data, requires massive computational resources to study different protein properties, such as expressions, changes in protein structures, and the interaction with other proteins. The protein molecules are too large to be identified by spectrometer and therefore are broken into smaller fragments called peptides. The mass spectrometer outputs the graphical output where each spectrum of data points is shown using Gaussian curves for peptide identification. The preprocessing step of proteomics data analysis is the identification of curves also called the 2D peaks. Each of the samples submitted to the spectrometer takes around 100 min to 4 h for complete analysis. During the passage of peptides, the spectrometer takes snapshots of spectrum every second where each peptide remains visible for several spectrums. The authors proposed a map-reduce implementations for proteomics data analysis where 2D peaks are picked at map level and further analyzed at reduce level [63]. The data reduction takes place at map level by applying preprocessing techniques for decoding the arrays, noise removal, and management of the overlapping peaks in the spectrum. Experimental results show that the given map-reduce implementation completes the data analysis in 22 min.

Recently light detection and ranging (LiDAR) technology enabled the generation of big 3D spatial data [64]. A cloud computing-based LiDAR processing system (CLiPS) processes big 3D spatial data effectively. The CLiPS uses several preprocessing techniques for data reduction to deal with large size of data. The data reduction is performed using a vertex decimation approach to provide a user's preferred parameters to reduce the big data. The results show the advantage of cloud computing technologies over the conventional systems comparing performance and time consumption.

The literature review of these techniques reveals that data preprocessing techniques are highly dependent on the nature of big data and also encourage further investigation of the underlying problem. Therefore, these techniques could not be generalized for all types of big data streams.

3.5 Dimension Reduction

Big data reduction is mainly considered to be the dimension reduction problem because the massive collection of big data streams introduces the 'curse of dimensionality' with millions of features (variables and dimensions) that increases the storage and computational complexity of big data systems [5]. A wide range of dimension reduction methods are proposed in the existing literature. The methods are based on clustering, map-reduce implementations of existing dimension reduction methods, feature selection techniques, and fuzzy logic implementations. Table 2 presents the summary of the above-mentioned methods.

The dynamic quantum clustering (DQC) enables powerful visualization of high-dimensional big data [8]. It outlines subsets of the data on the basis of density among all of the correlated variables in high-dimensional feature space. The DQC is scalable to very large systems due to its support for highly distributed data in parallel environments. The DQC is based on quantum mechanics techniques from physics. It works by constructing a potential proxy function to estimate the density of data points. The function named as parzen estimator, $\emptyset(\vec{x})$, is applied over n-dimensional feature space, and it is the sum of Gaussian functions centered at each data point, $\vec{x}$ (see Eq. 14). The DQC next defines a vector function that satisfies the Schrodinger equation (see Eq. 15). Afterward, the DQC computes Gaussians functions from subsets using Hamiltonian operator defined in the potential function and multiplies the results by quantum-time evolution operator $e^{-i\delta tH}$ (where δt is set as small, i is the ith iteration, and H is the Hamiltonian distance). The DQC then computes the new center of each Gaussian and iterates the whole procedure. The results show that large and complex datasets could be analyzed using the DQC without any prior assumption about the number of clusters or using any expert information. In addition, the DQC could be applied to noisy data to identify and eliminate unimportant features to produce better results. This data reduction strategy makes DQC useful for big data analysis.

$$\varphi(\vec{x}) = \sum_{l=1}^{m} e^{\frac{-1}{2\sigma^2}\left(\vec{x} - \vec{x_l}\right)^2} \qquad (14)$$

The potential function $V(\vec{x})$ can be defined over the same n-dimensional feature space and defined as the function for which $\varphi(\vec{x})$ satisfies the time-independent Schrodinger equation.

$$\frac{-1}{2\sigma^2}\nabla^2\varphi + V(\vec{x})\varphi = E\varphi = 0 \qquad (15)$$

Conventional dimensionality reduction algorithms that use Gaussian maximum likelihood estimator could not handle the datasets with over 20,000 variables. The BIG-Quic addresses the issue by applying a parallel divide-and-conquer strategy that can be applied up to 1-million variables in the feature space for dimensionality reduction [9]. The results show that the proposed algorithm is highly scalable and faster than the existing algorithms, such as Glasso and ALM [65, 66].

Knowledge discovery from high-dimensional big social image datasets is quite challenging. The authors proposed a new framework called twister which is a map-reduce implementation of k-means algorithm for dimensionality reduction [67]. The authors proposed a topology-aware pipeline-based method to accelerate broadcasting and to overcome the limitations of existing massively parallel infrastructure (MPI) implementations. In addition, the performance of the system was improved using local reduction techniques. This technique reduces local data before shuffling. The amount of data reduced is estimated using Eq. 16.

$$\text{Amount of data} = \frac{\text{No. of nodes}}{\text{No. of maps}} \times 100\% \qquad (16)$$

Normally, online learning techniques take the full feature set as the input, which is quite challenging when dealing with high-dimensional features space. The authors proposed an online feature selection (OFS) approach where the online learners only work on small and fixed-length feature sets. However, the selection of active features for accurate prediction is a key issue in the approaches presented in [68]. The authors investigated sparsity regularization and truncation techniques and proposed a new algorithm called the OFS. The results showed that the OFS outperformed RAND and PE$_{trun}$ algorithms for UCI datasets and it works best in online learning mode as compared to batch-mode learning.

The corsets are the small set of points that represent the larger population of data and maintain the actual properties of overall population. These properties vary by nature of knowledge discovery algorithms. For example, the corsets representing first k-components maps with first k-components in the big data. Similarly, the corsets containing k-clusters with radius r approximate the big data and obtain the k-clusters with same r. In this way, the authors [11] applied corsets to reduce the big data into small and

Table 2 Dimension reduction methods

References	Methods	Description	Strengths	Weaknesses
Weinstein et al. [8]	DQC	Visual data mining method	Ability to expose hidden structures and determine their significance in high-dimensional big data	Lacks efficiency Requires a combination of statistical tools
Hsieh et al. [9]	BIGQuic	Applying a parallel divide-and-conquer strategy	Supports parallelization Allowing for inexact computation of specific components	Lacks accuracy and reliability
Hoi et al. [68]	OFS	Selection of active features for accurate prediction	Works best in online learning mode as compared with batch-mode learning	Lacks efficiency
Feldman et al. [11]	Corsets	Applying corsets to reduce big data	High significance when used for data complexity	Works well on small datasets only
Azar and Hassanien [71]	LHNFCSF	Linguistic hedges fuzzy classifier	Data reduction	Lack of efficiency
Cichocki [72]	TNs	Tensor decomposition and approximation	Reduction in feature spaces	High computational complexity
Dalessandro [73]	FH	Maps features from high-dimensional space to low-dimensional spaces	Reduces feature space randomly	Compromise on data quality
Liu et al. [77]	CF	Classifier training with minimal feature spaces	Outlines critical feature dimensions and adequate sampling size	Assumptions need to be more accurate to outline critical feature dimension
Zeng and Li [74]	IPLS	Performs incremental analysis of streaming data	Computationally efficient Highly accurate	Needs to handle change detection in streaming data

manageable size, which reduces the overall data complexity. The authors mapped corsets with *k*-means, principal component analysis (PCA) and projective clustering algorithms deployed with massively parallel streaming data [69, 70]. The big data is reduced in such a way that high dimensions of input space do not affect the cardinalities of corsets. In addition, the corsets are merged by maintaining the property that union of two corsets represents the reduced set of union of two big datasets. The experimental results showed that corsets are suitable to address NP-hard problems in massively parallel and streaming data environments where big data complexity is reduced by application of data processing algorithms on small datasets that are approximated from big data. In addition, the corsets are paradigm shift in big data analysis where the focus of research remains on big data reduction instead of improving the computational efficiency of existing algorithms.

Medical big data comes across several issues regarding extraction of structures, storage of massive data streams, and uncovering the useful knowledge patterns. Research shows that fuzzy classification methods are good choice to cope with the above-mentioned issues. Recently, the authors of [71] presented linguistic hedges fuzzy classifier with selected features (LHNFCSFs) to reduce dimensions, select features, and perform classification operations. The integration of linguistic hedges in adaptive neural-fuzzy

classifier enhances the accuracy. The LHNFCSF reduces the feature space effectively and enhances the performance of the classifier by removing unimportant, noisy, or redundant features. The results depict that the LHNFCSF addresses the medical big data issues by reducing the dimensions of large datasets and speeding up the learning process and improves the classification performance.

Tensors are multi-dimensional representations of data elements with at least one extra dimension as compared to matrices. The increasing numbers of elements demand more computational power to process the tensors. Tensor processing works fine with small tensors. However, processing large tensors is a challenging task [10]. Tensor decomposition (TD) schemes are used to extract small but representative tensors from large tensors [72]. Three widely used TD strategies include canonical polyadic decomposition (CPD), tucker decomposition, and tensor trains (TT). The TD schemes represent the large tensors linked with their small representations. These decomposition schemes reduce the high dimensionality in big datasets and establish the interconnection among tensors to form tensor networks (TNs). These TNs enable to further reduce the data size by using optimization-based algorithms to find factor matrices and optimize using linear and nonlinear least square methods. The case studies show that tensor decomposition strategies could be used to alleviate/

eliminate dimensionality in large scientific computing datasets and have many potential applications for feature extraction, cluster analysis, classification, data fusion, anomaly detection, pattern recognition, integration, time-series analysis, predictive modeling, multi-way component analysis, and regression.

The feature hashing (FH) method reduces feature dimensionality by randomly assigning each feature in the actual space to a new dimension in a lower-dimensional space [73]. This is done by simply hashing the ID of the original features. Usually, all dimensional reduction techniques degrade the data quality. However, most of them preserve the geometric qualities of the data. Alternately, the FH does not preserve the data quality. Research shows that the degradation of data quality is so minimal that its benefits are outweighed by the cost. The FH scales linearly with simple preprocessing and preservation of data sparsity, if exists. The scalability property of the FH makes it a natural choice for million (or even billion) feature datasets. For example, the FH method applied to email spam filtering shows its power when applied upon sparse and streaming data with real-time requirements of mass customization. The results show that the feature set is reduced from one billion to one million features.

Big data streams enter with episodic information and create high-dimensional feature spaces. Normally, the feature extraction methods need whole data in the memory that increases the computational complexity of big data systems and degrades the performance of classifiers. The incremental feature extraction methods are the best choice to handle such issues [74]. Incremental partial least squares (IPLSs) is a variant of the partial least squares method that effectively reduces dimensions from large-scale streaming data and improves the classification accuracy. The proposed algorithm works in two-stage feature extraction process. First, the IPLS adopts the target function to update the historical means and to extract the leading projection direction. Second, the IPLS calculates the rest of projection directions that are based on the equivalence between the Krylov sequence and the partial least square vectors [75]. The comparison of the IPLS was performed with incremental PCA algorithm, incremental inter-class scatter method, and incremental maximum margin criterion technique. The results revealed that the IPLS showed improved performance in terms of accuracy and computational efficiency.

Systems of systems (SoS)—case study The integration of heterogeneous and independent operating computing systems to collectively maximize the performance as compared to the individual settings leads toward the SoS [76]. Nowadays, SoS is contributing to generate big data and raises the need for data reduction. Few examples of statistical and computational intelligence tools for data

reduction in SoS include the PCA, clustering, fuzzy-logic, neuro-computing, and evolutionary computing, such as genetic algorithms, and Bayesian networks. The authors applied data reduction methods at different stages of analyzing photovoltaic data that were collected from different sources. The original dataset contained 250 variables, which is highly dimensional and is not practical due to limitations of execution time and memory constraints on a desktop computer. Two approaches for data reduction at this stage were considered: (1) labeling the interesting attributes by domain expert and (2) development of an adaptive learning algorithm for automatic attribute selection. The authors employed the first approach for data reduction. The authors further cleaned-up the data and removed all invalid data points from the dataset. For example, solar irradiance in night hours generates data points with negative values, therefore not feasible for contribution in the study. After removing the invalid data, the data points containing very low values for global horizontal irradiance (GHI), direct normal irradiance (DNI), and direct horizontal irradiance (DHI) are removed to create more crispy data for further analysis.

The cleaned data are further fed into two nonparametric model generation tools, namely the fuzzy inference system generator and back-propagation neural network training tools using MATLAB fuzzy logic toolbox and the neural network toolbox. The initial evaluation of both of the tools revealed that the input variables should be further reduced for performance maximization in terms of execution time and memory consumption. The authors expanded the non-linear data by using additional variables that in turn increased the performance of the training model but also increased time and space complexity. Therefore, the PCA is applied for dimension reduction to compress the data without significant information loss. After application of the PCA, further dimension reduction was performed using genetic algorithm (GA). First, the data were reduced using the GA on the full set of initial data and remaining data were expanded nonlinearly. Finally, the expanded dataset is used to train a neural network to assess the overall effectiveness of the GA. In practice, the time- and computation-related constraints were limited to the selection of training data to first 1000 samples. The first iteration of GA took initially 244 samples and reduced it to 74. The results showed that the GA reduced the number of attributes up to 70%.

3.6 Data Mining and Machine Learning (DM and ML)

Recently, several DM and ML methods have also been proposed for big data reduction. The methods are either applied to reduce data immediately after its acquisition or customized to address some specific problems. For example, the authors [78] proposed a context-aware big data forwarding scheme using distributed wearable sensors. The scheme is based on hidden markov model (HMM) to enable context-aware features in the distributed sensor model and forwards only relevant information when there is some significant change in the data [78]. The proposed scheme reduces the communication and storage overhead in big data environment. The authors compared the result of proposed locality-sensitive hash (LSH)-based method with linear perception (LP)-based dimensionality reduction algorithm and argued on the effectiveness of the proposed scheme as compared to the LP-based dimensionality reduction methods.

The problem of mining uncertain big data due to existential probabilities becomes worse and requires huge efforts and computational power to explore the incrementally growing uncertain search space. Therefore, the search space is needed to be reduced for uncovering the maximum certain and useful patterns. The authors of [79] proposed a map-reduce algorithm to reduce the search space and mine frequent patterns from uncertain big data. The algorithm facilitates the users to confine their search space by setting some succinct anti-monotone (SAM) constraints for data analysis and subsequently mines the uncertain big data to uncover frequent patterns that satisfy the user-specified SAM constraints. The input of the algorithm is uncertain big data, user-specified minimum support (minsup) threshold, and the SAM constraints. Two sets of map-reduce implementations are used to uncover singleton and non-singleton frequent patterns. Experimental results show that the user-specified SAM (termed as selectivity) is directly proportional to multiple parameters which are derived from algorithm's runtime, the pairs returned by map function, the pairs sorted and shuffled by reduce function, and the required constraints checks.

Artificial intelligence methods, for example, artificial neural networks (ANNs) have also potential for big data reduction and compression. The authors in [80] proposed a self-organized Kohonen network-based method to reduce big hydrographic data acquired from the deep seas. The proposed system first converts the raw data into 'swath' files using a combination of four filters: (1) limit filter, (2) amplitude filter, (3) along track filter, and (4) across track filter. The appropriate combinations of the filters ensure the optimal dataset size. Despite filtering, the sample size is still large to be considered as big data. The self-organized Kohonen networks are trained and optimized using filtered hydrographic data to cluster the incoming data streams. The experimental results exhibited the feasibility of self-organized Kohonen networks for big hydrographic data for further analysis.

In addition to conventional machine learning algorithms, based on shallow learning models, deep learning is creating

space as an option for big data reduction methods [81]. Deep learning models are hierarchical representations of supervised and unsupervised classification methods that are best suitable for large-scale, high-dimensional big data streams [22]. Deep learning models become computationally inefficient with the increase in big data complexity. However, the availability of MPIs (clusters/clouds) can address the aforementioned issue. Conventionally, deep learning models work at multiple layers with different granularities of information and predictive abilities. Two well-established deep learning architectures are deep belief networks (DBNs) and convolutional neural networks (CNNs). The DBN learning models are developed in two stages: (1) the initial models are developed using unsupervised learning methods with unlabeled data streams and (2) the models are fine-tuned using supervised learning methods and labeled data streams. The typical architecture of the DBN in Fig. 2 shows the multilayer representation of the deep learning model. The architecture is based on an input and output layer with multiple intermediate hidden layers. The output of each $(n-1)$th layer becomes the input of the nth layer in the architecture. In addition, the learning models are fine-tuned using back-propagation methods to support generative performance and judicial power of the DBNs. Although the CNNs are based on learning models, they differ from the DBNs. The CNNs layers are either the convolutional layers to support the convolution of several input filters or sub-sampling layers to reduce the size of output variable from previous layers. Effective utilization of these deep learning models in conjunction with MPIs can significantly reduce big data streams.

Deep learning models are inherently computationally complex and require many-core CPUs and large-scale computational infrastructures. Some recent learning approaches for such large-volume, complex data include locally connected networks [82, 83], improved optimizers, and deep stacking networks (DSNs). The authors of [84] proposed the hybrid deep learning model, called DisBelief, to address the issue of high dimensionality in big data streams. Disbelief utilizes a large-scale cluster to parallelize both the data and the learning models using synchronization, message passing, and multi-threading techniques. The DisBelief model first achieves parallelism by partitioning large-scale networks into small blocks that are mapped to a single node and then achieves data parallelism using two separate distribution optimization procedures called stochastic gradient descent (SGD) for online optimization and sandblaster for batch optimization. Although feasible for big data reduction, the deep learning models are resource hungry and require MPIs based on clusters of CPUs or GPUs. Therefore, there is a need to develop optimized deep learning strategies to achieve resource efficiency and reduce communication burdens inside the MPIs.

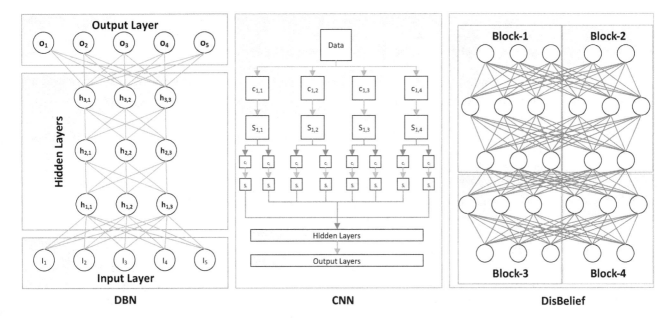

Fig. 2 Deep learning models

The wide spectrum view of the proposed methods for big data reduction uncovers the fact that the research on big data reduction methods is being carried out at several levels of big data architecture and in different forms.

4 Open Research Issues

The discussion on the open research issues, limitations, and possible future research directions is presented in this section.

Network theory The extraction of topological network and ranking of network nodes from big data is a complex process due to inherent big data complexity. In addition, the complex interactions among different nodes of the extracted networks increase the computational complexity of existing network theory-based methods. The scale-free networks and random networks can effectively reduce complex big datasets. However, the full network extraction from inconsistent and missing data is the key challenge [16, 40]. Big data systems contain many small and manageable datasets, but finding the connections among these datasets is a crucial task. The similarity graph is generated from big data where vertices represent datasets and the weighted edges are defined on the basis of similarity measure. The graph is further reduced by merging similar datasets to reduce the number of nodes. The similarity-based big data reduction methods are good choice for network extraction and reduction. However, a range of new similarity measures are required to deal with the evolving complexity and to fully comply with 6Vs of big data [17].

Persistent homology is a good solution for topological data analysis, but it involves high computational complexity. The solutions like selective collapse algorithms represent datasets in the form of forests, and the nodes are collapsed in a way to improve the speed of persistent homology and maintain strong collapse. The persistent homology tools for reducing and analyzing big data still need to be further explored in the future research [18, 42]. Similarly, the automated extraction of events and their representation in network structures is an emerging research area. The assessment of events co-occurrence and their mutual influences is the key challenge for big data reduction. The authors in [41] performed the influence assessment among different concepts (events or datasets) based on the co-occurrence of two events. The co-occurrence is assessed based on the preferential attachment property which determines that new nodes are most likely connected with highly connected nodes as compared to less connected nodes. In addition, the influence relationship among network nodes can be effectively derived from conditional dependencies among variables. However, the mathematical and probabilistic constraints increase the computational complexity in network extraction methods. Therefore, efforts are required to optimize the influence assessment methods for computationally efficient and better approximated network structures [41].

Compression Big data processing in cloud computing environments involves challenges relevant to inefficiency, parallel memory bottlenecks, and deadlocks. The spatiotemporal compression is a key solution for processing big graph data in the cloud environment. In spatiotemporal compression-based methods, the graph is partitioned and edges are mapped into different clusters where compression operations are performed for data reduction. The spatiotemporal compression is an effective approach for big data reduction. However, the research is required to find new parameters that are helpful in finding additional spatiotemporal correlations for maximum big data reduction [45].

The gap between computations and I/O capacity in the HEC systems degrades the system performance significantly. Although in situ analytics are useful for decreasing the aforementioned gap, the cost of computation increases abruptly. The compression methods can significantly reduce the transferred data and narrow the gap between computations and I/O capacity. The authors in [43] suggested that the number of available processors and the data reduction ratio (compression ratio) are two key factors that need attention in future research in this area. Alternately, the AST is a new way of compressing digitized data by selectively stretching and warping the signal. The technique is primarily based on self-adaptive stretch where more samples are associated with sharp features and fewer samples are associated with redundant coarse features. The AST performs data compression of the signal extracted on frequency domain. The method also performs inverse transformation of the constructed signal. The method specifically works with big data involving signal processing. However, the generalization to other domains is a bottleneck in this research [47].

Compressed sensing is a compressible and/or sparse signal that projects a high-dimensional data in low-dimensional space using random measurement matrix. The proposed scheme performs data acquisition and compression in parallel for improved performance as compared with Nyquist sampling theory-based compression methods. The probability of poor data quality and information fidelity loss increases when the analysis is performed on reduced and compressed data [48]. The RED encoding scheme proposed by authors in [48] is used to manage massively generated voluminous electrophysiology data. The scheme performs best when encoding of invariant signals is performed. However, while encoding time-series signals, the performance varies but the scheme achieves high compression rate with improved computational speed in lossless compression. The performance of the RED encoding methods degrades with high variance in signals [50].

Parallel compression methods can be used to reduce the data size with low computational cost. It uses proper orthogonal decomposition to compress data because it can effectively extract important features from the data and resulting compressed data can also be linearly decompressed. The parallel compression methods balance between feature retention error and compression ratio and

perform fast decompression for interactive data visualization. However, the standard deviation of error is significant due to noise in the dataset [55]. The sketching method uses count-min sketch algorithm to compress vehicular movement data and achieve compact communication. Although it ensures data reduction by preserving some important characteristics of the original data, the probability of information fidelity loss is more when sketching is applied with inconsistent and noisy data stream [46].

Data deduplication (redundancy elimination) Cluster-level data deduplication is a key requirement to comply with service-level agreements (SLAs) for privacy preserving in cloud environments. The main challenge is the establishment of trade-off between high deduplication ratio and scalable deduplication throughput. The similarity-based deduplication scheme optimizes the elimination process by considering the locality and similarity of data points in both the intra-node and inter-node scenarios. The approach is effective for data reduction, but it requires to be implemented with very large-scale cluster data deduplication systems [12]. The I/O latency and extra computational overhead of cluster-level data deduplication are among the key challenges. The authors in [13] characterized the deduplication schemes in terms of energy impact and performance overhead. The authors outlined three sources of redundancy in cluster environment including: (1) the deployment of additional nodes in the cluster, (2) the expansion of big datasets, and (3) the usage of replication mechanisms. The outcomes of the analysis reveal that the local deduplication, at cluster level, can reduce the hashing overhead. However, local deduplication cannot achieve the maximum redundancy. In contrast, global deduplication can achieve maximum redundancy but compromises on the hashing overheads. In addition, fine-grained deduplication is not suitable for big datasets especially in streaming data environments [13].

Data routing is a key issue in multi-node data deduplication systems. The availability of sufficient throughput is the main bottleneck for data movement among backup and recovery systems. The stateful data routing schemes, as compared to stateless approaches, have higher overhead with low imbalance in the data which minimizes the utility of data deduplication systems. The open issues for data routing include the characterization of parameters which causes the data skew. In addition, the scalability of routing methods to large-scale cluster systems and the impact of feature selection and super-chunk size are needed to be explored in future research. Moreover, the addition of new nodes is needed to be considered for effective bin migration strategies [14].

The in-network data processing methods facilitate in data reduction and reduce the bandwidth consumption, and the efforts are required for on-the-path data reduction and redundancy elimination. The reduced bandwidth consumption by in-network data processing methods enable enhanced query processing throughput. The future implementation of in-network data processing is envisioned as the provision of network-as-a-service (NaaS) in the cloud environment which is fully orchestrated for redundancy elimination and query optimization [57]. In addition, there is a need to devise new network-aware query processing and optimization models, and integration of these models in distributed data processing systems. Research shows that co-operative sensing methods can aid in significant data reduction in large-scale sensing infrastructures [58]. Current co-operative sensing methods lack in low-level contextual features and adaptive global learning models to handle the change detection in streaming data environments. Future research work to integrate current low-level contextual models and adaptive machine learning methods can aid in maximum data reduction as well as collection of a high-quality data.

Data preprocessing The investigations of research problems relevant to preprocessing techniques of big data are still at the initial level. Most of the works are based on the adoption of existing preprocessing methods that were earlier proposed for historical large datasets and data streams. The forefront deployment of data preprocessing methods in the big data knowledge discovery process requires new, efficient, robust, scalable, and optimized preprocessing techniques for both historical and streaming big data. The application of appropriate and highly relevant preprocessing methods not only increases data quality but also improves the analytics on reduced datasets. The research on new methods for sketching, anomaly detection, noise removal, feature extraction, outliers detection, and pre-filtering of streaming data is required to reduce big data effectively. In addition, the deployment of adaptive learning models in conjunction with said methods can aid in dynamic preprocessing of big streaming data [21].

Dimension reduction Big data reduction is traditionally considered to be a dimension reduction problem where multi-million features spaces are reduced to manageable feature spaces for effective data management and analytics. Unsupervised learning methods are the key consideration for dimensionality reduction problem. However, this literature review revealed several other statistical and machine learning methods to address this issue. The techniques to combine conventional dimension reduction methods with statistical analysis methods can increase the efficiency of big data systems [8]. This approach may aid in targeting highly dense and information oriented structures (feature sets) to achieve maximum and efficient big data reduction. Alternately, tensor decomposition and approximation methods are useful to cope with the curse of dimensionality that arises due to high-dimensional complex and sparse feature spaces [10]. The main application of TD-based methods is witnessed in the scientific computing and quantum information theory domain. This literature review revealed that the issue of dimensionality reduction in big data could be handled by adopting front-end data processing, online feature selection from big data streams, constant-size corsets for clustering, statistical methods, and fuzzy classification-based soft computing approaches. These adoptions open new research avenues for interdisciplinary research and develop novel big data reduction methods. The strengths and weaknesses of these methods are already presented in detail in Table 2.

DM and ML The DM and the ML methods for big data reduction could be used at various levels of big data architectures. These methods enable to find interesting knowledge patterns from big data streams to produce highly relevant and reduced data for further analysis. For example, HMM as applied in [78] enables the context-aware features to filter the raw data streams to transmit only highly relevant and required information. In addition, the scheme enables to project high-dimensional data streams in manageable low-dimensional feature spaces. Although the application of these methods is convenient for data reduction, the trade-off between energy consumptions in local processing with raw data transmission is a key challenge that is needed to be considered. The DM and ML methods also have potential to be deployed in map-reduce implementations of Hadoop architecture. The authors in [79] parallelized the frequent pattern mining algorithms using the map-reduce programming model to reduce the massively high-dimensional feature space produced by uncertain big data. However, there exists a huge research gap for the implementation of other DM and ML methods for big data reduction that include supervised, unsupervised, semi-supervised, and hierarchical deep learning models [85]. In addition, the implementation of statistical methods, both descriptive and inferential, for big data reduction using approximation and estimation properties in uncertain big data environments is also useful for data reduction in map-reduce programming models. Moreover, the DM and ML methods are equally useful for big data reduction when coupled with artificial intelligence-based optimization methods. However, supervised, unsupervised, and semi-supervised learning methods need more attention for future research [80].

Deep learning models have recently gained attention by the researchers. The deployment of deep learning models for big data reduction is potential research direction that can be pursued in future. The deep learning models are initially developed from certain data and gradually evolve with uncertain data to effectively reduce big data streams. However, the increasing computational complexities of operating in uncertain big data environments and optimization of learning models to discover patterns from maximum data are the issues that can be further investigated [84].

In this section, we thoroughly discussed the open issues, research challenges, the limitations of proposed methods for big data reduction and presented some future research directions. The survey reveals that big data reduction is performed at many levels during the data processing life-cycle that include data capturing, data preprocessing, data indexing and storage, data analysis, and visualization. Therefore, the relevant reduction methods and systems should be designed to handle the big data complexity at all stages of big data processing. In addition, the future research work should focus on considering all 6Vs to process big data in computing systems with different form factors from fine-grained mobile computing systems to large-scale massively parallel computing infrastructures.

5 Conclusions

Big data complexity is a key issue that is needed to be mitigated. The methods discussed in this article are an effort to address the issue. The presented literature review reveals that there is no existing method that can handle the issue of big data complexity single-handedly by considering the all 6Vs of big data. The studies discussed in this article mainly focused on data reduction in terms of volume (by reducing size) and variety (by reducing number of features or dimensions). However, further efforts are required to reduce the big data streams in terms of velocity and veracity. In addition, the new methods are required to reduce big data streams at the earliest immediately after data production and its entrance into the big data systems. In general, compression-based data reduction methods are convenient for reducing volume. However, the decompression overhead needs to be considered to improve efficiency. Similarly, network theory-based methods are effective for extracting structures from unstructured data and to efficiently handle the variety in big data. The data deduplication methods are useful to improve the data consistency. Therefore, the aforementioned methods are a suitable alternative to manage the variability issues in big data. Likewise, data preprocessing, dimension reduction, data mining, and machine learning methods are useful for data reduction at different levels in big data systems. Keeping in view the outcomes of this survey, we conclude that big data reduction methods are emerging research area that needs attention by the researchers.

References

1. Wu X et al (2014) Data mining with big data. IEEE Trans Knowl Data Eng 26(1):97–107
2. Che D, Safran M, Peng Z (2013) From big data to big data mining: challenges, issues, and opportunities. In: Database systems for advanced applications
3. Battams K (2014) Stream processing for solar physics: applications and implications for big solar data. arXiv preprint arXiv:1409.8166
4. Zhai Y, Ong Y-S, Tsang IW (2014) The emerging "big dimensionality". Comput Intell Mag IEEE 9(3):14–26
5. Fan J, Han F, Liu H (2014) Challenges of big data analysis. Nat Sci Rev 1(2):293–314
6. Chandramouli B, Goldstein J, Duan S (2012) Temporal analytics on big data for web advertising. In: 2012 IEEE 28th international conference on data engineering (ICDE)
7. Ward RM et al (2013) Big data challenges and opportunities in high-throughput sequencing. Syst Biomed 1(1):29–34
8. Weinstein M et al (2013) Analyzing big data with dynamic quantum clustering. arXiv preprint arXiv:1310.2700
9. Hsieh C-J et al (2013) BIG & QUIC: sparse inverse covariance estimation for a million variables. In: Advances in neural information processing systems
10. Vervliet N et al (2014) Breaking the curse of dimensionality using decompositions of incomplete tensors: tensor-based scientific computing in big data analysis. IEEE Signal Process Mag 31(5):71–79
11. Feldman D, Schmidt M, Sohler C (2013) Turning big data into tiny data: constant-size coresets for k-means, pca and projective clustering. In: Proceedings of the twenty-fourth annual ACM-SIAM symposium on discrete algorithms
12. Fu Y, Jiang H, Xiao N (2012) A scalable inline cluster deduplication framework for big data protection. In: Middleware 2012. Springer, pp 354–373
13. Zhou R, Liu M, Li T (2013) Characterizing the efficiency of data deduplication for big data storage management. In: 2013 IEEE international symposium on workload characterization (IISWC)
14. Dong W et al (2011) Tradeoffs in scalable data routing for deduplication clusters. In: FAST
15. Xia W et al (2011) SiLo: a similarity-locality based near-exact deduplication scheme with low RAM overhead and high throughput. In: USENIX annual technical conference
16. Trovati M, Asimakopoulou E, Bessis N (2014) An analytical tool to map big data to networks with reduced topologies. In: 2014 international conference on intelligent networking and collaborative systems (INCoS)
17. Fang X, Zhan J, Koceja N (2013) Towards network reduction on big data. In: 2013 international conference on social computing (SocialCom)
18. Wilkerson AC, Chintakunta H, Krim H (2014) Computing persistent features in big data: a distributed dimension reduction approach. In: 2014 IEEE international conference on acoustics, speech and signal processing (ICASSP)
19. Di Martino B et al (2014) Big data (lost) in the cloud. Int J Big Data Intell 1(1–2):3–17
20. Brown CT (2012) BIGDATA: small: DA: DCM: low-memory streaming prefilters for biological sequencing data
21. Lin M-S et al (2013) Malicious URL filtering—a big data application. In 2013 IEEE international conference on big data
22. Chen J et al (2013) Big data challenge: a data management perspective. Front Comput Sci 7(2):157–164
23. Chen X-W, Lin X (2014) Big data deep learning: challenges and perspectives. IEEE Access 2:514–525
24. Chen Z et al (2015) A survey of bitmap index compression algorithms for big data. Tsinghua Sci Technol 20(1):100–115
25. Hashem IAT et al (2015) The rise of "big data" on cloud computing: review and open research issues. Inf Syst 47:98–115
26. Gani A et al (2015) A survey on indexing techniques for big data:

taxonomy and performance evaluation. In: Knowledge and information systems, pp 1–44

27. Kambatla K et al (2014) Trends in big data analytics. J Parallel Distrib Comput 74(7):2561–2573

28. Jin X et al (2015) Significance and challenges of big data research. Big Data Res 2(2):59–64

29. Li F, Nath S (2014) Scalable data summarization on big data. Distrib Parallel Databases 32(3):313–314

30. Lohr S (2014) For big-data scientists, 'janitor work' is key hurdle to insights. http://www.nytimes.com/2014/08/18/technology/for-big-data-scientists-hurdle-to-insights-is-janitor-work.html

31. Ma C, Zhang HH, Wang X (2014) Machine learning for big data analytics in plants. Trends Plant Sci 19(12):798–808

32. Ordonez C (2013) Can we analyze big data inside a DBMS? In: Proceedings of the sixteenth international workshop on data warehousing and OLAP

33. Oliveira J, Osvaldo N et al (2014) Where chemical sensors may assist in clinical diagnosis exploring "big data". Chem Lett 43(11):1672–1679

34. Shilton K (2012) Participatory personal data: an emerging research challenge for the information sciences. J Am Soc Inform Sci Technol 63(10):1905–1915

35. Shuja J et al (2012) Energy-efficient data centers. Computing 94(12):973–994

36. Ahmad RW et al (2015) A survey on virtual machine migration and server consolidation frameworks for cloud data centers. J Netw Comput Appl 52:11–25

37. Bonomi F et al (2014) Fog computing: a platform for internet of things and analytics. In: Big data and internet of things: a roadmap for smart environments. Springer, pp 169–186

38. Rehman MH, Liew CS, Wah TY (2014) UniMiner: towards a unified framework for data mining. In: 2014 fourth world congress on information and communication technologies (WICT)

39. Patty JW, Penn EM (2015) Analyzing big data: social choice and measurement. Polit Sci Polit 48(01):95–101

40. Trovati M (2015) Reduced topologically real-world networks: a big-data approach. Int J Distrib Syst Technol (IJDST) 6(2):13–27

41. Trovati M, Bessis N (2015) An influence assessment method based on co-occurrence for topologically reduced big data sets. In: Soft computing, pp 1–10

42. Dey TK, Fan F, Wang Y (2014) Computing topological persistence for simplicial maps. In: Proceedings of the thirtieth annual symposium on computational geometry

43. Zou H et al (2014) Flexanalytics: a flexible data analytics framework for big data applications with I/O performance improvement. Big Data Res 1:4–13

44. Ackermann K, Angus SD (2014) A resource efficient big data analysis method for the social sciences: the case of global IP activity. Procedia Comput Sci 29:2360–2369

45. Yang C et al (2014) A spatiotemporal compression based approach for efficient big data processing on Cloud. J Comput Syst Sci 80(8):1563–1583

46. Monreale A et al (2013) Privacy-preserving distributed movement data aggregation. In: Geographic information science at the heart of Europe. Springer, pp 225–245

47. Jalali B, Asghari MH (2014) The anamorphic stretch transform: putting the squeeze on "big data". Opt Photonics News 25(2):24–31

48. Wang W et al (2013) Statistical wavelet-based anomaly detection in big data with compressive sensing. EURASIP J Wirel Commun Netw 2013(1):1–6

49. He B, Li Y (2014) Big data reduction and optimization in sensor monitoring network. J Appl Math. doi:10.1155/2014/294591

50. Brinkmann BH et al (2009) Large-scale electrophysiology: acquisition, compression, encryption, and storage of big data. J Neurosci Methods 180(1):185–192

51. Zou H et al (2014) Improving I/O performance with adaptive data compression for big data applications. In: 2014 IEEE international parallel & distributed processing symposium workshops (IPDPSW)

52. Lakshminarasimhan S et al (2011) Compressing the incompressible with ISABELA: in situ reduction of spatio-temporal data. In: Euro-Par 2011 parallel processing. Springer, pp 366–379

53. Ahrens JP et al (2009) Interactive remote large-scale data visualization via prioritized multi-resolution streaming. In: Proceedings of the 2009 workshop on ultrascale visualization

54. Compression utility, gzip. http://www.gzip.org

55. Bi C et al (2013) Proper orthogonal decomposition based parallel compression for visualizing big data on the K computer. In: 2013 IEEE symposium on large-scale data analysis and visualization (LDAV)

56. Bhagwat D, Eshghi K, Mehra P (2007) Content-based document routing and index partitioning for scalable similarity-based searches in a large corpus. In: Proceedings of the 13th ACM SIGKDD international conference on knowledge discovery and data mining

57. Rupprecht L (2013) Exploiting in-network processing for big data management. In: Proceedings of the 2013 SIGMOD/PODS Ph.D. symposium

58. Zhao D et al (2015) COUPON: a cooperative framework for building sensing maps in mobile opportunistic networks. IEEE Trans Parallel Distrib Syst 26(2):392–402

59. Zerbino DR, Birney E (2008) Velvet: algorithms for de novo short read assembly using de Bruijn graphs. Genome Res 18(5):821–829

60. Cheng Y, Jiang P, Peng Y (2014) Increasing big data front end processing efficiency via locality sensitive Bloom filter for elderly healthcare. In: 2014 IEEE symposium on computational intelligence in big data (CIBD)

61. Dredze M, Crammer K, Pereira F (2008) Confidence-weighted linear classification. In: Proceedings of the 25th international conference on machine learning

62. Crammer K et al (2006) Online passive-aggressive algorithms. J Mach Learn Res 7:551–585

63. Hillman C et al (2014) Near real-time processing of proteomics data using Hadoop. Big Data 2(1):44–49

64. Sugumaran R, Burnett J, Blinkmann A (2012) Big 3d spatial data processing using cloud computing environment. In: Proceedings of the 1st ACM SIGSPATIAL international workshop on analytics for big geospatial data

65. Friedman J, Hastie T, Tibshirani R (2008) Sparse inverse covariance estimation with the graphical lasso. Biostatistics 9(3):432–441

66. Scheinberg K, Ma S, Goldfarb D (2010) Sparse inverse covariance selection via alternating linearization methods. In: Advances in neural information processing systems

67. Qiu J, Zhang B (2013) Mammoth data in the cloud: clustering social images. Clouds Grids Big Data 23:231

68. Hoi SC et al (2012) Online feature selection for mining big data. In: Proceedings of the 1st international workshop on big data, streams and heterogeneous source mining: algorithms, systems, programming models and applications

69. Hartigan JA, Wong MA (1979) Algorithm AS 136: a k-means clustering algorithm. In: Applied statistics, pp 100–108

70. Wold S, Esbensen K, Geladi P (1987) Principal component analysis. Chemometr Intell Lab Syst 2(1):37–52

71. Azar AT, Hassanien AE (2014) Dimensionality reduction of medical big data using neural-fuzzy classifier. Soft Comput 19(4):1115–1127

72. Cichocki A (2014) Era of big data processing: a new approach via tensor networks and tensor decompositions. arXiv preprint arXiv: 1403.2048
73. Dalessandro B (2013) Bring the noise: embracing randomness is the key to scaling up machine learning algorithms. Big Data 1(2):110–112
74. Zeng X-Q, Li G-Z (2014) Incremental partial least squares analysis of big streaming data. Pattern Recogn 47(11):3726–3735
75. Ruhe A (1984) Rational Krylov sequence methods for eigenvalue computation. Linear Algebra Appl 58:391–405
76. Tannahill BK, Jamshidi M (2014) System of systems and big data analytics–Bridging the gap. Comput Electr Eng 40(1):2–15
77. Liu Q et al (2014) Mining the big data: the critical feature dimension problem. In: 2014 IIAI 3rd international conference on advanced applied informatics (IIAIAAI)
78. Jiang P et al (2014) An intelligent information forwarder for healthcare big data systems with distributed wearable sensors. IEEE Syst J PP(99):1–9

79. Leung CK-S, MacKinnon RK, Jiang F (2014) Reducing the search space for big data mining for interesting patterns from uncertain data. In: 2014 IEEE international congress on big data (BigData congress)
80. Stateczny A, Wlodarczyk-Sielicka M (2014) Self-organizing artificial neural networks into hydrographic big data reduction process. In: Rough sets and intelligent systems paradigms. Springer, pp 335–342
81. Hinton GE, Osindero S, Teh Y-W (2006) A fast learning algorithm for deep belief nets. Neural Comput 18(7):1527–1554
82. LeCun Y et al (1998) Gradient-based learning applied to document recognition. Proc IEEE 86(11):2278–2324
83. Kavukcuoglu K et al (2009) Learning invariant features through topographic filter maps. In: 2009 IEEE conference on computer vision and pattern recognition, CVPR 2009
84. Dean J et al (2012) Large scale distributed deep networks. In: Advances in neural information processing systems
85. Martens J (2010) Deep learning via Hessian-free optimization. In: Proceedings of the 27th international conference on machine learning (ICML-10), June 21–24, Haifa, Israel

7

Fine-Grained Access Control Within NoSQL Document-Oriented Datastores

Pietro Colombo[1] · Elena Ferrari[1]

Abstract The recent years have seen the birth of several NoSQL datastores, which are getting more and more popularity for their ability to handle high volumes of heterogeneous and unstructured data in a very efficient way. In several cases, NoSQL databases proved to outclass in terms of performance, scalability, and ease of use relational database management systems, meeting the requirements of a variety of today ICT applications. However, recent surveys reveal that, despite their undoubted popularity, NoSQL datastores suffer from some weaknesses, among which the lack of effective support for data protection appears among the most serious ones. Proper data protection mechanisms are therefore required to fill this void. In this work, we start to address this issue by focusing on access control and discussing the definition of a fine-grained access control framework for document-oriented NoSQL datastores. More precisely, we first focus on issues and challenges related to the definition of such a framework, considering theoretical, implementation, and integration aspects. Then, we discuss the reasons for which state-of-the-art fine-grained access control solutions proposed for relational database management systems cannot be used within the NoSQL scenario. We then introduce possible strategies to address the identified issues, which are at the basis of the framework development. Finally, we shortly report the outcome of an experience where the proposed framework has been used to enhance the data protection features of a popular NoSQL database.

Keywords Fine-grained access control · Document stores · NoSQL · MongoDB

1 Introduction

NoSQL datastores are getting popularity in a variety of scenarios, and their diffusion is growing especially within the data management back-end of modern web applications, and the data storage and analysis layer of Internet of Things platforms. The reasons of NoSQL datastores diffusion range from outstanding performance and scalability, to the provided support for handling high volumes of data, as well as to the ease of interaction with external applications. As a matter of fact, NoSQL datastores outperform relational database management systems (RDBMSs) with respect to the efficiency of data analysis, the flexibility, and the scalability of data management. Current surveys[1] show that MongoDB,[2] which is the current most popular NoSQL datastore, immediately follows, in terms of diffusion, widely used RDBMSs, such as Oracle Database[3] or MySQL.[4] This shows that NoSQL datastores are affirmed solutions which compete in terms of diffusion with RDBMSs.

Different from RDBMSs, characterized by a standard reference data model and query language, a variety of proprietary query languages have been proposed for NoSQL datastores, as well as different data models have been introduced for them. Recent surveys have classified NoSQL databases into three main categories on the basis of

✉ Pietro Colombo
pietro.colombo@uninsubria.it

[1] DiSTA, University of Insubria, Via Mazzini, 5, Varese, Italy

---

[1] http://db-engines.com/en/ranking.

[2] https://www.mongodb.com.

[3] https://www.oracle.com.

[4] https://www.mysql.com.

the adopted data model, namely key value, wide column, and document-oriented datastores [7]. Each of these classes is characterized by features that make the related datastores suited to specific application scenarios. Key-value datastores (e.g., Redis)[5] handle data modeled as pairs of keys and values. Data can be of primitive type or complex objects and are uniquely identified by a key. Such systems allow executing basic queries which retrieve values corresponding to given keys. They are very efficient in terms of used computational resources. Wide column stores (e.g., Cassandra)[6] are an evolution of key-value datastores, with more advanced data organization and analysis features. Data are collected into flexible tables, and they are modeled as heterogeneous records of variable size. Tables are flexible in that each row can be composed of a different set of columns, and columns, in turn, can be organized into column families. Finally, document-oriented datastores (e.g., MongoDB) model data as heterogeneous, hierarchical records, denoted as documents, which in turn are composed of sets of key-value pairs, each specifying a document field. Documents are grouped into collections, which in turn compose a database. Document-oriented datastores provide complex data management and analysis features and query languages and appear as the most flexible and complex currently available NoSQL datastores.

Even though the advanced data analysis and management features of NoSQL datastores are making them very popular, these platforms show several shortcomings, and, as highlighted in [18], one of the most serious is related to the poor data protection mechanisms they currently offer. For instance, Okman et al. [18] analyze the basic authentication and authorization features of MongoDB and Cassandra and propose possible strategies to enhance them.

In this work, we focus on access control features of NoSQL datastores, since access control is the core data protection module of any DBMS. Most of NoSQL systems adopt basic access control mechanisms operating at coarse-grained level. For instance, within document-oriented datastores, access control is enforced at the level of database or at the level of collection of documents. Even MongoDB, the most popular NoSQL datastore, integrates a role-based access control model operating at collection level only. While collection level protection is a good step forward with respect to several other systems operating at database level, it is still not sufficient to provide customized data protection levels, which could further raise the usability and diffusion of these systems.

It is well recognized that data management systems that handle sensitive data could greatly benefit from the integration of fine-grained access control (FGAC) features.

FGAC has been recognized as a fundamental requirement in a variety of application scenarios, which range from data management and analysis systems (e.g., [8, 9, 22]), to social networks (e.g., [3, 5, 14]), and service oriented and mobile applications (e.g., [14]). Few NoSQL datastores provide a native support for FGAC, such as the key-value datastore Accumulo,[7] which enforces access control at cell level. However, the great majority of the existing systems do not enforce FGAC, and in this work, we aim at starting to fill this void.

Recent surveys on database popularity[1] rank document-oriented NoSQL datastores in the top position. This is probably due to the flexibility of these systems, the provided advanced analysis features, and the native support for the management of JSON[8] data, which, at present, is among the most common data exchange format of modern applications. For these reasons, in this work, we target document-oriented datastores. Unfortunately, as we will discuss throughout the paper, the schemaless data model of document-oriented datastores do not allow to straightforwardly reuse the FGAC enforcement mechanisms defined for RDBMSs. Moreover, so far no standard NoSQL query language has emerged yet (neither in general nor for a specific datastore category), and each datastore adopts a different language. This reduces the interoperability among the existing systems, for instance, up to now, it is not possible to write a query, even of basic type, which can be executed within several systems. Similarly, data portability can be problematic. For instance, even though within MongoDB and Counchbase[9] data are serialized as JSON objects, the importing of a MongoDB dataset into Couchbase requires preliminary data manipulation activities. The heterogeneity of NoSQL systems as well as of their query languages make the definition of a general FGAC enforcement solution a complex and ambitious task.

In this paper, we survey issues and challenges related to the development of FGAC enforcement monitors and their integration into document-oriented NoSQL datastores. The analysis of the literature lead us to identify possible strategies to address issues related to the definition of policy specification criteria, enforcement strategies, the implementation of the proposed mechanisms by an enforcement monitor, and aspects related to integration of the monitor into existing document-oriented datastores. The analysis described in this paper is partially based on early research experiences on NoSQL datastores that we did with MongoDB [10, 12], as well as on ongoing research activities finalized to the generalization of the approach in [10, 12].

---

[5] http://redis.io.

[6] http://cassandra.apache.org.

[7] https://accumulo.apache.org.

[8] http://www.json.org.

[9] https://www.couchbase.com.

The remainder of the paper is organized as follows. Section 2 surveys related work. Section 3 describes the main issues related to the definition of a FGAC framework for document-oriented datastores. Section 4 discusses FGAC enforcement strategies, describing possible ways to address the previously identified issues. Section 5 shortly presents an application that shows how the proposed strategies can be actually applied for the enhancement of the access control features of MongoDB with FGAC. Finally, in Sect. 6, we conclude the paper shortly describing the state of our current research on access control within NoSQL systems, as well as introducing future research goals.

2 Related Work

FGAC has been integrated into several relational access control models, such as, for instance, the purpose-based model proposed in [6], and the action aware access control model in [9]. It has been also successfully deployed into some commercial RDBMSs (e.g., Oracle Virtual Private Database),[10] as well as in modern non-relational systems (e.g., Accumulo[7]).

Oracle Virtual Private Database (VPD) [4] is among the most known fine-grained access control framework for relational database management systems. Oracle VPD regulates the access to table rows by means of access control policies, which specify content- and context-based predicates that refer to properties of the protected data and the execution environment. Policy enforcement is achieved by means of query rewriting, appending the specified policy predicates to the *where* clause of the submitted SQL query. In [20], the enforcement approach used by Oracle VPD has been classified as a Truman model, where each data analyst has a partial view of the database. Rizvi et al. [20] claim that the user view may be inconsistent with respect to the information included in the database and propose an enforcement mechanism which only authorizes the execution of queries whose rewritten version do not bring to inconsistent views. Other approaches for RDBMSs enforce access control at a finer granularity level. For instance, LeFevre et al. [17] propose a SQL-based query rewriting approach which allows enforcing FGAC by means of dynamically generated authorized views of database tables. In [17], access control is enforced at cell level, generating views where all unauthorized cells are nullified. Agrawal et al. [1] describe an approach to transform RDBMSs into privacy-aware DBMSs, which relies on a language that supports the specification of grant commands at cell level.

Research efforts have also been recently focused on the integration of FGAC into NoSQL datastores (e.g., [10, 12, 16]) and map-reduce analytics platforms (e.g., [22]). For instance, Kulkarni [16] has proposed a fine-grained access control model for key-value systems denoted K-VAC, which has been first designed to operate with Cassandra,[11] and then extended for the integration into HBase.[12] However, the proposed solution is an ad hoc implementation and cannot be easily ported or adapted to other systems.

In [10], we have proposed the integration of a purpose-based model operating at document level into MongoDB. The successful experience brought us to refine the granularity and generalize the supported policies. Thus, in [12], we have proposed an access control model operating at field level which supports content- and context-based access control policies similar to those of Oracle VPD.

In [22], we have considered the enforcement of FGAC policies within map-reduce systems. The pairs key-value extracted from an accessed resource by a map-reduce job are dynamically modified on the basis of the specified FGAC policies, before the mapping phase starts the processing.

Overall, the research on the integration of FGAC into NoSQL datastores is still in the early stages. More specifically, for what document-oriented datastores are concerned, although the initial experiences that we had with MongoDB allowed us to identify some approaches to the definition and integration of FGAC into NoSQL systems, the proposed solutions need to be generalized to increase their applicability.

3 FGAC Within NoSQL Document-Oriented Datastores: Issues and Challenges

As briefly introduced in Sect. 1, the goal of this paper is to discuss how FGAC can be deployed within document-oriented NoSQL datastores. Although the goal is similar to the one already addressed within traditional DBMSs, intrinsic characteristics of the NoSQL scenario make this a challenge for data security researchers. Table 1 summarizes the main reasons for which we believe that the enhancement of document-oriented datastores with FGAC features is a far more complex and challenging tasks than designing a FGAC framework for RDBMSs.

In the remainder of this section, we shortly consider each of these points.

Generality A first aspect that should be taken into consideration is the heterogeneity of the existing NoSQL

---

[10] http://docs.oracle.com/database/121/DBSEG/vpd.htm.

[11] http://cassandra.apache.org.

[12] https://hbase.apache.org.

Table 1 Aspects affecting the complexity of FGAC solutions for data management systems

Aspect	Relational DBMSs	Document-oriented NoSQL datastores
Generality	Eased by a reference data model	Multiple declinations of the same data model
	Eased by a reference standard query language	Multiple proprietary query languages
FGAC granularity	Access control granularity up to cell level	Field level granularity is often a must due to data modeling choices
	Cell level policy specification based on a priori known tables schema	No a priori assumption on documents structure for specification purposes
	Cell level enforcement mechanisms based on a priory known tables schema	No a priori assumption on documents structure for enforcement purposes
Performance	Efficiency is important, but no very strict constraint, due to the size of traditional datasets	Efficiency is a must due to the high volumes of data. A proper trade-off between performance and security is needed, taking into consideration that performance is among the reasons for which NoSQL datastores are getting popularity
Enforcement mechanisms	Query rewriting to enforce access control at row and cell level	Techniques in the literature not applicable at field level, due to the schemaless nature of documents
	Native support for views	No systematic support for views

datastores and the need to define a general solution rather than an ad hoc solution operating with a unique NoSQL database (e.g., [10]). The complexity of the problem is partially due to the lack of a standard query language. Indeed, the enforcement approaches defined for RDBMSs rely on the presence of the relational model and SQL as unique data model and query language. In contrast, the variety of NoSQL datastores that have been defined so far, most of which operating with a different query language, make the definition of a general approach a very ambitious task. In addition, the lack of a reference standard has caused the definition of multiple implementations of the document-oriented data model, which differ for data organization features and terminology. For instance, some document stores do not integrate the concept of collection (e.g., CouchDB).[13]

FGAC granularity Let us now start to consider why the FGAC solutions developed for RDBMSs cannot be reused for the NoSQL scenario. To make the discussion more concrete, let us consider Oracle VPD, one of the most popular FGAC solutions developed for RDBMSs. Oracle VPD considers table rows as the finest protection objects. From a data management perspective, table rows of relational databases correspond to documents of document-oriented NoSQL datastores, even though documents model data resources in a less abstract way than rows, as they do not abstract from the intrinsic structure of a resource, and thus they do not require one to flatten the resource content.

Example 1   Let us consider a dataset of emails. An email has a structure providing meta information related to the message content. For instance, it includes a header and a body, where the header is in turn characterized by properties specifying, among others, the email sender, all the receivers, and the email subject. Within a document store, emails can be straightforwardly modeled as a document whose fields are hierarchically organized to match the email structure. In contrast, the modeling of the same dataset with the relational model requires to flatten the structure of an email by removing fields hierarchy.

At a first sight, due to the parallelism of concepts between the relational and document-oriented data model, fine-grained enforcement mechanisms operating at document level could be defined starting from the mechanisms proposed for RDBMSs. However, additional important aspects need to be considered. To be more concrete, let us consider again Oracle VPD. Within Oracle VPD, the key element of an access control policy is a boolean expression specified over table attributes and contextual properties. For instance, referring to the application scenario in Example 1, an access control policy could grant the access only to those emails that have been sent to a specific email address. Within the relational model the fields to, cc, and bcc are attributes of the email table scheme. In contrast, the schemaless data model of document-oriented NoSQL datastores brings to the definition of documents that include these fields only when the modeled email specify a receiver of that type, as for instance, an email may not have a bcc receiver or a cc receiver. As a consequence, a content-based policy could refer to fields which may not be included in all the documents. This implies the need to specify content-based access control policies under a different perspective, that is, not only considering fields values, but also even considering the structural characteristics of a document, such as the presence of a field.

---

[13] http://www.couchdb.apache.org.

For what access control granularity is concerned, it is worth noting that depending on the application context and the adopted modeling choices, document level granularity may be too coarse grained. As above mentioned, the hierarchical structure supported by the document-oriented data model allows representing data without abstracting from their structural characteristics. This brings one to define documents with a potential complex structure and many fields, and, as a consequence, access control policies can be defined to protect the access to a single field of a complex document with a hierarchical structure.

Example 2 Let us consider the application scenario introduced in Example 1, and an access control policy that regulates the access to field *from* of an email.[14] Let us suppose that a query that aims at accessing such an email is submitted for execution, and the access control policy that regulates the access to *from* is not satisfied. An access control framework similar to Oracle VPD cannot prevent the access to a single unauthorized sender field. In contrast, it would prevent the access to the whole document containing such a field. Such a mechanism is too restrictive as all other fields of the considered document could be freely accessed.

Within relational databases, the limits of row level access control brought researchers to define cell level access control mechanisms. For instance, Lefevre et al. [17] proposed to enforce cell level access control policies by means of query rewriting. The idea of the proposed mechanism is that a query q submitted for execution is rewritten as q', in such a way that q' integrates a subquery that derives an authorized view of each table t accessed by q and performs the analysis tasks of q on such a view. The subquery either projects or nullifies the value of cells on the basis of the satisfaction of the policies specified for them [17]. This technique requires to know in advance the scheme of the accessed data, as well as the name of the attributes that should be projected. In contrast, the schemaless nature of NoSQL datastores prevents the systematic use of similar techniques, as each document in a collection can be characterized by a different set of fields.

Example 3 Let us suppose to specify an access control policy which prevents the access to the fifth bcc receiver of an email when a given condition is not satisfied. The policy is applied to a single email, whose structure is potentially different from all other documents of the collection as it may be the only email with 5 bcc receivers. According to the approach in [17], one should know in advance the existence of an email with 5 bcc receivers within the dataset, in order to rewrite the query.

On the basis of the above-mentioned considerations, we believe that the heterogeneity of the documents collected within a NoSQL database makes the definition of a field level access control mechanism a challenging problem.

Performance An additional challenging aspect is related to the strict performance requirements that commonly characterize NoSQL systems, as the access control enforcement overhead should not compromise the efficiency of the considered systems. Indeed, NoSQL systems are often used in the back-end of applications where performance and scalability are first class requirements. We believe that reasonable trade-offs among security, performance, and scalability of the proposed enforcement mechanisms need to be identified, as secure systems with poor performance may suffer from low usability, but the same applies to highly efficient insecure databases.

Enforcement mechanisms The literature presents two main categories of enforcement approaches for FGAC, namely view-based and query rewriting mechanisms. The view-based mechanism consists in deriving authorized views of a resource, on the basis of the specified access control policies, and granting the permit to access that views instead of the original data resources. This approach suffers from several drawbacks. Indeed, different from relational databases, views are not supported by all NoSQL datastores, and thus ad hoc implementations are required within several NoSQL datastores.

The most straightforward solution probably consists in defining views as temporary collections, which store copies of authorized documents. Although this naive approach allows satisfying security requirements, from the engineering perspective the generation and storage of multiple views of the same resource appears quite impractical, both in terms of memory and time required for view generation and serialization. This naive approach suffers from low efficiency, large memory usage, difficulties to handle resource updates, and it is not scalable. On the other hand, disk view serialization may not be a practical solution due to the variety of views of the protected resources that must be generated and to the time required for write operations. Indeed, write on disk operations typically suffer from high latency, and the definition of multiple views of the same collection may not be possible for the collection size. In addition, even assuming that this naive approach can be used in some application scenarios, this solution requires to regenerate all views every time the protected resource is updated. As such, the cost of handling updates depends on the number of views that have been generated for a protected resource, and the number of documents that must be modified within each view.

Let us consider, for instance, the dataset of emails introduced in Example 1, and let us suppose that the collected emails are stored within a collection cl. The

---

[14] *from* is a sub-field of the email header.

authorized view of cl is derived by considering all access control policies specified for cl documents and related fields. Several different views could be defined for the same dataset, which differ for the number of documents characterizing the protected collection, and the number of fields that characterize any generated image of cl documents. In addition, every time a document of cl is updated, it is also necessary to update the corresponding document of each derived view.

On the basis of the above-mentioned considerations, we believe that the view-based naive approach can only work with small datasets, in scenarios with a low number of stakeholders, which are inherently static.

A second type of enforcement mechanism is based on query rewriting. To the best of our knowledge, in the literature on RDBMSs, two different approaches have been proposed, which operate at row and cell level, respectively. The first one, implemented by Oracle VPD, operates by modifying the where clause of a submitted query q through the conjunction of the selection criteria of q with policy compliance predicates. This solution does not require any serialization, as in practice the rewritten query generates an authorized view at query execution time restricting the selection criteria of the original query. Oracle VPD operates at row level, and thus in the NoSQL counter part, it can only work at document level.

The second mechanism, introduced by Lefevre et al. [17], operates at cell level, either projecting or nullifying the value of each cell. The rewritten query is defined in such a way to include a subquery for each accessed table t, which substitutes the content of t with an authorized view of this resource, generated starting from the cell level access control policies. However, the schema of the accessed tables must be known in order to perform the rewriting, and thus, it cannot be directly applied to document-oriented datastores, as each document structure is potentially different from the ones of all other documents belonging to the same collection.

On the basis of the previous considerations, neither the view based, nor the query rewriting approaches proposed for RDBMSs can be directly applied with NoSQL document-oriented datastores.

4 Enforcement Strategies

The enhancement of NoSQL datastores with FGAC requires to identify proper engineering solutions for the encoding of fine-grained access control policies, the definition of enforcement monitors and the monitors integration into a target NoSQL system. In the remainder of this section, we discuss possible strategies to address the above-mentioned open issues.

4.1 Policy Encoding

The first considered issue is related to the approach to be used for the specification of FGAC policies. In the literature on relational DBMSs, several approaches have been proposed. For instance, in [6], purpose-based policies operating at different granularity levels are specified in dedicated tables. We believe that within NoSQL datastores, a similar specification approach can be used for access control policies operating at the collection level. The policies can be either coarse grained, thus implicitly regulating the access to the whole referred collection, or fine grained, thus regulating the access to documents of the referred collection which satisfy given selection criteria. However, we believe that FGAC policies should not be specified within dedicated collections, as, currently, join operations are not systematically supported by NoSQL datastores. In contrast, they can be stored within dedicated fields of the protected documents. In our previous work, we have used this approach for document level [10] and field level policies [12].

4.2 Enforcement

Abstracting from language and platform dependent aspects, we believe that a promising strategy to enforce FGAC within document-oriented NoSQL datastore consists in combining query rewriting with in memory view generation. Aware of the efficiency and consistency issues that affect naive implementations of the view-based approach (cfr. Sect. 3) and aligned with [17] principles, we believe that an effective enforcement approach should combine view generation and query rewriting, taking maximum benefit from the two mechanisms. According to the proposed approach, the views: (1) should not be serialized on disk, but derived in memory at run time and (2) should be directly generated by the rewritten queries, on the basis of the execution environment of the access request. More precisely, let q be a query that is submitted for execution. At an high level of abstraction, the overall goal of the approach consists in rewriting q as a query q' which derives an authorized view cl' of each collection cl accessed by q and performs the same analysis tasks as q accessing the derived views instead of the original collections. Given a query q, the idea is to first derive the selection criteria sc of q and the set of collections to be accessed by q. For each collection cl accessed by q, the criteria specified by sc as well as the access control policies specified for cl are used to select candidate documents of cl to be stored into cl'. Denoted with cl'', the set of candidate documents, for each document d in cl'', the approach prunes out from d any field f of d such that f is referred to by at least a policy p specified for d fields, but no policy referring to f is satisfied.

At an high level of abstraction, the rationale of view generation is aligned with the basic principles proposed in [17], but the schemaless nature of the document-based model requires a different rewriting mechanism as well as a different view derivation approach. As pointed out in Sect. 3, Lefevre et al. approach [17] requires to know in advance the scheme of the accessed tables. This cannot occur within the NoSQL scenario, where the structure of each accessed document is potentially unique and thus may differ from the ones of all other accessed documents. For instance, within the email dataset previously considered, the emails can have a varying number of to/cc/bcc receivers, whereas some of them may have no to/cc/bcc receiver. The goal is thus carrying out the projection, without knowing in advance the fields which characterize the accessed documents. As such, a possible solution is the one that operates by analyzing the structure of each document at execution time and thus differs from the methodology in [17], which relies on the a priori knowledge of the accessed tables schema. The idea is to consider the candidate documents as JSON objects, characterized by properties representing the document fields. These properties, which are modeled as key-value pairs, are iteratively accessed and modified by means of JSON manipulation functions. Different from [17], where the attributes to be projected are referred to by name within the rewritten queries, a possible approach for the NoSQL scenario consists in referring to the fields to be projected by position, iteratively considering any property of the documents.

In order to exemplify the rationale of the proposed approach and the differences with the one proposed for the relational model, let us consider again the dataset of emails referred to in Example 1 and the followings. Let us consider a query q that derives all types of receivers and the body of the emails that specify a given object. For the sake of simplicity and the lack of a standard query language for NoSQL databases, let us consider the SQL representation of q, which can be straightforwardly defined as *select to, cc, bcc, body from emails where object like "party"*.

Let us now consider how q can be rewritten on the basis of Lefevre et al. approach [17] within a RDBMS. For the sake of simplicity, let us assume that the scheme of an email is characterized by the fields from, to, cc, bcc, obj and body, and let us suppose that the access to any email field is regulated by a policy specified within field p. Let us suppose the existence of a function compliesWith that evaluates whether q execution complies with the access control policies specified for each email field. Listing 1 shows the pseudocode of the rewritten SQL query that derives the authorized view on email.

Listing 1 Query rewriting for FGAC at table cell level

```
select av.cc, av.to, av.subject, av.body from
(select
  case when compliesWith(p) then from
    else null end as from,
  case when compliesWith(p) then to
    else null end as to,
  case when compliesWith(p) then cc
    else null end as cc,
  case when compliesWith(p) then bcc
    else null end as bcc,
  case when compliesWith(p) then obj
    else null end as obj,
  case when compliesWith(p) then body
    else null end as body
  from emails where obj like "party" and
compliesWith(cd,p)) av
```

According to Listing 1, the outer query accesses the view generated by the subquery, whereas the subquery projects email fields, provided that the access control policies specified for those fields are satisfied. As shown in Listing 1, any field of emails is explicitly referred to by name in the subquery.

Let us now consider a possible approach for the NoSQL scenario. Listing 2 shows the SQL-like pseudocode of the rewritten query.

Listing 2 Query rewriting for FGAC at field level within document stores

```
select av.cc, av.to, av.subject, av.body
from (select
  object <k,v> for <k,v> in object_pairs(e)
    when compliesWith(cd,p) end
  from emails e
  where obj like "party"
    and compliesWith(cd,p)) av
```

Similar to Listing 1, the derivation of the authorized view is achieved by a subquery, whereas the outer query simply projects fields of the derived view. In this case, the subquery generates an authorized image of each email using JSON manipulation operators. In the pseudo code, we have used the N1QL operator *object*,[15] which allows building an object by composition of key-value pairs of another object, which satisfies a condition. The authorized email images are thus defined in such a way to include any field of the original email e for which the specified access control policies are satisfied. In this case, we do not need to explicitly refer to the fields to be projected by name, and thus, it is not required to know in advance the fields composing the documents.

---

[15] For the sake of simplicity, Listing 2 reports a simplified syntax.

4.3 Monitor Implementation and Integration

The heterogeneity and variety of existing NoSQL datastores represent one of the main obstacles to the definition of a general development and integration approach. NoSQL document-oriented datastores typically provide APIs, often available for different programming languages, which support the programmatic interaction with the analysis and management features. Each set of APIs is a different interface to the provided services, and the enforcement monitor should be defined in such a way to regulate the fruition of these services, regardless they are invoked trough the APIs or by means of queries expressed with the supported data analysis languages. Although a possible integration strategy consists in the programmatic modification of the provided services, we believe that this cannot be a general and portable solution, as it strictly depends on the technological and architectural characteristics of each datastore, as well as on the availability of the source code, while the definition of a general solution requires to abstract from these aspects.

Due to the client–server nature of NoSQL systems, a possible way to handle the interaction with the datastore services is to define the enforcement monitor as a proxy. More precisely, the monitor should be responsible of the interaction of the datastore clients with the target server, exposing services to the clients and executing additional checks whenever a service is invoked.

Within several NoSQL datastores, the client–server interaction is achieved by means of dedicated, ad hoc defined, communication protocols, which regulate the information exchanged by the counterparts and the related format. Each message either encodes a client request or a server response to a client request. Client requests encode the invocation of analysis or management services provided by the server, whereas server responses encode the data that are returned by the server. Whenever a user invokes the execution of a service, either through an application or by means of a graphical interface, the request is first encoded and then sent to the server. Similarly, whenever the server completes the computation of a command, it encodes the response as a message sending it to the connected clients. In order to specify a client for a specific programming language, it is thus sufficient to implement an interpreter of the considered communication protocol, which is capable of encoding service invocations as messages. This suggests that, in order to enforce FGAC, one could focus on the messages exchanged by the clients and the server, rather than focusing on syntactical aspects of the query languages.

The proxy should thus be defined as an interpreter of the communication protocol supported by the considered datastore. This solution has the advantage of ensuring independence from APIs and programming languages, which are typically subject of continuous changes. In contrast, communication protocols are expected to be enhanced, to guarantee the interoperability of multiple client–server versions.

5 An Application Scenario: Enhancing MongoDB with FGAC

In this section, we discuss a possible implementation of the strategies proposed in Sect. 4 for MongoDB. A thorough presentation of technical aspects related to design, implementation, and integration of the proposed enforcement monitor can be found in [10, 12], which also provides a thorough discussion related to the efficiency and scalability of the proposed framework. In this section, we summarize relevant aspects related to policy specification and the developed enforcement mechanism.

5.1 Policy Specification

On the basis of the experience illustrated in [10], hereafter we describe a possible implementation of purpose-based access control policies, which are one of the most relevant type of FGAC policies. In this scenario, a policy p is a pair $\langle r, e \rangle$, where r specifies the list of resources for which p has been specified and e is the list of purposes for which the access to the protected resources is authorized, which are selected from a purpose set Ps. Access to a resource referred to within r is granted, if the access purpose ap associated with the access request complies with the purposes specified within component e of p. Coarse-grained policies regulating the access to collections of a database db have been specified within a dedicated collection cgp. In contrast, FGAC policies at document and field level have been directly specified within the protected documents.

Example 4 Let us consider the email dataset introduced in Example 1, and let us suppose that the considered dataset collects all the emails in collection cl. Let us now suppose that three purposed-based access control policies have been specified, which, respectively, grant: (1) the access to the collection of emails cl for marketing purposes; (2) the access to email em of cl for analysis purposes; and (3) the access to the list of receivers of em for research purposes. The first policy is specified as $\langle \{cl\}, \{marketing\} \rangle$ and encoded as a document of collection *cgp*, whereas the second and third policies are directly specified within a dedicated field of em.

5.2 Enforcement Strategies

The enforcement mechanisms for the considered scenario have been defined on the basis of the strategies introduced

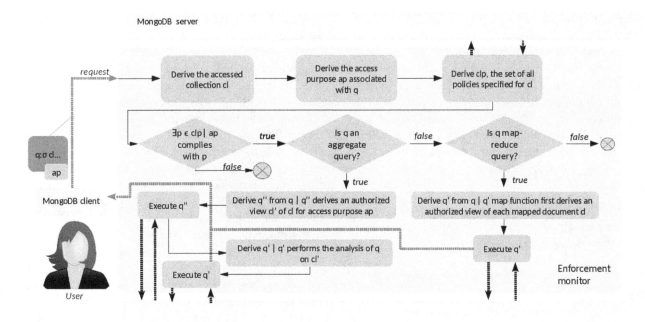

Fig. 1 Enforcement of FGAC within MongoDB

in Sect. 4. For space limitation, in this paper, we shortly discuss selected aspects related to the enforcement mechanism abstracting from model specific aspects as well as aspects related to authorization and compliance analysis within the purpose-based access control model.

The process, illustrated in Fig. 1, starts considering the query q which is submitted for execution and deriving the collection cl that is accessed by q. Afterwords, the process extracts from cgp all the access control policies that have been specified for cl. Then, the compliance of the access purpose of q with the purposes specified within the policies specified for cl is checked. If purpose compliance is satisfied for at least one policy, the process continues, otherwise it is immediately blocked due to the missing authorizations.

The process goes on considering FGAC policies specified for the documents to be accessed by q. Due to limitations of the supported query language, the mechanism is differentiated on the basis of the type of operation encoded by q. In particular, we focus here on aggregate and map-reduce operations, which represent the most advanced analysis operations of MongoDB. As introduced in Sect. 4, the enforcement mechanisms should derive an authorized view cl' of the collection accessed by q, and rewrite q as q' in such a way that q' executes the analysis specified by q on cl'. Two different rewriting approaches have been used for the considered operations, as MongoDB adopts a proprietary notation for aggregate queries, and Javascript for map-reduce queries. Abstracting from query language specific aspects which require a technical background on MongoDB, the main differences between the proposed approaches are related to the generation of the authorized

view. In the case of map-reduce queries, the view is generated using the approach introduced in Sect. 4 and exemplified in Listing 2. However, different from Listing 2, where SQL-pseudocode is used, map-reduce queries are defined using Javascript functions. Listing 3 presents an example of a map-reduce query mrq, which counts the emails sent to addresses which have received at least one email.

Listing 3 An example of MongoDB map-reduce query

```
db.runCommand({
  mapReduce: clName,
  map: function() {
    var toF = this["headers"]["To"];
    for(i in toF){emit(toF[i], 1);}
  },
  reduce: function(key, values) {
    return Array.sum(values);
  },
  out: { inline: 1 }
})
```

The authorized view is derived by means of Javascript instructions which precede those performing the analysis and aggregation. Referring to the example in Listing 3, the query is rewritten in such a way that the first instructions of function map derive the authorized view of the mapped document. This is achieved by analyzing all field level policies regulating the access to the document, which according to the strategy proposed in Sect. 4, are referred to within a dedicated field. Given a document d, for each analyzed policy p specified for d fields, if the policy predicate of p is not satisfied, the fields referred by p are pruned out from d.

In contrast, limitations of MongoDB query language do not allow defining aggregate queries performing the derivation of the authorized view at the head of the operations pipeline. In this case, it is not possible to apply the approach introduced in Sect. 4, and the naive view generation approach comprising the serialization appears as the only viable solution. As such, this case is handled with the generation and sequential execution of two queries, which generate and serialize the view to a temporary collection and execute q processing activities on such a temporary collection.

Example 5   Let us consider an aggregate query agq, which counts the emails sent to given addresses, whose source code is shown in Listing 4.

Listing 4 An example of MongoDB aggregate query

```
var aliases = ["kenneth.lay@enron.com",
 "kenneth_lay@enron.net", "klay@enron.com"]
db.emails.aggregate([
  {$match: {"headers.To" :{"$in":aliases}}},
  {$group: {"_id":"sum", "num":{$sum:1}}}
]);
```

In this case, the rewriting is operated through the sequential execution of two queries: 1) a map-reduce query which derives an authorized view of the accessed collection on the basis of the policy compliance, as introduced for the example related to Listing 3; and 2) an aggregate query almost equivalent to agq.

5.3 Implementation

Let us briefly consider selected aspects related to the development of the enforcement monitor. According to the guidelines proposed in Sect. 4, the monitor has been defined as a proxy which analyzes the interaction of MongoDB clients and server. MongoDB client/server interaction is achieved by means of the Wire[16] communication protocol, which supports a request–response interaction initiated by the clients. The proposed monitor, which has been designed as an interpreter of the Wire protocol, analyzes all the requests that are issued by the clients to the server, rewrites the query execution requests in accordance with the previously discussed enforcement criteria, and executes complementary functionalities in support of access control enforcement, such as deriving access control policies applied to a resource, evaluating purpose compliance, handling the profiling of the users that issue query execution requests. The monitor has been developed as a Java multi-thread application deployed on a node which is at the interface of the network that hosts the MongoDB cluster.

We have extensively tested the developed monitor using both synthetic datasets and a real dataset, that is, the Enron corpus, a dataset of email messages comprising over 500K emails (1.5 GB of data) exchanged by around 150 employees of the Enron corporation [15]. The experiments targeting the synthetic datasets have considered a benchmark of 20 find, aggregate and map reduce queries, which have been defined in such a way to ensure different complexity and selectivity levels.[17] Similarly, the benchmark targeting the Enron dataset includes 9 queries of type find, aggregate and map-reduce which have been inspired by the analysis functions presented in [21].

For our experiments, we have synthetically defined FGAC policies in such a way that these provide given selectivity levels. The experiments have assessed the enforcement overhead for the considered queries varying the selectivity of the considered policies. The results have shown that overall the overhead decreases with the increase in policy selectivity, due to the reduction of data that are accessed and analyzed by the queries. The experiments have shown that the overhead is negligible for find and map-reduce queries, but it is significant for aggregate queries. This confirms that the naive implementation of the view-based approach (cfr Sect. 3), which appears as the only viable solution for aggregate queries, suffers from low efficiency. The interested readers can refer to [10, 12] for a detailed presentation of the empirical results.

The experiences described in [10, 12] show significant differences between the measured overhead for document and field level access control policies. The overhead introduced with document level access control policies is low. Due to the effect of policy selectivity[18] with several queries of the considered benchmark, the execution time of the rewritten version of the queries is even lower than the execution time of the original queries. In contrast, the experience with field level access control policies reveals that the enforcement overhead varies with the type of the considered query. More precisely, aggregate queries suffer from a significant time overhead, whereas the overhead that has been measured with map-reduce queries is reasonably low.

---

[16] https://docs.mongodb.com/manual/reference/mongodb-wire-protocol/.

[17] By policy selectivity we mean the percentage of fields which are pruned out from the documents due to policy specification.

[18] We mean the effect of policy enforcement which brings to reduce the number of documents that are actually accessed.

6 Conclusions and Future Work

NoSQL datastores are getting increasing interest by users for their outstanding levels of flexibility, scalability, and performance, and their ability to manage huge data volumes. Despite this popularity, NoSQL datastores suffer from inappropriate data protection features. We believe that these shortcoming can be significantly addressed with the integration of FGAC features into the datastores. The integration of FGAC into a NoSQL datastore is a novel research topic that has been only recently addressed and that can open new research areas and applications. In this paper, we have discussed issues and challanges arising from the integration of FGAC features into NoSQL datastores. We have also described our experience with the MongoDB NoSQL datastore.

Our research is still progressing. In particular, we are currently focusing on recent standardization effort for NoSQL datastores, such as for instance SQL++ [19], a query language defined with the goal to become the reference query language for NoSQL datastores. SQL++ has been designed to keep compliance with SQL syntax, so that data analysts with a background on relational databases can easily migrate to a NoSQL datastore with a small initial effort. SQL++ is currently supported by AsterixDB[19] [2] and a few other datastores. A proprietary partial implementation of SQL++, denoted N1QL, is currently supported by the last version of Couchbase.[20] We believe that the involvement of industrial partners like Couchbase shows a concrete commercial interest in such a unifying solution. The availability of a general query language is an interesting basis for the specification of platform independent FGAC enforcement mechanisms, as well as for the development of multi-platform enforcement monitors.

Compliance with Ethical Standards

Competing of interest The authors declares that they have no competing of interests.

References

1. Agrawal R, Bird P, Grandison T, Kiernan J, Logan S, Rjaibi W (2005) Extending relational database systems to automatically enforce privacy policies. In: Proceedings of the 21st IEEE international conference on data engineering (IEEE ICDE)
2. Alsubaiee S, Altowim Y, Altwaijry H, Behm A, Borkar VR, Bu Y (2014) Asterixdb: a scalable, open source BDMS, PVLDB '14, pp 841–852
3. Bahri L, Carminati B, Ferrari E, Lucia W (2016) LAMP Label-based access control for more privacy in online social networks. In: Proceedings of the 10th WISTP international conference on information security theory and practice (WISTP 2016)
4. Browder K, Davidson MA (2002) The virtual private database in oracle9ir2. Oracle corporation, technical report 2002, oracle technical white paper
5. Buccafurri F, Lax G, Nicolazzo S, Nocera A (2016) A middleware to allow fine-grained access control of twitter applications. In: Proceedings of the international conference on mobile, secure and programmable networking (MSPN'2016)
6. Byun J, Li N (2008) Purpose based access control for privacy protection in relational database systems. VLDB J 17(4):603–619
7. Cattell R (2011) Scalable SQL and NoSQL data stores. SIGMOD Rec 39(4):12–27
8. Colombo P, Ferrari E (2014) Enforcement of purpose based access control within relational database management systems. IEEE Trans Knowl Data Eng (TKDE) 26(11):2703–2716
9. Colombo P, Ferrari E (2015) Efficient enforcement of action-aware purpose-based access control within relational database management systems. IEEE Trans Knowl Data Eng 27(8):2134–2147
10. Colombo P, Ferrari E (2015) Enhancing MongoDB with purpose based access control. In: IEEE transactions on dependable and secure computing (in press)
11. Colombo P, Ferrari E (2015) Privacy aware access control for big data: a research roadmap. Big Data Res 2(4):145–154. ISSN 2214-5796, Elsevier
12. Colombo P, Ferrari E (2016) Towards virtual private NoSQL datastores. In: 2016 IEEE 32nd international conference on data engineering (ICDE), Helsinki, Finland, pp 193–204
13. Jahid S, Mittal P, Borisov N (2011) EASiER: encryption-based access control in social networks with efficient revocation. In: Proceedings of the 6th ACM symposium on information, computer and communications security (ACM ASIACCS 2011)
14. Jin X, Wang L, Luo T, Du W (2013) Fine-grained access control for HTML5-based mobile applications in android. In: Proceedings of the 16th information security conference (ISC)
15. Klimt B, Yang Y (2004) The enron corpus: a new dataset for email classification research. In: Machine learning: ECML 2004. Springer, pp. 217–226
16. Kulkarni D (2013) A fine-grained access control model for key-value systems. In: Proceedings of the third ACM conference on data and application security and privacy, pp 161–164. ACM
17. LeFevre K, Agrawal R, Ercegovac V, Ramakrishnan R, Xu Y, DeWitt D (2004) Limiting disclosure in hippocratic databases. In: Mario A, Nascimento M, Tamer Z, Donald K, Rene JM, Jos A, Blakeley B, Schiefer K (eds) Proceedings of the thirtieth international conference on very large data bases (VLDB '04), vol 30. VLDB Endowment, pp 108–119
18. Okman L, Gal-Oz N, Gonen Y, Gudes E, Abramov J (2011) Security issues in NoSQL databases. In IEEE TrustCom
19. Ong KW, Papakonstantinou Y, Vernoux R (2014) The SQL++ unifying semi-structured query language, and an expressiveness benchmark of SQL-on-Hadoop, NoSQL and NewSQL databases. CoRR, abs/1405.3631
20. Rizvi S, Mendelzon A, Sudarshan S, Roy P (2004) Extending query rewriting techniques for fine-grained access control. In: Proceedings of the 2004 ACM SIGMOD international conference on management of data (SIGMOD '04). ACM, New York, NY, USA, pp 551–562
21. Russell MA (2013) Mining the social web: data mining Facebook, Twitter, LinkedIn, Google+, GitHub, and More. OReilly Media, Inc
22. Ulusoy H, Colombo P, Ferrari E, Kantarcioglu M, Pattuk E (2015) GuardMR: fine-grained security policy enforcement for MapRe- duce systems. In: ACM ASIACCS

---

[19] https://asterixdb.apache.org.

[20] http://www.couchbase.com.

8

Graph Partitioning for Distributed Graph Processing

Makoto Onizuka[1] · Toshimasa Fujimori[1] · Hiroaki Shiokawa[2]

Abstract There is a large demand for distributed engines that efficiently process large-scale graph data, such as social graph and web graph. The distributed graph engines execute analysis process after partitioning input graph data and assign them to distributed computers, so the quality of graph partitioning largely affects the communication cost and load balance among computers during the analysis process. We propose an effective graph partitioning technique that achieves low communication cost and good load balance among computers at the same time. We first generate more clusters than the number of computers by extending the modularity-based clustering, and then merge those clusters into balanced-size clusters until the number of clusters becomes the number of computers by using techniques designed for graph packing problem. We implemented our technique on top of distributed graph engine, PowerGraph, and made intensive experiments. The results show that our partitioning technique reduces the communication cost so it improves the response time of graph analysis patterns. In particular, PageRank computation is 3.2 times faster at most than HDRF, the state-of-the art of streaming-based partitioning approach.

✉ Makoto Onizuka
onizuka@ist.osaka-u.ac.jp

Toshimasa Fujimori
fujimori@ist.osaka-u.ac.jp

Hiroaki Shiokawa
shiokawa@cs.tsukuba.ac.jp

[1] Graduate School of Information Science and Technology, Osaka University, 1-5, Yamadaoka, Suita, Osaka 565-0871, Japan

[2] Center of Computational Sciences, University of Tsukuba, 1-1-1, Tennoudai, Tsukuba, Ibaraki 305-8573, Japan

Keywords Graph partitioning · Graph mining · Distributed processing

1 Introduction

Large-scale graph data such as social graphs and web graphs have emerged in various domains. As an example of social graph, the number of daily active users in Facebook reached 1.13 billion on average for June 2016 an increase of 17% year-over-year reported in the Facebook reports second quarter 2016 results:[1] vertexes and edges represent users and their relationships, respectively.

To analyze such large-scale graph data efficiently, distributed graph engines have been developed and they are widely used in graph analysis field. Some examples are Pregel [1], GraphLab [2], PowerGraph [3], and GraphX [4]. Distributed graph engines commonly (1) partition input graph data into sub-graphs, (2) assign each sub-graph to each computer, and (3) make graph analysis over the distributed graph. Each computer iteratively analyzes the assigned sub-graph by updating the parameters assigned to the vertexes/edges. Notice that the sub-graph assignment to computers largely affects the communication cost and load balance during graph analysis. The commutation cost increases to the number of cross-partition vertexes/edges, because communication between different computers is required when parameters are updated by referring to adjacent vertexes/edges in remote computers. The computation cost of each computer depends on the number of vertexes/edges assigned to the computer [5], so load imbalance occurs among computers when the number of assigned vertexes/edges imbalances.

---

[1] https://investor.fb.com/investor-news/default.aspx.

Our goal is to design a graph partitioning technique that achieves low communication cost and good load balance among computers. The state-of-the art of graph partitioning techniques is *Oblivious* [3] and *HDRF* [6] that are actually implemented in PowerGraph. These techniques generate balanced-size clusters while attempting to reduce communication overhead. However, the communication overhead tends to be high and this degrades the performance, in particular, the number of commuters is large. In contrast, there are other graph clustering techniques [7–9] that are designed to reduce the number of cross-cluster edges. They are expected to reduce the communication overhead; however, the size of the obtained clusters is imbalanced as reported in [8] so we cannot directly apply these techniques to our goal just as they are.

We propose an effective graph partitioning technique that achieves low communication cost and good load balance among computers at the same time. So as to obtain balanced-size clusters, we first generate much more balanced-size clusters than the number of computers by extending the modularity-based clustering, and then merge those clusters into balanced-size clusters by employing the techniques designed for the packing problem [10]. Finally, we convert edge-cut graph into vertex-cut graph, because the modularity clustering is edge-cut-based clustering and most of the recent distributed graph engines are based on vertex-cut graph. We implemented our technique on top of PowerGraph and made evaluations. The results show that our partitioning technique reduces the communication cost so it improves the response time of graph analysis patterns. In particular, it improves the response time of PageRank computation 3.2 times faster at most than HDRF. In addition, we also evaluated how the major graph metrics (the replication factor and load balance factor) correlate with the physical performance measures, the response time, the amount of data transfer between computers, and the imbalance runtime ratio among computers.

The remainder of this paper is organized as follows. Section 2 describes the background of this work. Section 3 describes the detailed design of our technique. Section 4 reports the results of experiments. Section 5 addresses related work, and Sect. 6 concludes this paper.

2 Preliminary

2.1 Replication Factor and Load Balance Factor

Recent distributed graph processing frameworks (e.g., GraphLab [2] and PowerGraph [3]) have employed vertex-cut method [2, 6] for the graph partitioning since it provides better performance in terms of load balancing among distributed computers. Vertex-cut method is a graph

partitioning technique for distributed graph processing; it divides a graph into multiple partitions by replicating cross-cluster vertexes, and it assigns each partition to each computer in the distributed computation environment. In order to qualify the effectiveness of graph partitioning, it is natural choice to use two major metrics called *replication factor* [2] and *load balance factor* [3].

Replication factor [2] is a metric that evaluates communication cost among distributed computers. Replication factor quantifies how many vertexes are replicated over computers compared with the the number of vertexes of the original input graph. The vertex-cut method takes a strategy to replicate cross-cluster vertex and assign the replicas to the computers the adjacent edges of the vertex belong to. In order to keep the consistency of analysis results among distributed computers, we need to communicate and exchange the analysis results among the computers in which the replicated vertexes are located. Thus, we can mitigate the communication cost by keeping the replication factor small. By following the literature [2], we formally define the replication factor RF as follows:

$$\text{RF} = \frac{1}{|V|} \sum_{v \in V} |R(v)|, \tag{1}$$

where V are a set of vertexes, and $R(v)$ is a set of vertexes replicated from vertex v.

Load balance factor is another metric of distributed graph processing that evaluates skewness of loads among distributed computers. Distributed graph processing frameworks using vertex-cut method employ the following equation for evaluating load balance factor:

$$\max_{m \in M} |E(m)| < \lambda \frac{|E|}{|M|}, \tag{2}$$

where E and M are a set of edges and a set of computers, respectively; $E(m)$ is a number of edges that are assigned to computer m. λ is a user-specified parameter that determines the acceptable skewness; user needs to set a value for λ that satisfies $\lambda \in \mathbb{R}$ and $\lambda \geq 1$. That is, Eq. (2) indicates that how large size is acceptable for $E(m)$ compared with the expected number of edges for each computer (i.e., $\frac{|E|}{|M|}$). From Eq. (2), we can conduct the following equation:

$$\lambda = \frac{|M|}{|E|} \max_{m \in M} |E(m)|. \tag{3}$$

In this paper, we call Eq. (3) as *load balance factor*. We employ Eq. (3) for evaluating the load balance efficiency of graph partitioning results.[2]

---

[2] A partitioning result is well balanced when λ is small.

2.2 Modularity

Our proposed method merges partition pairs for increasing a graph partitioning measure, namely *modularity* [7], so as to reduce the total number of cross-partition edges. In this section, we formally introduce modularity.

Modularity, proposed by Girvan and Newman [7], is widely used to evaluate the quality of graph partitions from global perspective. Modularity is a quality metric of graph partitioning based on *null model*; it measures the difference of the graph structure from the corresponding random graph. Intuitively, graph clustering is to find groups of vertexes that have a lot of inner-group edges and few outer-group edges; optimal partitions are achieved when the modularity is maximized. The modularity Q is formally defined as follows:

$$Q = \sum_{i \in C} \left\{ \frac{|E_{ii}|}{2|E|} - \left(\frac{\sum_{j \in C} |E_{ij}|}{2|E|} \right)^2 \right\}, \quad (4)$$

where C and $|E|$ are a set of partitions and the total number of edges included in graph G, respectively, and E_{ij} is a number of edges between partition i and j.

For finding good partitions, traditional modularity-based algorithms [9, 11, 12] greedily select and merge partition pairs so as to maximize the increase in modularity. However, Eq. (4) is inefficient to evaluate the modularity increase made by merging partition pairs since Eq. (4) needs to compute the complete modularity score for all merging partitions. Instead of computing complete modularity score, existing algorithms (i.e., CNM [11] and Louvain method [12]) conducted an equation of the *modularity gain* $\triangle Q_{ij}$ for efficiently evaluating the modularity increase after merging two partitions i and j as follows:

$$\triangle Q_{ij} = 2 \left\{ \frac{|E_{ij}|}{2|E|} - \left(\frac{\sum_{k \in C} |E_{ik}|}{2|E|} \right) \left(\frac{\sum_{k \in C} |E_{jk}|}{2|E|} \right) \right\}, \quad (5)$$

where $\triangle Q_{ij}$ indicates the modularity gain after merging partition i and j. As we described above, the modularity-based algorithms find a set of partitions that with high modularity Q by iteratively selecting and merging partition pairs that maximize Eq. (5).

In our proposed method, we modify Eq. (5) for finding balanced-size partitions for efficient distributed graph processing; we introduce a new term for balancing the partitioning size [8] into Eq. (5). We present its details in Sect. 3.1.

3 Balanced-Size Clustering Technique

Our goal is to design a graph partitioning technique that achieves low communication cost and good load balance among computers at the same time. We propose an effective graph partitioning technique that achieves low replication factor and good load balance factor. Our technique consists of three phases, balanced-size modularity clustering phase, cluster merge phase, and graph conversion phase as follows.

Balanced-size modularity clustering phase	We first employ a modified modularity proposed by Wakita and Tsurumi [8] that achieves good modularity and mitigates the imbalance of cluster size.
Cluster merge phase	Since modularity clustering generates large number of clusters in general, we need to have additional phase to merge clusters more. Moreover, even if we employ the modified modularity that mitigates imbalanced size of clusters, we still have the imbalance of cluster size. So, we generate much more clusters than the number of computers in the 1st phase, and then merge those clusters into balanced-size clusters until the number of clusters becomes the number of computers by employing techniques designed for graph packing problem.
Graph conversion phase	Finally, we convert edge-cut graph into vertex-cut graph, because the modularity clustering is edge-cut-based clustering and most of the recent distributed graph engines are based on the vertex-cut graph.

3.1 Balanced-Size Modularity Clustering Phase

The goal of this balanced-size modularity clustering phase is to produce fine-grained and well-balanced clusters. In this phase, we iteratively merge cluster pair into clusters so as to increase modularity score while keeping the size of clusters balanced. As we described in Sect. 1, modularity-based clustering algorithms, e.g., CNM [11], generally tend to produce imbalanced sizes of clusters. For mitigating the imbalanced cluster size, we first employ a modified modularity gain $\triangle Q'$, proposed by Wakita and Tsurumi [8], which introduces a heuristic into Eq. (5) for controlling the size of the merged cluster. The modified modularity gain $\triangle Q'_{ij}$ between cluster i and j is defined as follows:

$$\triangle Q'_{ij} = \min\left(\frac{|E_i|}{|E_j|}, \frac{|E_j|}{|E_i|}\right) \triangle Q_{ij}, \qquad (6)$$

where E_i is a set of edges included in cluster i. As shown in Eq. (6), we can find clusters that are expected to increase the modularity score since we have $\triangle Q_{ij}$ term in the right-hand side on the equation. In addition, Eq. (6) also evaluates $\min\left(\frac{|E_i|}{|E_j|}, \frac{|E_j|}{|E_i|}\right)$ term, which clearly takes large value when $|E_i|$ and $|E_j|$ are almost same sizes. Hence, the modified modularity gain $\triangle Q'_{ij}$ prefers to merge two clusters whose sizes are similar each other. As a result, Eq. (6) gives large score when two clusters i and j not only contain similar number of inner edges but also show better modularity gain.

For finding fine-grained and well-balanced clusters efficiently, we apply Eq. (6) to the state-of-the-art modularity-based clustering called *incremental aggregation method* [9]. The incremental aggregation method is a modularity-based clustering algorithm that is able to process large-scale graphs with more than a few billion edges within quite short computation time. This is because the method effectively reduces the number of edges to be referenced during the modularity gain computation by incrementally merging cluster pairs. By combining the method and the modified modularity gain shown in Eq. (6), this phase finds the fine-grained and well-balanced clusters efficiently.

In addition, this phase attempts to produce larger number of clusters than user-specified parameter k. The reasons are twofold: (1) Although Eq. (6) is effective in balancing the cluster size, it is not sufficient for the load balance. For further balancing the size of clusters, we additionally perform first-fit algorithm [10] in the next phase, which is an approximation algorithm for the bin packing problem. (2) If we run modularity-based clustering methods until convergence, they automatically determine the number of clusters relying on the input graph topology. In order to control the number of clusters for the distributed machines, this phase needs to run until (a) we can find no cluster pairs that increase the modularity score, or (b) the number of clusters produced in this phase reaches $a \times k$ where $a \in \mathbb{R}$ is a user-specified parameter such that $a > 1$.

3.2 Cluster Merge Phase

Algorithm 1 Cluster merge

Input: $\mathbb{C}, k$
Output: $\mathbb{R}$
 1: $\mathbb{R} \leftarrow top\_k\_clusters(\mathbb{C}, k)$
 2: $\mathbb{C} \leftarrow \mathbb{C} - \mathbb{R}$
 3: **while** $\mathbb{C} \neq \emptyset$ **do**
 4: $\quad m \leftarrow \arg\min_{r \in \mathbb{R}}\{|inner\_edges(r)|\}$
 5: $\quad \mathbb{N} \leftarrow neighbors(m) \cap \mathbb{C}$
 6: $\quad$ **if** $\mathbb{N} = \emptyset$ **then**
 7: $\qquad$ **break**
 8: $\quad$ **end if**
 9: $\quad$ **for each** $n \in \mathbb{N}$ **do**
10: $\qquad$ merge cluster m and n, generate cluster m'
11: $\qquad$ delete n from $\mathbb{C}$
12: $\qquad$ delete m from $\mathbb{R}$, insert m' into $\mathbb{R}$
13: $\qquad$ **if** $m' \neq \arg\min_{r \in \mathbb{R}}\{|inner\_edges(r)|\}$ **then**
14: $\qquad\quad$ **break**
15: $\qquad$ **end if**
16: $\quad$ **end for**
17: **end while**
18: $merge\_flag = true$
19: **while** $\mathbb{C} \neq \emptyset$ and $merge\_flag$ **do**
20: $\quad merge\_flag = false$
21: $\quad$ **for each** $c \in \mathbb{C}$ **do**
22: $\qquad \mathbb{N} \leftarrow neighbors(c) \cap \mathbb{R}$
23: $\qquad$ **if** $\mathbb{N} \neq \emptyset$ **then**
24: $\qquad\quad merge\_flag = true$
25: $\qquad\quad m \leftarrow \arg\min_{n \in \mathbb{N}}\{|inner\_edges(n)| + |cut\_edges(n,c)|\}$
26: $\qquad\quad$ merge cluster m and c, generate cluster m'
27: $\qquad\quad$ delete c from $\mathbb{C}$
28: $\qquad\quad$ delete m from $\mathbb{R}$, insert m' into $\mathbb{R}$
29: $\qquad$ **end if**
30: $\quad$ **end for**
31: **end while**
32: **for each** $c \in \mathbb{C}$ **do**
33: $\quad$ delete c from $\mathbb{C}$
34: $\quad \mathbb{N} \leftarrow neighbors(c) \cap \mathbb{C}$
35: $\quad$ **while** $\mathbb{N} \neq \emptyset$ **do**
36: $\qquad$ **for each** $n \in \mathbb{N}$ **do**
37: $\qquad\quad$ merge cluster c and n, generate cluster c'
38: $\qquad\quad$ delete n from $\mathbb{C}$
39: $\qquad\quad c \leftarrow c'$
40: $\qquad$ **end for**
41: $\qquad \mathbb{N} \leftarrow neighbors(c) \cap \mathbb{C}$
42: $\quad$ **end while**
43: $\quad m \leftarrow \arg\min_{r \in \mathbb{R}}\{|inner\_edges(r)|\}$
44: $\quad$ merge cluster m and c, generate cluster m'
45: $\quad$ delete m from $\mathbb{R}$, insert m' into $\mathbb{R}$
46: **end for**
47: **return** $\mathbb{R}$

The idea of producing balanced-size clusters is to employ the techniques developed for the packing problem [10]. That is, given various size of items, we pack them into fixed number of containers with the same size. Since we generated more clusters than the number of computers at the last phase, we pack those clusters into balanced-size containers by performing first-fit algorithm. In addition, we choose an adjacent cluster of a given cluster and pack them into the same container during first-fit algorithm, so that we can keep the number of cross-cluster edges small.

The detail is as follows. Given we have many clusters produced at the balanced-size modularity clustering phase, we choose k (number of computers) largest clusters as seed clusters and put them into different containers. Then, we repeatedly merge the smallest seed cluster with its adjacent cluster until there is no adjacent cluster to seed clusters. After that, there may be clusters that are not connected to any seed clusters, that is, the clusters are isolated from any seed clusters. We pick up a cluster from the isolated ones, merge reachable clusters from it, and put the merged cluster into the container with the smallest number of inner edges.

The pseudocode of this phase is shown in Algorithm 1. The symbols and their definitions used in the code are summarized in Table 1. The input is clusters $\mathbb{C}$, and the specified number of output clusters is k. Clusters $\mathbb{C}$ are obtained at the balanced-size modularity clustering phase. First, we choose k clusters that have the largest number of inner edges from input clusters $\mathbb{C}$. We treat them as seed clusters and put them into output clusters $\mathbb{R}$ (line 1). In the following procedure, we pick up other clusters from $\mathbb{C}$ and merge them with the seed clusters until no cluster is left in $\mathbb{C}$. The procedure consists of three steps. In the first step, so as to balance the size of the seed clusters while keeping the number of cross-cluster edges small, we choose the smallest seed cluster, pick up its adjacent cluster in $\mathbb{C}$, and merge the seed cluster with the adjacent cluster (line 3–17). We repeat this merge process until there is no adjacent cluster to the smallest seed clusters left in $\mathbb{C}$. In the second step, we pick up a cluster in $\mathbb{C}$ and merge it with its adjacent and the smallest seed cluster (line 18–33). We repeat this merge process until there is no adjacent cluster to the seed clusters left in $\mathbb{C}$. Now, there may be clusters in

Table 1 Definitions of symbols used in Algorithm 1

Symbol	Definition
$\mathbb{C}$	Input cluster set
k	Specified number of output clusters
$\mathbb{R}$	Output cluster set
$top\_k\_clusters(\mathbb{C}, k)$	Top-k clusters $\in \mathbb{C}$
$inner\_edges(c)$	Inner edges of cluster c
$neighbors(c)$	Adjacent clusters of cluster c
$cut\_edges(n, m)$	Cut edges between cluster n and m

$\mathbb{C}$ that are not connected to any seed clusters. In the final step, we treat the seed clusters in $\mathbb{R}$ as containers of the packing problem. We pick up a cluster in $\mathbb{C}$ (line 32–33), merge it with its reachable clusters in $\mathbb{C}$ (line 34–42), and put it to the smallest seed cluster (container) (line 43–45).

Example 1 Figure 1 depicts an example of the cluster merge phase, the initial state is on the left, and the final state is on the right. Each circle represents cluster, and the number located at the center of the circle shows the number of inner edges in the cluster. The number assigned to an edge shows the number of the cross-cluster edges. The dotted shape represents seed cluster (container). (1) In the initial state, two largest clusters (cluster 1 and cluster 2) are chosen as seed clusters. (2) The smallest seed cluster (cluster 2) and its one of adjacent clusters (cluster 3) are merged. (3) Still the merged seed cluster (containing cluster 2 and cluster 3) is the smallest seed cluster [the size is 35 (20 + 5 + 10)], so we continue to merge it with its adjacent cluster, cluster 5. (4) Now the merged seed cluster size is 55, the smallest cluster changes to cluster 1. Then, cluster 1 is merged with its adjacent cluster, cluster 4, and the size becomes 65. (5) Now, there is no adjacent cluster to any seed clusters, so we put the isolated cluster, cluster 6, into the smallest seed cluster, cluster 2, as shown in the final state in Fig. 1.

3.3 Graph Conversion Phase

So far, we have obtained k clusters of edge-cut graph. In this final phase, we convert edge-cut graph into vertex-cut graph, since most of the recent distributed graph engines are based on the vertex-cut graph. This design is based on the fact that vertex-cut graph is more efficiently balanced than edge-cut graph [3, 13]. To convert edge-cut graph to vertex-cut graph, we have to convert cross-cluster edge to cross-cluster vertex by choosing either two sides of cross-cluster edge as cross-cluster vertex. Let u is chosen as cross-cluster vertex and v is not for cross-cluster edge $e(u, v)$. The cross-cluster edge $e(u, v)$ is assigned to the cluster to which non-cross-cluster vertex v belong. We choose cross-cluster vertexes so that the size of the clusters to be balanced. This procedure is simple but affects largely the load balance.

4 Experiments

We implemented our proposal, balanced-size clustering technique, on top of one of the recent distributed graph processing frameworks, PowerGraph [3]. We made following experiments to validate the effectiveness of our graph partitioning technique.

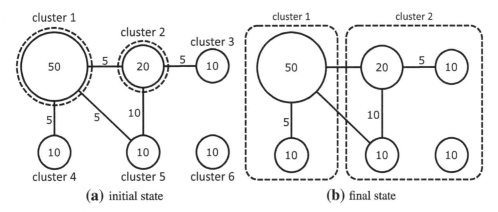

(a) initial state   **(b)** final state

Fig. 1 Example in cluster merge phase. The initial state is on the *left*, and the final state is on the *right*. *Each circle* represents cluster, and the number located at the center of the circle shows the number of inner edges in the cluster. The number assigned to an edge shows the number of the cross-cluster edges. The *dotted shape* represents seed cluster (container) **a** initial state, **b** final state

Partitioned graph quality	We evaluated the effectiveness of partitioned graph by using the major metrics, replication factor [Eq. (1)] and load balance factor [Eq. (2)].
Performance for graph analysis	We evaluated the runtime, the amount of data transfer between computers, and the imbalance runtime ratio among computers during graph analysis. In addition, we also evaluated how the major graph metrics, the replication factor and load balance factor, correlate with the physical performance measures, the response time, the amount of data transfer between computers, and the imbalance runtime ratio among computers.
Scalability	We evaluated the response time of graph analysis, graph partitioning time, and the sum of both by varying the number of computers.

We compared our graph partitioning technique to other techniques, a random partition, *Oblivious* [3], and *HDRF* [6]. The random partitioning is a naive approach that randomly assigns vertexes/edges to distributed computers. The Oblivious is a heuristic technique that balances the size of partitions and reduces the replication factor. The HDRF is a technique improved from Oblivious and actually provides better graph partitions than Oblivious does for various graphs. We used two variations of our graph partitioning technique in the 1st phase; the original modularity clustering and the balanced-size modularity clustering. They are denoted as *modularity* and *balanced-size*

in figures, respectively. For the parameter setting, we choose the number of clusters the 1st phase generates according to the graph size; we set more clusters to generate as input graph size increases.

4.1 Benchmark

We used real graph data shown in Table 2 and three typical graph analysis patterns as follows.

1. PageRank [14]: one of the link-based ranking techniques designed for web pages.
2. SSSP (single-source shortest path): computing the shortest paths to all vertexes from a given vertex.
3. CC (connected component): detecting sub-graphs (components) connected with edges.

4.2 Setting

The experiments were made on Amazon EC2, r3.2xlarge Linux instances. Each instance has CPU Intel(R) Xeon(R) CPU E5-2670 v2, 2.50 GHz (four cores) with 64 GB RAM. The network performance between instances was 1.03 Gbps. The hard disks delivered 103 MB/s for buffered reads. We used g++4.8.1 with –O3 optimization for PowerGraph and all partitioning techniques. We chose synchronous engine of PowerGraph to ensure the preciseness of the analysis results.

4.3 Partitioned Graph Quality

We evaluated the effectiveness of partitioned graph by using the major metrics, replication factor [Eq. (1)] and load balance factor [Eq. (2)] for the graph data in Table 2.

Table 2 Real-world graph data

Dataset	Short name	$|V|$	$|E|$	Modularity
email-EuAll [15]	Eu	265,214	420,045	0.779
web-Stanford [15]	St	281,903	2,312,497	0.914
com-DBLP [15]	DB	317,080	1,049,866	0.806
web-NotreDame [15]	No	325,729	1,497,134	0.931
amazon0505 [15]	am	410,236	3,356,824	0.852
web-BerkStan [15]	Be	685,230	7,600,595	0.930
web-Google [15]	Go	875,713	5,105,039	0.974
soc-Pokec [15]	Po	1,632,803	30,622,564	0.633
roadNet-CA [15]	CA	1,965,206	2,766,607	0.992
wiki-Talk [15]	Ta	2,394,385	5,021,410	0.566
soc-LiveJournal1 [15]	Li	4,847,571	68,993,773	0.721
uk-2002 [16]	uk	18,520,486	298,113,762	0.986
webbase-2001 [16]	ba	118,142,155	1,019,903,190	0.976

4.3.1 Relationship Between Modularity and Replication Factor

Our technique is based on modularity clustering so as to decrease the number of cross-cluster edges. We investigated the relationship between the modularity value[3] of the real graph data and how our technique improves replication factor for those data compared with random partitioning and HDRF. In Fig. 2, X-axis shows the modularity value and Y-axis shows the replication factor ratio of the partitions obtained by our technique to those obtained by random partitioning and HDRF. As expected, we observe that our technique provides better replication factors than other techniques and that the replication factor is improved more as the modularity value of the graph increases.

4.3.2 Replication Factor

Figure 3 shows the results of the experiments for replication factor by varying the number of computers, 8, 16, 32, 48, 64. The figure includes only the three largest graph data, soc-LiveJournal1, uk-2002, webbase-2001. We omit others here because they are similar results to the above three graph data. We set the number of clusters the 1st phase generates at 4000, 8000, 160,000 for soc-LiveJournal1, uk-2002, webbase-2001, respectively.

We observe that our technique achieves the best among others and the advantage increases as the number of computers increases. Only for soc-LiveJournal1, the variation that uses the original modularity clustering in the 1st phase performs better than the variation that uses the balanced-size modularity clustering. We guess this is caused by the fact that the modularity of soc-LiveJournal1 (0.721) is relatively lower than those (0.986 and 0.976) of uk-2002

and webbase-2001 (see Fig. 2), so the balanced-size modularity clustering could not improve the replication factor as the original modularity clustering.

4.3.3 Load Balance Factor

Figure 4 shows the results of the experiments for load balance factor. We observe that the variation that uses the original modularity clustering seriously inferior to others. This is because the primary goal of the Oblivious and HDRF is to generate balanced-size clusters and decreasing the replication factor is secondary. We also observe that the balanced-size modularity clustering effectively mitigates the load balance factor to the original modularity clustering.

4.4 Performance for Graph Analysis

We evaluated the runtime time, the amount of data transfer between computers, and the imbalance runtime ratio among computers during graph analysis executed on PowerGraph. We fixed the number of computers at 64.

4.4.1 Runtime

Figure 5 shows the runtime results for analysis patterns. The runtime results in Y-axis are normalized to random partitioning result. As we can see in the figure, our technique performs best among others. In general, our technique is more effective as the modularity of graph increases (soc-LiveJournal1 $0.721 \rightarrow$ webbase-2001 $0.976 \rightarrow$ uk-2002 0.986), mainly because the amount of data transfer is reduced more for the graph with larger modularity (we will see in Fig. 6). Also the response time is not correlated so much with the imbalance runtime ratio (we will see in Fig. 7). For the largest modularity case of uk-2002, our

---

[3] We set the number of partitions at 64.

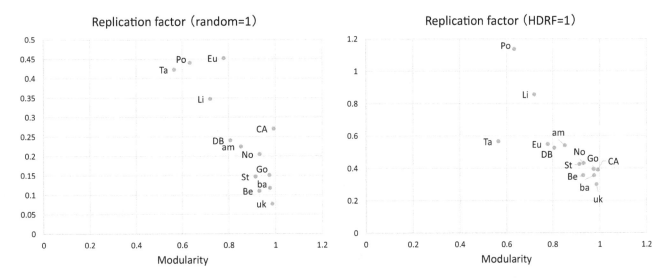

Fig. 2 Relationship between Modularity and replication factor for graph data in Table 2. Y-axis shows the replication factor ratio of the partitions obtained by our technique to those obtained by random partitioning and HDRF

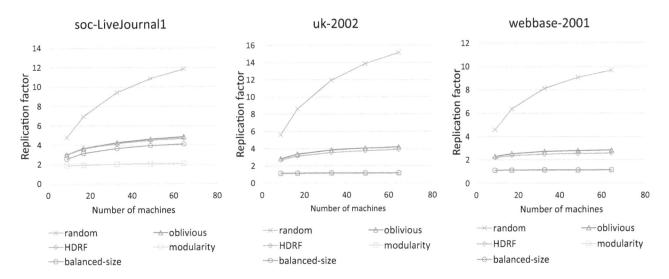

Fig. 3 Scalability experiments for replication factor

technique is 3.2, 1.2, 2.2 times faster in PageRank, SSSP, CCC, respectively, than HDRF. For soc-LiveJournal1, where the modularity is the smallest among others, the variation that uses the balanced-size modularity clustering in the 1st phase provides higher performance than the one that uses the original modularity clustering.

4.4.2 Amount of Data Transfer

Figure 6 shows the average amount of data transfer between computers for analysis patterns. The results in Y-axis are normalized to random partitioning result. By comparing this figure with the replication factor experiments in Fig. 3, the amount of data transfer is highly correlated with the replication factor. For the largest modularity case of uk-2002, our technique most effectively

reduces the amount of data transfer by 94%, 62%, 95% of HDRF in PageRank, SSSP, CCC, respectively. We guess the runtime improvement achieved by our technique is caused by not only the reduction ratio of data transfer but also its actual amount of data transfer. Our technique improves the runtime of PageRank most, because both the reduction rate of data transfer and the actual amount of data transfer are large. The actual amount of data transfer is 21 GB in PageRank, 0.17 GB in SSSP, 1.5 GB in CC for the case of uk-2002 in random partitioning.

4.4.3 Imbalance Runtime Ratio

Figure 7 shows the imbalance runtime ratio for analysis patterns. The runtime indicates CPU time and excludes network IO wait. The imbalance runtime ratio is defined as

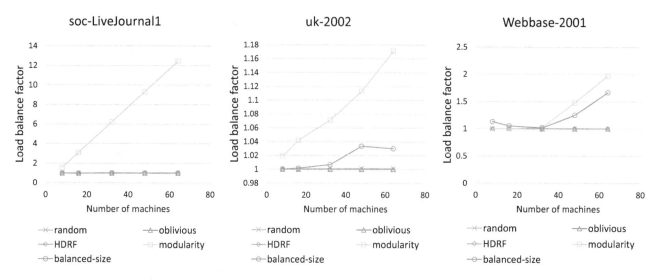

Fig. 4 Scalability experiments for load balance factor

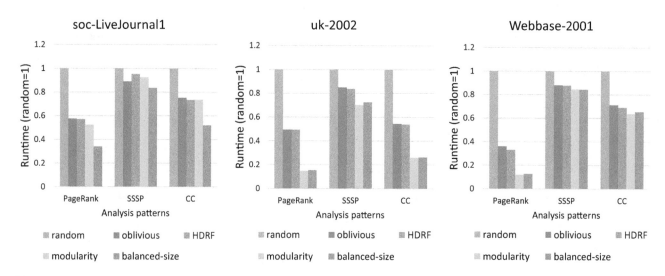

Fig. 5 Runtime experiments for analysis patterns (*Y*-axis is normalized to random partitioning result)

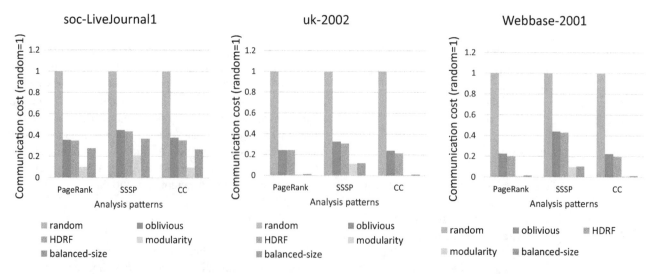

Fig. 6 Average amount of data transfer between computers for analysis patterns (*Y*-axis is normalized to random partitioning result)

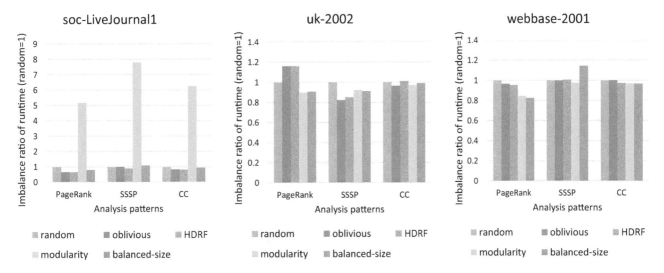

Fig. 7 Imbalance runtime ratio for analysis patterns (*Y*-axis is normalized to random partitioning result)

the ratio of the slowest computer's runtime to the average runtime. Again, the results in *Y*-axis are normalized to random partitioning result. By comparing this figure with the load balance factor experiments in Fig. 4, the imbalance runtime ratio is correlated with the load balance factor. In particular for the case of the variation that uses the original modularity clustering in the 1st phase for soc-LiveJournal1. Except that, the results are comparable to all techniques for all graph data. Notice that, for our technique that uses the balanced-size modularity clustering in the 1st phase, even if its load balance factor is inferior to others (see in Fig. 4), the imbalance runtime is comparable to others. In addition, the imbalance ratio changes to analysis patterns. So, we conjecture that there should be other factors than load balance factor that affect the imbalance runtime depending on analysis patterns.

4.5 Scalability

We evaluated the response time of graph analysis, graph partitioning (ingress) time, and the sum of both (total time) by varying the number of computers. Figure 8 shows runtime results for the largest graph data, webbase-2001, and PageRank analysis pattern. The analysis results show that our technique scales well to the number of computers and achieves best among others. For the graph ingress time, random partitioning is fastest because it chooses a computer to assign a new edge randomly. Our technique is scalable since we extend to use the state-of-the-art modularity-based clustering [9] in the 1st phase and the cost of the 2nd and 3rd phases does not depend on the number of computers. Notice that both Oblivious and HDRF are not scalable. The ingress time of Oblivious and HDRF gets worse to the number of computers. We investigated the implementation of Oblivious and HDRF and found that

they made a linear search on the computer list to determine which computer stores the smallest number of assigned edges. For the total time, our technique is the best, in particular, the variation that uses the balanced-size modularity clustering in the 1st phase.

5 Related Work

In the line of the work for efficient distributed graph processing, the problem of finding better graph partitions has been studied in recent decades. A recent survey paper on vertex-centric frameworks summarizes various types of graph partitioning techniques [17]. The major approach is twofold: *edge-cut method* and *vertex-cut method*.

Edge-cut method The edge-cut method is a graph partitioning approach that divides a graph into sets of sub-graphs by cutting edges so as to reduce the number of cross-partition edges. In the distributed graph processing, the edge-cut method assigns each sub-graph to each computer. METIS, proposed by Karypis and Kumar in 1998 [18], is one of the representative partitioning algorithms that focuses on reducing the number of cross-partition edges via the edge-cut method. The problem of edge-cut method is that it cannot avoid load imbalance for typical graphs that follow the power law distribution [19]. We explain the detail more in the vertex-cut method part.

Vertex-cut method The vertex-cut method is another type of partitioning technique that attempts to reduce the number of cross-partition vertexes. As we described above, the edge-cut method splits a graph into sets of sub-graphs by cutting edges. In contrast, the vertex-cut method divides a graph by splitting vertexes. Most of the recent distributed graph engines use vertex-cut methods, because vertex-cut graph is more efficiently balanced than edge-cut

Fig. 8 Scalability experiments for analysis runtime, graph ingress time, and total time (for webbase-2001 dataset and PageRank analysis pattern)

graph [3, 13]. Typically, graph usually follows the power law distribution so it tends to include super-vertexes, that is, the number of their connected edges is tremendously large. Those super-vertexes affect largely load imbalance, so the idea of the vertex-cut method is to reduce the load imbalance by splitting the super-vertexes. In the family of the vertex-cut methods, Oblivious [2] and HDRF (High-Degree (are) Replicated First) [6] are the state-of-the-art algorithms. These algorithms are stream-based algorithms: Every edge is read from input file, and it is immediately assigned to a computer; and thus, they are scalable to large-scale graphs and achieve better load balance performance. Specifically, Oblivious assigns an incoming edge to a computer, so that it can reduce the number of cross-vertexes spanned among computers. HDRF divides edges into partitions by splitting high-degree vertexes in order to reduce the total number of cross-vertexes.

6 Conclusion

We proposed a graph partitioning technique that efficiently partitions graphs with good quality so that it achieves high performance for graph analysis by reducing the communication cost and by keeping good load balance among computers. We extend modularity-based clustering and integrate it with the techniques for the graph packing problem. We implemented our technique on top of distributed graph engine, PowerGraph, and made intensive experiments. The results show that our partitioning technique reduces the communication cost so it improves the response time of graph analysis patterns. In particular, PageRank computation is 3.2 times faster at most than HDRF, the state-of-the art of streaming-based partitioning approach. In addition, we observed that the replication

factor and load balance factor correlate with the amount of data transfer and the imbalance runtime ratio, respectively, and that the response time is correlated with the replication factor but not with the load balance factor so much.

Possible future work is as follows. (1) There is a trade-off between the communication cost and load balance depending on the number of computers. We optimize the trade-off problem by fixing the number of computers in this paper, but one future work is to optimize the number of computers depending on the input graph and analysis patterns. (2) There is a still room improving more on the replication factor and load imbalance and achieving efficient graph clustering.

References

1. Malewicz G, Austern MH, Bik AJ, Dehnert JC, Horn I, Leiser N, Czajkowski G (2010) Pregel: a system for large-scale graph processing. In: Proceedings of SIGMOD
2. Low Y, Bickson D, Gonzalez J, Guestrin C, Kyrola A, Hellerstein JM (2012) Distributed GraphLab: a framework for machine learning and data mining in the cloud. PVLDB, 5(8):716–727
3. Gonzalez JE, Low Y, Gu H, Bickson D, Guestrin C (2012) PowerGraph: distributed graph-parallel computation on natural graphs. In: Proceedings of OSDI
4. Xin RS, Gonzalez JE, Franklin MJ, Stoica I (2013) GraphX: a resilient distributed graph system on Spark. In: Proceeding of GRADES
5. Suri S, Vassilvitskii S (2011) Counting triangles and the curse of the last reducer. In: Proceedings of WWW
6. Petroni F, Querzoni Leonardo, Daudjee K, Kamali S, Iacoboni G (2015) HDRF: stream-based partitioning for power-law graphs. In: Proceeding of CIKM
7. Newman MEJ, Girvan M (2004) Finding and evaluating community structure in networks. Phys Rev E 69, 026113
8. Wakita K, Tsurumi T (2007) Finding community structure in mega-scale social networks. In: Proceedings of WWW
9. Shiokawa H, Fujiwara Y (2013) Fast algorithm for modularity-based graph clustering. In: Proceeding of AAAI, Onizuka

10. Dósa G, Sgall J (2013) First fit bin packing: a tight analysis. In: Proceeding of STACS

11. Clauset A, Newman MEJ, Moore C (2004) Finding community structure in very large networks. Phys Rev E 70:066111

12. Blondel VD, Guillaume J, Lambiotte R, Lefebvre E (2008) Fast unfolding of communities in large networks. J Stat Mech Theory Exp. doi:10.1088/1742-5468/2008/10/P10008

13. Bourse F, Lelarge M, Vojnovic M (2014) Balanced graph edge partition. In: Proceeding of KDD

14. Page L, Brin S, Motwani R, Winograd T (1999) The PageRank citation ranking: bringing order to the web. Technical report

15. Stanford Large Network Dataset Collection (2014) http://snap.stanford.edu/data/. Accessed 31 Jan 2017

16. Laboratory for Web Algorithmics (2002) http://law.di.unimi.it. Accessed 31 Jan 2017

17. McCune RR, Weninger T, Madey G (2015) Thinking like a vertex: a survey of vertex-centric frameworks for large-scale distributed graph processing. ACM Comput Surv 48(2):25

18. Karypis G, Kumar V (1999) A fast and high quality multilevel scheme for partitioning irregular graphs. SIAM J Sci Comput 20(1):359–392

19. Faloutsos M, Faloutsos P, Faloutsos C (1999) On power-law relationships of the internet topology. In: Proceeding of SIGCOMM

9

Private Blocking Technique for Multi-party Privacy-Preserving Record Linkage

Shumin Han[1] · Derong Shen [1] · Tiezheng Nie[1] · Yue Kou[1] · Ge Yu[1]

Abstract The process of matching and integrating records that relate to the same entity from one or more datasets is known as record linkage, and it has become an increasingly important subject in many application areas, including business, government and health system. The data from these areas often contain sensitive information. To prevent privacy breaches, ideally records should be linked in a private way such that no information other than the matching result is leaked in the process, and this technique is called privacy-preserving record linkage (PPRL). With the increasing data, scalability becomes the main challenge of PPRL, and many private blocking techniques have been developed for PPRL. They are aimed at reducing the number of record pairs to be compared in the matching process by removing obvious non-matching pairs without compromising privacy. However, most of them are designed for two databases and they vary widely in their ability to balance competing goals of accuracy, efficiency and security. In this paper, we propose a novel private blocking approach for PPRL based on dynamic k-anonymous blocking and Paillier cryptosystem which can be applied on two or multiple databases. In dynamic k-anonymous blocking, our approach dynamically generates blocks satisfying k-anonymity and more accurate values to represent the blocks with varying k. We also propose a novel similarity measure method which performs on the numerical attributes and combines with Paillier cryptosystem to measure the similarity of two or more blocks in security, which provides strong privacy guarantees that none information reveals even collusion. Experiments conducted on a public dataset of voter registration records validate that our approach is scalable to large databases and keeps a high quality of blocking. We compare our method with other techniques and demonstrate the increases in security and accuracy.

Keywords Privacy-preserving record linkage · Private blocking · k-anonymity · Paillier cryptosystem · Scalability

1 Introduction

As the world is moving into the Big Data era, large amounts of data from several organizations require to be integrated. Due to privacy and confidentiality concerns, these organizations are not willing or allowed to reveal their sensitive and personal data to other database owners. Therefore, we need to protect these data from unauthorized disclosure. For example, in a decentralized health-care system, where the personal medical records are distributed among several hospitals, it is critical to integrate the information belonging to a patient without disclosing his/her sensitive attributes. Thus, making sure that privacy of individuals is maintained whenever databases are linked across organizations is vital.

Privacy-preserving record linkage (PPRL) [1] is the process of identifying records from two or more data sources that refer to the same individuals, without revealing any private or sensitive information. PPRL has been widely used in many fields. For example, Microsoft has acquired Yahoo, by applying record linkage technique on their client databases, and we can not only obtain common clients between them, but also acquire the potential new clients from Yahoo, which has significant business value for

✉ Shumin Han
hanshumin_summer@yeah.net

[1] College of Computer Science and Engineering, Northeastern University, Shenyang, China

Microsoft. However, the client databases are confidential, and exposing client data to other companies would cause heavy loss. Therefore, comparing client databases without data disclosure excepting matched records is crucial.

Considering the growing large volumes of available data and the increasing number of parties, blocking [2] is a possible solution aimed at improving scalability, which is used to divide records into mutually exclusive blocks, and only the records within the same block can be linked. A naive pair-wise comparison across P databases of n records is n^P. The computation and communication complexities increase significantly with multiple parties. Thus, concentrating on the study of multi-party blocking techniques is the key to improve scalability.

Private blocking [3] aims to generate candidate record pairs which are remained to perform PPRL without revealing any sensitive information that can be used to infer individual records and their attribute values. So far, there have been many private blocking techniques proposed for two or more databases, and there still exist some drawbacks to be solved. As to the approaches between two databases: In [3], the two-party private blocking (TPPB) method avoids the use of a third party and cryptographic techniques and instead trades off privacy for blocking quality. In [4], Inan et al. suggest creating forming generalized hierarchies (FGH) for reducing the cost of PPRL. However, the forming hierarchies may cause the blocks over-generalization and reduce the accuracy of blocking. As to the approaches among multiple parties: In multiple parties, the risk of collusion increases, where a subset of parties collude in order to learn about other parties' sensitive data. In [5] and [6], the degree of privacy preserving cannot against collusion among the database owners. We propose a novel private blocking technique based on dynamic k-anonymous blocking and Paillier cryptosystem which can deal with the problems above. Our approach accurately creates blocks without revealing any private information and takes less time than previous approaches which apply cryptographic techniques.

The contributions of this paper are: (1) We propose a novel dynamic k-anonymous blocking algorithm which generates k-anonymous blocks and more accurate values to represent the blocks with varying k, and the values are called representative values (RVs). (2) We apply a cryptographic technique Paillier cryptosystem on the RVs of each block without revealing any information, which provides stronger privacy than previous approaches. And we propose a novel measure method which performs on the numerical attributes and combines with Paillier cryptosystem to measure the similarity of two or more blocks in security. (3) We propose a multi-party private blocking approach which can against collusion among multiple owners and reduce time cost by multi-thread concurrent mechanism. (4) Experimental evaluation conducted on a real-world dataset shows our method has an advantage of keeping a high accuracy even k becoming very large. We compare our method with other techniques and demonstrate the increases in security and accuracy.

The remainder of this paper is organized as follows. In the following section, we mention some previous works related to ours. In Sect. 3, we introduce definitions and background. In Sect. 4, we describe our approach. In Sect. 5, we analyze the privacy of our approach. In Sect. 6, we show its experimental evaluation. Finally, we summarize our findings in Sect. 7.

2 Related Work

Due to the growing size of databases, various private blocking methods have been developed in recent years. As to the methods between two databases, most methods rely on the use of a third party. Al-Lawati et al. [7] proposed a secure three-party blocking protocol in 2005 which achieves high-performance PPRL by using secure hash encoding for computing the TF–IDF distance measure in a secure fashion. Inan et al. [4] proposed a hybrid approach that combines generalization and cryptographic techniques to solve the PPRL problem in 2008. An approach to PPRL was proposed by Karakasidis et al. [8] in 2011 a secure blocking based on phonetic encoding algorithms. The records that have similar (sounding) values are divided into the same block. In 2012, a k-anonymous private blocking approach based on a reference table was proposed by Karakasidis et al. [9] for three-party PPRL techniques. Durham [10] proposed a framework for PPRL using Bloom filters in 2012. Recently, Karakasidis [11] proposed a novel privacy-preserving blocking technique based on the use of reference sets and Multi-Sampling Transitive Closure for Encrypted Fields (MS-TCEF). As to the two-party techniques, Inan et al. [12] in 2010 presented an approach for PPRL based on differential privacy. The approach combines differential privacy and cryptographic methods to solve the PPRL problem in a two-party protocol. A two-party approach based on the use of Bloom filters for approximate private matching was developed by Vatsalan et al. [13] in 2012. Vatsalan [3] proposed an efficient two-party private blocking based on privacy techniques k-anonymous clustering and public reference values. As to the methods among multiple parties, there only few have been proposed. The latest two methods [5, 6] were, respectively, proposed in 2015 and 2016. In these two papers, they preserve the privacy of records by applying Bloom filters.

The methods in [3, 4] are closest to our approach. However, the approach in [3] uses public reference values as the RVs, although the attributes values of records are not revealed, and to a certain degree, public reference values also expose some information about corresponding block. And when k becomes very large, the public reference values cannot sufficiently represent the blocks. So the quality of blocking reduces heavily. The approach in [4] uses forming generalized hierarchies to generate k-anonymous blocks, which may make the RVs over-generalization and reduces the accuracy of generating candidate pairs. The approaches applying Bloom filters in [5, 6] protect the privacy of records to some degree, but they still cannot against collusion among multiple owners.

We create blocks using dynamic k-anonymous blocking instead of forming hierarchies, which generates the RVs more accurately and flexibly. Applying Paillier cryptosystem provides a stronger guarantee of privacy against collusion, which takes less time than previous approaches that apply cryptographic techniques.

3 Preliminaries

3.1 Problem Formulation

We assume P databases of n records $D_1, D_2, \ldots, D_P$ are to be matched, and potentially each record from D_i ($1 \le i \le P$) needs to be compared with each record from D_j ($1 \le j \le P$), resulting in a maximum number of n^P comparisons among P databases. Private blocking contributes to removing obvious non-matching pairs and generating candidate record pairs without revealing any information about the originating plaintexts, which reduces the complexity of comparisons. Considering the privacy, the process of private blocking is different from the traditional blocking. In private blocking, the records of one database should not be exposed to other parties. Further details involved in private blocking are outlined as follows [14]:

Blocking Key Selection Blocking key is the criteria by which the records are partitioned.

Block Partitioning Once a blocking key has been selected, this blocking key is as an input to partition each database, respectively, by the same principle where the output is a set of blocks and their RVs.

Candidate Blocks Generation Given the blocks of each database, through measuring the similarity among the RVs, we can decide whether the records in multiple blocks compare; then, the candidate record pairs would be generated.

3.2 k-anonymity

We now give the definitions of k-anonymity [15].

- Explicit Identifier is a set of attributes, such as name and social security number (SSN), containing information that explicitly identifies record owners;
- Quasi Identifier (QI) is a set of attributes that could potentially identify record owners;
- Sensitive Attributes consist of sensitive person-specific information such as disease, salary and disability status;
- Non-Sensitive Attributes contain all attributes that do not fall into the previous three categories.

To prevent record linkage through QI, Samarati and Sweeney proposed [15] the notion of k-anonymity:

k-anonymity: If one record in table T has some value QI, at least k–1 other records also have the value QI. Table T is k-anonymity with respect to the QI.

In other words, the minimum group size on QI is at least k. In a k-anonymous table, each record is indistinguishable from at least k–1 other records with respect to QI. Consequently, the probability of linking a victim to a specific record through QI is at most $1/k$. Consider a table T contains no sensitive attributes (such as the voter list). An attacker could possibly use the QI in T to link to the sensitive information in an external source. A k-anonymous T can still effectively prevent this type of record linkage without revealing the sensitive information. In this paper, the RVs are QI.

3.3 Paillier Cryptosystem

The Paillier cryptosystem [16], named and invented by Pascal Paillier in 1999, is a probabilistic asymmetric algorithm for public-private key cryptosystem. The scheme is an additive homomorphic cryptosystem, and this means that given only the public key and the encryption of m_1 and m_2, one can compute the encryption of $m_1 + m_2$. More formally, let Enc_{kpub} and Dec_{kpriv} be the Paillier encryption and decryption functions with keys k_{pub} and k_{priv}, m_1 and m_2 be messages, $c(m_1)$ and $c(m_2)$ be ciphertexts such that $c(m_1) = Enc_{kpub} (m_1)$, $c(m_2) = Enc_{kpub} (m_2)$. So homomorphic addition can be expressed by operators "·" and "+" as follows:

$$Dec_{kpriv}(c(m_1) \cdot c(m_2)) = m_1 + m_2 . \tag{1}$$

4 Proposed Solution

Our proposed solution conducts private blocking by dynamic k-anonymous blocking and Paillier cryptosystem. It is composed of three parts: Data Preparation, Local k-anonymous Blocks Construction and Candidate Blocks Generation. The framework is described in Fig. 1.

Fig. 1 Framework of our
approach

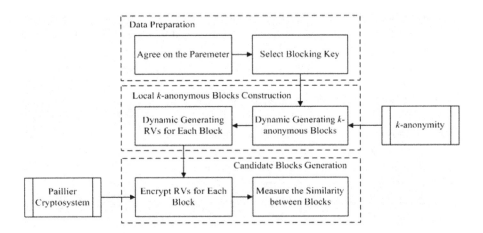

4.1 Data Preparation

In Data Preparation, we agree on the parameters used in our approach and select one or more attributes as blocking keys.

Agree on the Parameter We assume p $(p \geq 2)$ participants in our method $P_1, P_2, \ldots, P_p$ who participate in the protocol to perform private blocking on their databases. Decision unit (DU) is used to generate candidate blocks or in other words decide whether to compare the records among n blocks. $P_1, P_2, \ldots$, and P_p agree on the parameter k the minimum number of elements in a block.

Select Blocking Key Blocking key is used to partition the records into blocks. Selecting an appropriate blocking key is necessary. To protect the privacy of blocks, our approach generates blocks satisfying k-anonymity and protects the RVs by Paillier cryptosystem. The method in [3] also uses k-anonymity and select given name and surname as blocking keys. However, when k becomes large, the RVs in method [3] cannot sufficiently represent the blocks causing the quality of blocking reduces heavily. The RVs also expose some information about corresponding blocks. To avoid the deficiency above, our approach selects the numerical attributes such as age, zip code (consisting of numbers) or salary as the blocking key. The numerical attributes represent the blocks more accurately and flexibly with varying k. And when we apply Paillier cryptosystem, the computational demand for numeric attributes is much less than for string attributes. Thus, selecting numerical attributes as blocking key can improve the scalability and be applied in many real-world scenarios.

4.2 Local k-anonymous Blocks Construction

The local blocks construction phase partitions the records into blocks by blocking key. To construct blocks on distinct data sources without leaking any private information, our approach utilizes k-anonymity and Paillier cryptosystem

privacy techniques. We generate k-anonymous blocks and obtain the RVs of each block using dynamic k-anonymous blocking algorithm.

Dynamic Generating k-anonymous Blocks We suppose A_N (numerical attribute) is selected to be the blocking key; then, we form blocks on the databases of $P_1, P_2, \ldots$, and P_p $(p \geq 2)$, respectively. The blocks are divided by the values of blocking key, and each value of blocking key constructs one block. After this, we obtain equivalence classes and sort them by the blocking key values (BKVs). Considering privacy, we merge equivalence classes until the number of records in a block being at least k. It provides k-anonymous privacy characteristics, as each record in the database can be seen as similar to at least k–1 other records. Algorithm 1 (which is executed independently by p databases) shows the main steps involved in the merging of equivalence classes to create k-anonymous blocks (Algorithm 1, lines 4–7).

Algorithm 1: Dynamic k-anonymity Blocking

Input:
- E: Equivalence classes divided and sorted by A_N $\{E_1, E_2, E_3, \ldots, E_n\}$
- Minimum number of elements in a block k

Output:
- L_A: Set of k-anonymous blocks $\{ L_{A1}, L_{A2}, L_{A3}, \ldots, L_{Am} \}$

- $V[L_{Am}]$: RVs of L_{Am}

1:    $i=1; j=1; L_{Aj} = \emptyset$;

2:    **while** $i \leq n$ **do:**

3:       $Kset = \emptyset$

4:         **while** $\left| L_{Aj} \right| \leq k$ **do:**

5:           $L_{Aj} = L_{Aj} \cup E_i$

6:           $Kset.\text{add}(E_i . A_N)$

7:           $i++$

8:        $V[L_{Aj}] = [Kset[0], Kset[size-1]]$

9:       $j++$

Dynamic Generating RVs for Each Block We assume L is a block satisfying k-anonymity, and x, y are the smallest and biggest BKVs in L. The RVs are composed by $[x, y]$. Then, the BKVs of each record in block L are replaced by $[x, y]$; more specifically, each record in block L has at least $k{-}1$ records with the same BKVs. Therefore, the block L is k-anonymity respecting to $[x, y]$ and $[x, y]$ is the RVs of the block L. Comparing the approach in [4], which uses forming generalized hierarchies may lead to the RVs over-generalization and reduce the accuracy of generating candidate blocks, our approach dynamically adjusts the RVs with the change of k and has a good influence on keeping high accuracy even k becoming very large. Algorithm 1 shows the main steps involved in dynamic generating the RVs of each block (Algorithm 1, lines 8).

4.3 Candidate Blocks Generation

After generating k-anonymous blocks and corresponding RVs, we need to decide candidate blocks to eliminate record pairs that are expected to be non-matches. Firstly, in Sect. 4.3.1, to protect the privacy of RVs and generate candidate blocks, we encrypt the RVs with Paillier and propose a novel measure method on the encrypted RVs to measure the similarity between two blocks. Then, we extend the method to measure the similarity among multiple blocks and reduce the time cost by using the multi-thread concurrent mechanism in Sect. 4.3.2. At last, we take an example between two blocks to illustrate our method.

4.3.1 Approach for Two Datasets

In this part, we assume two participants in our method Alice (A) and Bob (B) who are the owners of databases D_A and D_B. Decision unit (DU) is used to decide whether to compare the records between two blocks.

Encrypt RVs for Each Block To measure the similarity between blocks, the RVs of blocks should be released by at least one data owner. Before releasing, the RVs in both A and B are encrypted by Paillier to guarantee privacy. DU generates Paillier public–private key and sends the public key to A and B. Then, A and B, respectively, encrypt their RVs with the public key (Algorithm 2, lines 3–5). We assume that the RVs of block L_A (from A) are $[a, b]$ and the RVs of block L_B (from B) are $[c, d]$. The RVs are encrypted as follows:

$$c(-a) = Enc_{kpub}(-a); c(b) = Enc_{kpub}(b) \tag{2}$$

$$c(-c) = Enc_{kpub}(-c); c(d) = Enc_{kpub}(d)$$
$$c(-d) = Enc_{kpub}(-d) \tag{3}$$

Measure the Similarity between Blocks After getting encrypted RVs in A and B, we pass the encrypted RVs in A to part B. In part B who lacks the private key, Bob cannot infer the plaintexts of records in A. As to the party B, Bob has gained the encrypted RVs from A; then, he uses the encrypted RVs of two blocks from A and B to decide whether two blocks match. We design a novel similarity measure method which combines with Paillier cryptosystem to measure the similarity between blocks (Algorithm 2, lines 7–16). The novel similarity measure method is expressed as follows:according to

$b < c$ or $d < a$,

$b < d$,

but L_A does not match with other blocks in B $\qquad$ (4)

otherwise,

According to the Homomorphic addition in Paillier cryptosystem:

$$Dec_{kpriv}(c(m_1) \cdot c(m_2)) = m_1 + m_2 \tag{5}$$

We can express our measure method as:

$$Dec_{kpriv}(c(b) \cdot c(-c)) = b - c$$
$$Dec_{kpriv}(c(d) \cdot c(-a) = d - a \tag{6}$$
$$Dec_{kpriv}(c(b) \cdot c(-d) = b - d$$

As Eq. (4) shows, if $b < c$ or $d < a$, it means L_A and L_B have no intersection. So, they are non-match. Otherwise, L_A and L_B are match. If we assume $b_1 < d_1$ in L_{A1} and L_{B1}, as algorithm 1 shows, we know $c_2 gt$ d_1, so we can infer $b_1 < c_2$, L_{A1} and L_{B2} are non-match. By that analogy, L_{A1} also does not match with $L_{B3}, L_{B4}, \ldots, L_{Bm}$.

Our novel similarity measure method combines well with the Paillier cryptosystem. We perform the secure computation $c(m_1)c(m_2)$ which is designed in (6) in party B and send the results to DU. Then, DU decrypts the results by the private key to get real results. Through judging the real results by (4), we could decide whether two blocks become candidate blocks. Therefore, in the whole process, our approach is unconditioned safe with none of the information revealing.

The last step PPRL conducts on each candidate record pairs individually by using a private matching technique, which should not reveal any information regarding the sensitive attributes and non-matches (this step is outside of our approach).

Algorithm2: Generating Candidate Blocks

Input:
- $V(L_A)$: RVs of each block in A $\{[a_1, b_1], [a_2, b_2], \ldots, [a_n, b_n]\}$
- $V(L_B)$: RVs of each block in B $\{[c_1, d_1], [c_2, d_2], \ldots, [c_m, d_m]\}$

Output:
- Candidate blocks match or non-match

```
1:   for i=1; i≤n; i++ do
2:       for j=1; j≤m; j++ do
3:           c(-a_i) = Enc_{k_pub}(-a_i); c(b_i) = Enc_{k_pub}(b_i);
4:           c(-c_j) = Enc_{k_pub}(-c_j); c(d_j) = Enc_{k_pub}(d_j);
5:           c(-d_j) = Enc_{k_pub}(-d_j);
6:           send c(-a_i) and c(b_i) to B
7:           S_1 = c(b_i)· c(-c_j); S_2 = c(d_j)· c(-a_i);
8:           S_3 = c(b_i)· c(-d_j);
9:           send S_1, S_2, S_3 to C
10:          if Dec_{k_prv}(s_1)<0 or Dec_{k_prv}(s_2)<0 then
11:              return non-match;
12:          else if Dec_{k_prv}(s_3)<0 then
13:              return match;
14:              break;
15:          else
16:              return match;
```

4.3.2 Approach for Multiple Datasets

In this part, we assume p participants in our method $P_1, P_2, \ldots, P_p$ who are the owners of databases $D_1, D_2, \ldots, D_p$. Decision unit (DU) is used to decide whether to compare the records among multiple blocks.

Encrypt RVs for Each Block As similar with the measure method between two blocks, at first, DU generates Paillier public–private key and sends the public key to each block. Then, each block, respectively, encrypts its RVs with the public key. We assume that the RVs of block L_i (from P_i) are $[a_i, b_i]$ $(1 \le i \le p)$.

Measure the Similarity between Blocks After getting encrypted RVs in each block, we transmit the encrypted RVs to next part starting from P_1. Gaining the encrypted RVs from P_1, P_2 performs the secure computations on the encrypted RVs (Algorithm 3, lines 1–3). Then, we send the computation results c_1 and s_1 to the DU. By receiving the R_1 from DU, we transmit the bigger a and the smaller b to

the next part. And so on, we obtain a_{max} and b_{min} until the last part (Algorithm 3, lines 4–8). At last, we design a novel similarity measure method which combines with Paillier cryptosystem to measure the similarity among multiple blocks (Algorithm 3, lines 9–13). The whole process is shown in Fig. 2, and the novel similarity measure method is expressed as follows:

$$c(a_{max}) \cdot c(-b_{min}) \le 0, \quad L_1 L_2, \ldots, \text{and } L_p \text{ match}$$

$$\text{otherwise}, \quad L_1 L_2, \ldots, \text{and } L_p \text{ non-match} \tag{7}$$

As Eq. (7) shows, if $c(a_{max}) \cdot c(-b_{min}) \le 0$, it means the p blocks have intersection, so we decide the p blocks match. Otherwise, they are non-match.

Algorithm3: Generating Candidate Blocks for Multiple Databases

Input:
- Set of $[a_i, b_i]$ belonging to parties P_i, $1 \le i \le p$

Output:
- Candidate blocks match or non-match

```
1:   a_max=a_1; b_min=b_1;
2:   c_1=c(a_max)· c(-a_i+1)
3:   s_1=c(b_min)· c(-b_i+1)
4:   for i=1; i≤p; i++ do
5:       if c_1<0 then
6:           a_max=a_i+1;
7:       else if s_1≥0 then
8:           b_min=b_i+1
9:   D= c(a_max)· c(-b_min)
10:  if D≤0 then
11:      return match;
12:  else
13:      return non-match;
```

Reduce the Time Cost From the algorithm 3, we know that there are $p-1$ secure computations in it. Each secure computation takes much more time than the time used to compare the plaintexts. Therefore, we propose using the multi-thread concurrent mechanism to deal with the algorithm 3 as shown in algorithm 4 which can reduce half of time than the algorithm before.

Fig. 2 Process of generating candidate blocks among multiple parties

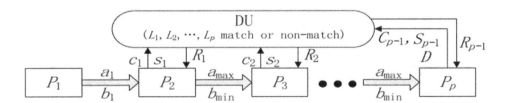

Algorithm4: Generating Candidate Blocks for Multiple Databases

---

Input:
-Set of $[a_i, b_i]$ belonging to parties P_i, $1 \le i \le p$
Output:
- Candidate blocks match or non-match
1:   *findmami* $(1, p)$;
2:   $g=2/p$
3:   **if** $n>1$ **then**
4:         Thread a = **new** Thread (*findmami*$(1, g)$).start();
5:         Thread b = **new** Thread (*findmami*$(g+1, p)$).start();
6:   Thread.join();
7:   **else return** a_{max}, b_{min};

4.3.3 Example of Our Approach Between Two Blocks

In this part, we take an example to illustrate our approach except the part of Paillier cryptosystem and describe the process of generating candidate blocks in privacy. We select age as blocking key and $k = 3$. In Fig. 3a, we choose twelve records in D_A and D_B to perform private blocking. In Fig. 3b, A and B sort by BKVs and generate k-anonymous blocks, respectively. In Fig. 3c, we obtain the RVs in A and B. Then in Fig. 3d, we apply proposed similarity measure method to decide which blocks match. For example, as shown in Fig. 3c, we choose the block L_A which ID = 2 to compare with the block L_B which ID = 2. The RVs are respective [19, 20] and [20, 21] of L_A and L_B, so $a = 19$, $b = 20$, $c = 20$, $d = 21$. Firstly, we compute $c(r_1) = c(20)c(-20), c(r_2) = c(21)c(-19), c(r_3) = c(20)$ $c(-21)$ according to 4.3 (6) in B. Then, we send the results to C and decrypt them. We would get $r_1 = 0, r_2 = 2$ $> 0, r_3 = -1 < 0$, and through judging by 4.3 (4), we decide L_A and L_B match, but L_A does not match with other blocks in B.

5 Privacy Analysis

In this section, we will discuss the privacy guarantees offered by our approach. We assume that all parties will follow the protocol honestly, but may try to infer private information based on messages they receive during the process or collusion [15]. Next we summarize the information that our approach discloses to each of the participants. Firstly, a pair of private and public keys is generated for encrypting and decrypting the RVs. The public key is known to all parties while the private key is known only to the DU. $P_i(1 \le i \le n)$: Each party receives encrypted RVs of blocks and sends the encrypted results of secure computation to the DU. Without knowing the private key, a party cannot decrypt the received RVs, and therefore, colluding with a party to learn another party's RVs would be impossible. DU: This party only receives the encrypted results of secure computation from $P_i(1 \le i \le p)$. After decrypting the encrypted results with private key, the real results only show the final results without revealing the specific information from each part. Thus, we can conclude Paillier cryptosystem can guarantee our approach is unconditioned safe.

6 Experiments

To perform the experimental analysis, we selected a publicly available dataset of real personal identifiers, derived from the North Carolina voter registration list (NCVR) [17]. We selected attribute age as the blocking key. To evaluate the scalability of multi-part blocking method, we need to generate two different sizes of datasets which are 10,000 and 100,000 for 2, 3, 5, 7 and 10 parties. Therefore,

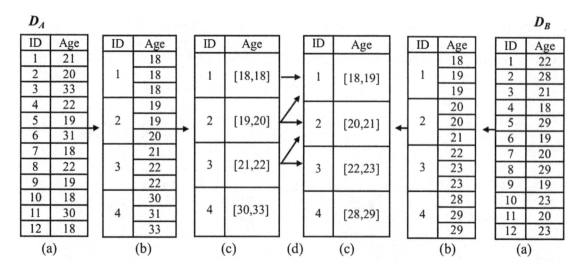

Fig. 3 (a) Example databases held by $A(D_A)$ and $B(D_B)$ with blocking key values based on age. (**b–d**) Illustrate the protocol, which is described in Sect. 4.3.1, $k = 3$

we, respectively, sampled 10,000 and 100,000 records randomly drawn from NCVR for each party. Of these records, 8000 (80,000) were randomly selected from NCVR (excluding those in other parties), while 2000 (20,000) were selected the same as other parties. The goal was to privately identify the 2000 (20,000) matching records between two or more blocks. Our experiments also perform on datasets of different sizes, and we sampled 0.1%, 1%, 10% and 100% of records in the full database for each part. All tests were conducted on a computer server with a 64-bit, 8.0G of RAM Intel Core (3.30 GHz) CPU.

6.1 Evaluation Measures

We use the following measures to evaluate the performance of private blocking techniques in terms of complexity and quality of blocking. Complexity is evaluated by the total time required for blocking. We utilize reduction ratio (RR) and pair completeness (PC) as evaluation metrics for private blocking approaches [18]. Specifically, suppose c is the number of candidate record pairs produced by the private blocking, c_m is the number of true matches among c candidate pairs, $n = |D_A||D_B|$ is the number of all possible pairs, and n_m is the number of true matches among all pairs. Then, RR and PC are defined as follows:

$$RR = 1 - c/n \qquad PC = c_m/n_m . \qquad (8)$$

6.2 Performance Evaluation

As to the two datasets, we compare our approach with previous two approaches TPPB [3] and FGH [4]. The approach TPPB generates candidate blocks satisfying k-anonymity and uses public reference values as the RVs of blocks. Since each block consists of at least k records, only when revealing one reference value from each block can guarantee k-anonymity privacy. If several reference values are released by a block, the k-anonymity privacy would not be guaranteed. As to FGH, it generates k-anonymous blocks by forming generalized hierarchies.

We set the parameters of two approaches according to the settings provided by the authors [3, 4]. We compared three private blocking techniques on two different sizes of datasets which are 10,000 and 100,000 to measure the change of RR, PC and blocking time against k. The changing trends of RR, PC and blocking time against k are similar in two datasets. We also measure the blocking time with different dataset sizes for the three approaches. Then, we discuss the results of our experiments.

As to the multiple databases, we evaluate our multi-party private blocking method by RR, PC and blocking time against k and the number of participants p. We also

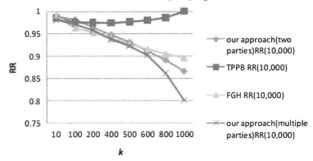

Reduction ratio(RR) aginst k

Fig. 4 RR with different values for k, dataset size $= 10,000$

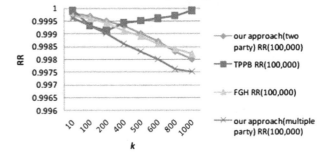

Reduction ratio(RR) against k

Fig. 5 RR with different values for k, dataset size $= 100,000$

evaluate the improved algorithm which uses the multi-thread concurrent mechanism by blocking time.

RR with Varying k Figures 4 and 5 show the RR with varying k in three approaches and our multi-part blocking method, $P = 3$. Our approach (two parties) and FGH keep a high RR with the increasing k. When k increases to 1000, RR is still above 0.86 in the smaller dataset. Toward TPPB, at first RR reduces when k is less than 200. Then, with k becoming bigger, RR increases and at last RR almost closes to 1. It can be explained that when k becomes larger, in TPPB, representing a block by only one reference value is not sufficient to represent all the values in block, which might lead to the number of candidate blocks reduces and the RR increases. The RR of our approach (multiple parties) is a little lower than the RR of our approach (two parties).

PC with Varying k Because of the reason above, some true candidate blocks being missed with the increasing k; therefore, the PC reduces heavily in TPPB as shown in Figs. 6 and 7. In FGH, PC also reduces heavily with the reason that the bigger the k the higher level in the VGHs the records are generalized which may cause over-generalization. With regard to our approach (two and multiple parties), PC is always 1 on both datasets. This owns to our better similarity measure method.

Blocking Time with Varying k To the aspect of *blocking time* in Figs. 8 and 9, the *blocking time* reduces with k in three approaches because the number of resulting blocks

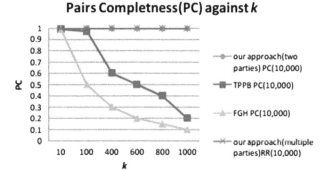

Fig. 6 *PC* with different values for k, dataset size $= 10,000$

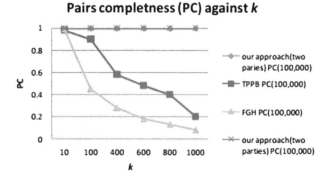

Fig. 7 *PC* with different values for k, dataset size $= 100,000$

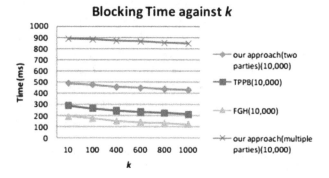

Fig. 8 *Blocking time* with different values for k, dataset size $= 10,000$

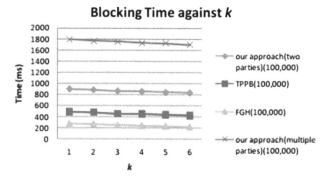

Fig. 9 *Blocking Time* with different values for k, dataset size $= 100,000$

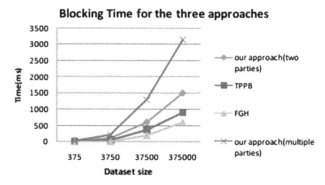

Fig. 10 *Blocking Time* with different dataset sizes for the four approaches

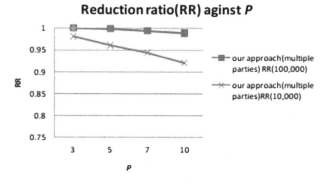

Fig. 11 (*RR* with varying p for multi-part private blocking

(n/k) becomes less as k gets bigger. As shown in Figs. 8 and 9, the blocking time of our approach is more than the other two approaches. It is because that our approach applies Paillier cryptosystem.

Blocking Time with Varying Database Sizes In Fig. 10, we compare the blocking time for three approaches with different dataset sizes. Our approach takes a little more time than the others with different dataset sizes. All the three approaches do not consider the communication cost. Through inferring, we can get the knowledge that all encrypted RVs are totally transmitted at most 500 times in our approach, which are far less than the communication

cost of previous approaches applying cryptographic techniques.

RR with Varying p In Fig. 11, we assume $k=10$ and measure the *RR* of our multi-part private blocking approach with the change of p. As Fig. 11 shows, *RR* reduces with the change of p.

PC with Varying p In Fig. 12, we assume $k=10$ and measure the *PC* of our multi-part private blocking approach with the change of p. As Fig. 12 shows, *PC* always keeps 1 with the change of p.

Blocking Time with Varying p In Fig. 13, we assume $k = 10$ and measure the blocking time of our multi-part private

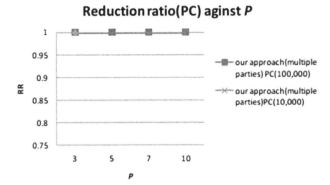

Fig. 12 *PC* with varying *p* for multi-part private blocking

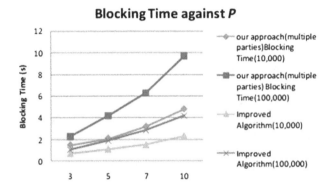

Fig. 13 *Blocking Time* with varying *p* for multi-part private blocking

blocking approach with the change of *p*. We also evaluate the blocking time of improved algorithm which uses the multi-thread concurrent mechanism. As Fig. 13 shows, the improved algorithm reduces the time effectively. Hence, we conclude that our approach performs better in accuracy and privacy with a little loss of efficiency.

7 Conclusion

We present a novel scalable private blocking technique which is more accurate and secure than previous approaches. Dynamic *k*-anonymity blocking guarantees that each block has at least *k* records and meanwhile generates more accurate RVs with varying *k*. We also propose a novel similarity measure method which combines with Paillier cryptosystem and guarantees absolute security without revealing any information. We extend this effective measure method to multiple parties which can avoid collusion. As experiments show, our approach exhibits high performance both in accuracy and security with a little loss of blocking time.

Acknowledgements This work is supported by the National Basic Research 973 Program of China under Grant No. 2012CB316201 and the National Natural Science Foundation of China under Grant Nos. (61472070, 61672142).

References

1. Vatsalan D, Christen P, Verykios VS (2013) A taxonomy of privacy-preserving record linkage techniques. Inf Syst 38(6):946–969
2. Christen P (2011) A survey of indexing techniques for scalable record linkage and deduplication. IEEE Trans Knowl Data Eng
3. Vatsalan D, Christen P, Verykios VS (2013) Efficient two-party private blocking based on sorted nearest neighborhood clustering. In: ACM CIKM
4. Inan A, Kantarcioglu M, Bertino E, Scannapieco M (2008) A hybrid approach to private record linkage. In: ICDE. pp 496–505
5. Ranbaduge T, Vatsalan D, Christen P (2015) Clustering-based scalable indexing for multi-party privacy-preserving record linkage. In: PAKDD. pp 549–561
6. Ranbaduge T, Vatsalan D, Christen P, Verykios V (2016) Hashing-based distributed multi-party blocking for privacy-preserving record linkage. In: PAKDD. pp 415–427
7. Al-Lawati A, Lee D, McDaniel P (2005) Blocking-aware private record linkage. In: IQIS. pp 59–68
8. Karakasidis A, Verykios VS (2011) Secure blocking + secure matching = secure record linkage. J Comput Sci Eng 5:223–235
9. Karakasidis A, Verykios VS (2012) Reference table based *k*-anonymous private blocking. In: 27th annual ACM symposium on applied computing. Trento
10. Durham E (2012) A framework for accurate, efficient private record linkage. Ph.D. Thesis, Vanderbilt University
11. Karakasidis A, Verykios VS (2015) Scalable blocking for privacy preserving record linkage. In: ACM KDD. Sydney
12. Inan A, Kantarcioglu M, Ghinita G, Bertino E (2010) Private record matching using differential privacy. In: EDBT. Lausanne, Switzerland, pp 123–134
13. Vatsalan D, Christen P (2012) An iterative two-party protocol for scalable privacy-preserving record linkage. In: Aus DM, CRPIT, vol 134. Sydney, Australia
14. Durham EA (2012) A framework for accurate, efficient private record linkage. Ph.D. Thesis, Graduate School of Vanderbilt University, Nashville
15. Sweeney L (2002) k-anonymity: a model for protecting privacy. Int J Uncertain Fuzziness Knowl Based Syst 10:557–570
16. Paillier P (1999) Public-key cryptosystems based on composite degree residuosity classes. In: EUROCRYPT'99. pp 223–238
17. Vatsalan D, Christen P (2014) Scalable privacy-preserving record linkage for multiple databases. In: ACM CIKM. Shanghai, pp 1795–1798
18. Kuzu M, Inan A (2013) Efficient privacy-aware record integration. In: ACM EDBT

10

An I/O-Efficient Buffer Batch Replacement Policy for Update-Intensive Graph

Ningnan Zhou[1,2] · Xuan Zhou[1,2] · Xiao Zhang[1,2] · Shan Wang[1,2]

Abstract With the proliferation of graph-based applications, such as social network management and Web structure mining, update-intensive graph databases have become an important component of today's data management platforms. Several techniques have been recently proposed to exploit locality on both data organization and computational model in graph databases. However, little investigation has been conducted on buffer management of graph databases. To the best of our knowledge, current buffer managers of graph databases suffer performance loss caused by unnecessary random I/O access. To solve this problem, we develop a novel batch replacement policy for buffer management. This policy enables us to maximally exploit sequential I/O to improve the performance of graph database. However, trivial solution produces impractical maintenance for replacement plan with maximal sequential I/O. To enable the policy, we first devise a segment tree-based buffer manager to efficiently maintain a optimal replacement plan. Unfortunately, segment tree-based solution becomes bottleneck in multi-core environment. To remedy this weakness, a B-tree-based buffer manager is further proposed. Extensive experiments on real-world and synthetic datasets demonstrate the superiority of our method.

Keywords Batch replacement · Buffer manager · Graph database

✉ Xuan Zhou
zhou.xuan@outlook.com

[1] MOE Key Laboratory of DEKE, Renmin University of China, Haidian, China

[2] School of Information, Renmin University of China, Beijing 100872, China

1 Introduction

The rapid growth of graph data fosters a market of specialized graph databases such as Neo4j,[1] Titan[2] and DEX [16]. To meet the needs of various graph-based applications [12, 28], these disk-based graph databases offer both database functionality such as insert/delete/update and analytical graph algorithms such as PageRank computation [7]. The evolving social network and the nature of some graph algorithms require graph databases to be update friendly and update efficient. For instance, to maintain a social network, each time a new friendship/connection establishes, a link connecting the pair of users should be inserted into the graph to reflect the change. In PageRank computation, the ranking score of every vertex needs to be updated in each iteration. This paper focuses on such update-intensive applications.

To support large scale graph databases, existing research work has mainly investigated the data organization and computational models. To achieve efficient data organization, the associated edges of each vertex are normal stored together. For example, in social networks, the friends of a user are usually stored in continuous data pages in neo4j. As a result, frequent requests such as "return the friends of a specific user" in Facebook or Twitter[3] can benefit from low latency of sequential I/O. As to computational model, the dominant vertex-centric [15] or edge-centric [21] processing models partition a graph based on vertices or edges, and treat each partition as a unit of computation. They can also benefit from sequential I/O.

[1] http://neo4j.com/.

[2] http://thinkaurelius.github.io/titan/.

[3] https://dev.twitter.com/rest/reference/get/friends/list.

Although existing graph databases widely adopt I/O efficient data organization and computational models, they rarely consider buffer replacement policies. In fact, they still adopt variants of least recently used (LRU) or least frequently used (LFU) policies [8, 17], which evict one buffer page at a time and thus to some degree cancel out the effects of the specialized data organization and computational models. Figure 1 illustrates such a scenario. After the insertion of some new friends of user u, the data pages containing u's information, b_{u_1}, b_{u_2} and b_{u_3}, will be cached in the buffer. Note that b_{u_1}, b_{u_2} and b_{u_3} should be continuously located on disk. When a query such as "return the friend list of user v" is issued, the buffer manager requires to read in a new set of continuously located data pages, v_1, v_2 and v_3, which contain the friends of the user v. As the buffer is currently full, the buffer manager decides to evict b_{u_1}, b_{u_2} and b_{u_3} to make room for the incoming data pages. Following the existing replacement policy, the system will first seek to the position of u_1 to evict b_{u_1} and then seek to the position of v_1 to read in a new page. Iteratively, the system will perform 6 random I/Os according to the order marked by the arrows in Fig. 1. This is inefficient. If we can evict b_{u_1}, b_{u_2} and b_{u_3} in a batch, and read in v_1, v_2 and v_3 in a batch, we only need to perform two random disk seeks, and the other I/Os can be performed sequentially. Thus, such batch replacement can save 4 out of 6 random I/Os.

In this paper, we propose a batch replacement buffer manager for update-intensive graph databases. To the best of our knowledge, it is the first buffer replacement policy that exploits sequential I/O to speed up graph databases. Our design considers the following aspects: (1) the buffer manager should provide an unchanged interface to other layers of the graph database; (2) it should figure out the optimal replacement plan each time it needs to replace buffered pages; (3) it should minimize computational and memory overhead. To address these challenges, we first define the optimal replacement plan as the criteria to evict pages via sequential I/O. Then, we propose a segment tree-based structure to organize buffered pages and to efficiently generate the optimal replacement plan.

Since there is no specific optimized concurrency control strategy for segment tree, our segment tree-based buffer manager suffers from concurrent updates. To remedy this weakness, we propose to transform the replacement plans into B-tree organization and thus it benefits from sophisticated B-tree concurrency control techniques.

To evaluate the performance of our batch replacement buffer manager, we tried it on both real-world and synthetic datasets using typical workloads of database manipulation and graph algorithms. The experiment results show that (1) the batch replacement policy is able to achieve significant performance improvement by exploiting sequential I/O and (2) it is practical for graph databases.

The contributions of this paper are fourfold:

- We show the importance of exploiting sequential I/O in buffer management of graph databases.
- We propose a batch buffer replacement policy. Based on it, we define the optimal replacement plan and devise a segment tree-based structure to manage buffered data pages and efficiently maintain the optimal plan.
- We propose to transform the replacement plans in segment tree-based buffer manager to B-tree organization. Consequently, our batch replacement buffer manager can benefit from sophisticated concurrency control techniques for B-tree.
- We conduct extensive experiments on real-world and synthetic datasets to verify the effectiveness of the batch replacement policy.

2 Related Work

Our work builds upon the existing techniques of graph databases, especially their data organization and computational models.

2.1 Data Organization

Conventionally, graph organization is built on top of the relational (*a.k.a.*, SQL) storage and graphs are stored as triplets [6, 22]. In other words, each edge e directed from a vertex u to a vertex v in the graph is transformed into a triplet $\langle u, e, v \rangle$. However, it is known that RDBMS organization is not good at answering traversal types of graph queries [24]. Considering the locality of data manipulation, such as queries like "return the friends of a specific user," it is more efficient to pack in-edges and out-edges of the same vertex in two lists and store them together [19, 26]. This has been adopted by most disk-based graph databases such as Neo4j. Therefore, we also assume such graph-specific data organization.

2.2 Computational Model

Recently, a general iterative framework is adopted to process various graph algorithms such as PageRank and shortest path computation. In the framework, every vertex and edge in the graph are associated with a value and at each iteration, the value on a vertex or an edge is updated in vertex-centric or edge-centric model.

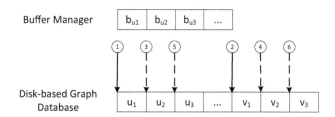

Fig. 1 An illustrative example for the effect of existing buffer manager and batch replacement in terms of random access, where the dashed arrow indicates the additional random access performed by existing buffer managers

2.2.1 Vertex-centric Model

Vertex-centric model is explored by initial works such as GraphLab [13] and Pregel [15]. In vertex-centric model, each vertex and its associated edges are regarded as a unit of computation so that if the main memory can hold any single vertex and its associated edges, only sequential I/O for loading data and updating results is required for each computation unit. To improve scalability, MOCgraph further reduces the memory footprint using message online computing [27].

2.2.2 Edge-centric model

Because a single vertex in real-world graph data, such as a celebrity, may be associated with so many edges that they cannot fit in main memory, edge-centric model is proposed [12, 21]. Edge-centric model partitions edges into disjoint sets, and each set and its associated vertices form the unit of computation. In this way, each set can be hold in main memory to avoid random I/O access [10, 28, 29].

There is a significant body of work on distributed graph databases [9, 20, 23]. As our work focuses on speeding up a disk-based graph database on a single machine, our research is orthogonal and complementary to them.

2.3 Buffer Manager on Database

Existing buffer managers in graph databases usually adopt the variants of the LRU/LFU policy to reduce disk I/O. Neo4j adopts the LRU policy while TurboGraph [10] maintains frequently used pages in memory. These works follow the same paradigm—when the buffer manager requires to read in a new page and the buffer gets overflow, only one buffered data page is evicted at a time. As a result, it introduces unnecessary random I/Os. To deal with this drawback, one recent work has proposed to remove buffer managers [14]. Besides, there are also alternative approaches which utilize index structures such as log structured merge tree [18] or fractal tree [4] to handle update-intensive workload. Both index structures process updates in a

key range in a batch. However, as the physical pages of a key range may not be located consecutively on disk, random I/O still cannot be avoided completely.

In this paper, we aim to leverage sequential I/O by evicting buffered pages in a batch way rather following the existing paradigm which repeats evicting and reading one page at a time. Thus, our approach can benefit from the data organization and computational models for graph databases.

3 Batch Replacement Buffer Manager

In this section, we first present the problem definition for our batch replacement buffer manager. Then, we present the structure and algorithms of the proposed buffer manager.

3.1 Problem Formulation

As we have shown in Fig. 1, it is inefficient to follow the existing paradigm of buffer manager, which evicts only one buffered data page at a time. In this paper, we extend the single page-based replacement plan to the one that considers a set of pages. Thus, the new definition of replacement plan subsumes that of the existing buffer managers.

Definition 1   Replacement Plan. When the buffer manager gets overflow, a replacement plan is a set of buffered data pages that will be evicted before the buffer manager performs any subsequent read operation.

For example, the ideal replacement plan in Fig. 1 is $\{b_{u_1}, b_{u_2}, b_{u_3}\}$.

Observing that evicting continuous buffered dirty data pages can maximize sequential I/O, the ideal batch replacement plan is to evict the longest sequence of such data pages.

Definition 2   Optimal batch replacement plan. Given a set of buffered pages with positions on the disk as $S = \{p_1, p_2, ..., p_n\}$, the optimal batch replacement plan is a subset $\mathcal{P} \subseteq S$ satisfying the following two conditions:

(1)   Pages in $\mathcal{P}$ are continuous in disk, namely, there are $n-1$ pairs of p_i and p_j in $\mathcal{P}$, such that $p_i \rightarrow p_j$ or $p_j \rightarrow p_i$, where $p_i \rightarrow p_j$ means that p_j is the successor data block in disk to p_i.

(2)   Any other subset $\mathcal{P}' \subseteq S$ satisfying Condition 1 contains less data pages than $\mathcal{P}$, namely, $|\mathcal{P}'| < |\mathcal{P}|$.

For example, in Fig. 1, the optimal batch replacement plan is $\{p_{b_1}, p_{b_2}, p_{b_3}\}$. Although its subset such as $\{p_{b_1}, p_{b_2}\}$ satisfies the first condition, they violate the second condition and are not the optimal batch replacement plan.

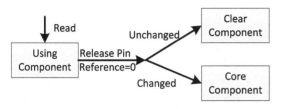

Fig. 2 The three components for batch replacement buffer manager

3.2 Overview

We would like a buffer manager to change its replacement policy to the optimal batch replacement plan. However, we also prefer the change is transparent to other components of a graph database. We identify three properties the batch replacement buffer manager should possess: (1) *transparency* requires to export the same interface to other layers in a graph database; (2) *effectiveness* requires to identify the exact optimal replacement plan; and (3) *efficiency* requires to minimize the computation and space cost of buffer manager.

inserted into the "using" component and only when the data page is unpinned and all queries referring to it terminate, it will be moved to the "clear" component or the core component, depending on if it has been updated. When the buffer overflows, the buffered data pages in the "clear" component will be evicted first. When the "clear" component is empty, the batch replacement plans will be used.

To obtain an optimal replacement plan, the most straightforward approach is to sort all buffered data pages based on their positions in disk and then scan the sorted page list to find the longest continuous sequence. As shown in Algorithm 1, once we meet a continuous data page, we increase the length of the continuous page list (Line 7–10) and once the continuous data pages terminate, we update the replacement plan (Line 11–13). Although simple, this baseline algorithm is expensive, as it needs to sort and scan all buffered data pages.

Algorithm 1 Trivial Algorithm

Require: $\mathcal{S} = \{p_1, p_2, ..., p_n\}$, the set of all buffered pages free to evict
Ensure: $\mathcal{P}$, the optimal replacement plan
1: Compute the list $\mathcal{L}$ by sorting pages in $\mathcal{S}$ in increasing order of positions in disk
2: $\mathcal{P} = \emptyset$
3: $len_\mathcal{P} = 0$
4: $\mathcal{P}' = \{\mathcal{L}[0]\}$
5: $len_{\mathcal{P}'} = 1$
6: **for** $i = 1$ to $n - 1$ **do**
7:     **if** $\mathcal{L}[i-1] \rightarrow \mathcal{L}[i]$ **then**
8:         $len_{\mathcal{P}'} + +$
9:         $\mathcal{P}' = \mathcal{P}' \cup \{\mathcal{L}[i]\}$
10:     **else**
11:         **if** $len_{\mathcal{P}'} > len_\mathcal{P}$ **then**
12:             $\mathcal{P} = \mathcal{P}'$
13:             $len_\mathcal{P} = len_{\mathcal{P}'}$
14: Return $\mathcal{P}'$

When a data page is being updated, if it is surrounded by a number of continuous buffered dirty pages, batch replacement may evict such an active page and cause thrashing. Therefore, we use a "using" component to keep track of such active data pages to avoid them from being evicted. Although our batch replacement buffer manager is designed for update-intensive applications, we also need to ensure transparency for mixed workloads of read and write. Therefore, we use a "clear" component to keep track of unchanged data pages.

Besides the above-mentioned two components, the core component for our batch replacement buffer manager store all dirty data pages that can be evicted. Figure 2 shows the transitions of a data page among the three components. Whenever the buffer manager reads a data page, it is

3.3 Segment Tree-based Buffer Manager

To avoid sorting and scanning, we adopt a segment tree-based structure that maintains the buffered data pages that are continuous in disk.[4] In this way, each insertion routine actually amortizes the time for sorting and scanning.

To amortize the overhead of sorting, we represent each set of continuous data pages as an interval $[a, b]$, which indicates that these data pages start at the position a and end at the position b on disk. Note that such an interval represents individual data pages and continuous data pages in a unified way—the interval of an individual data page at

---

[4] For continence, the term "buffer manager" refers to the core component in the rest of the paper.

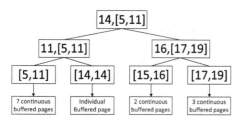

Fig. 3 An example segment tree, where leaf node represents intervals and internal node is associated with a key value and the longest interval among its descendants

position a on disk will be $[a, a]$. *To avoid the overhead of scanning*, we associate each interval with its interval length, on which the priority of eviction is based. In other words, the interval with the largest interval length will be chosen as the optimal replacement plan.

As Fig. 3 illustrates, a segment tree is a balanced binary tree of height $O(\log n)$, using $O(n)$ space. It can support indexing of intervals with logarithmic computational complexity for insertion, deletion and querying [5]. Such a segment tree has the following 2 properties: (1) a key value is associated with each internal node. The intervals in its left branch end with positions no more than the key value and the intervals in its right branch start with positions larger than the key value; (2) an interval is associated with each internal node; it records the longest interval among all the intervals of its descendants.

For example, given the root node associated with the key value 14 and the interval [5, 11], we know that: the interval [17, 19] must be in its right branch because it starts at 17 which is larger than 14 (Property 1); the associated interval [5, 11] is the longest interval in the buffer and its length is 7 (Property 2). In the figure, the interval [14, 14] actually represents an individual data page at the position 14 on disk.

The original segment tree is unable to maintain continuous data pages or the longest interval. It is our proposed insertion algorithm that utilizes the segment tree to maintain continuous data pages and the optimal replacement plan. The main idea is twofold: (1) whenever a buffered data page is inserted into the buffer manager, if its predecessor interval or successor interval exists, the inserted data page will extend the interval to a new longer interval and (2) whenever an interval is updated, the longest intervals on the path percolated from the root down to the interval itself will be updated. As Algorithm 2 illustrates, if the inserted data page d is at position $d.pos$ on disk, its predecessor interval should end with $d.pos - 1$ and its successor interval should start with $d.pos + 1$ (Line 2–3). If any one of the two intervals is found, it will be removed from the segment tree, and the intervals maintained by each internal node on the path from the root percolating to the interval will be updated (Line 7,11). Then, a new interval combining the predecessor/successor interval and the inserted data page will be inserted into the segment tree, and the longest intervals on the path from the root to the new interval will also be updated (Line 12–13). In this way, an insertion involves at most two queries, two deletions and one insertion on the segment tree. Thus its time complexity is $O(\log n)$, where n denotes the number of intervals and is normally less than the number of buffered data pages.

For example, given the segment tree in Fig. 3, if we want to insert a page with position 12, we first find its predecessor interval [5, 11], and combine it with the inserted page to form the new interval [5, 12]. Since no successor interval starting with $12 + 1 = 13$ is found in the segment tree, only the interval [5, 11] is removed from the

---

Algorithm 2 Buffer Insert Algorithm

Require: d, the page to be inserted into the buffer
　　　　$tree$, the segment tree organizing buffered pages in the batch replacement buffer
　　　　manager
1: New Interval $new = [d.pos, d.pos]$
2: Predecessor interval $p = tree.search(d.pos - 1)$
3: Successor interval $s = tree.search(d.pos + 1)$
4: **if** p exists **then**
5:　　$new = [p.start, d.pos]$
6:　　$tree$.delete(p)
7:　　update longest intervals along the path from root to p
8: **if** s exists **then**
9:　　$new = [new.start, s.end]$
10:　　$tree$.delete(s)
11:　　update longest intervals along the path from root to s
12: $tree$.insert(new)
13: update longest intervals along the path from root to new

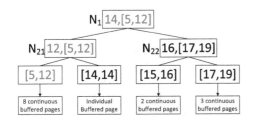

Fig. 4 The example segment tree after the page with position 12 at disk is inserted, where the updated nodes are marked in *red*

tree and the new interval is inserted. The longest intervals are updated correspondingly as marked in red in Fig. 4.

Since the segment tree maintains the longest interval at the root node, whenever the buffer overflows, we simply pick up the data pages corresponding to the longest interval as the optimal replacement plan. After the eviction, we can remove the corresponding interval and update the segment tree with amortized and worst case time complexity of $O(\log n)$. This procedure is efficient.

4 Concurrency Control

Our segment tree-based buffer manager suffers from concurrent updates from two aspects: (1) lack of optimized concurrency control strategies and (2) the binary structure of segment tree reduces granularity of concurrency control. To this end, we propose to transform all the replacement plans hold by the segment tree into B-tree organization. In this way, we can use the concurrency sophisticated B-tree to handle concurrent updates on the buffer manager. In this paper, we adopt a sophisticated multi-version B-tree implementation [3]. Note that any concurrency-supporting B-tree can be adopted such as the recently proposed multicore environment specific Bw tree [11]. In the following, we first describe the transformation from the segment tree-based buffer manager to B-tree organization and then present how to maintain optimal replacement plan.

The transformation from the segment tree structure to a B-tree organization is based on the following observation: each candidate replacement plan, e.g., continuous pages in disk, is regarded as an interval and all candidate plans are disjoint. For example, there are totally 4 candidate replacement plans in Fig. 3, namely [5,11], [14,14], [15,16]

and [17,19]. These intervals can also be represented in key-length pairs in the form of $\langle k, l \rangle$, where the key k denotes the start position of each candidate plan in disk and the length l indicates the number of pages that can be flushed in sequential I/O. For example, these 4 candidate replacement plans can be represented by four key-length pairs $\langle 5,7 \rangle$, $\langle 14,1 \rangle$, $\langle 15,2 \rangle$ and $\langle 17,19 \rangle$. In this way, each replacement plan can be organized in B-tree in a natural way. As Fig. 5 illustrates, the B-tree indexes the keys in each key-length pairs and the length is stored in leaf nodes. Similar to the segment tree-based buffer manager, each internal node of the B-tree also refers to the optimal replacement plan underlying itself. For example, the root node contains three keys separating the four candidate replacement plans and indicates that the candidate plan with start position less than 14 is the optimal replacement plan.

When a new page is buffered, it will be merged into one existing replacement plan or become an individual replacement plan. Since the new page with position p in disk can be merged into an existing replacement plan if and only if it is the successor or predecessor of an existing key-length pair, we search two potential key-length pairs $\langle k_1, l_1 \rangle$ and $\langle k_2, l_2 \rangle$ in the B-tree such that (1) $k_1 < p$ and $\forall k' < p, k_1 \geq k'$ and (2) $k_2 > p$ and $\forall k' > p, k_2 \leq k'$. The first condition is the necessary condition that the new page is a successor of the replacement plan $\langle k_1, l_1 \rangle$, and the second condition is the necessary condition that the new page is a predecessor of the replacement plan $\langle k_2, l_2 \rangle$. If the new page is a successor of the replacement plan $\langle k_1, l_1 \rangle$, it should hold that $p = k_1 + l$; if the new page is a predecessor of the replacement plan $\langle k_2, l_2 \rangle$, it should hold that $p + 1 = k_2$.

The maintenance under B-tree is similar to segment tree-based maintenance, and in the following, we use an example to reveal the details. As Fig. 6 illustrates, given the original B-tree shown in Fig. 5, when a new page with position 12 becomes free to evict, B-tree first finds that $\langle 5,7 \rangle$ is the first replacement plan with start position less than the new page position in disk and $\langle 14,1 \rangle$ is the first replacement plan with start position greater than the new page position in disk. For the key-length pair $\langle 5,7 \rangle$, we can determine the new page is the successor of this replacement plan because $p = k_1 + l$, where $p = 12$, $k_1 = 5$ and $l = 7$. Therefore, the new page is merged into a new replacement

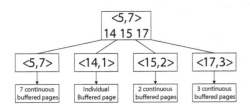

Fig. 5 An example for replacement plans organized by B-tree

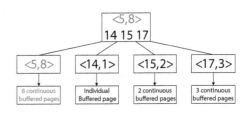

Fig. 6 An example for replacement plan maintenance in B-tree

Table 1 Statistics of our datasets

Dataset	# Vertex	# Edges	Raw size
Live Journal	4, 847, 571	68, 993, 773	2.3GB
Friendster	65, 608, 366	1, 806, 067, 135	150GB
LinkBench	10^6–10^7	10^8–10^9	5–60GB

plan. Meantime, in each internal node up toward the root node, the optimal replacement plan is updated.

5 Experiment

In this section, we report experiment results on real-world and synthetic datasets. We demonstrate the effectiveness of our method on both database manipulation and graph algorithm execution. We also analyze the properties of the proposed batch replacement method.

5.1 Experimental Setting

5.1.1 Dataset

Two public real-world graph datasets were used, namely *Live Journal* [2] and *Friendster* [25]. Both datasets follow power-law distribution with parameter $\alpha \approx 1.4$, while the Friendster dataset is much larger than the Live Journal dataset. The parameter α controls the skewness of the power-law distribution, that is, with a small α such as 0.5, all vertices have similar number of edges, while with a large α such as 1.5, a small number of vertices have much more edges than others. The synthetic dataset is generated by *LinkBench* and the graph database benchmark published by Facebook [1]. It is able to generate graphs with power-law distribution under varying α. The detailed statistics are shown in Table 1.

5.1.2 Workload

The workloads included typical graph algorithms and database manipulation. Following [12, 14, 20, 29], we ran typical graph algorithms including PageRank (PR), single-source shortest paths (SSSP), weakly connected components (WCC) and sparse matrix multiplication (SMM). LinkBench also provides a mix of insert/delete/update operations on vertices and edges as basic graph database manipulation.

All experiments were conducted on a machine with 2.5 Ghz Intel Core 2 CPU, 8GB of RAM and 10TB, 15, 000 rpm hard drive. We implemented the proposed batch replacement buffer manager on Neo4j[5] (Neo4j-BR) and

GraphChi-DB[6] (ChIDB-BR). Neo4j is a leading industry standard graph database that adopts LRU-based buffer manager and vertex-centric programming model, while GraphChi-DB (ChIDB) is a research prototype that discards buffer manager and adopts edge-centric programming model. For database manipulation, we also report the performance of a relational database MySQL, only for the purpose of reference. ChIDB also has an option to adopt log-structured merge tree (ChIDB-LSM) for write-optimized database manipulation. We explicitly created appropriate indexes for all databases during the experimental study.

5.2 Performance Comparison

In this section, we first show the effectiveness of our batch replacement buffer manager for data manipulation and graph algorithms. Then, we show that our approach is robust for various buffer sizes and workloads.

Figure 7 shows the average execution time for the typical graph algorithms. The buffer size *BS* is set to 5% of the dataset size. We have three observations: (1) for all graph algorithms on all datasets, the batch replacement variants of the two graph databases outperform their original versions. This shows that our batch replacement policy is superior to the LRU-based policy and the approach that does not use buffer manager; (2) on both real-world datasets, ChIDB-BR and ChIDB outperform Neo4j-BR and Neo4j. This shows edge-centric programming model is more suitable for graph algorithms on real-world datasets. The high value of $\alpha \approx 1.4$ indicates that a few vertices may contain a huge number of edges so that data pages involved in these vertices are read and evicted repeatedly in Neo4j and Neo4j-BR. However, our batch replacement policy exhibits better performance than the LRU-based policy; (3) on the synthetic dataset, Neo4j-BR outperforms ChIDB. This is because under $\alpha = 0.5$ edges are distributed more uniformly on vertices and thus Neo4j-BR benefit from less buffered page eviction.

Table 2 shows the average execution time for various manipulation workload on a small dataset (5GB) and a large dataset (50GB), respectively. We have the following observations: (1) on both datasets, both Neo4j-BR and ChIDB-BR outperform the original databases equipped with LRU-based buffer manager or log structure merge tree or no buffer manager; this indicates that batch replacement buffer manager is more suitable for graph databases; (2) Neo4j-BR and ChIDB-BR outperform MySQL, which shows the superiority of specialized graph database; (3) Neo4j outperforms ChIDB on small dataset, while ChIDB outperforms Neo4j on large dataset, revealing that LRU-

---

[5] http://neo4j.com/.

[6] https://github.com/graphchi/graphchiDB-scala.

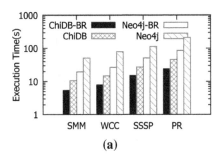
(a)

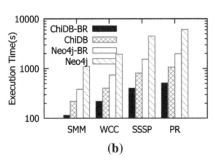
(b)

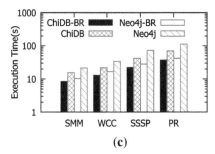
(c)

Fig. 7 Execution time for graph algorithms on three datasets, where the synthetic dataset contains 10^6 vertices and 10^8 edges with $\alpha = 0.5$. $BS=$ 5% of dataset size. **a** Live Journal, **b** Friendster, **c** LinkBench

Table 2 Execution time (ms) for graph database manipulation on synthetic dataset with $\alpha = 1.5$ and $BS = 5GB$

Data Size	Operation	ChiDB-BR	ChiDB	ChiDB-LSM	Neo4j-BR	Neo4j	MySQL
10^6 vertices, 10^8 edges	node_insert	0.09	12.9	0.10	**0.08**	0.13	0.11
	node_delete	0.10	16.7	0.14	**0.07**	0.12	0.17
	node_update	0.12	19.1	0.16	**0.09**	0.13	0.21
	edge_insert	0.15	24.6	0.17	**0.09**	0.19	0.25
	edge_delete	0.15	26.3	0.19	**0.12**	0.19	0.34
	edge_update	0.19	29.5	0.22	**0.14**	0.22	0.41
10^7 vertices, 10^9 edges	node_insert	**31**	94	37	36	259	42
	node_delete	**33**	105	41	39	268	45
	node_update	**34**	116	46	41	280	49
	edge_insert	**42**	136	55	47	295	64
	edge_delete	**48**	152	63	57	323	69
	edge_update	**51**	159	67	62	344	73

based buffer management is sensitive to the scale of dataset, while batch replacement buffer management is more robust.

Both batch replacement buffer manager and log-structured merge tree are designed for update-intensive applications by leveraging sequential I/O. However, ChiDB-BR outperforms ChiDB-LSM in most cases. This is because LSM-tree does not consider the optimal replacement plan. Sometimes, LSM-tree's data accesses will be scattered across a wide range on disk, which incurs numerous random I/Os.

Figure 8 validates the robustness of our approach on various ratios of buffer size to data size. On Live Journal dataset, we continuously increased the buffer size until the whole dataset was hold in main memory. The execution time of the PageRank algorithm keeps dropping. We can see: (1) until the buffer holds half the dataset, graph databases employing the batch replacement policy always outperform their counterparts; therefore, our approach can exploit available main memory efficiently; (2) when the buffer holds the whole dataset and buffer replacement is no longer needed, our approach consumes 1% less execution time than their counterparts; this shows that our method for identifying optimal replacement plans is efficient.

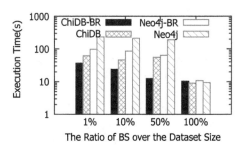

Fig. 8 Effect of RAM size on Live Journal

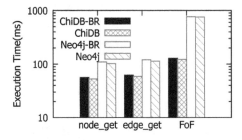

Fig. 9 Query time on Friendst., $BS = 2GB$

Figure 9 shows the query performance on the Friendster dataset for typical read-only workloads, including retrieval of a specific vertex/edge and a traversal-heavy Friends-of-

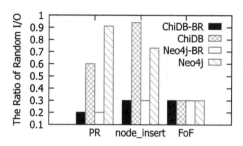

Fig. 10 Ratio of random I/O access on Friendster dataset

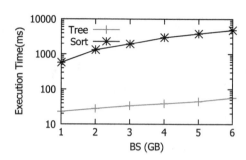

Fig. 12 CPU time for replacement plan

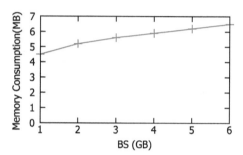

Fig. 13 Memory overhead

Friends (FoF) query. The FoF query is defined to find all vertices which can reach a specific vertex via any proxy vertex. We can see that although maintaining intervals of continuous buffered pages is of no use since there is no replacement for dirty pages, the overhead is still low. Therefore, although our batch replacement buffer manager is designed for update-intensive applications, its performance is acceptable for read-only applications as well.

Figure 14 compares the performance under different number of threads. We can see that on graph algorithms, the performance of all methods does not increases much because processing is blocked by I/O. Instead, for data manipulations, we can see that our B-tree-based buffer manager does not incur performance drop and still outperforms other methods under parallel processing, while the segment tree-based method suffers from high concurrency no matter which concurrency control is adopted.

5.3 Property of Batch Replacement

In this section, we evaluate the effectiveness of our batch replacement policy in terms of I/O and the computational overhead.

Figure 10 plots the ratios of random I/O to all disk I/O for the workloads of PageRank, node insertion and FoF query, respectively, which represent typical workloads of graph algorithm, database manipulation and read-only query. We can observe that both Neo4j-BR and ChiDB-BR used the least random I/O access. Therefore, it is not surprising their execution time is the shortest in aforementioned experiments. Figure 11 depicts the distribution of

buffered interval lengths when running the PageRank Algorithm on the Friendster dataset. We can see that on most datasets there are sufficient segments of continuous buffered data pages. Therefore, it is always possible for our batch replacement buffer manager to exploit sequential I/Os. The distribution of random I/O and interval lengths for other graph algorithms and data manipulation are similar to Figs. 10 and 11.

Figure 12 shows the average execution time for each batch replacement using our segment tree-based solution (Tree) and the trivial sort-based algorithm (Sort, Algorithm 1) on the Friendster dataset for the PageRank Algorithm. We can see that as the buffer size increases, our segment tree-based solution outperforms the trivial sort-based solution significantly. Figure 13 shows the additional memory consumption for maintaining the segment tree of continuous pages on the Friendster dataset for the PageRank Algorithm. We can see that the segment tree only consumes less than 1% of the buffer size. Note that the computational and memory overhead are normally only influenced by buffer size, rather than the variation of workloads and datasets (Fig. 14).

6 Conclusion

In this paper, we propose a novel approach to batch replacement buffer management for graph databases. Taking the specific data organization and vertex-centric or edge-centric programming models into consideration, the

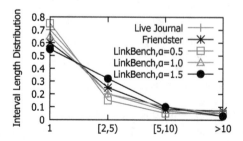

Fig. 11 Interval length distribution for PageRank

Fig. 14 Effect of multi-threads on Friendster dataset with $BS =$ 5% of dataset size **a** Page Rank, **b** data manipulation

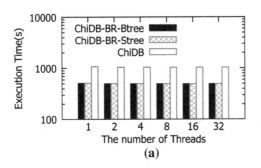
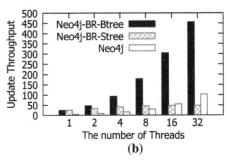

proposed method enables graph databases to make the best of sequential I/O. In addition to a sort-based trivial solution to find optimal replacement plan, we propose a segment tree-based buffer structure to efficiently maintain optimal replacement plans. To utilize multi-core environment, we propose to transform all replacement plans in segment tree-based buffer manager into B-tree organization. As a result, our batch replacement buffer manager benefits from sophisticated concurrency control techniques for B-tree. Extensive experiments on real-world and synthetic datasets show that our approach significantly improves the performance of existing graph databases and outperforms the LRU-based approaches and a recently proposed no-buffer approach. The experiment results also show that our approach incurs minimum computational and memory overhead and therefore is practical for real-world applications.

References

1. Armstrong TG, Ponnekanti V, Borthakur D, Callaghan M (2013) Linkbench: a database benchmark based on the facebook social graph. SIGMOD, pp 1185–1196
2. Backstrom L, Huttenlocher D, Kleinberg J, Lan X (2006) Group formation in large social networks: membership, growth, and evolution. KDD, pp 44–54
3. Becker B, Gschwind S, Ohler T, Seeger B, Widmayer P (1996) An asymptotically optimal multiversion b-tree. VLDB J 5(4):264–275
4. Bender MA, Demaine ED, Farach-Colton M (2005) Cache-oblivious b-trees. SIAM J Comput 35(2):341–358
5. Berg M, Otfried C, Marc van K, Mark O (2008) Computational geometry: algorithms and applications, 3rd edn. Springer, Berlin
6. Bornea MA, Dolby J, Kementsietsidis A, Srinivas K, Dantressangle P, Udrea O, Bhattacharjee B (2013) Building an efficient rdf store over a relational database. SIGMOD, pp 121–132
7. Brin S, Page L (1998) The anatomy of a large-scale hypertextual web search engine. Comput Netw 30(1–7):107–117
8. Effelsberg W, Haerder T (1984) Principles of database buffer management. ACM Trans Database Syst 9(4):560–595
9. Gonzalez JE , Xin RS, Dave A, Crankshaw D, Franklin MJ, Stoica I (2014) Graphx: graph processing in a distributed dataflow framework. OSDI, pp 599–613
10. Han WS, Lee S, Park K, Lee J-H, Kim M-S, Kim J, Yu H (2013) Turbograph: a fast parallel graph engine handling billion-scale graphs in a single pc. KDD, pp 77–85
11. Sengupta S, Levandoski J, Lomet D (2013). The bw-tree: a b-tree for new hardware. ICDE

12. Kyrola A, Blelloch G, Guestrin C (2012) Graphchi: large-scale graph computation on just a pc. In: Proceedings of the 10th USENIX conference on operating systems design and implementation, OSDI, pp 31–46
13. Low Y, Bickson D, Gonzalez J, Guestrin C, Kyrola A (2012) Hellerstein JM Distributed graphlab: a framework for machine learning and data mining in the cloud. PVLDB 5(8):716–727. doi:10.14778/2212351.2212354
14. Macko P, Marathe VJ, Margo DW, Seltzer MI (2015) Llama: Efficient graph analytics using large multiversioned arrays. ICDE, pp 363–374
15. Malewicz G, Austern MH, Bik AJC, Dehnert JC, Horn I, Leiser N, Czajkowski G(2010) Pregel: a system for large-scale graph processing. SIGMOD, pp 135–146
16. Martínez-Bazan N, Muntés-Mulero V, Gómez-Villamor S, Nin J, Sánchez-Martínez MA, Larriba-Pey JL (2007) Dex: high-performance exploration on large graphs for information retrieval. CIKM, pp 573–582
17. O'Neil EJ, O'Neil PE, Weikum G (1999) An optimality proof of the lru-k page replacement algorithm. J ACM 46(1):92–112
18. O'Neil P, Cheng E, Gawlick D, O'Neil E (1996) The log-structured merge-tree (lsm-tree). Acta Inf 33(4):351–385
19. Robinson I, Webber J, Emil E (2013) Graph databases. O'Reilly Media, Inc, Sebastopol
20. Roy A, Bindschaedler V, Malicevic J, Zwaenepoel W (2015) Chaos: scale-out graph processing from secondary storage. SOSP, pp 472–488
21. Roy A, Mihailovic I, Zwaenepoel W (2013) X-stream: edge-centric graph processing using streaming partitions. SOSP, pp 472–488
22. Rudolf M, Paradies M, Bornhövd C, Lehner W (2013) The graph story of the SAP HANA database. BTW, pp 403–420
23. Shao B, Wang H, Xiao Y (2012) Managing and mining large graphs: systems and implementations. SIGMOD, pp 589–592
24. Xia Y, Tanase IG, Nai L, Tan W, Liu Y, Crawford J, Lin CY (2014) Graph analytics and storage. IEEE Big Data, pp 942–951
25. Yang J, Leskovec J (2012) Defining and evaluating network communities based on ground-truth. MDS, pp 3:1–3:8
26. Zeng K, Yang J, Wang H, Shao B, Wang Z (2013) A distributed graph engine for web scale rdf data. PVLDB, pp 265–276
27. Zhou C, Gao J, Sun B, Yu JX (2014) Mocgraph: scalable distributed graph processing using message online computing. pp 377–388
28. Zhou Y, Liu L, Lee K, Zhang Q (2015) Graphtwist: fast iterative graph computation with two-tier optimizations. PVLDB, pp 1262–1273
29. Zhu X, Han W, Chen W (2015) Gridgraph: large-scale graph processing on a single machine using 2-level hierarchical partitioning. ATC, pp 375–386

11

Time for Addressing Software Security Issues: Prediction Models and Impacting Factors

Lotfi Ben Othmane[1] · Golriz Chehrazi[1] · Eric Bodden[1] · Petar Tsalovski[2] ·
Achim D. Brucker[2]

Abstract Finding and fixing software vulnerabilities have become a major struggle for most software development companies. While generally without alternative, such fixing efforts are a major cost factor, which is why companies have a vital interest in focusing their secure software development activities such that they obtain an optimal return on this investment. We investigate, in this paper, quantitatively the major factors that impact the time it takes to fix a given security issue based on data collected automatically within SAP's secure development process, and we show how the issue fix time could be used to monitor the fixing process. We use three machine learning methods and evaluate their predictive power in predicting the time to fix issues. Interestingly, the models indicate that vulnerability type has less dominant impact on issue fix time than previously believed. The time it takes to fix an issue instead seems much more related to the component in which the potential vulnerability resides, the project related to the issue, the development groups that address the issue, and the closeness of the software release date. This indicates that the software structure, the fixing processes, and the development groups are the dominant factors that impact the time spent to address security issues. SAP can use the models to implement a continuous improvement of its secure software development process and to measure the impact of individual improvements. The development teams at SAP develop different types of software, adopt different internal development processes, use different programming languages and platforms, and are located in different cities and countries. Other organizations, may use the results—with precaution—and be learning organizations.

Keywords Human factors · Secure software · Issue fix time

1 Introduction

Fixing vulnerabilities, before and after a release, is one of the most costly and unproductive software engineering activities. Yet, it comes with few alternatives, as code-level vulnerabilities in the application code are the basis of increasingly many exploits [1]. Large software development enterprises, such as SAP, embed in their development process activities for identifying vulnerabilities early, such as dynamic and static security testing [2]. Next to that, SAP's security development lifecycle (see, e.g., [3] for Microsoft's security development lifecycle) includes a process for fixing vulnerabilities after a software release.

Analyzing and fixing security issues is a costly undertaking that impacts a software's time to market and increases its overall development and maintenance cost. In result, software development companies have an interest to determine the factors that impact the effort, and thus, the time it takes to fix security issues, in particular to:

- identify time-consuming factors in the secure development process,
- better understand affecting factors,
- focus on important factors to enhance software's security level,
- accelerate secure software development processes, and
- enhance security cost planning for software development projects.

✉ Lotfi Ben Othmane
  lotfi.ben.othmane@sit.fraunhofer.de

[1] Fraunhofer Institute for Secure Information Technology, Darmstadt, Germany

[2] SAP SE, Walldorf, Germany

In a previous study, Othmane et al. [4] conducted expert interviews at SAP to identify factors that impact the effort of fixing vulnerabilities. SAP collects data about fixing security issues (potential vulnerabilities that need to be analyzed further manually to ensure whether they are vulnerabilities or false positive issues) both during a software's development and after its release. With this study we supplement the previous qualitative, interview-based results with objectively gathered system data. In this study, we used these data to identify and quantify, using machine learning, to what extent automatically measured factors impact a given issue's fix time. By *issue fix time*, we mean the duration between the time at which a security issue is reported to SAP and the time at which the issue is marked as closed in number of days. For simplicity, we use the term issue to refer to a security issue in the remaining of the paper.

Vulnerabilities are subset of software defects; they allow violation of constraints that can lead to malicious use of the software. The information, tools, and expertise that help to analyze faults (functionalities errors) apply with limited efficacy to analyze vulnerabilities. Zimmermann et al. [5] reported, for example, that the number of vulnerabilities is highly correlated with code dependencies, while the metrics that are correlated with faults such as size of changed code have only small effect. In addition, detecting faults requires exercising the specified functionalities of the software, while vulnerabilities analysis requires the software developers to have the knowledge and expertise to think like attackers [6]. Moreover, vulnerabilities detection tools do not provide often sufficient information to locate the issue easily, besides that they report high number of false positive. Thus, it is believed that "finding vulnerabilities is akin to finding a needle in a haystack" [6]. Also vulnerabilities issues occur much less frequently then faults. Thus, models derived from data related to faults and vulnerabilities issues have to deal with unbalanced datasets, c.f., [7]. Therefore, better prediction models of issue fix time should use only security issues data and consider the characteristics of issues.

For the analysis, we use five data sources based on distinct system tools available at SAP. The first three main data sources relate to security issues; issues found by code scanners for the programming language ABAP [8] (Data source 1) and for Java, JavaScript, and C (Data source 2), as well as issues found in already released code, which are communicated through so-called security messages, for instance reported by customers, security experts or SAP's own security team (Data source 3). The other two data sources comprise support data. They describe the components, i.e., a group of applications that performs a common business goal such as sales order or payroll (Support data 1), and the projects (Support data 2).

After cleaning the data, we used three methods to develop prediction models, based on (1) linear regression, (2) Recursive PARTitioning (RPART), and (3) Neural Network Regression (NNR). Next, we measured the models' accuracy using three different metrics. Interestingly, the models indicate that the impact of a vulnerability's type (buffer overflow, cross-site-scripting, etc.) is less dominant than previously believed. Instead, the time it takes to fix an issue is more related to the component in which the vulnerability resides, the project related to the issue, to the development groups that address the issue, and to the closeness of the software release date.

SAP can use the results of this study to identify costly pain points and important areas in the secure development process and to prioritize improvements to this process. Such models can be used to establish a learning organization, which learns and improves its processes based on the company-specific actual facts reflected in the collected data [9]. Since SAP collects the models' input data continuously, the models can be used to analyze the company's processes and measure the impact of enhancements over time.

This paper is organized as follows. First, we give an overview of related work (Sect. 2), discuss SAP's approach to secure software development (Sect. 3), and provide an overview of the regression methods and model accuracy metrics that we use in the study (Sect. 4). Next, we describe the research methodology that we applied (Sect. 5), report about our findings (Sect. 6), and analyze the factors that impact the issue fix time (Sect. 7). Subsequently, we discuss the impacts and the limitations of the study (Sect. 8) and the main lessons (and surprises) that we learned (Sect. 9), and conclude the paper.

2 Related Work

There is related work on prediction models for development efforts and time to fix bugs but work in the area of effort estimation for fixing security issues is scarce. Thus, we discuss in this section related work that investigates influencing factors on issue fix time or vulnerability fix time and also the development of prediction models for effort estimations, and differentiates them from our work.

Cornell measured the time that the developers spent fixing vulnerabilities in 14 applications [10]. Table 1 shows the average time the developers in the study take to fix vulnerabilities for several vulnerability types. Cornell found that there are vulnerability types that are easy to fix, such as dead code, vulnerability types that require applying prepared solutions, such as a lack of authorization, and vulnerability types that, although simple conceptually, may require a long time to fix for complex cases, such as SQL

Table 1 Examples of time required for fixing vulnerabilities [10]

Vulnerability type	Average fix time (min)
Dead code (unused methods)	2.6
Lack of authorization check	6.9
Unsafe threading	8.5
XSS (stored)	9.6
SQL injection	97.5

injection. The vulnerability type is thus one of the factors that indicate the vulnerability fix time but is certainly not the only one [4].

In previous work, Othmane et al. [4] reported on a qualitative study conducted at SAP to identify the factors that impact the effort of fixing vulnerabilities and thus the vulnerability fix time. The study involved interviews with 12 security experts. Through these interviews, the authors identified 65 factors that include, beside the vulnerabilities characteristics, the structure of the software involved, the diversity of the used technologies, the smoothness of the communication and collaboration, the availability and quality of information and documentation, the expertise and knowledge of developers and security coordinators, and the quality of the code analysis tools.

Several studies aim at predicting the time to fix bugs [11–17]. Zhang et al. [18] conducted an empirical study on three open-source software to examine what factors affect the time between bug assignment to a developer and the time bug fixing starts, that is the developer's delay (when fixing bugs), along three dimensions: bug reports, source code, and code changes. The most influencing factor found was the issue's level of severity. Other factors are of technical nature, such as sum of code churn, code complexity or number of methods in changed files as well as the maximum length of all comments in a bug report. Similar to our study, Zhang et al. were interested in revealing the factors that impact time, but as opposed to them we focus on security issues, not on bugs, and include in our analysis not only automatically collected information about security issues before and after release, but additionally component- and project-related factors from which human-based and organizational factors can be derived. In contrast to Zhang et al., we consider the overall fix time that starts at the time when a security issue is reported and ends when the issue is marked as closed.

Menzies et al. [19] estimated projects development effort, using project-related data, such as the type of teams involved, the development time of the projects, and the number of high-level operations within the software. They found that it is better to use local data based on related projects instead of global data, which allows to account for project-related particularities that impact the development

effort. Their data sample is a "global dataset" that includes data from several research software projects conducted by different entities. We believe that the issue is related to contextual information that are not captured by the data and are related to the entities. Instead, our data are related to thousands of projects developed by quasi-independent development teams that use, for example, different programming languages and platforms (e.g., mobile, cloud, Web), adopt different internal processes, and are located in several countries and cities.

In another study, Menzies et al. [20] reassured the usefulness of static code attributes to learn defect predictors. They showed that naive Bayes machine learning methods outperform rule-based or decision tree learning methods and they showed, on the other hand, that the choice of learning methods used for defect predictions can be much more important than used attributes. Unlike this previous work, we use static code attributes to predict issue fix time and we use neural networks as additional method for prediction.

Following the objective to reduce effort for security inspection and testing, Shin et al. [21] used in their empirical study code complexity, code churn, and developer activity metrics obtained to predict vulnerable code locations with logistic regressions. They also used J48 decision trees, random forest, and Bayesian network classification techniques based on data obtained from two large-scale open-source projects using code characteristics and version control data. They found out that the combination of these metrics is effective in predicting vulnerable files. Nevertheless, they state that further effort is necessary to characterize differences between faults and vulnerabilities and to enhance prediction models. Unlike Shin et al., our empirical research focuses on predictions using system-based data to predict vulnerability fix time.

Hewett and Kijsanayothin [17] developed models for defect repair time prediction using seven different machine learning algorithms, e.g., decision trees and support vector machines. Their predictive models are based on a case study with data from a large medical software system. Similar to our approach they consider the whole repair time including all phases of a defect lifecycle. They use twelve defect attributes selected by domain experts for their estimations such as component, severity, start and end date, and phase. Unlike them we are interested in estimating vulnerability fix time not defect fix time.

In contrast to prior work, which often is based on open-source software, we estimate the vulnerability fix time based on an industrial case study of a major software development company, based on distinct datasets that include security issues before and after release and combine them with project and component-related data. Our objective is to identify the impacting strength of the factors on vulnerability fix time as well as to predict issue fix time in general.

3 Secure Software Development at SAP

To ensure a secure software development, SAP follows the SAP Security Development Lifecycle (S²DL). Figure 1 illustrates the main steps in this process, which is split into four phases: preparation, development, transition, and utilization.

To allow the necessary flexibility to adapt this process to the various application types (ranging from small mobile apps to large-scale enterprise resource-planning solutions) developed by SAP as well as the different software development styles and cultural differences in a worldwide distributed organization, SAP follows a two-staged security expert model:

1. a central security team defines the global security processes, such as the S²DL, provides security trainings, risk identification methods, offers security testing tools, or defines and implements the security response process;
2. local security experts in each development area/team are supporting the developers, architects, and product owners in implementing the S²DL and its supporting processes.

For this study, the *development* and *utilization* phases of the S²DL are the most important ones, as the activities carried out during these phases detect most of the vulnerabilities that need to be fixed:

- during the actual software development (in the steps *secure development* and *security testing*) vulnerabilities are detected, e.g., by using manual and automated as well as static and dynamic methods for testing application security [2, 22]. Most detected vulnerabilities are found during this step, i.e., most vulnerabilities are fixed in unreleased code (e.g., in newly developed code that is not yet used by customers);
- *security validation* is an independent quality control that acts as "first customer" during the transition from software development to release, i.e., security validation finds vulnerabilities after the code freeze (called correction close) and the actual release;

- *security response* handles issues reported after the release of the product, e.g., by external security researchers or customers.

If an issue is confirmed (e.g., by an analysis of a security expert), from a high-level perspective developers and their local security experts implement the following four steps: 1. analyze the issue, 2. design or select a recommended solution, 3. implement and test a fix, and 4. validate (e.g., by retesting the fixed solution) and release this fix. Of course, the details differ depending on the development model of the product team and, more importantly, depending on whether the issue is detected in code that is used by customers or not.

While the technical steps for fixing an issue are the same regardless of whether the issue is in released code or currently developed code, the organizational aspects differ significantly: For vulnerabilities in unreleased development code, detecting, confirming, and fixing vulnerabilities are lightweight process defined locally by the development teams. Vulnerabilities detected by security validation, e.g., after the code freeze, even if in unreleased code, involve much larger communication efforts across different organizations for explaining the actual vulnerabilities to development as well as ensuring that the vulnerability is fixed before the product is released to customers.

Fixing vulnerabilities in released code requires the involvement of yet more teams within SAP, as well as additional steps, e.g., for back-porting fixes to older releases and providing patches (called *SAP Security Notes*) to customers.

Let us have a closer look on how an externally reported vulnerability in a shipped software version is fixed: First, an external reporter (e.g., customer or independent security researcher) contacts the *security response team*, which assigns a case manager. The case manager is responsible for driving the decision if a reported problem is a security vulnerability that needs to be fixed, and for ensuring that the confirmed vulnerability is fixed and that a patch is released. After vulnerability is confirmed, the case manager contacts the development team and often also a dedicated maintenance team (called IMS) to ensure that a fix is developed and back-ported to all necessary older releases (according to SAP's support and maintenance contracts). The developed fixes are subject to a special security test by the security validation team and, moreover, the response

Fig. 1 Overview of the SAP Security Development Lifecycle (S²DL)

teams reviews the SAP Security Note. If the technical fix as well as the resulting Security Note passes the quality checks, the Security Note is made available to customers individually and/or in the form of a support package (usually on the first Tuesday of a month). Support packages are functional updates that also contain the latest security notes.

4 Background

Assume a response variable y and a set of independent variables x_i such that $y = f(x_1, x_2, \ldots, x_n)$ where f represents the systematic information that the variables x_i provide about y [23]. Regression models relate the *quantity* of a response factor, i.e., dependent variable to the independent variables.

Different regression models have different capabilities, e.g., in terms of their resistance to outliers, their fit for small datasets, and their fit for a large number of predicting factors [24]. However, in general, a regression model is assumed to be good, if it predicts responses close to the actual values observed in reality. In this study, the performance of a given model is judged by its prediction errors; the low are the errors, the better is the performance of the model.

This section provides background about the regression methods, model's performance metrics, and a metric for measuring the relative importance of the prediction factors used in the models.

4.1 Overview of Used Regression Methods

We give next an overview of the three methods used in this study.

Linear Regression This method assumes that the regression function is linear in the input [25], i.e., in the prediction factors. The linear method has the advantage of being simple and allows for an easy interpretation of the correlations between the input and output variables.

Tree-Based Regression This method recursively partitions the observations, i.e., the data records of the object being analyzed, for each of the prediction factors (aka features) such that it reduces the value of a metric that measures the information quantity of the splits [26]. In this study, we use the method *recursive partitioning and regression trees (RPART)* [27].

Neural Network Regression This method represents functions that are nonlinear in the prediction variables. It uses a multi-layer network that relates the input to the output through intermediate nodes. The output of each intermediate node is the sum of weighted input of the nodes of the previous layer. The data input is the first layer [28].

These three regression methods are the basic ones that are commonly used in data analytics. In this study, we use their implementations in packages for the statistics language R:[1] rpart[2] for RPART, and nnet[3] for NNR. The implementation "lm" of the linear regression (LR) is already contained within the core of R.

4.2 Model Performance Metrics

Regression methods infer prediction models from a given set of training data. Several metrics have been developed to compare the performance of the models in terms of accuracy of the generated predictions [29]. The metrics indicate how well the models predict accurate responses for future inputs. Next, we describe the three metrics that we used in this work, the coefficient of determination (R^2) [30], the Akaike information criterion (AIC) [29] and the prediction at a given level (PRED) [30].[4]

Coefficient of Determination (R^2) This metric "summarizes" how well the generated regression model fits the data. It computes the proportion of the variation of the response variable as estimated using the generated regression compared to the variation of the response variable computed using the null model, i.e., the mean of the values [29]. The following equation formulates the metric.

$$R^2 = 1 - \frac{\sum_{i=0}^{n} (x_i - \hat{x}_i)^2}{\sum_{i=0}^{n} (x_i - \bar{x})^2} \tag{1}$$

Here n is the number of observations, x_i is the actual value for observation i, $\hat{x}_i$ is the estimated value for observation i, and $\bar{x}$ is the mean of x_i values.

The LR method focuses on minimizing R^2. Thus, Spiess and Neumeyer, for example, consider that the metric is not appropriate for evaluating nonlinear regression models [32]. Nevertheless, the metric is often used to compare models, e.g., [29]. In this study, we use the metric to evaluate the performance of the prediction models in predicting the test dataset and not the training dataset. The metric provides a "summary" of the errors of the predictions.

Akaike Information Criterion This metric estimates the information loss when approximating reality. The following equation formulates the metric [29].

$$AIC = n \times log \left(\sum_{k=0}^{n} (x_i - \hat{x}_i)^2 / n \right) + 2(k + 2) \tag{2}$$

---

[1]　https://www.r-project.org/about.html.

[2]　https://cran.r-project.org/web/packages/rpart/rpart.

[3]　https://cran.r-project.org/web/packages/nnet/nnet.

[4]　We avoided the metric Mean of the Magnitude of the Relative Error (MMRE) as it was shown to be misleading [31].

Here n is the number of observations, x_i is the actual value for observation i, $\hat{x}_i$ is the estimated value for observation i, and k is the number of variables.

A smaller AIC value indicates a better model.

Prediction at a Given Level This metric computes the percentage of prediction falling within a threshold h [33]. The following equation formulates the metric

$$PRED(h) = \frac{100}{n} \times \sum_{i=1}^{n} \begin{cases} 1 & \text{if} \quad \dfrac{x_i - \hat{x}_i}{x_i} \leq h \\ 0 & \text{otherwise} \end{cases} \qquad (3)$$

Here n is the number of observations, x_i is the actual value for observation i, $\hat{x}_i$ is the estimated value for observation i, and h is the threshold, e.g., 25 %.

The perfect value for the PRED metric is 100 %.

4.3 Variable Importance

This metric measures the relative contributions of the different predicting factors used by the regression method to the response variable. For statistical use, such metric could be, for example, the statistical significance while for business use, the metric could be the "impact on the prediction factor" on the (dependent) response variable. In this work, we use the variable importance metric employed in the RPART regression method.[5] The metric measures the sum of the weighted reduction in the impurity method (e.g., the Shannon entropy and the variance of response variable) attributed to each variable [34, 35].[6] It associates scores with each variable, which can be used to rank the variables based on their contribution to the model.

5 Methodology

Figure 2 depicts the process that we used in this study; a process quite similar to the one used by Bener et al. [36]. First, we define the goal of the data analytics activity, which is to develop a function for predicting the issue fix time using the data that SAP collects on its processes for fixing vulnerabilities in pre-release and post-release software. The following steps are: collect data that could help achieve the goal; prepare the data to be used to derive insights using statistical methods; explore the collected datasets to understand the used coding scheme, its content, and the relationships between the data attributes; develop prediction models for each of the collected datasets; compute metrics on the model; and try to find explanations

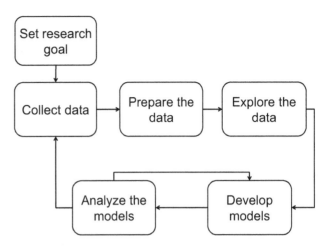

Fig. 2 Analysis method

and arguments for the results. The results of the models analysis were used to identify ways to improve the models. The improvements included the collection of new datasets for dependent information, e.g., about projects. We discuss next the individual steps in more details.

5.1 Data Collection

SAP maintains three datasets on fixing security vulnerabilities, which we refer to as our main *data sources*. In addition, it maintains a dataset about components, and a dataset about projects, which we call *support data*. Table 2 lists the different datasets we use. The datasets used in our study span over distinct time periods for each dataset (e.g., about 5 years).

The security testing process records data about fixing issues in two datasets. First, ABAP developers use SLINT for security code analysis. In Data source 1, the tool records data related to a set of attributes about each of the issues it discovers and the tasks performed on these issues. Table 3 lists these attributes.

Second, Java and JavaScript developers use Fortify[7] and C++ developers use Coverity to analyze software for security issues. In Data source 2, these tools record data related to a set of attributes about each of the vulnerabilities they discover and the tasks performed on these vulnerabilities. Table 4 lists these attributes.

In Data source 3, the security response process maintains data about fixing issues discovered in released software. The data are collected and maintained through a Web form; it is not collected automatically as in the case of Data sources 1 and 2. The attributes of this Data source are listed in Table 5.

---

[5] We use function `varImp()`.

[6] There are other methods for ranking variables. We choose this method, which comes with RPART, because most the variables are categorical.

[7] Since 2013, SAP uses Checkmarx for analyzing JavaScript. Thus, the use of Fortify by JavaScript developers declines since then.

Table 2 Datasets collected from SAP's tools

Dataset	Description
Data source 1	Vulnerabilities found in ABAP code
Data source 2	Vulnerabilities found in Java and C++ code
Data source 3	Security messages
Support data 1	Components
Support data 2	Projects
Extended data source 2	Extend data source 2 with information about the projects (support data 2)
Extended data source 3	Extend data source 3 with information about the components (support data 1)

Table 3 List of the attributes of ABAP issue fixing (Data source 1)

Attribute	Description
Date_found	Date on which the issue was found
Date_solved	Date on which the issue was closed
Vulnerability_name	Vulnerability types such as memory corruption and buffer overflow
Project_ID	Project identifier
Priority	The priority of fixing the vulnerability. Range: 1 to 4, with 1 highest, 4 lowest priority
Vulnerability_count	Number of issues of the same vulnerability found at once. This indicates that the issues might be related to the same problem

Table 4 List of the attributes of Java and C++ issue fixing (Data source 2)

Attribute	Description
Date_found	Date on which the issue was found
Date_solved	Date on which the issue was closed
Vulnerability_name	Vulnerability types such as memory corruption and buffer overflow
Scan_source	Tool that performed the scan, i.e., Coverity (for C++ code) or Fortify (for Java code)
Project_name	Project identifier
Folder_name	Indicates the required behavior of the developer toward the issue, e.g., must fix, fix one of the sets, optional, etc
Scan_status	Status of the issues, i.e., new, updated, removed, and reintroduced (i.e., removed but reopened). It allows to identify whether the issue is addressed or not, and is a false positive or not
Vulnerability_count	Number of issues of the same vulnerability found at once
Priority	The priority of fixing the vulnerability. Range: 1 to 4, with 1 highest and 4 lowest priority

Each issue can relate to a concrete component. Components are groups of applications that perform a common business goal. A system consists of a set of components. Table 6 lists the components attributes.

A software is developed in the context of a project. Table 7 lists the attribute of the projects dataset (Support data 2). We Extended data source 2 with project descriptions data; we joined Data source 2 and Support data 2. We also added three computed fields to the dataset:

1. FixtoRelease_period: The time elapsed from fixing the given issue to releasing the software.
2. Dev_period: The time elapsed from starting the development to closing the development of the software that contains the issue.
3. FoundtoRelease_period: The time elapsed from discovering the issue to the releasing of the software that contains the issue.

The number of records for each of the basic datasets ranges from thousands of records to hundred of thousands of records. We did not provide the exact numbers to avoid their misuse (in combination with potentially other public data) to derive statistics about vulnerabilities in SAP products, which would be outside the scope of this work.

5.2 Data Preparation

Using the collected data required us to prepare them for the model generation routines. The preparation activities

Table 5 List of the attributes for security messages (Data source 3)

Attribute	Description
CVSS_score	Common Vulnerability Scoring System (CVSS). The score indicates also the urgency of fixing the vulnerability
Processor	Identifier of development team/area and, thus, implicitly for the local instantiation of the S^2DL
Reporter	Identifier of the external researcher/company who reported the issue
Source	The source of the reported issue such as internal, security testing tool, customers
Vulnerability_type	Vulnerability type
Priority	Priority of the issue to be fixed: low, medium, or high
Component	Group of applications that perform a common business goal such as sales order or payroll

Table 6 List of the attributes for the components (support data 1)

Attribute	Description
PTU_area	The area of the component, e.g., CRM, IMS, ERP
Gr_component	Component group, i.e., semantic aggregation of components based on superordinate level
Language	The language(s) used to develop the component: ABAP, Java, ABAP and Java, or unknown
PPMS_product	The name of product that the component is part of, as stated in PPMS (Projects Management System)
Comp_owner	The component's development group
Product_owner	The product's development group

Table 7 List of the attributes for projects (support data 2)

Attribute	Description
Project_name	The name of the project (internal program name)
Prg_typ_id	Release related vs release unrelated (RR / UR)
Rel_type_id	Project type (standard, etc.)
Rel_typ_id	Release type ID (standard, pilot, etc.)
Delivery_mode_id	Mode of delivery to the customer. Values are on premise, on demand, on mobile, etc
Maintstrategy_id	Maintenance strategy. There is a codification for the strategies
Deploy_type	Deployment type. There is a codification for the deployment
D2t_date	Planned end of the test period. The period starts after the development closes
Devclose_date	Closing date of the development
P2d_date	Planned development starting date
P2r_date	Planned release date
Prg_lead_resp	Development team responsible for the project
Risk_expert	Identifier of risk expert (anonymized data)

required cleaning the data and transforming them as needed for processing.

Data Cleaning First, we identified the data columns where data are frequently missing. Missing values impact the results of the regression algorithms because these algorithms may incorrectly assume default values for the missing ones. We used plots such as the one in Fig. 3 to identify data columns that require attention.

Second, we developed a set of plots to check outliers—values that are far from the common range of the values of the attributes. We excluded data rows that include semantically wrong values, e.g., we removed records from

Data source 1 where the value of "Date_found" is 1 Dec. 0003.

Third, we excluded records related to issues that are not addressed yet; we cannot deduce issue fix time of such records.

Fourth, we excluded records that include invalid data. For example, the vulnerability type attribute of Data source 2 includes values such as "not assigned," "?," and "&novuln." The records that have these values are excluded. There is no interpretation of prediction results that include these values.

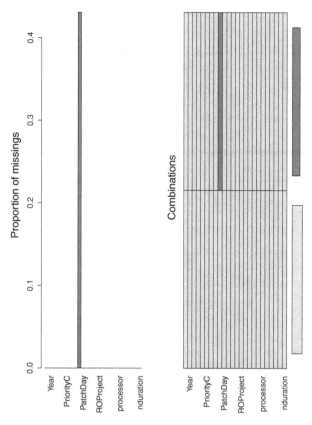

Fig. 3 Plot that visualizes missing data for Data source 3

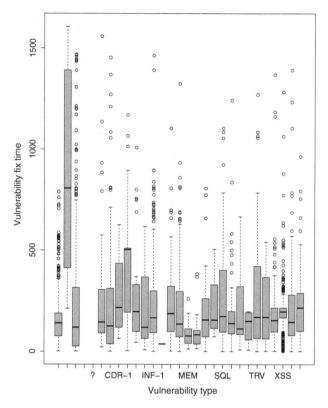

Fig. 4 Relationship between issue fix time (in days) and vulnerability types in the context of Data source 3. CDR-1, INF-1, MEM, SQL, TRV, XSS are internal codes for vulnerabilities types and code "?" indicates unknown or uncategorized type of reported vulnerabilities. (Some vulnerability types do not appear on the X axis to ensure clarity)

Fifth, we excluded non-useful data attributes. These include, for example, the case where the attribute is derived from other attributes considered in the models.

Data Transformation First, we transformed the data of some columns from type text to appropriate types. For instance, we transformed the data of the CVSS column to numeric. Next, we computed new data columns from the source (original) data. For example, we computed the issue fix time from the issue closing date and issue discovery date or we performed some attributes' value transformations to obtain machine readable data for model generation. Some attributes contain detailed information that reduces the performance of the regression algorithms. We addressed this issue by developing a good level of data aggregation for the prediction algorithm. For example, the original dataset included 511 vulnerability types. We grouped the vulnerabilities types in vulnerability categories, which helps to derive better prediction models. Also, we aggregated the "component" variable to obtain "Gr_component" to include in our regression.

5.3 Data Exploration

We developed a set of plots and statistics about the frequencies of values for the factors and the relationship between the issue fix time and some of the prediction factors. For example, Fig. 4 shows the relationship between the issue fix time in days and vulnerability type. This gives us a first impression of the relations among the attributes of a given dataset. Also, Table 8 shows the coefficients of the linear regression (LR) of the issue fix time using the factor message source, that identifies the source of the reported issue. The table shows that the coefficients in this categorical factor indicate the different contributions of the factor on the issue fix time. The results indicate different impacting strengths of the different sources of security messages (e.g., external parties, customers, or the security department) on the issue fix time.

5.4 Models Development

We partitioned each prepared Data source into a training set that includes 80 % of the data and a test set (used to validate the developed model) that includes the remaining 20 %.[8] We used the training set to develop the prediction

---
[8] We used 80 % of the data for developing the prediction models and not 60 % of the data because the size of Extended data source 3 is limited: 380 records. (We wanted to use the same ratio for all datasets.)

Table 8 Coefficients of the linear regression of issue fix time to security message dataset (Data source 3)

Message source	Coefficient	p value
(Intercept)	249.17	<0.001
Code scan tool	−50.04	<0.001
Central security department	−38.05	<0.001
Customers	−60.68	<0.001
External research organizations	−102.78	<0.001
Internal development departments	−12.21	0.304
Test services	−124.74	<0.001
Validation services	−21.88	0.136

models, or fits, and the test set to assess the goodness of the generated models. The selection of the records for both sets is random.

Next, we performed three operations for each of the main data sources. First, we generated three prediction models using the training set, one using the linear regression method, one using the RPART method, and one using the NNR method. The three data sources have different data attributes and cannot be combined. Thus, we cannot use them together to develop a generic prediction model.

5.5 Models Analysis

We used the variable importance metric described in Sect. 4.3 to assess the impact of the different prediction factors on the issue fix time for each of the three data sources. The metric indicates that the factor "project name" is very important for Data source 2 and the factor "component" is very important for Data source 3. The results and their appropriateness were discussed with the security experts at SAP. We Extended data source 2 with Support data 2 (i.e., projects dataset) and we Extended data source 3 with Support data 1 (i.e., components dataset). Next, we performed the model development phase (Sect. 5.4) using the extended datasets. Then, we used each of the prediction models to predict the issue fix time for the test dataset and computed the performance metrics (see Sect. 4.2) for each model. We discuss the results in the next section.

6 Study Results

This section discusses the developed prediction models addressing issue fix time and their performance, the relative importance of the prediction factors, and the evolution of mean vulnerability fix time over time.

6.1 Issue Fix Time Prediction Models

This section aims to address the question: How well do the chosen models (LR, RPART, and NNR) predict the issue fix time from a set of given factors?

Most of the data that we use are not numeric; they are categorical variables, e.g., vulnerability types and component IDs. The number of categories in each of these variables can be very high. For instance, there are about 2300 components. This makes the prediction models large, e.g., in the order of a couple of hundred of nodes for the tree-based model and few thousands for the neural network model. This problem of large sets for the categorical factors limits the ability to generate accurate prediction models.

The regression algorithms cluster the elements of the categorical variables automatically; this clustering does not follow a given semantics, such as aggregation on superordinate component level, i.e., "Gr_component" in Support data 1. Because of this, it is impractical to plot the prediction models. Figure 5, for instance, shows a prediction model that we generated from Data source 3 by using the RPART method. The big number of (categorical) values for many of the prediction variables makes visualizing the generated models clearly difficult.

Interestingly, we observe that the component factor is built upon a set of distinct component classes (i.e., the first three digits indicate the superordinate component level, e.g., CRM for customer relationship management). An investigation of underlying reasons for such clustering might reveal, e.g., coherence with process-related factors.

6.2 Performance of Selected Regression Methods on the Prediction of Issue Fix Time

This subsection addresses the question: Which of the developed regression models gives the most accurate predictions? It reports and discusses the measurements of the performance metrics (introduced in Sect. 4.2) that we performed on the models that we generated for predicting the issue fix time. Table 9 summarizes the measurements that we obtained.

Coefficient of Determination Metric We observe that the LRs method outperforms the RPART and NNR methods for the five datasets. The metric values indicate that the prediction models generated using LR explain about half of the variation of the real values for Data source 1 and for Data source 2 and explains most of the variations for the remaining data sources. Indeed, the estimates of the model for the Extended data source 2 perfectly match the observed values. We note also that the residues metric values indicate that the prediction models generated using

84) vulnerabilitytype=,&OTHER,ACI-1,CDR-1,INF-1,MAC-1,MEM,XSS,XS
S-2 270 5063771.00 286.53700

    168) Component=AP-RC-ANA-UI-XLS,BC-BSP,BC-CST-DP,BC-C
ST-IC,BC-CTS-SDM,BC-CTS-TMS,BC-DOC-HLP,BC-DOC-TTL,BC-I18,BC
-JAS-ADM-MON,BC-JAS-DPL,BC-SEC,BC-SEC-DIR,BC-SRV-ARL,BC-SR
V-FSI,BC-UPG-SLM,BC-UPG-TLS-TLJ,BC-WD-CMP-FPM,BC-XI-CON-AX
S,BC-XI-IBD,BC-XI-IBF,BI-BIP-AUT,BI-OD-STW,BI-RA-WBI,BW-BEX-OT-
MDX,CA-GTF-IC-BRO,CA-GTF-IC-SCR,CA-GTF-RCM,CRM-BF,CRM-BF-
SVY,CRM-CIC,CRM-IC-EMS,CRM-IC-FRW,CRM-IPS-BTX-APL,CRM-ISA,
CRM-ISA-AUC,CRM-ISE,CRM-LAM-BF,CRM-MD-PRO,CRM-MKT-DAM,C
RM-MKT-MPL,CRM-MSA,FS-CM,FS-SR,IS-A-DP,IS-U-CS-ISS,LO-AB-BS
P,LO-GT,MFG-ME,MOB-APP-EMR-AND,PA-GE,PLM-PPM-PDN,PLM-WUI
-RCP,PSM-CPR-SN,SBO-INT-B1ISN,SCM-EWM-RF,XAP-IC-IDM,XX-PRO
J-CDP-TEST-296 119 1015233.00 205.82350 *

    169) Component=AP-CFG,AP-LM-MON-HC,AP-LM-SUP,AP-RC-
ANA-RT-MDA,AP-RC-RSP,AP-RC-UIF-RT,AP-SDM-EXC,BC-CCM-MON-
OS,BC-CCM-SLD-JAV,BC-CST,BC-CUS-TOL-CST,BC-DB-ORA-INS,BC-D
OC-TER,BC-ESI-WS-ABA,BC-ESI-WS-JAV-RT,BC-FES-BUS-RUN,BC-JA
S-ADM-ADM,BC-JAS-COR,BC-JAS-SEC-UME,BC-MID-RFC,BC-SEC-SA
L,BC-SRV-COM,BC-SRV-COM-FTP,BC-SRV-KPR-CS,BC-SRV-MCM,BC-
SRV-SSF,BC-WD-ABA,BC-WD-

Fig. 5 Part of the prediction model generated from Data source 3 using RPART method. (It shows that there is a long list of component IDs (among a set of about 2300 components) for the selection of nodes 168 and 169 while also the parent node uses a set of vulnerability types)

the NNR perform worse than the null model, that is, taking the average of the values.

AIC Metric We observe that the LR method outperforms the RPART and NNR methods for two datasets and that the RPART method outperforms the LR and NNR methods for the remaining three datasets. Thus, this metric gives mixed results with respect to performance of the three regression methods.

PRED Metric We observe that the LR method outperforms the RPART and NNR methods for two datasets, the RPART method outperforms the LR and NNR methods for

one dataset, and the NNR method outperforms the RPART and LR methods for two datasets. This gives mixed results with respect to performance of the three regression methods. However, the NNR performance improves when the dataset is extended with related data. For instance, the PRED value increased from 0.73 % in the case of Data source 3–65.05 % for the case of the Extended data source 3. We acknowledge that the PRED value improved also for the LR method for the case of Data source 2 and Extended data source 2. However, the number of records (N) for the Extended data source 2 is low ($N = 380$); the result should be taken with caution.

Different regression methods have shown conflicting performance measurements toward the problem of effort estimation. For example, Gray and MacDonell [24] compared a set of regression approaches using MMRE and PRED metrics. The methods have shown conflicting results; their rank change based on the used performance metrics. For example, they found that based on the MMRE metric, LR outperforms NNR and based on the PRED metric, NNR outperforms LR. This finding was confirmed by Wen et al. [37] who analyzed the performance of several other regression methods. The regression methods have different strengths and weaknesses. Most importantly, they perform differently in the presence of small datasets, outliers, categorical factors, and missing values. We found in this study that it is not possible to claim that a regression method is better than the other in the context of predicting the issue fix time. This result supports the findings of Gray and MacDonell [24] and of Wen et al. [37].

Table 9 Measurement of the performance metrics of the prediction models

Dataset	LR	RPART	NN	Best method
Residuals metric				
Data source 1	0.526	0.498	−1.252	LR (0.526)
Data source 2	0.461	0.44	−0.294	LR (0.461)
Extended data source 2	1	0.956	−0.587	LR (1)
Data source 3	0.944	0.6585	1.944	LR (0.944)
Extended data source 3	0.909	0.701	1.97	LR (0.909)
AIC metric				
Data source 1	122,465	123,157	141,462	LR (122,465)
Data source 2	334,565	335,936	365,665	LR (334,565)
Extended data source 2	−4877	463	793	RPART (463)
Data source 3	6632	6507	6958	RPART (6507)
Extended data source 3	6581	6421	7057	RPART (6421)
PRED metric				
Data source 1	31.81 %	31.74 %	0.156 %	LR (31.81 %)
Data source 2	14.93 %	13.96 %	33.81 %	NN (33.81 %)
Extended data source 2	100 %	30.32 %	39.40 %	LR (100 %)
Data source 3	33.98 %	34.71 %	0.73 %	RPART (34.71 %)
Extended data source 3	35.41 %	34.52 %	65.05 %	NN (65.05 %)

Table 10 Importance factors for the main datasets

Factor	Data source 1		Data source 2		Data source 3	
Rank	Factor	Metric	Factor	Metric	Factor	Metric
1	Project_ID	0.408	Scan_status	1.231	Component	3.653
2	Vulnerability_name	0.179	Project_name	0.956	Processor	3.352
3	Vulnerability_count	0.097	Vulnerability_name	0.841	Reporter	1.813
4	Priority	0.042	Folder_name	0.522	Vulnerability_type	0.879
5			Scan_source	0.238	Source	0.443
6			Priority	0.358	CVSS_score	0.230
7			Vulnerability_count	0.078		

6.3 Relative Importance of the Factors Contributing to Issue Fix Time

This section aims to address the question: What are the main factors that impact the issue fix time? To answer this question, we computed the variable importance metric (see Sect. 4.3) for each factors [38]. Given that the factors used in the datasets are different, we present, and shortly discuss, each dataset separately, and we used the variable importance metric discussed in Subsection 4.3 to compute the importance of each factor.

Data source 1 Table 10 reports the importance of the factors used in Data source 1 on issue fix time. The most important factor in this dataset is "Project_ID," followed by "Vulnerability_name." This implies that there is a major contribution of the project characteristics to issue fix time. Unfortunately, there were no additional metadata available on the projects that could have been joined with Data source 1 to allow us to further investigate aspects of projects that impact the fixing time.

Data source 2 Table 10 reports the importance of the factors used in Data source 2 on issue fix time. The most important factor in this dataset is "Scan_status." This shows that depending on whether the issue is false positive or not impacts the issue fix time.[9] The second ranking factor is "Project_name," followed by "Vulnerability_name." This results support the observation we had with Data source 1. We observe also that the factor "Scan_source," which indicates the static code analysis tool used to discover the vulnerabilities (i.e., Fortify or Coverity) is ranked at place 5.

Extended data source 2 We Extended data source 2 with data that describe the projects and computed three additional variables: the time elapsed between fixing the vulnerability and releasing the software, called FixtoRelease_period; the development period, called Dev_period; and the time elapsed between discovering the vulnerability and releasing the software, called FoundtoRelease_period.

Table 11 reports the importance of the factors used in the Extended data source on issue fix time. We observe that the most important factor is FixRelease_period while a related factor, FoundtoRelease_period has less importance (rank 6). The other main important factors include the development period (Dev_period), the project (Project_name), the risk expert (Risk_expert), the project development team (Prg_lead_resp), and the vulnerability name (Vulnerability_name). We observe that vulnerability name is ranked at the seventh position.

Data source 3 Table 10 reports the importance of the factors used in Data source 3 on the issue fix time. The most important factor in this dataset is the software component that needs to be changed (Component) followed by the development team who addresses the issue (Processor). We observe that the vulnerability name (Vulnerability_type) has a moderate importance, ranked 4th, while the CVSS (CVSS_score) is ranked on the sixth position.

Extended data source 3 We Extended data source 3 with data that describe the components. Table 11 reports the importance of the factors used in the Extended data source 3 on the issue fix time. The most important factors in this extended dataset is the component (Component), followed by the development team (Processor), the development team responsible for the component (Dev_comp_owner), the reporter of the vulnerability (Reporter), and a set of other factors. We observe that the vulnerability name (Vulnerability_type) has a moderate importance, ranked eighth, and the CVSS score (CVSS_score) decreased considerably to be 0.

6.4 Evolution of the Issue Fix Time

This section aims to address the question: Is the company improving in fixing security issues? The tendency of the issue fix time could be used as "indicator" of such improvement. For instance, increasing time indicates deteriorating capabilities and decreasing time indicates improving capabilities. The information should not be used as an evidence but as indicator of a fact that requires further investigation.

---

[9] As indicated before, issues marked as, e.g., new and updated are not considered in the models; they are for issues that are not addressed yet.

Table 11 Importance factors for the extended datasets

Rank	Extended data source 2		Extended data source 3	
	Factor	Metric	Factor	Metric
1	FixtoRelease_period	0.946	Component	2.434
2	Dev_period	0.634	Processor	2.363
3	Project_name	0.634	Dev_comp_owner	1.380
4	Risk_expert	0.634	Reporter	1.207
5	Prg_lead_resp	0.672	Dev_product_owner	0.633
6	FoundtoRelease_period	0.433	PPMS_product	0.407
7	Vulnerability_name	0.429	PTU_area	0.407
8	Priority	0.045	Vulnerability_type	0.058
9	Vulnerability_count	0.045		
10	Folder_name	0.045		

We modeled the evolution of the mean issue fix time for the resolving (closing) issue month[10] for the three data sources using the LR, which shows the trend of the response variable over time. Figure 6 depicts, respectively, the mean issue fix time for (a) Data source 1 (pre-release ABAP-based code), (b) Data source 2 (pre-release Java, C++, and JavaScript-based code), and (c) Data source 3 (post-release security issues).

The figure indicates a fluctuation of the mean issue fix time but with an increasing trend. This trend indicates a deteriorating performance with respect to fixing security issues. A close look at the figure shows that there is a recent reverse in the tendency, which indicates a response to specific events such as dedicated quality releases or the development of new flag ship products. So-called quality releases are releases that focus on improving the product quality instead of focusing on new features. To ensure a high level of product quality and security of SAP products, top-level managements plans, once in a while, for such quality releases. Also the development of new flagship products that change the development focus of a large fraction of all developers at SAP can have an influence. Such a shift might result in significant code simplifications of the underlying frameworks.

Figure 6 shows that the increasing global trend applies to pre-release as well as post-release issues. We believe that this indicates that the causes of the increase in the mean issue fix time apply to both cases. We again see that the management actions impacted both cases.

Berner et al. [36] advise that models are sensitive to time. This work supports the claim because it shows that the issue fix time is sensitive to the month of closing the issue.

7 Analysis of the Impacting Factors

We observe from Data source 1 and Data source 2 that projects (represented by, e.g., Project_ID, and Project_name data attributes) have major contributions to issue fix time for the case of pre-release issue fixing. The extension of Data source 2 with project-related data confirmed our observation: the most impacting factors of pre-release issues on the time to fix are project characteristics. Among these characteristics, we find the time between issue fixing and software release, project development duration, and the development team (data attribute Project_name). We believe that the factor time between issue fixing and software release indicates that developers tend to fix vulnerabilities as the release date becomes close. This is not surprising, since they must address all open issues before the software can pass the quality gate to be prepared for release. We expect that the factor project development duration is related to, e.g., the used development models, and the component-related characteristics. Further data analysis shall provide insights about the impact of the factors related to the project development duration (Dev_period), such as component complexity. For instance, updating smaller component could be easy and be performed in short development cycles while updating complex components requires long development cycles. In addition, we believe that the factor development team (Processor) indicates the level of expertise of the developers and the smoothness of communication and collaboration among the team. Nevertheless, it is interesting to observe that the influence of vulnerability type decreases when project-related factors are included.

There are two additional dominant factors for the issue fix time, based on the analysis of Data source 2: scan status and folder name. We believe that the factor scan status indicates that the developers address issues based on their perception of whether the given issue is a false positive or

---

[10] Compute the mean issue fix time for the vulnerabilities resolved (addressed) in the specified month.

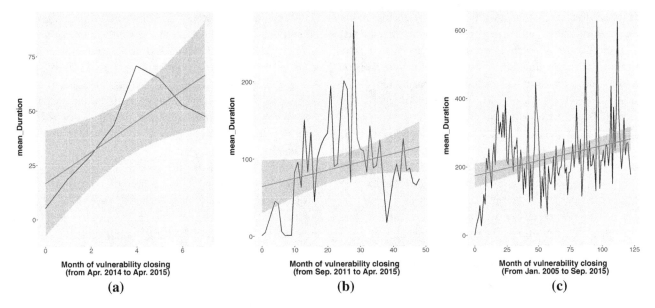

Fig. 6 Trend of the issue fix effort by closing month. The *x* axis indicates the number of months elapsed since the start date of the data. The *y* axis indicates the mean issue fix time in number of days. **a** Data source 1. **b** Data source 2. **c** Data source 3

not and whether it is easy to address or not. For example, they may close false positive issues that are easy to analyze and postpone addressing issues that are difficult to analyze and/or fix to, e.g., when the time for the quality gates becomes close. We also expect that the factor "folder name" indicates that the developers behave differently toward issues flagged must fix, fix one of the sets, or optional to fix.

The analysis of Data source 2 reveals that the security scan tools (represented by the data attribute Scan_source) are not a leading factor of issue fix time. It is possible that the developers rely on their expertise in analyzing security issues and not on the tool features as they get experts in addressing security issues. Further analysis may explain the finding better.

The results obtained from the analysis of Data source 3 (and its extension) suggest that the software structure and development team characteristics are the dominant factors that impact the issue fix time for the case of post-release issue fixing. (Note that issues for post-release are not related to projects but to released components.). The analysis results show that the component factor is among the most impacting factors on the issue fix time, which indicates the impact of software structure characteristics. Unfortunately, we do not have, at this moment, data that describe the components, such as the component's complexity, which could be used to get detailed insights about these characteristics.

The results obtained from the analysis of Data source 3 shows the dominance of the impact of processor and reporter on the issue fix time and thus the importance of human-related factors. The importance of the reporter

factor is aligned with the results of Hooimeijer and Weimer [39], who found a correlation between a bug reporter's reputation and triaging time: We confirm the importance of the reporting source on vulnerability fix time. Unlike Zhang et al. [18] finding, we found that severity, represented by the "CVSS_score" in our study, is not a leading factor.

The qualitative study [4], which was based on expert interviews at SAP, revealed several factors that impact the issue/vulnerability fix time, such as communication and collaboration issues, experience and knowledge of the involved developers and security coordinators, and technology diversification. The results of this study confirm the impact of some of these factors and show their importance. For example, the category technology diversification included factors related to technologies and libraries supported by the components associated with the given vulnerability. The impact of the component, found in our current study, reflects these underlying factors. Unfortunately, it was only possible to relate components' attributes to security messages, i.e., post-release issues, not to pre-release issues to further investigate the components' impact on these. The impact of the development groups reflects the importance of the experience and vulnerability- and software-related knowledge of the teams as well as the importance of the smoothness of communication and collaboration between the involved stakeholders.

At SAP, the project development teams work independently; e.g., they choose their own development model and tools, as long as they confirm to the corporate requirements, such as the global security policies. Further investigation of component-, project-, human-, and process-related characteristics of the development teams might reveal more insights on the underlying factors that impact the issue fix time. Such investigation may reveal why certain products/teams are more efficient than others. Reasons may, for example, include the local setup of the communication structures, the used development model (i.e., SCRUM, DevOps.) and the security awareness of teams. Another potential factor to check its impact is the number of people involved in fixing the given issue. This factor was found to impact the fix time of bugs [15, 40]. Controlling these factors allows to control the issue fix time and thus the cost of addressing security issues.

A question worth also investigating is: Are the factors that impact the time for addressing pre-release and post-release issues similar? We argue in Sect. 3 that the processes for fixing pre- and post-release issues are different, which shall impact the issue fix time for both cases. Nevertheless, acquiring evidence to answer this question requires using the same data attributes for both cases, which may not be possible, at the moment, with data collected at SAP.

8 Study Validity and Impacts

This section discusses the impacts of the finding and the limitations of the study.

8.1 Impacts of the Findings

This study showed that the models generated using the LR, RPART, and NNR methods have conflicting accuracy measurements in predicting the issue fix time. This implies that the conflict in the performance measurements in estimating software development effort, e.g., in [37], applies to security issues. We infer from this result that there is no better regression method, from the analyzed ones, when it comes to predicting security issue time. We believe that more work needs to be done to develop regression methods appropriate for predicting issue fix time.

The second main finding of this study is that vulnerability type is not the dominant impacting factors for issue fix time. Instead, the dominant factors are the component in which the vulnerability resides, the project related to the issue, the development groups that address the issue, and the closeness of the software release date, which are process-related information. This result implies that we should focus on the impact of software structure, developers' expertise and knowledge, and secure software development process when investigating ways to reduce the cost of fixing issues.

The third main finding is that the monthly mean issue fix time changes with the issue closing month. We can infer

from this result that the prediction models are time sensitive; that is, they depend on the data collection period. This supports Berner et al. advice to consider recently collected data when developing prediction models [36]. We infer, though, that prediction models are not sufficient for modeling issue fix time since they provide a static view. We believe that prediction methods should be extended to consider time evolution, that is, combine prediction and forecasting.

Finally, SAP can use the models to implement a continuous improvement of its secure software development process and to measure the impact of individual improvements. Other companies can use similar models and mechanism to realize a learning organization.

8.2 Limitations

There is a consensus among the community that there are many "random" factors involved in software development that may impact the results of data analytics experiments [36]. This aligned with Menzies et al.'s [19] findings about the necessity to be careful about generalization of results related to effort estimations in a global context.

The data analysis described in this report suffers from the two common threats to validity that apply to effort estimation [20]. First, the conclusions are based on the data that SAP collects about fixing vulnerabilities in its software. Changes to the data collection processes, such as changes to the attributes of the collected data, could impact the predictions and the viability of producing predictions in the first place. Second, the conclusions of this study are based on the regression methods we used, i.e., LR, RPART, and NNR. There are many other single and ensemble regression methods that we did not experiment with. We note that performance issues due to the size of the datasets inhibit us from using random forest [23] and boosting [23], two ensemble regression methods.

In addition, the data are collected over 5 years. During that time SAP refined and enhanced its secure software development processes. This could bias our results. The identification of major process changes along with the times of the changes and a partitioning of the data accordingly might reduce such bias and reveal measurable insights about impacts of process changes on issue fix time.

On the positive side, the conclusions are not biased by the limited data size and the subjectivity in the responses. First the number of records of each of the dataset was high enough to derive meaningful statistics. Second, the data are generated automatically and do not include subjective opinions, except the CVSS score of Data source 3. This score is generated based on issue-related information that is assessed by the security coordinator responsible for the issue.

Our findings are based on particular datasets of SAP and might mirror only the particularities of time to fix issues for this organization. However, SAP has a diversified software portfolio, the development teams are highly independent in using development processes and tools (as long as they follow generic guidelines such as complying with corporate security requirements), teams are located in different countries, and software are developed using several programming languages (e.g., ABAP, C++, and Java). These characteristics encourage us to believe that the findings apply to industrial companies in general and therefore contribute to the discussion about predicting the issue fix time.

Vulnerabilities, such as SQL injection, cross-site scripting (XSS), buffer overflow, and directory path traversal are commonly identified using the same techniques, such as taint analysis [41], but by applying different patterns. This may explain why vulnerability type is not a dominant factor of issue fix time—because the time to analyze many of the vulnerability types using the techniques is the same. These techniques may be used to detect other defect types besides vulnerabilities, but not all (or most) defects. Thus, the fact that vulnerability type is not a dominant factor of issue fix time does not imply that the study results apply to defects in general.

9 Lessons Learned

Data analytics methods are helpful tools to make generalizations about past experience [36]. These generalizations require considering the context of the data being used. In our study, we learned few lessons in this regard.

Anonymization Companies prefer to provide anonymized data for data analytics experiments and keep the anonymization map to trace the results to the appropriate semantics. There is a believe that the analyst would develop models and the data expert (from the company) would interpret them using the anonymization map. We initially applied the technique and we found that it prevents the analyst from even cleaning the data correctly. We worked closely with the owner of the data to understand them, interpret the results, and correct or improve the models. The better the data analyst understands the data, the more they are able to model them.

Prediction Using Time Series Data We initially sliced the data sequentially into folds (sliced them based on their order in the dataset) and used the cross-validation method in the regression.[11] We found that the performance metrics of the generated prediction models deviate considerably.

---

[11] This slicing method allows for easily splitting all the data among the folds.

Table 12 Predicted values for automatically clustered component factor and Gr_component

Error metric	LR		RPART		NNR	
	AC	MC	AC	MC	AC	MC
RSQ	0.98	0.76	0.80	0.7045	2.02	1.92
AIC	6586	6187	6461	6139	7033	6733
PRED	33.88	34.12	33.48	32.6915	0.48	0.67

AC is for automatic clustering of components and MC is for manual clustering of components

To explore this further, we developed the tendency of the mean issue fix time shown in Fig. 6. The figure shows a fluctuation of the issue fix time over time. This leads to believe that the prediction models are of temporal relevance as claimed by Berner et al. [36]. The lesson warns to check whether the data are time series or not when using cross-validation with sequential slicing of the data in the regression.

A more generic lesson that we learned concerns *attribute values clustering*. We found in this study an insignificant small difference in the performance of the prediction models that automatically cluster components and the ones that use semantically clustered components instead. The latter aggregates components based on a semantic based on superordinate level, i.e., Gr_component. Manual investigation is necessary to infer the component characteristics that the algorithms silently used in the clustering. Table 12, for example, shows that the performance of the prediction models using the automated clustering and using the manual clustering are similar. This implies that manual clustering does not provide additional information.

10 Conclusions

We developed in this study prediction models for issue fix time using data that SAP, one of the largest software vendors worldwide, and the largest in Germany, collects about fixing security issues in the software development phase and also after release. The study concludes that none of the regression methods that we used (linear regression (LR), Recursive PARTitioning (RPART), Neural Network Regression (NNR)) outperforms the others in the context of predicting issue fix time. Second, it shows that vulnerability type does not have a strong impact on the issue fix time. In contrast, the development groups involved in processing the issue, the component, the project, and the closeness of the release date have strong impact on the issue fix time.

We also investigated in this study the evolution of the mean issue fix time as time progresses. We found that the issue fix time fluctuates over time. We suggest that better models for predicting issue fix time should consider the temporal aspect of the prediction models; they shall combine both prediction technique and forecasting techniques.

Acknowledgments This work was supported by SAP SE, the BMBF within EC SPRIDE, the Scientific and Economic Excellence in Hesse (LOEWE), and a Fraunhofer Attract grant.

References

1. McGraw, G.: Software security: building security. In: Addison-Wesley software security series. Pearson Education Inc, Boston (2006)
2. Bachmann R, Brucker AD (2014) Developing secure software: a holistic approach to security testing. Datenschutz und Datensicherheit (DuD) 38:257–261
3. Howard M, Lipner S (2006) The security development lifecycle: SDL—a process for developing demonstrably more secure software. Microsoft Press
4. ben Othmane L, Chehrazi G, Bodden E, Tsalovski P, Brucker A, Miseldine P (2015) Factors impacting the effort required to fix security vulnerabilities. In: Proceedings of information security conference (ISC 2015), Trondheim, Norway, pp 102–119
5. Zimmermann T, Nagappan N, Williams L (2010) Searching for a needle in a haystack: predicting security vulnerabilities for windows vista. In: Proceedings of the 2010 third international conference on software testing, verification and validation, Washington, DC, pp 421–428
6. Shin Y, Williams L (2013) Can traditional fault prediction models be used for vulnerability prediction? Empir Softw Eng 18:25–59
7. Morrison P, Herzig K, Murphy B, Williams L (2015) Challenges with applying vulnerability prediction models. In: Proceedings of the 2015 symposium and bootcamp on the science of security, pp 4:1–4:9
8. Keller H, Krüger S (2007) ABAP objects. SAP Press
9. Chehrazi G, Schmitz C, Hinz O (2015) QUANTSEC—ein modell zur nutzenquantifizierung von it-sicherheitsmaßnahmen. In: Smart enterprise engineering: 12. Internationale Tagung Wirtschaftsinformatik, WI 2015, Osnabrück, Germany, March 4–6, 2015. pp 1131–1145
10. Cornell D (2012) Remediation statistics: what does fixing application vulnerabilities cost? In: RSAConference, San Fransisco, CA
11. Zeng H, Rine D (2004) Estimation of software defects fix effort using neural networks. In: Proceedings of the 28th annual international computer software and applications conference (COMPSAC 2004), vol 2, Hong Kong, China, pp 20–21
12. Weiss C, Premraj R, Zimmermann T, Zeller A (2007) How long will it take to fix this bug? In: Proceedings of the fourth international workshop on mining software repositories. MSR '07, Washington, DC, p 1
13. Panjer LD (2007) Predicting eclipse bug lifetimes. In: Proceedings of the fourth international workshop on mining software repositories. MSR '07, Washington, DC, IEEE Computer Society, p 29
14. Bhattacharya P, Neamtiu I (2011) Bug-fix time prediction models: can we do better? In: Proceedings of the 8th working conference on mining software repositories. MSR '11, ACM, New York, NY, pp 207–210
15. Giger E, Pinzger M, Gall H (2010) Predicting the fix time of bugs. In: Proceedings of the 2nd international workshop on recommendation systems for software engineering. RSSE '10, ACM, New York, NY, pp 52–56
16. Hamill M, Goseva-Popstojanova K (2014) Software faults fixing effort: analysis and prediction. Technical Report 20150001332, NASA Goddard Space Flight Center, Greenbelt, MD USA
17. Hewett R, Kijsanayothin P (2009) On modeling software defect repair time. Empir Softw Eng 14:165–186
18. Zhang F, Khomh F, Zou Y, Hassan A (2012) An empirical study on factors impacting bug fixing time. In: 19th Working conference on reverse engineering (WCRE), Kingston, Canada, pp 225–234
19. Menzies T, Butcher A, Marcus A, Zimmermann T, Cok D (2011) Local versus global models for effort estimation and defect prediction. In: Proceedings of the 2011 26th IEEE/ACM international conference on automated software engineering. ASE '11, Washington, DC, pp 343–351
20. Menzies T, Greenwald J, Frank A (2007) Data mining static code attributes to learn defect predictors. IEEE Trans Softw Eng 33:2–13
21. Shin Y, Meneely A, Williams L, Osborne J (2011) Evaluating complexity, code churn, and developer activity metrics as indicators of software vulnerabilities. IEEE Trans Softw Eng 37:772–787
22. Brucker AD, Sodan U (2014) Deploying static application security testing on a large scale. In: GI Sicherheit 2014, vol 228 of lecture notes in informatics, pp 91–101
23. James G, Witten D, Hastie T, Tibshirani R (2013) An introduction to statistical learning with applications in R. Springer, New York
24. Gray AR, MacDonell SG (1997) A comparison of techniques for developing predictive models of software metrics. Inf Softw Technol 39:425–437
25. Hastie T, Tibshirani R, Friedman J (2013) The elements of statistical learning, 2nd edn. Springer, Berlin
26. Menzies T (2013) Data mining: a tutorial. In: Robillard MP, Maalej W, Walker RJ, Zimmermann T (eds) Recommendation systems in software engineering. Springer, Berlin, pp 39–75
27. Breiman L, Friedman J, Stone CJ, Olshen R (1984) Classification and regression trees. Chapman and Hall/CRC, Belmont
28. Specht DF (1991) A general regression neural network. IEEE Trans Neural Netw 2:568–576
29. Hyndman R, Athanasopoulos G (2014) Forecasting: principles and practice. Otexts
30. Menzies EKT, Mendes E (2015) Transfer learning in effort estimation, empirical software engineering. Empir Softw Eng 20:813–843
31. Foss T, Stensrud E, Kitchenham B, Myrtveit I (2003) A simulation study of the model evaluation criterion mmre. IEEE Trans Softw Eng 29:985–995
32. Spiess ANN, Neumeyer N (2010) An evaluation of R2 as an inadequate measure for nonlinear models in pharmacological and biochemical research: a Monte Carlo approach. BMC Pharmacol 10:6
33. Kocaguneli E, Menzies T, Keung J (2012) On the value of ensemble effort estimation. IEEE Trans Softw Eng 38:1403–1416
34. Louppe G, Wehenkel L, Sutera A, Geurts P (2013) Understanding variable importances in forests of randomized trees. In: Burges C, Bottou L, Welling M, Ghahramani Z, Weinberger K (eds) Advances in neural information processing systems, vol 26, pp 431–439

35. Eisenhardt KM (1989) Building theories from case study research. Acad Manag Rev 14:532–550
36. Bener A, Misirli A, Caglayan B, Kocaguneli E, Calikli G (2015) Lessons Learned from software analytics in practice. In: The art and science of analyzing software data, 1st edn. Elsevier, Waltham, pp 453–489
37. Wen J, Li S, Lin Z, Hu Y, Huang C (2012) Systematic literature review of machine learning based software development effort estimation models. Inf Softw Technol 54:41–59
38. Therneau TM, Atkinson EJ (2011) An introduction to recursive partitioning using the rpart routines. Technical Report 61, Mayo Foundation for Medical Education and Research; Mayo Clinic; and Regents of the University of Minnesota, Minneapolis, USA
39. Hooimeijer P, Weimer W (2007) Modeling bug report quality. In: Proceedings of the twenty-second IEEE/ACM international conference on automated software engineering. ASE '07, ACM, New York, NY, pp 34–43
40. Guo PJ, Zimmermann T, Nagappan N, Murphy B (2011) "not my bug!" and other reasons for software bug report reassignments. In: Proceedings of the ACM 2011 conference on computer supported cooperative work. CSCW '11, ACM, New York, NY, pp 395–404
41. Chess B, West J (2007) Secure programming with static analysis, 1st edn. Addison-Wesley, Reading

12

Homomorphic Pattern Mining from a Single Large Data Tree

Xiaoying Wu[1] · Dimitri Theodoratos[2]

Abstract Finding interesting tree patterns hidden in large datasets is a central topic in data mining with many practical applications. Unfortunately, previous contributions have focused almost exclusively on mining-induced patterns from a set of small trees. The problem of mining homomorphic patterns from a large data tree has been neglected. This is mainly due to the challenging unbounded redundancy that homomorphic tree patterns can display. However, mining homomorphic patterns allows for discovering large patterns which cannot be extracted when mining induced or embedded patterns. Large patterns better characterize big trees which are important for many modern applications in particular with the explosion of big data. In this paper, we address the problem of mining frequent homomorphic tree patterns from a single large tree. We propose a novel approach that extracts non-redundant maximal homomorphic patterns. Our approach employs an incremental frequency computation method that avoids the costly enumeration of all pattern matchings required by previous approaches. Matching information of already computed patterns is materialized as bitmaps, a technique that not only minimizes the memory consumption, but also the CPU time. Our contribution also includes an optimization technique which can further reduce the search space of homomorphic patterns. We conducted detailed experiments to test the performance and scalability of our approach. The experimental evaluation shows that our approach mines larger patterns and extracts maximal homomorphic patterns from real and synthetic datasets outperforming state-of-the-art embedded tree mining algorithms applied to a large data tree.

1 Introduction

Extracting frequent tree patterns which are hidden in data trees is central for analyzing data and is a base step for other data mining processes including association rule mining, clustering and classification. Trees have emerged in recent years as the standard format for representing, exporting, exchanging and integrating data on the web (e.g., XML and JSON). Tree data are adopted in various application areas and systems such as business process management, NoSQL databases, key-value stores, scientific workflows, computational biology and genome analysis.

Because of its practical importance, tree mining has been extensively studied [2, 3, 5, 6, 8–11, 14–19, 25–27]. The approaches to tree mining can be basically characterized by two parameters: (a) the type of morphism used to map the tree patterns to the data structure and (b) the type of mined tree data.

Mining homomorphic tree patterns The morphism determines how a pattern is mapped to the data tree. The morphism definition depends also on the type of pattern considered. In the literature, two types of tree patterns have been studied: patterns whose edges represent parent-child

The research of Wu was supported by the National Natural Science Foundation of China under Grant Nos. 61202035 and 61272110.

✉ Dimitri Theodoratos
dth@njit.edu

Xiaoying Wu
xiaoying.wu@whu.edu.cn

[1] State Key Laboratory of Software Engineering, Wuhan University, Wuhan, China

[2] New Jersey Institute of Technology, Newark, NJ, USA

relationships (*child* edges) and patterns whose edges represent ancestor-descendant relationships (*descendant* edges). Over the years, research has evolved from considering isomorphisms for mining patterns with child edges (*induced patterns*) [2, 5] to considering embeddings for mining patterns with descendant edges (*embedded patterns*) [17, 26, 27]. Because of the descendant edges, embeddings are able to extract patterns "hidden" (or embedded) deep within large trees which might be missed by the induced pattern definition [26]. Nevertheless, embeddings are still restricted because: (a) They are injective (one-to-one), and (b) they cannot map two sibling nodes in a pattern to two nodes on the same path in the data tree. On the other hand, homomorphisms are powerful morphisms that do not have those two restrictions of embeddings. We term patterns with descendant edges, mined through homomorphisms, *homomorphic* patterns. Formal definitions are provided in Sect. 2. As homomorphisms are more relaxed than embeddings, the mined homomorphic patterns are a superset of the mined embedded patterns.

Figure 1a shows four data trees corresponding to different schemas to be integrated through the mining of large tree patterns. The frequency threshold is set to three. Figure 1b shows induced mined tree patterns, embedded patterns and non-redundant homomorphic patterns. Figure 1b includes the largest patterns that can be mined in each category. As one can see, the shown embedded patterns are not induced patterns, and the shown homomorphic patterns are neither embedded nor induced patterns. Further, the homomorphic patterns are larger than all the other patterns.

Large patterns are more useful in describing data. Mining tasks usually attach much greater importance to patterns that are larger in size, e.g., longer sequences are usually of more significant meaning than shorter ones in bioinformatics [29]. As mentioned in [28], large patterns have become increasingly important in many modern applications.

Therefore, homomorphisms and homomorphic patterns display a number of advantages. First, they allow the extraction of patterns that cannot be extracted by embedded patterns. Second, extracted homomorphic patterns can be larger than embedded patterns. Finally, homomorphisms can be computed more efficiently than embeddings. Indeed, the problem of checking the existence of a homomorphism of an unordered tree pattern to a data tree is polynomial [13], while the corresponding problem for an embedding is NP-complete [12].

Mining patterns from a large data tree The type of mined data can be a collection of small trees [2, 5, 17, 26, 27] or a single large tree. Surprisingly, the problem of mining tree patterns from a single large tree has only very recently been touched even though a plethora of interesting datasets from different areas are in the form of a single large tree. Examples include encyclopedia databases like Wikipedia, bibliographic databases like PubMed, scientific and experimental result databases like UniprotKB, and biological datasets like phylogenetic trees. These datasets grow constantly with the addition of new data. Big data applications seek to extract information from large datasets. However, mining a single large data tree is more complex than mining a set of small data trees. In fact, the former setting is more general than the latter, since a collection of small trees can be modeled as a single large tree rooted at a virtual unlabeled node. Existing algorithms for mining embedded patterns from a collection of small trees [26] cannot scale well when the size of the data tree increases. Our experiments show that these algorithms cannot scale beyond some hundreds of nodes in a data tree with low-frequency thresholds.

The problem Unfortunately, previous work has focused almost exclusively on mining-induced and embedded patterns from a set of small trees. The issue of mining *homomorphic patterns* from a *single large data tree* has been neglected.

The challenges Mining homomorphic tree patterns is a challenging task. Homomorphic tree patterns are difficult to handle as they may contain redundant nodes. If their structure is not appropriately constrained, the number of frequent patterns (and therefore the number of candidate patterns that need to be generated) can be infinite.

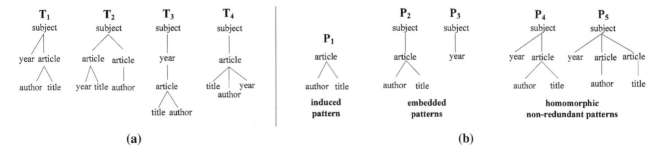

(a)   (b)

Fig. 1 Different types of mined tree patterns occurring in three of the four data trees. **a** Data trees, **b** mined tree patterns

Even if homomorphic patterns are successfully constrained to be non-redundant, their number can be much larger than that of frequent embedded patterns from the same data tree. In order for the mining algorithm to be efficient, new, much faster techniques for computing the support of the candidate homomorphic tree patterns need to be devised.

The support of patterns in the single large data tree setting cannot be anymore the number of trees that contain the pattern as is the case in the multiple small trees setting. A new way to define pattern support in the new setting is needed which enjoys useful monotonic characteristics.

Typically, one can deal with a large number of frequent patterns, by computing only maximal frequent patterns. In the context of induced tree patterns, a pattern is maximal if there is no frequent superpattern [5]. A non-maximal pattern is not returned to the user as there is a larger, more specific pattern, which is frequent. However, in the context of homomorphic patterns, which involve descendant edges, the concept of superpattern is not sufficient for capturing the specificity of a pattern. A tree pattern can be more specific (and informative) without being a superpattern. For instance, the homomorphic pattern P_4 of Fig. 1b is more specific than the homomorphic pattern P_5 without being a superpattern of P_5. Therefore, a new sophisticated definition for maximal patterns is required which takes into account both the particularities of the homomorphic patterns and the single large tree setting.

Contribution In this paper, we address the problem of mining maximal homomorphic unordered tree patterns from a single large data tree. Our main contributions are:

- We define the problem of extracting homomorphic and maximal homomorphic unordered tree patterns with descendant relationships from a single large data tree. This problem departs from previous ones which focus on mining-induced or embedded tree patterns from a set of small data trees.
- We constrain the extracted homomorphic patterns to be non-redundant in order to avoid dealing with an infinite number of frequent patterns of unbounded size. In order to define maximal patterns, we introduce a strict partial order on patterns characterizing specificity. A pattern which is more specific provides more information on the data tree.
- We design an efficient algorithm to discover all frequent maximal homomorphic tree patterns. Our algorithm wisely prunes the search space by generating and considering patterns that are maximal and frequent or can contribute to the generation of maximal frequent patterns. It also exploits an optimization technique which relies on pattern ordering to further reduce the space of homomorphic patterns.

- Our algorithm employs an incremental frequency computation method that avoids the costly enumeration of all pattern matchings required by previous approaches. An originality of our method is that matching information of already computed patterns is materialized as bitmaps. Exploiting bitmaps not only minimizes the memory consumption, but also reduces CPU costs.
- We run extensive experiments to evaluate the performance and scalability of our approach on real datasets. The experimental results show that: (a) The mined maximal homomorphic tree patterns are *larger* on the average than maximal embedded tree patterns on the same datasets, (b) our approach mines homomorphic maximal patterns up to *several orders of magnitude faster* than state-of-the-art algorithms mining embedded tree patterns when applied to a large data tree, (c) our algorithm consumes only a *small fraction of the memory space* and *scales smoothly* when the size of the dataset increases, and (d) the optimization technique substantially improves the time performance of the algorithm.

Paper outline The next section introduces various related concepts and formally defines the problem. Section 3 presents our algorithm that discovers all frequent maximal homomorphic tree patterns. Our comparative experimental results are presented and analyzed in Sect. 4. Related work is reviewed in Sect. 5. Section 6 concludes and suggests future work.

2 Preliminaries and Problem Definition

Trees and inverted lists We consider rooted labeled trees, where each tree has a distinguished root node and a labeling function lb mapping nodes to labels. A tree is called *ordered* if it has a predefined left-to-right ordering among the children of each node. Otherwise, it is *unordered*. The *size* of a tree is defined as the number of its nodes. In this paper, unless otherwise specified, a tree pattern is a rooted, labeled, unordered tree.

For every label a in an input data tree T, we construct an inverted list L_a of the data nodes with label a ordered by their pre-order appearance in T. Figure 2a, b shows a data tree and inverted lists of its labels.

Tree morphisms There are two types of tree patterns: patterns whose edges represent child relationships (child edges) and patterns whose edges represent descendant relationships (descendant edges). In the literature of tree pattern mining, different types of morphisms are employed to determine whether a tree pattern is included in a tree.

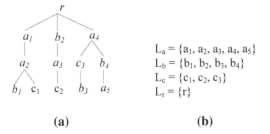

		pattern	occurrences	occur. lists	bitmaps	sup.

pattern	occurrences	occur. lists	bitmaps	sup.
P: A ／＼ B　C	$\{a_1b_1c_1,\ a_2b_1c_1,$ $a_4b_3c_3,\ a_4b_4c_3\}$	$L_A=\{a_1,a_2,a_4\}$ $L_B=\{b_1,b_3,b_4\}$ $L_C=\{c_1,c_3\}$	$L_A=11010$ $L_B=1011$ $L_C=101$	2

$L_a = \{a_1, a_2, a_3, a_4, a_5\}$
$L_b = \{b_1, b_2, b_3, b_4\}$
$L_c = \{c_1, c_2, c_3\}$
$L_r = \{r\}$

(a)   (b)   (c)

Fig. 2 A tree T, its inverted lists and occurrence info. of pattern P on T. **a** A tree T, **b** inverted lists, **c** occurrence information for pattern P on tree T

Given a pattern P and a tree T, a *homomorphism* from P to T is a function m mapping nodes of P to nodes of T, such that: (1) for any node $x \in P$, $lb(x) = lb(m(x))$; and (2) for any edge $(x, y) \in P$, if (x, y) is a child edge, $(m(x), m(y))$ is an edge of T, while if (x, y) is a descendant edge, $m(x)$ is an ancestor of $m(y)$ in T.

Previous contributions have constrained the homomorphisms considered for tree mining in different ways. Let P be a pattern with descendant edges. An *embedding* from P to T is an injective function m mapping nodes of P to nodes of T, such that: (1) for any node $x \in P$, $lb(x) = lb(m(x))$; and (2) (x, y) is an edge in P *iff* $m(x)$ is an ancestor of $m(y)$ in T. Clearly, an embedding is also a homomorphism. Notice that, in contrast to a homomorphism, an embedding cannot map two siblings of P to two nodes on the same path in T. Patterns with descendant edges mined using embeddings are called *embedded* patterns. We call patterns with descendant edges mined using homomorphisms *homomorphic* patterns. In this paper, we consider mining homomorphic patterns. The set of frequent embedded patterns on a data tree T is a subset of the set of frequent homomorphic patterns on T since embeddings are restricted homomorphisms.

Pattern nodes occurrence lists We identify an occurrence of P on T by a tuple indexed by the nodes of P whose values are the images of the corresponding nodes in P under a homomorphism of P to T. The set of occurrences of P under all possible homomorphisms of P to T is a relation OC whose schema is the set of nodes of P. If X is a node in P labeled by label a, the *occurrence list of X on T* is a sublist L_X of the inverted list L_a containing only those nodes that occur in the column for X in OC.

As an example, in Fig. 2c, the second and third columns give the occurrence relation and the node occurrence lists, respectively, of the pattern P on the tree T of Fig. 2a.

Support We adopt for the support of tree patterns root frequency: The support of a pattern P on a data tree T is the number of distinct images (nodes in T) of the root of P under all homomorphisms of P to T. In other words, the *support* of P on T is the size of the occurrence list of the root of P on T.

A pattern S is *frequent* if its support is no less than a user-defined threshold *minsup*. We denote by F_k the set of all frequent patterns of size k, also known as a *k-pattern*.

Constraining patterns When homomorphisms are considered, it is possible that an infinite number of frequent patterns of unrestricted size can be extracted from a dataset. In order to exclude this possibility, we consider and define next non-redundant patterns. We say that two patterns P_1 and P_2 are *equivalent*, if there exists a homomorphism from P_1 to P_2 and vice-versa. A node X in a pattern P is *redundant* if the subpattern obtained from P by deleting X and all its descendants is equivalent to P. For example, the rightmost node C of P_3 and the rightmost node B of P_5 in Fig. 3 are redundant. Adding redundant nodes to a pattern can generate an infinite number of frequent equivalent patterns which have the same support. These patterns are not useful as they do not provide additional information on the data tree. A pattern is *non-redundant* if it does not have redundant nodes. In Fig. 3, patterns P_3 and P_5 are redundant, while the rest of the patterns are non-redundant. Non-redundant patterns correspond to minimal tree pattern queries [1] in tree databases. Their number is finite. We discuss later how to efficiently check patterns for redundancy by identifying redundant nodes. We set forth to extract only frequent patterns which are non-redundant, but in the process of finding frequent non-redundant patterns, we might generate also some redundant patterns.

Maximal patterns In order to define maximal homomorphic frequent patterns, we introduce a specificity relation on patterns: A pattern P_1 is *more specific* than a pattern P_2 (and P_2 is *less specific* than P_1) iff there is a homomorphism from P_2 to P_1 but not from P_1 to P_2. If a pattern P_1 is more specific than a pattern P_2, we write $P_1 \prec P_2$. For instance, in Fig. 3, $P_1 \prec P_i$, $i = 2, \ldots, 7$, and $P_2 \prec P_6$. Similarly, in Fig. 1, $P_2 \prec P_1$, $P_5 \prec P_3$, $P_4 \prec P_2$ and $P_4 \prec P_5$. Note that P_4 is more specific than P_5 even though it is smaller in size than P_5. Clearly, $\prec$ is a strict partial order. If $P_1 \prec P_2$, P_1 conveys more information on the dataset than P_2.

Fig. 3 A data tree and homomorphic patterns. **a** A data tree T, **b** Homomorphic patterns on T

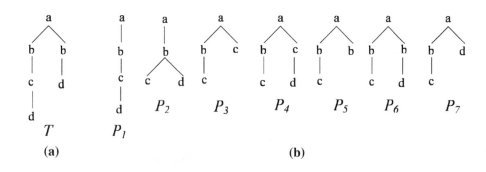

(a)   (b)

A frequent pattern P is *maximal* if there is no other frequent pattern P_1, such that $P_1 \prec P$. For instance, in Fig. 1, all the patterns shown are frequent homomorphic patterns and P_4 is the only maximal pattern.

Problem statement Given a large tree T and a minimum support threshold *minsup*, our goal is to mine all maximal homomorphic frequent patterns from T.

3 Proposed Approach

Our approach for mining homomorphic tree patterns from a large tree iterates between the candidate generation phase and the support counting phase. In the first phase, we use a systematic way to generate candidate patterns that are potentially frequent. In the second phase, we develop an efficient method to compute the support of candidate patterns.

3.1 Candidate Generation

To generate candidate patterns, we adapt in this section the equivalence class-based pattern generation method proposed in [26, 27] so that it can address pattern redundancy and maximality. A candidate pattern may have multiple alternative isomorphic representations. To minimize the redundant generation of the isomorphic representations of the same pattern, we employ a canonical form for tree patterns [7].

3.1.1 Equivalence Class-Based Pattern Generation

Let P be a pattern of size k-1. Each node of P is identified by its *depth-first position* in the tree, determined through a depth-first traversal of P, by sequentially assigning numbers to the first visit of the node. The *rightmost leaf* of P, denoted *rml*, is the node with the highest depth-first position. The *immediate prefix* of P is the subpattern of P obtained by deleting the *rml* from P. The *equivalence class* of P is the set of all the patterns of size k that have P as their immediate prefix. We denote the equivalence class of P as $[P]$. Any two members of $[P]$ differ only in their *rml*s.

We use the notation P_x^i to denote the k-pattern formed by adding a child node labeled by x to the node with position i in P as the *rml*.

Given an equivalence class $[P]$, we obtain its successor classes by expanding patterns in $[P]$. Specifically, candidates are generated by *joining* each pattern $P_x^i \in [P]$ with any other pattern P_y^j in $[P]$, including itself, to produce the patterns of the equivalence class $[P_x^i]$. We denote the above join operation by $P_x^i \otimes P_y^j$. There are two possible outcomes for each $P_x^i \otimes P_y^j$: One is obtained by making y a sibling node of x in P_x^i (*cousin expansion*), the other is obtained by making y a child node of x in P_x^i (*child expansion*). We call patterns P_x^i and P_y^j the *left parent* and *right parent* of a join outcome, respectively.

As an example, in Fig. 3, patterns P_1, P_2, P_3, P_5, and P_7 are members of class $[a \ / \ b \ / \ c]$; P_4 is a join outcome of $P_3 \otimes P_7$, obtained by making the *rml* d of P_7 a child of the *rml* c of P_3.

3.1.2 Checking Pattern Redundancy

The pattern generation process may produce candidates which are redundant (defined in Sect. 2). We discuss below how to efficiently check pattern redundancy by identifying redundant nodes. We exploit a result of [1] which states that: A node X of a pattern P is redundant iff there exists a homomorphism h from P to itself such that $h(X) \neq X$. A brute-force method for checking whether a pattern is redundant computes all the possible homomorphisms from P to itself. Unfortunately, the number of the homomorphisms can be exponential on the size of P. Therefore, we have designed an algorithm called *computeHoms* which, given patterns P and Q, compactly encodes all the homomorphisms from P to Q in polynomial time and space. This algorithm enhances the previous one presented in [13] which checks whether there exists a homomorphism from one tree pattern to another, while achieving the same time and space complexity.

Algorithm computeHoms Algorithm *computeHoms* is presented in Fig. 4. It deploys a standard dynamic programming technique for computing a Boolean matrix $\mathcal{M}(p,$

Input: two patterns P and Q.
Output: a Boolean matrix $\mathcal{M}$ that encodes all the homomorphisms from P to Q.

1. Initialize a boolean matrix $\mathcal{C}(p, q)$, $p \in \text{nodes}(P)$, $q \in \text{nodes}(Q)$;
2. **if** (BottomUpTraversal($\mathcal{C}$)) **then**
3. $\mathcal{M} := \text{TopDownTraversal}(\mathcal{C})$;
4. **else**
5.   there is no homomorphism from P to Q;

Function BottomUpTraversal(Matrix $\mathcal{C}$)

1. Initialize a boolean matrix $\mathcal{D}(p, q)$, $p \in \text{nodes}(P)$, $q \in \text{nodes}(Q)$;
2. **for** (every node q of Q in bottom-up order) **do**
3.   **for** (every node p of P in bottom-up order) **do**
4. $\mathcal{C}(p,q) := (lb(q) = lb(q)) \wedge$
         $\bigwedge_{u \in children(p)}(\bigvee_{v \in children(q)} \mathcal{D}(u, v))$;
5. $\mathcal{D}(p, q) := \mathcal{C}(p, q) \vee \bigvee_{v \in children(q)} \mathcal{D}(p, v)$;
6. **return** $\mathcal{D}(\text{root}(p), \text{root}(q))$;

Function TopDownTraversal(Matrix $\mathcal{C}$)

1. Initialize two boolean matrices $\mathcal{P}(p, q)$ and $\mathcal{A}(p, q)$, $p \in \text{nodes}(P)$, $q \in \text{nodes}(Q)$;
2. **for** (every node q of Q in top-down order) **do**
3.   **for** (every node p of P in top-down order) **do**
4. $\mathcal{P}(p, q) := (\mathcal{C}(p, q)) \wedge \mathcal{A}(\text{parent of } p, \text{parent of } q)$;
5. $\mathcal{A}(p, q) := \mathcal{P}(p, q) \vee \mathcal{A}(p, \text{parent of } q)$;
6. **return** $\mathcal{P}$;

Fig. 4 Algorithm computeHoms

q), $p \in \text{nodes}(P)$, $q \in \text{nodes}(Q)$, such that $\mathcal{M}(p, q)$ is true if: (1) There exists a homomorphism from the subpattern rooted at p to the subpattern rooted at q (Function *BottomUpTraversal*); and (2) there exists a homomorphism from the prefix path of p to the prefix path of q, where *prefix path* of a node is the path from the pattern root to that node (Function *TopDownTraversal*). Without loss of generality, we assume that both P and Q have a virtual root r. We now describe the algorithm in more detail.

The algorithm first performs a bottom-up traversal of P and Q (Function *BottomUpTraversal*) to compute a Boolean matrix $\mathcal{C}$. Entry $\mathcal{C}(p, q)$ is true if there exists a homomorphism from the subpattern rooted at p to the subpattern rooted at q. To eliminate redundant computations, the bottom-up traversal also computes a second matrix $\mathcal{D}$. Entry $\mathcal{D}(p, q)$ is true if there exists a homomorphism from the subpattern rooted at p to some subpattern of Q whose root is either q or a descendant of q.

If *BottomUpTraversal* returns true, the algorithm proceeds to perform a top-down traversal of P and Q (Function *TopDownTraversal*) to compute a Boolean matrix $\mathcal{P}$. Entry $\mathcal{P}(p, q)$ is true if $\mathcal{C}(p, q)$ (computed by the bottom-up traversal) is true and there exists a homomorphism from the prefix path of p to the prefix path of q. As with the bottom-up traversal, a second matrix $\mathcal{A}$ is computed. Entry $\mathcal{A}(p, q)$ is true if there exists a homomorphism from the prefix path of p to some prefix path of either q or an ancestor of q.

Proposition 1 *There exists a homomorphism from pattern P to pattern Q that maps node $p \in P$ to node $q \in Q$ iff entry $\mathcal{M}(p,q)$ is true, where $\mathcal{M}$ is the Boolean matrix computed by Algorithm computeHoms on P and Q.*

The proof of Proposition 1 is straightforward by the definition of pattern homomorphisms and the construction process of Boolean matrix $\mathcal{M}$.

We now analyze the complexity of Algorithm *computeHoms*. The entry $\mathcal{D}(u, v)$ of function *BottomUpTraversal* is checked once for every pair of nodes ($u \in children(p)$, $v \in children(q)$) (line 4). The entry $\mathcal{D}(p, v)$ is checked once for every pair of nodes ($p \in P$, $v \in children(q)$) (line 5). Therefore, the total number of times these two entries are checked is no more than $|P| \times |Q|$.

The entry $\mathcal{A}(\text{parent of } p, \text{parent of } q)$ in line 4 and the entry $\mathcal{A}(p, \text{parent of } q)$ in line 5 of function *TopDownTraversal* are checked once for every pair of nodes ($p \in P, q \in Q$). The total number of times these two entries are checked is no more than $|P| \times |Q|$. Therefore, the time and memory complexities of Algorithm *computeHoms* are both $O(|P| \times |Q|)$.

During the candidate generation, we cannot, however, simply discard candidates that are redundant, since they may be needed for generating non-redundant patterns. For instance, the pattern P_5 shown in Fig. 3b is redundant, but it is needed (as the left operand in a join operation with P_7) to generate the non-redundant pattern P_6 shown in the same figure. Clearly, we want to avoid as much as possible generating patterns that are redundant. In order to do so, we introduce the notion of *expandable* pattern.

Definition 1 *(Expandable pattern)* A pattern P is *expandable*, if it does not have a redundant node X such that: (1) X is not on the rightmost path of P, or (2) X is on the rightmost path of P and L_X is equal to $L_{X_1} \cup \ldots \cup L_{X_k}$, where $X_1, \ldots, X_k$ are the images of node X under a homomorphism from P to itself.

Based on Definition 1, if a pattern is not expandable, every expansion of it is redundant. Therefore, only expandable patterns in a class are considered for expansion.

3.1.3 Expandable Pattern Refining

The number of expandable patterns enumerated by the equivalence class expansion process can still be very large, particularly when the frequent patterns to find have both a high depth and a high branching factor. In order to further reduce the number of generated patterns, we present below a pattern refining method which exploits properties of the equivalence class-based pattern expansion. We observe that the specificity relation $\prec$ induces a linear order on patterns in a given equivalence class whose rightmost leaf nodes have the same label: for any two patterns P_x^i and P_x^j in the equivalence class $[P]$, $P_x^i \prec P_x^j$ if $i > j$. Clearly, the occurrence set of $P_x^i(x)$ is a subset of the occurrence set of $P_x^j(x)$, for $i > j$.

Let $P_1, P_2, \ldots, P_n$ stand for a sequence of n expandable patterns satisfying the above linear order. Each pattern in the sequence has a rightmost leaf node x. For a pattern P_k, if the occurrence set of $P_k(x)$ is the same as the union of the occurrence sets of $P_i(x)$, $i = 1, \ldots, k - 1$, then the set of occurrences of P_k is the same as the union of occurrence sets of P_i's. In this case, it is not useful to further expand P_k, since it is refined by a set of more specific patterns. We call P_k a *refinable* pattern. In Fig. 7, pattern Q_2 is refined by Q_1.

In order to efficiently identify refinable patterns, we keep the patterns P_x^i in each class sorted by the node label x primarily and by the position p (in descending order) secondarily. Figure 6 shows patterns of a class in sorted order. Given a sorted pattern list; the equivalence class expansion process considers ordered pairs of patterns in the class for expansion. This way, the candidate generation process outputs a new class list which is also sorted based on this order, and no explicit sorting is needed.

In the implementation, we scan patterns of a given class in descending order. For each pattern P under consideration, we check whether it has a preceding pattern Q, such that the rightmost leaf nodes of P and Q have the same label and the same occurrence list. If it is the case, P is a refinable pattern and is excluded from further expansion. The process is summarized in Procedure *CheckClassElements* shown in Fig. 5. Our experiments show that the pattern pruning technique can effectively reduce the pattern search space.

3.1.4 Finding Maximal Patterns

One way to compute the maximal patterns is to use a post-processing pruning method. That is, first compute the set S of all frequent homomorphic patterns, and then do the maximality check and eliminate non-maximal patterns by

---

Procedure CheckClassElements(Class $[P]$)
1. **for** (each $P_x^i \in [P]$ in descending order) **do**
2.   check if P_x^i is expandable; {Ref. Definition 1 and Algorithm *computeHoms* of Fig. 4}
3.   **if** (P_x^i is not expandable and contains a redundant node not on the rightmost path) **then**
4.   remove P_x^i from $[P]$;
5.   check if P_x^i is refinable;   {Ref. Section 3.1.3}
6.   **if** (P_x^i is refinable) **then**
7.   remove P_x^i from $[P]$;

Fig. 5 Procedure CheckClassElements

checking the specificity relation on every pair of patterns in S. However, the time complexity of this method is $O(|S|^2)$. It is, therefore, inefficient since the size of S can be exponentially larger than the number of maximal patterns.

We have developed a better method which can reduce the number of frequent patterns that need to go through the maximality check. During the course of mining frequent patterns, the method locates a subset of frequent patterns called locally maximal patterns. A pattern P is *locally maximal* if it is frequent and there exists no frequent pattern in the class $[P]$. Clearly, a non-locally maximal pattern is not maximal. Then, in order to identify maximal patterns, we check only locally maximal patterns for maximality. Our experiments show that this improvement can dramatically reduce the number of frequent patterns checked for maximality.

3.2 Support Computation

Recall that the support of a pattern P in the input data tree T is defined as the size of the occurrence list L_R of the root R of P on T (Sect. 2). To compute L_R, a straightforward method is to first compute the relation OC which stores the set of occurrences of P under all possible homomorphisms of P to T and then "project" OC on column R to get L_R. Fortunately, we can do much better using a twig-join approach to compute L_R without enumerating all homomorphisms of P to T. Our approach for support computation is a complete departure from existing approaches.

A holistic twig-join approach In order to compute L_X, we exploit a holistic twig-join approach (e.g., *TwigStack* [4]), the state-of-the-art technique for evaluating tree pattern queries on tree data. Algorithm *TwigStack* works in two phases. In the first phase, it computes the matches of the individual root-to-leaf paths of the pattern. In the second phase, it merge-joins the path matches to compute the results for the pattern. *TwigStack* ensures that each solution to each individual query root-to-leaf path is guaranteed to be merge-joinable with at least one solution of each of the other root-to-leaf paths in the pattern. Therefore, the algorithm can guarantee worst-case performance *linear* to the size of the data tree inverted lists (the input) and the size of the pattern matches in the data tree (the output), i.e., the algorithm is optimal.

By exploiting the above property of *TwigStack*, we can compute the support of P at the first phase of *TwigStack* when it finds data nodes participating in matches of root-to-leaf paths of P. There is no need to enumerate the occurrences of pattern P on T (i.e., to compute the occurrence relation OC).

The time complexity of the above support computation method is $O(|P| \times |T|)$, where $|P|$ and $|T|$ denote the size of

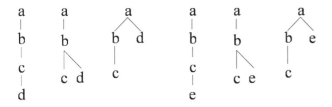

Fig. 6 Sorted patterns in class $[a \ / \ b \ / \ c]$

pattern P and of the input data tree T, respectively. Its space complexity is the $min(|T|, |P| \times heigh(T))$. We note that, on the other hand, the problem of computing an unordered embedding from P to T is NP-complete [12]. As a consequence, a state-of-the-art unordered embedded pattern mining algorithm *Sleuth* [26] computes pattern support in $O(|P| \times |T|^{2|P|})$ time and $O(|P| \times |T|^{|P|})$ space.

Nevertheless, the *TwigStack*-based method can still be expensive for computing the support of a large number of candidates, since it needs to scan fully the inverted lists corresponding to every candidate pattern. We present below an incremental method, which computes the support of a pattern P by leveraging the computation done at its parent patterns in the search space.

Computing occurrence lists incrementally Let P be a pattern and X be a node in P labeled by a. Using *TwigStack*, P is computed by iterating over the inverted lists corresponding to every pattern node. If there is a sublist, say L_X, of L_a such that P can be computed on T using L_X instead of L_a, we say that node X can be *computed using L_X on T*. Since L_X is non-strictly smaller than L_a, the computation cost can be reduced. Based on this idea, we propose an incremental method that uses the occurrence lists of the two parent patterns of a given pattern P to compute P.

Let pattern Q be a join outcome of $P_x^i \otimes P_y^j$. By the definition of the join operation, we can easily identify a homomorphism from each parent P_x^i and P_y^j to Q.

Proposition 2 *Let X' be a node in a parent Q' of Q and X be the image of X' under a homomorphism from Q' to Q. The occurrence list L_X of X on T is a sublist of the occurrence list $L_{X'}$ of X' on T.*

Sublist L_X is the inverted list of data tree nodes that participate in the occurrences of Q to T. By Proposition 2, X can be computed using $L_{X'}$ instead of using the corresponding label inverted list. Further, if X is the image of nodes X_1 and X_2 defined by the homomorphisms from the left and right parent of Q, respectively, we can compute X using the *intersection*, $L_{X_1} \cap L_{X_2}$, of L_{X_1} and L_{X_2} which is the sublist of L_{X_1} and L_{X_2} comprising the nodes that appear in both L_{X_1} and L_{X_2}.

Using Proposition 2, we can compute Q using only the occurrence list sets of its parents. Thus, we only need to store with each frequent pattern its occurrence list set. Our method is space efficient since the occurrence lists can encode in linear space an exponential number of occurrences for the pattern [4]. In contrast, the state-of-the-art methods for mining embedded patterns [26, 27] have to store information about all the occurrences of each given pattern in T.

Occurrence lists as bitmaps The occurrence list L_X of a pattern node X labeled by a on T can be represented by a bitmap on L_a. This is a bit array of size $|L_a|$ which has a "1" bit at position i iff L_X comprises the tree node at position i of L_a. Then, the occurrence list set of a pattern is the set of bitmaps of the occurrence lists of its nodes. Figure 2c shows an example of bitmaps for pattern occurrence lists.

As verified by our experimental evaluation, storing the occurrence lists of multiple patterns as bitmaps results in important space savings. Bitmaps offer CPU cost saving as well by allowing the translation of pattern evaluation to bitwise operations. This bitmap technique is initially introduced and exploited in [20, 21, 23, 24] for materializing tree pattern views and for efficiently answering queries using materialized views.

Example 1 Figure 7 shows an example of the incremental method for computing the support of Q_1 and Q_2, the two outcomes of $P_1 \otimes P_2$ on the data tree T of Fig. 2a. We assume *minsup* is one. Each node of the patterns P_1 and P_2 is associated with its occurrence list together with the corresponding bitmap vector. To compute Q_1 and Q_2, the bitmaps of P_1 and P_2 are ANDed and the resulting bitmaps are attached to nodes of Q_1 and Q_2. These bitmaps are used as input to compute Q_1 and Q_2 using *TwigStack*. The bitmap output associated with each pattern node indicates the occurrence list of that node on T. Note that pattern Q_2 is refined by Q_1 and thus will not be further expanded.

3.3 The Tree Pattern Mining Algorithm

We present now our homomorphic tree pattern mining algorithm called *HomTreeMiner* (Fig. 8). The first part of the algorithm computes the sets containing all frequent 1-patterns F_1 (i.e., nodes) and 2-patterns F_2 (lines 1–2). F_1 can be easily obtained by finding inverted lists of T whose size (in terms of number of nodes) is no less than *minsup*. The total time for this step is $O(|T|)$. F_2 is computed by the following procedure: Let $X \ / \ Y$ denote a 2-pattern formed by two elements X and Y of F_1. The support of $X \ / \ Y$ is computed via algorithm *TwigStack* on the inverted lists $L_{lb(X)}$ and $L_{lb(Y)}$ that are associated with labels $lb(X)$ and

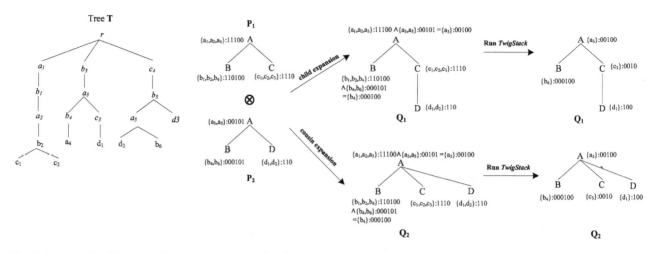

Fig. 7 An example of incremental support computation for the outcomes of $P_1 \otimes P_2$ on tree T

Input: inverted lists $\mathcal{L}$ of tree T and $minsup$.
Output: all the frequent maximal patterns $\mathcal{M}$ in T.

1. $F_1 := \{\text{frequent 1-patterns}\}$;
2. $F_2 := \{\text{classes } [P]_1 \text{ of frequent 2-patterns}\}$;
3. **for** (every $[P] \in F_2$) **do**
4. $MineHomPatterns([P], \mathcal{M} = \emptyset)$;
5.   run the maximality checking procedure on $\mathcal{M}$;
6. **return** $\mathcal{M}$;

Procedure $MineHomPatterns([P], \mathcal{M})$

1. **for** (each $P_x^i \in [P]$) **do**
2.   **if** (P_x^i is in canonical form and is expandable) **then**
3. $[P_x^i] := \emptyset$
4.   **for** (each $P_y^j \in [P]$) **do**
5. $Q :=$ the child expansion outcome of $P_x^i \otimes P_y^j$;
6.   add Q to $[P_x^i]$ if Q is frequent;
7. $Q :=$ the cousin expansion outcome of $P_x^i \otimes P_y^j$;
8.   add Q to $[P_x^i]$ if Q is frequent;
9.   CheckClassElements($[P_x^i]$);   {Ref. Fig. 5}
10.   add P_x^i to $\mathcal{M}$ if none of the elements of $[P_x^i]$ is in canonical form;
11. $MineHomPatterns([P_x^i], \mathcal{M})$;

Fig. 8 Homomorphic tree pattern mining algorithm

$lb(Y)$, respectively. The total time for each 2-pattern candidate is $O(|T|)$.

The main part of the computation is performed by procedure *MineHomPatterns* which is invoked for every frequent 2-pattern (Lines 3–4). This is a recursive procedure. It tries to join every $P_x^i \in [P]$ with any other element $P_y^j \in [P]$ including P_x^i itself. Then, it computes the support of the child expansion and the cousin expansion outcomes in that order and adds them to $[P_x^i]$ if they are frequent (Lines 1–8). Once all P_y^j have been processed, Procedure *CheckClassElements* of Fig. 5 is invoked on class $[P_x^i]$ (Line 9). Subsequently, the algorithm checks whether P_x^i is a locally maximal pattern. If so, P_x^i is added to the maximal pattern set $\mathcal{M}$ (Line 10). Then, the new class $[P_x^i]$ is

recursively explored in a depth-first manner (Line 11). The recursive process is repeated until no more frequent patterns can be generated.

Once all the locally maximal patterns have been found, the maximality check procedure described in Sect. 3.1 is run to identify maximal patterns among the locally maximal ones and the results are returned to the user (Lines 5–6).

Before expanding a class $[P]$, we make sure that P is expandable and is in canonical form (line 2 in *MineHomPatterns*). Our approach is independent of any particular canonical form; it can work with any systematic way of choosing a representative from isomorphic representations of the given pattern, such as those presented in [7, 26]. Efficient methods for checking canonicity can also be drawn from [7, 26].

Complexity The total cost for generating a new class $[P_x^i]$ is $O(n^2 \times |T| \times |P|)$, where n is the number of elements of $[P]$. In terms of memory consumption, observe that the algorithm only needs to load in memory the classes along a path in a depth-first traversal of the search space. In fact, it only needs to store in memory occurrence lists for two classes at a time: the current class $[P]$ and a new class $[P_x^i]$. Since occurrence lists of each pattern in a class are materialized as bitmaps, the memory footprint of the algorithm is very small. This is verified by our experimental results presented in Sect. 4.

4 Experimental Evaluation

We implemented our algorithm *HomTreeMiner* and we conducted experiments to: (a) compare the features of the extracted (maximal) homomorphic patterns with those of (maximal) embedded patterns and (b) study the performance of *HomTreeMiner* in terms of execution time, memory consumption and scalability. To evaluate the

Table 1 Dataset statistics

Dataset	Tot. #nodes	#labels	Max/avg depth	#paths
Treebank	2,437,666	250	36/8.4	1,392,231
XMark	83,533	74	12/5.6	60,853
CSlogs	772,188	13,355	86/4.4	59,691 (#trees)

effect of the pattern refining technique described in Sect. 3.1.3, we consider also a basic version of *HomTreeMiner* that does not employ that optimization in its mining process. That basic version was introduced in [22] and is called *HomTMBasic* in the following paragraphs.

To the best of our knowledge, there is no previous algorithm computing homomorphic patterns from data trees. Therefore, we compared the performance of our algorithm with state-of-the-art algorithms that compute embedded patterns on the same dataset.

Our implementation was coded in Java. All the experiments reported here were performed on a workstation equipped with an Intel Xeon CPU 3565 @3.20 GHz processor with 8 GB memory running JVM 1.7.0 on Windows 7 Professional. The Java virtual machine memory size was set to the default 4 GB.

Datasets We have ran experiments on three real and benchmark datasets with different structural properties. Their main characteristics are summarized in Table 1.

Treebank[1] is a real XML dataset derived from computation linguistics. It models the syntactic structure of English text and provides a hierarchical representation of the sentences in the text by breaking them into syntactic units based on part of speech. The dataset is deep and comprises highly recursive and irregular structures.

XMark[2] is an XML benchmark dataset generated using the data generator with *factor* = 0.05. It is deep and has many regular structural patterns. It includes very few recursive elements.

CSlogs[3] is a real dataset and is composed of users' access trees to the CS department Web site at RPI. The dataset contains 59,691 trees that cover a total of 13,355 unique web pages. The average size of each tree is 12.94.

4.1 Algorithm Performance

We compare the performance of *HomTreeMiner* with two unordered embedded tree mining algorithms *Sleuth* [26] and *EmbTreeMiner* [19]. *Sleuth* was designed to mine embedded patterns from a set of small trees. In order to

allow the comparison in the single large tree setting, we adapted *Sleuth* by having it return as support of a pattern the number of its root occurrences in the data tree. *EmbTreeMiner* is a newer embedded tree mining algorithm which, as *HomTreeMiner*, exploits the twig-join approach and bitmaps to compute pattern support.

To the best of our knowledge, direct mining of maximal embedded patterns has not been studied in the literature. We therefore use post-processing pruning which eliminates non-maximal patterns after computing all frequent embedded patterns. For this task, we implemented the unordered tree inclusion algorithm described in [12]. As our experiments show, the cost of this post-processing step is in general not significant compared to the frequent pattern mining cost.

To allow *Sleuth*—which is slower—to extract some patterns within a reasonable amount of time, we used a fraction of the Treebank dataset which consists of 35% of the nodes of the original tree. We measured execution times over the entire Treebank dataset in the scalability experiment.

Candidate pattern generated Figs. 9c, 10c and 11c compare the total candidates generated by *sleuth*, *EmbTreeMiner*, *HomTMBasic* and *HomTreeMiner*, respectively, under different support thresholds on the Treebank, XMark and CSlogs datasets.

As one can see, the search space of a homomorphic pattern mining can be larger than that of embedded pattern mining for low support levels. On Treebank, for instance, *HomTreeMiner* computes 17 times more candidates than *EmbTreeMiner* at *minsup* = 30 k. Since Treebank contains many deep, highly recursive paths, the search space of homomorphic patterns becomes substantially large at low support levels. Like Treebank, XMark has many deep paths, and therefore, the search space of homomorphic patterns becomes large at low support levels. For example, on XMark at *minsup* = 700, *HomTreeMiner* generates about 2.23 times more candidates than *EmbTreeMiner*. The number of candidates generated by *HomTreeMiner* and *EmbTreeMiner* is comparable on CSlogs. The difference in the number of candidates generated by *sleuth* and *EmbTreeMiner* is not noticeable on all the testing cases.

We notice that *HomTMBasic* generates substantially more candidates than *HomTreeMiner* for low support levels. For instance, on XMark at *minsup* = 650, *HomTMBasic* generates about 9 times more candidates than *HomTreeMiner*. On CSlogs at *minsup* = 250, *HomTMBasic* generates about 5 times more candidates than *HomTreeMiner*. This indicates that the pattern refining technique enables *HomTreeMiner* to reduce substantially the search space when it is applicable.

Execution time We measure the total elapsed time for producing maximal frequent patterns at different support

---

[1] http://www.cis.upenn.edu/∼treebank.

[2] http://monetdb.cwi.nl/xml/.

[3] http://www.cs.rpi.edu/∼zaki/software/.

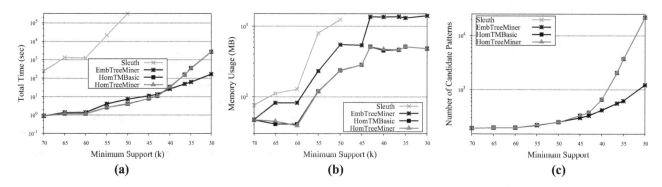

Fig. 9 Performance comparison on a fraction of treebank. **a** Run time versus support. **b** Memory usage. **c** Candidate patterns

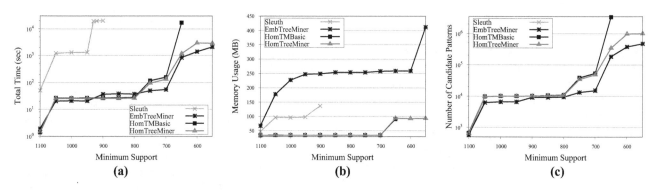

Fig. 10 Performance comparison on XMark. **a** Run time versus support. **b** Memory usage. **c** Candidate patterns

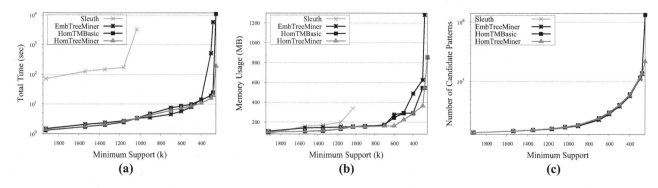

Fig. 11 Performance comparison on CSlogs. **a** Run time versus support. **b** Memory usage. **c** Candidate patterns

thresholds. The total time involves the time to generate candidate patterns, compute pattern support and check maximality of frequent patterns.

Figures 9a, 10a and 11a compare the total elapsed time of the four algorithms under different support thresholds on the Treebank, XMark and CSlogs datasets. Due to prohibitively long times, we stopped testing *Sleuth* when support levels are below certain values on each dataset.

We can see that *HomTreeMiner* runs orders of magnitude faster than *Sleuth*, especially for low support levels. The rate of increase of the running time for *HomTreeMiner* is slower than that for *Sleuth* as the support level decreases. This is expected, since *HomTreeMiner* computes the support of a homomorphic pattern in time linear to the input

data size, whereas this computation is exponential for embedded pattern miners (Sect. 3.2). Furthermore, *Sleuth* has to keep track of all possible embedded occurrences of a candidate to a data tree and to perform expensive join operations over these occurrences.

The large number of candidate homomorphic patterns can negatively affect the time performance of *HomTreeMiner* at low support levels. For instance, on Treebank, *HomTreeMiner* shows similar or better performance than *EmbTreeMiner* when support levels are above 40 K and both generate a similar number of candidates. When *minsup* decreases below 40 K, the execution time of *HomTreeMiner* increases noticeably faster than that of *EmbTreeMiner* due to the substantially larger number of candidates evaluated by *HomTreeMiner*. At *minsup* = 30k, in order to evaluate 17 times more candidates, *HomTreeMiner* runs about 15 times slower than *EmbTreeMiner*.

However, even though the number of (candidate and frequent) homomorphic patterns is always larger than the number of embedded patterns, this difference is not so pronounced in shallower datasets like CSlogs. As we can see from Fig. 11a, *HomTreeMiner* can largely outperform *EmbTreeMiner* at low support levels. This is due to its efficient computation of pattern support which does not require the enumeration of pattern occurrences and the embedding checking as is the case with *EmbTreeMiner* [19].

From the results, we observe that *HomTreeMiner* can largely outperform *HomTMBasic*, when it is able to substantially reduce the search space with the refinement technique. For instance, on XMark at *minsup* = 650, *HomTreeMiner* runs more than 13 times faster than *HomTMBasic*.

Memory usage We measured the memory footprint of the four algorithms with varying support thresholds. The results are shown in Figs. 9b, 10b and 11b. We can see that *HomTreeMiner* always has the best memory performance. It consumes substantially less memory than both *Sleuth* and *EmbTreeMiner* in all the test cases. This is mainly because *Sleuth* needs to enumerate and store in memory all the pattern occurrences for candidates under consideration. In contrast, *HomTreeMiner* avoids storing pattern occurrences by storing only bitmaps of occurrence lists which are usually of insignificant size. Although *EmbTreeMiner* does not store pattern occurrences, it still has to generate pattern occurrences as intermediate results, the size of which can be substantial at low support levels. The memory performance of *HomTMBasic* is similar to that of *HomTreeMiner*. The results indicate that the memory performance of a mining algorithm is mainly determined by its pattern support computation.

4.2 Algorithm Scalability

In our final experiment, we studied the scalability of the three algorithms *EmbTreeMiner*, *HomTMBasic* and *HomTreeMiner* as we increase the input data size. We omit the comparison with *sleuth*, since *sleuth* was unable to finish within a reasonable time even on the smallest size of input.

For Treebank, we generated ten fragments of increasing size and fixed *minsup* at 4.5%. For XMark, we generated 10 XMark trees by setting *factor* = 0.01, 0.02, ..., 0.1 and fixed *minsup* at 1%. For CSlogs, we generated 7 datasets of different sizes (from 40 k trees and up to 100 k) by randomly choosing trees from the original CSlogs. We fixed *minsup* at 400.

The results show that *HomTreeMiner* has the best time performance on both XMark and CSlogs (Fig. 12b, c); it runs slightly slower than *EmbTreeMiner* on Treebank (Fig. 12a). The reason is that, on both XMark and CSlogs, the number of candidates evaluated by *HomTreeMiner* is similar to that by *EmbTreeMiner*, whereas on Treebank, it needs to evaluate 56% more candidates on average. On CSlogs, the growth of the running time of *EmbTreeMiner* becomes much sharper with datasets containing 80 k trees and up. *EmbTreeMiner* is unable to finish within 5 hours on CSlogs containing 90 k trees and up. *HomTMBasic* has similar time performance with *HomTreeMiner* on both Treebank and XMark. However, on CSlogs of size 90 k and 100 k, *HomTreeMiner* outperforms *HomTMBasic* by a factor of more than 2.5. The reason is that, in these two cases, *HomTMBasic* has to evaluate about 47 k more candidates in total and generates twice as many frequent patterns on average than *HomTreeMiner*.

Figure 13a–c show that *HomTreeMiner* always has the smallest memory footprint. The growth of its memory consumption is much slower than that of *EmbTreeMiner*.

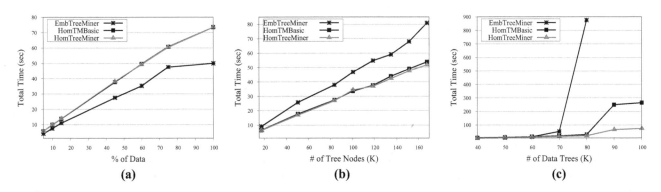

Fig. 12 Run time scalability comparison on the three datasets with increasing size. **a** Treebank (*minsup* = 4.5%). **b** XMark (*minsup* = 1%). **c** CSlogs (*minsup* = 400)

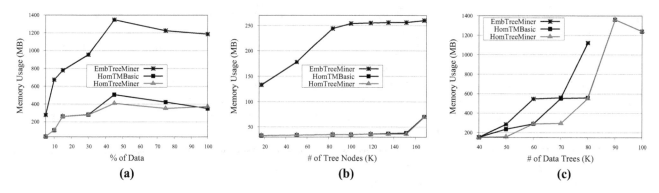

Fig. 13 Memory usage scalability comparison on the three datasets with increasing size. **a** Treebank (*minsup* = 4.5%). **b** XMark (*minsup* = 1%). **c** CSlogs (*minsup* = 400)

Table 2 Statistics for maximal frequent patterns mined from the three datasets

Dataset	Morphism	# freq. patterns	# loc.max patterns	# max. non. red.patterns	%max. over freq. patterns	Average #nodes	Average height	Average fanout	maximum #nodes	#common max.patterns
Treebank	Emb	78	n/a	2 (8)	2.6	0.63	0.375	0.25	3	1
(minsup = 35k)	Hom	521	158	9	1.7	5	2.11	2.11	8	
Treebank	Emb	175	n/a	13 (32)	7.4	1.47	0.66	0.78	5	5
(minsup = 30k)	Hom	2937	915	35	1.2	6.14	2.23	2.57	9	
XMark	Emb	934	n/a	14 (19)	1.5	2.63	1.05	1.58	5	6
(minsup = 800)	Hom	853	26	15	1.76	4.67	1.93	2.6	10	
XMark	Emb	43,441	n/a	27 (54)	0.06	3.33	1	2.09	15	14
(minsup = 550)	Hom	56,160	302	35	0.06	8.74	2.29	5.71	15	
CSlogs	Emb	638	n/a	133 (164)	20.8	2	0.896	1.1	5	119
(minsup = 400)	Hom	816	307	152	18.6	2.53	1.11	1.41	6	
CSlogs	Emb	2192	n/a	250 (375)	11.4	1.68	0.728	0.95	6	192
(minsup = 280)	Hom	1625	676	312	19.2	2.8	1.22	1.57	6	

4.3 Comparison of Mined Maximal Homomorphic and Embedded Patterns

We computed different statistics on frequent and maximal frequent patterns mined by *HomTreeMiner* and *EmbTreeMiner* from the three datasets varying the support; the results are summarized in Table 2. For the comparison, we considered only maximal embedded patterns that contain no redundant nodes. We show the total number of maximal embedded patterns in parenthesis in Column 5. We can make the following observations.

First, *HomTreeMiner* is able to discover larger patterns than *EmbTreeMiner* for the same support level. As one can see in Table 2, the maximum size of frequent homomorphic patterns and the maximum size and average number of nodes, height and fanout of maximum frequent homomorphic patterns is never smaller (substantially larger in many cases) than that of the embedded patterns for the same support level.

Second, the number of homomorphic and embedded frequent patterns is substantially reduced if only maximal patterns are selected (Column 6 of Table 2). However, the effect is larger on homomorphic patterns as the number of frequent homomorphic patterns is usually larger than that of embedded patterns for the same support level (Column 3 of Table 2).

Third, by further looking at the mined maximal patterns, we find that the embedded maximal patterns at a certain support level can be partitioned into sets which correspond one-to-one to the maximal homomorphic patterns at the same support level so that all the embedded patterns in a set are less specific than the corresponding homomorphic pattern. Figure 14 shows, for each of the three datasets, examples of embedded maximal patterns each from the same set in the partition and the corresponding maximal homomorphic pattern. Therefore, for a number of applications, maximal homomorphic patterns can offer more information in a more compact way.

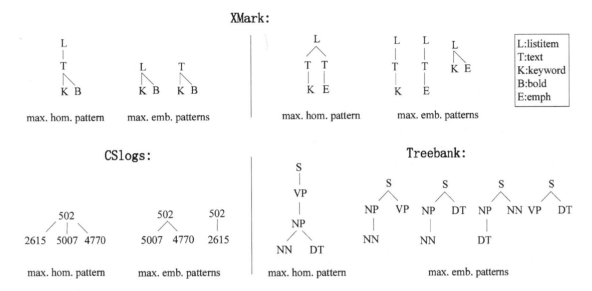

Fig. 14 Examples of maximal patterns mined from the three datasets

5 Related Work

We now discuss how our work relates to the existing literature. The problem of mining tree patterns from a set of small trees has been studied since the last decade. Among the many proposed algorithms [2, 3, 5, 6, 8–11, 14–19, 25–27], only few mine unordered embedded patterns [9, 17, 26].

Mining unordered embedded patterns TreeFinder [17] is the first unordered embedded tree pattern mining algorithm. It is a two-step algorithm. In the first step, it clusters the input trees by the co-occurrence of labels pairs. In the second step, it computes maximal trees that are common to all the trees of each cluster. A known limitation of *TreeFinder* is that it tends to miss many frequent patterns and is computationally expensive.

WTIMiner [9] transfers the frequent tree pattern mining to itemset mining. It first finds all the frequent itemsets, and then for each itemset found, it scans the database to count all the corresponding tree patterns. Although *WTIMiner* is complete, it is inefficient since the structural information is lost while mining for frequent itemsets. Further, the overhead for processing false positives may potentially reduce the performance.

Sleuth [26] extends the ordered embedded pattern mining algorithm *TreeMiner* [27]. Unlike *TreeFinder*, *Sleuth* uses the equivalence class pattern expansion method to generate candidates. To avoid repeated invocation of tree inclusion checking, *Sleuth* maintains a list of embedded occurrences with each pattern. It defines also a quadratic join operation over pattern occurrence lists to compute support for candidates. The join operation becomes inefficient when the size of pattern occurrence lists is large. Our approach relies on an incremental stack-based

approach that exploits bitmaps to efficiently compute the support in time linear to the size of input data.

Mining maximal and closed induced patterns There exist algorithms [5, 18, 25] which focus on mining closed and maximal (induced) patterns. A frequent pattern P is closed if none of P's proper superpatterns has the same support as that P has; P is maximal if none of P's proper superpatterns is frequent. The number of both maximal and closed patterns is usually much smaller, yet represents the same information as that of *all* frequent patterns. We below briefly mention about these algorithms.

CMTreeMiner [5] mines both closed and maximal frequent patterns from a set of small trees. Their method relies on a concept called *blanket*. The blanket of a pattern provides the set of immediate super patterns that are frequent. By comparing the occurrences of a given pattern with the occurrences of its blanket patterns, the algorithm determines whether the original pattern is closed or not. It uses pruning and heuristic techniques to reduce the search space. *CMTreeMiner* is the first algorithm which directly mines closed and maximal patterns without first generating all frequent patterns. However, it mines only for induced patterns; extending it to embedded patterns is not trivial.

PathJoin [25] finds maximal unordered induced patterns from a set of small trees. *PathJoin* assumes that no two siblings in data trees have the same label. It first discovers the set of maximal frequent paths and then it finds the tree patterns by joining the paths. After obtaining all frequent patterns, *PathJoin* keeps only maximal patterns by using a post-processing pruning, which eliminates those that are not maximal. Such a strategy will suffer from a significant overhead if the number of false positive paths is very high.

DryadeParent [18] mines closed induced patterns from a set of small trees. Observing that the performances of existing algorithms are dramatically affected by the branching factor of the tree patterns to find, *DryadeParent* makes the assumption that no two siblings in the data trees can have the same label (similar to *PathJoin*). The method first computes a set of tiles, which are closed frequent patterns of depth 1. Then, it develops a hooking strategy that reconstructs the closed frequent patterns from these tiles. Similar to *PathJoin*, *DryadeParent* is designed based on the assumption that no two siblings in the data trees can have the same label. While this simplifies the problem, it limits the usage of the method in real applications.

The work on mining tree patterns in a single large tree or graph setting has so far been very limited. The only known papers are [8, 10, 11] which focus on mining tree patterns with only child edges from a single graph and [19] which leverages homomorphisms to mine embedded tree patterns from a single tree. To the best of our knowledge, our work is the first one for efficiently mining (maximal) homomorphic tree patterns with descendant edges from a single large tree.

A preliminary version of algorithm *HomTreeMiner* was presented in [22]. The algorithm described in the present paper extends the previous version with an optimization technique which exploits the specificity relation to prune the space of candidate homomorphic patterns. The performance of the new version of *HomTreeMiner* is compared with that of its old version in the experimental section.

6 Conclusion

In this paper, we have addressed the problem of mining maximal frequent homomorphic tree patterns from a single large tree. We have provided a novel definition of maximal homomorphic patterns which takes into account homomorphisms, pattern specificity and the single tree setting. We have designed an efficient algorithm that discovers all frequent non-redundant maximal homomorphic tree patterns. Our approach employs an incremental stack-based frequency computation method that avoids the costly enumeration of all pattern occurrences required by previous approaches. An originality of our method is that matching information of already computed patterns is materialized as bitmaps, which greatly reduces both memory consumption and computation costs. An optimization technique further prunes the search space of candidate patterns. We have conducted extensive experiments to compare our approach with tree mining algorithms that mine embedded patterns when applied to a large data tree. Our results show that maximal homomorphic patterns are fewer and larger than maximal embedded tree patterns. Further, our algorithm is as fast as the state-of-

the-art algorithm mining embedded trees from a single tree while outperforming it in terms of memory consumption and scalability.

Several applications are interested in extracting not all the frequent patterns, but only those that comply with a number of restrictions. We are currently working on incorporating user-specified constraints to the proposed approach to enable constraint-based homomorphic pattern mining.

References

1. Amer-Yahia S, Cho S, Lakshmanan LVS, and Srivastava D (2001) Minimization of tree pattern queries. In: SIGMOD, pp 497–508
2. Asai T, Abe K, Kawasoe S, Arimura H, Sakamoto H, and Arikawa S (2002) Efficient substructure discovery from large semi-structured data. In: SDM, pp 158–174
3. Asai T, Arimura H, Uno T, Nakano S-I (2003) Discovering frequent substructures in large unordered trees. In: Discovery, Science, pp 47–61
4. Bruno N, Koudas N, and Srivastava D (2002) Holistic twig joins: optimal XML pattern matching. In: SIGMOD, pp 310–321
5. Chi Y, Xia Y, Yang Y, Muntz RR (2005) Mining closed and maximal frequent subtrees from databases of labeled rooted trees. IEEE Trans Knowl Data Eng 17(2):190–202
6. Chi Y, Yang Y, and Muntz RR (2004) Hybridtreeminer: an efficient algorithm for mining frequent rooted trees and free trees using canonical form. In: SSDBM, pp 11–20
7. Chi Y, Yang Y, Muntz RR (2005) Canonical forms for labelled trees and their applications in frequent subtree mining. Knowl Inf Syst 8(2):203–234
8. Dries A, Nijssen S (2012) Mining patterns in networks using homomorphism. In: SDM, pp 260–271
9. Feng Z, Hsu W, and Lee M-L (2005) Efficient pattern discovery for semistructured data. In: ICTAI, pp 294–301
10. Goethals B, Hoekx E, and den Bussche JV (2005) Mining tree queries in a graph. In: KDD, pp 61–69
11. Kibriya AM, Ramon J (2013) Nearly exact mining of frequent trees in large networks. Data Min Knowl Discov 27(3):478–504
12. Kilpeläinen P, Mannila H (1995) Ordered and unordered tree inclusion. SIAM J Comput 24(2):340–356
13. Miklau G, Suciu D (2004) Containment and equivalence for a fragment of xpath. J ACM 51(1):2–45
14. Nijssen S, Kok JN (2004) A quickstart in frequent structure mining can make a difference. In: KDD, pp 647–652
15. Tan H, Hadzic F, Dillon TS, Chang E, Feng L (2008) Tree model guided candidate generation for mining frequent subtrees from xml documents. TKDD 2(2):1–43
16. Tatikonda S, Parthasarathy S, Kurç TM (2006) Trips and tides: new algorithms for tree mining. In: CIKM, pp 455–464
17. Termier A, Rousset M-C, Sebag M (2002) Treefinder: a first step towards xml data mining. In: ICDM, pp 450–457
18. Termier A, Rousset M-C, Sebag M, Ohara K, Washio T, Motoda H (2008) Dryadeparent, an efficient and robust closed attribute tree mining algorithm. IEEE Trans Knowl Data Eng 20(3):300–320
19. Wu X, Theodoratos D (2015) Leveraging homomorphisms and bitmaps to enable the mining of embedded patterns from large data trees. In: DASFAA, pp 3–20
20. Wu X, Theodoratos D (2016) Template-based bitmap view selection for optimizing queries over tree data. Int J Coop Inf Syst 25(3):1–28

21. Wu X, Theodoratos D, Kementsietsidis A (2015) Configuring bitmap materialized views for optimizing XML queries. World Wide Web 18(3):607–632
22. Wu X, Theodoratos D, Peng Z (2016) Efficiently mining homomorphic patterns from large data trees. In: DASFAA, pp 180–196
23. Wu X, Theodoratos D, Wang WH (2009) Answering XML queries using materialized views revisited. In: CIKM, pp 475–484
24. Wu X, Theodoratos D, Wang WH, Sellis T (2013) Optimizing XML queries: bitmapped materialized views vs. indexes. Inf Syst 38(6):863–884
25. Xiao Y, Yao J-F, Li Z, Dunham MH (2003) Efficient data mining for maximal frequent subtrees. In: ICDM, pp 379–386
26. Zaki MJ (2005) Efficiently mining frequent embedded unordered trees. Fundam Inform 66(1–2):33–52
27. Zaki MJ (2005) Efficiently mining frequent trees in a forest: algorithms and applications. IEEE Trans Knowl Data Eng 17(8):1021–1035
28. Zhu F, Qu Q, Lo D, Yan X, Han J, Yu PS (2011) Mining top-k large structural patterns in a massive network. PVLDB 4(11):807–818
29. Zhu F, Yan X, Han J, Yu PS, Cheng H (2007) Mining colossal frequent patterns by core pattern fusion. In: ICDE, pp 706–715

13

Investigating TSP Heuristics for Location-Based Services

Weihuang Huang[1] · Jeffrey Xu Yu[1]

Abstract Travel planning is one of the important issues in the location-based services (*LBS*). Traveling salesman problem (*TSP*) is to find the optimal tour that traverses points exactly once in the minimum total distance. Given the hardness of *TSP* (NP-hard), *TSP* query for a given set of points, Q, is not widely studied for online *LBS*, and the nearest-neighbor heuristic is the only heuristic adapted to find *TSP*-like tours with additional constraints for *LBS*. The questions to ask are: Is the nearest-neighbor the best in terms of accuracy? Which heuristics among many should we use to process *TSP* queries online for *LBS*? In the literature, *TSPLIB* benchmarks are designed for special cases where the number of points used is large, and the existing synthetic datasets are based on uniform/normal distributions. Both do not reflect the real datasets used in real applications. Therefore, the best heuristics suggested by the *TSPLIB* and the existing benchmarks need to be reconsidered for *LBS* setting. In this work, we investigate 22 heuristics and show that the best heuristics in terms of accuracy for *LBS* are not the ones suggested by the existing work, and identify several heuristics by extensive performance studies over real datasets, *TSPLIB* benchmarks, the existing synthetic datasets and our new synthetic datasets. Among many issues, we also show that it is possible to get high-quality *TSP* by precomputing/indexing, even though it is hard to prove by theorem.

Keywords TSP · Heuristics · Sketch

1 Introduction

Location-based services (*LBS*) attract great attention from both research and industry communities, and various queries have been studied. In Refs. [7, 26] discover useful information from trajectory data generated in daily life. In Refs. [17, 24] optimize query processing on location-based social networks. In Refs. [12, 18, 25] combine *LBS* with traditional keyword search. Travel planning has also been studied, and becomes an important issue in location-based services (*LBS*), which are to find tours among points of interest (*POI*), where *POI*s are with latitude and longitude in a two-dimensional space or in a road network. In Refs. [9, 26] study on how to find trajectories from an existing trajectory set. There are works that try to construct routes satisfying certain requirements. In [8] constructs the most popular routes between two given points. In [35] defines different queries as finding the earliest arrival, latest departure and shortest duration paths on the transportation networks. Some recent work study finding the shortest tour connecting two *POI*s [34, 38] and searching the optimal meeting point for a set of *POI*s, which are to minimize the sum of distances from these *POI*s to the meeting point [36, 37].

As an important issue in travel planning, traveling salesman problem (*TSP*) has been extensively studied, which finds a tour that traverses all the points exactly once with the minimum overall distance, for a given set of points, and is known as NP-hard problem. The hardness is mainly due to two reasons. First, given n points, there are $n!$ possible routes to traverse, in order to find the one with minimum overall distance. Second, the local optimum

✉ Weihuang Huang
  whhuang@se.cuhk.edu.hk

  Jeffrey Xu Yu
  yu@se.cuhk.edu.hk

[1] The Chinese University of Hong Kong, Hong Kong, China

property does not hold. The state-of-the-art exact *TSP* solution, Concorde, is based on linear programming (http://www.math.uwaterloo.ca/tsp/concorde.html). By randomization, Arora in [1] finds $(1 + \frac{1}{c})$-approximate answer in $O(n(\log n)^{O(c)})$ time, for every fixed $c > 1$, which is known as the best theoretical result, but is difficult to implement. In the literature, numerous works have been proposed to study *TSP* [19]. A large number of heuristics are proposed to find a high-quality tour within reasonable time. In Refs. [5, 31] and the most recent [21] summarize and test many representative heuristics and compare them in both effectiveness and efficiency.

Given the hardness of *TSP*, *TSP* query is not well studied in database community. Recently, there are *TSP*-like problems being studied for *LBS*, which are with constraints to reduce the search space [6, 23, 33], and find a tour by adding nearest neighbors one by one in a manner of expanding the partial result found. In other words, the work reported [6, 23, 33] only use one heuristic, namely the nearest neighbor, among many possible heuristics. The questions that arise are as follows. Is the nearest neighbor the best in terms of accuracy? What are the other methods and which one should we use to process *TSP* if there are many? This issue is important, since it opens ways for us to explore different ways to deal *TSP* in *LBS* for real large datasets with different properties.

There are several attempts to study different heuristics. First, [21] studies heuristics for *TSP* queries that travel more than 1000 points. However, in many real applications, the number of points can vary in a large range. For *LBS*, the number of points can be much smaller than that number. Second, the *TSPLIB* benchmark (http://comopt.ifi. uni-heidelberg.de/software/TSPLIB95) studies about 150 difficult cases, which is not sufficient to understand the heuristics in real datasets. Third, there are synthetic datasets [20, 21], but they do not reflect all real datasets. Figure 1 shows 4 datasets. Figure 1a shows a dataset with 3038 points in *TSPLIB*. Figure 1b shows a dataset containing 3000 points that follow normal distribution generated [21]. Figure 1c shows 3000 randomly sampled *POIs* in a real dataset in New York (NY). Figure 1d shows 3000 randomly sampled check-ins in Los Angeles (LA) from the location-based social network, *Gowalla* (https://en.wikipedia.org/wiki/Gowalla). Fourth, there are no performance studies to study all heuristics. In this work, we study 22 heuristics for *TSP* queries.

The main contributions of this work are summarized below. First, we study 22 *TSP* construction heuristics. The reason to study such heuristics is due to the efficiency requirement in *LBS*, since construction heuristics [21] are

efficient to find *TSP* without any further refinement. Second, we propose new synthetic datasets to understand *TSP* in the real *LBS* setting. Third, we conduct extensive performance studies over the selected real datasets, *TSP* benchmarks, the existing synthetic datasets, and our new synthetic datasets. Fourth, we conclude that both the nearest-neighbor-based heuristics that are widely used in *LBS* and the best heuristics in *TSPLIB* for difficult setting are not the best to be used in *LBS*. We identify several that can achieve high accuracy efficiently. Among many issues, we also show that it is possible to get high-quality *TSP* by precomputing/indexing, even though it is hard to prove by theorem.

The rest of the paper is organized as follows. Section 2 discusses the preliminaries and gives the problem statement. We introduce all the 22 construction heuristics in Sect. 3. In Sect. 4, we discuss our new synthetic datasets generation in detail, and we report our finding over the 22 heuristics using real datasets, the selected 20 *TSPLIB* benchmarks, the existing synthetic datasets, and new synthetic datasets. We conclude this work in Sect. 5.

2 Preliminaries

Consider a set of points V in a two-dimensional space, where the distance between two points u and v in V is the Euclidean distance, denoted as $d(u, v)$.

$$d(u, v) = \sqrt{(u.x - v.x)^2 + (u.y - v.y)^2} \qquad (1)$$

We denote the two x and y coordinates of a point u as $u.x$ and $u.y$.

An edge-weighted complete undirected graph $G = (V, E)$ can be constructed for the set of given points. Here, V is the set of nodes for the same set of points, and E is a set of edges for every pair of nodes in V where an edge weight for an edge (u, v) is the distance between u and $v, d(u, v)$.

Let Q be a subset of nodes of size $n = |Q|$ in V. A Hamilton path over Q is a simple path, $(v_1, v_2, v_3, \ldots, v_{n-1}, v_n)$, that visits every node exactly once, where (v_i, v_{i+1}) is an edge in the graph G. A Hamilton circuit over Q is a simple cycle over all nodes in G. Both Hamilton path and Hamilton circuit can be regarded as a permutation of nodes (or points) in Q. Here, a permutation π over Q is a one-to-one mapping. In other words, a node can only appear at a specific position in a permutation. Below, we use π_i to indicate a specific node v in Q at the ith position. We indicate a permutation over Q as $T = (\pi_1, \pi_2, \ldots, \pi_n)$. Given a permutation T over Q, the

Fig. 1 Different datasets.
a *TSPLIB* (pcb3038). **b** Normal.
c New York (*POI*). **d** Los
Angeles (check-ins)

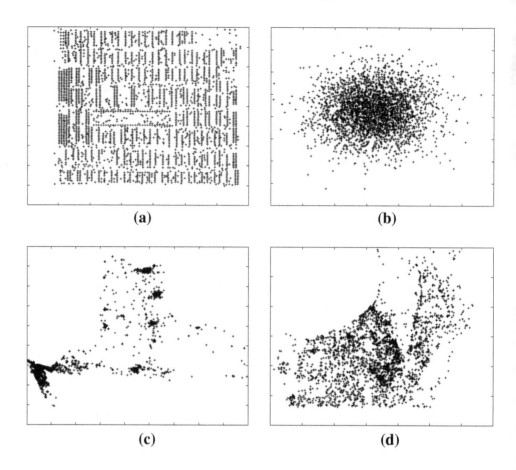

distance of a Hamilton path by T is defined as $d(T) = \sum_{1 \le i < n} d(\pi_i, \pi_{i+1})$, and the distance of a Hamilton circuit by T is defined as $d(T) = \sum_{1 \le i < n} d(\pi_i, \pi_{i+1}) + d(\pi_n, \pi_1)$. Let $\mathcal{T}$ be the set of all possible paths (circuits) for Q. The size of $\mathcal{T}$ is $|\mathcal{T}| = n!$ for Hamilton paths, and the size is $|\mathcal{T}| = \frac{(n-1)!}{2}$ for Hamilton circuits.

In this paper, we focus on Hamilton circuit, and may use "circuit," "tour" and "route" interchangeably, since they are all used in reported studies. Among all possible permutations in $\mathcal{T}$, the optimal Hamilton circuit over Q is the shortest Hamilton circuit, denoted as T^*, such that $d(T^*) = \min_{T \in \mathcal{T}} d(T)$. The problem of finding the optimal Hamilton circuit is known as traveling salesman problem (*TSP*), which is known to be NP-hard. The error-ratio for an approximate T is defined below.

$$\text{eratio}(T) = \frac{d(T) - d(T^*)}{d(T^*)} \qquad (2)$$

It is worth mentioning that the *TSP* problem we study in this paper is the symmetric and metric *TSP*. Here, by symmetric it implies $d(u, v) = d(v, u)$, and by metric it implies $\forall u, v, w \in V, d(u, w) + d(w, v) \ge d(u, v)$.

The Problem   In this paper, we study *TSP* query to find the shortest Hamilton circuit T^* for a given *TSP* query, Q,

which is a set of points, and explore the similarities and differences among 22 heuristics proposed for *TSP* using real datasets and new synthetic datasets in addition to the existing benchmarks and uniform/normal synthetic datasets.

3 The Heuristics

The *TSP* heuristics have been studied. In this work, we focus on tour construction heuristics [21]. By tour construction, it computes a tour (or a circuit) following some rules, and takes the resulting tour by the rules as the final result without further refinement. In [21], construction heuristics are divided into 3 categories: heuristics designed for speed, tour construction by pure augmentation and more complex tour construction. In this work, we cover more heuristics, and divide 22 construction heuristics into 3 new categories, namely (1) space-partitioning-based heuristics, (2) node-based heuristics and (3) edge-based heuristics. Table 2 lists all the 22 heuristics studied, where some are with guarantee of the approximate ratio. Below, we discuss 2 space-partitioning-based heuristics in Sect. 3.1, 4 edge-based heuristics in Sect. 3.3 and 16 node-based heuristics in Sect. 3.2.

3.1 Space-Partitioning-Based Heuristics

The space-partitioning-based methods compute *TSP* for a given set of points Q in three main steps: (1) partition nodes in Q into smaller subsets based on their pairwise Euclidean distances, (2) connect the nodes in the same subset into a Hamilton path and (3) determine the Hamilton circuit for Q by linking all Hamilton paths obtained for all subsets. We discuss two heuristics, namely Strip and Hilbert.

First, Strip computes the minimum bounding rectangle (*MBR*) in two-dimensional space that encloses all the query nodes Q of size $n = |Q|$, and partitions the *MBR* into $\sqrt{\frac{n}{3}}$ equal-width vertical strips. For each vertical strip, Strip sequences all the inside nodes according to y-coordinate by alternately top to bottom and bottom to top. The final circuit is determined by connecting all the sequences computed for all strips. Strip only involves sorting by x-coordinate and y-coordinate.

Algorithm 1: Greedy (Q)

Input: Q: a *TSP* query of a set of points
Output: T: the *TSP* for Q
1 **begin**
2     $T \leftarrow \emptyset$; $\mathcal{H} \leftarrow \emptyset$;
3   **for** *every* $u, v \in Q$ *s.t.* $u \neq v$ **do**
4   insert (u, v) with $d(u, v)$ into the min-heap $\mathcal{H}$;
5   **while** $|T| < |Q|$ **do**
6   let (u, v) be the edge with min cost deleted from $\mathcal{H}$;
7   **if** u *and* v *are not in the same subtree* **then**
8   **if** $deg(u) \leq 2$ *and* $deg(v) \leq 2$ **then**
9   insert (u, v) into T;
10   connect the two nodes in T with degree 1;
11   **return** T;

Second, the space filling curve is a widely used technique to map multidimensional data into one-dimensional data. The main idea behind the space filling curve is that it keeps the locality information of the original data after mapping such that two near nodes may still be close to each other after mapping. Therefore, visiting query nodes in Q in the order of their appearance along the space filling curve reduces the total length [29]. By space filling curve, it can recursively partition the whole plane into small units, where a unit is labeled with a string of binary digits based on where it is in the hierarchy. For instance, if the entire plane is divided into two units, one is labeled with "0," and the other is labeled with "1." Then it can get 4 units by further dividing each of the unit into another 2 smaller units in the similar manner. Such partitioning stops until there is at most one node at each unit. In this paper, we focus on the Hilbert curve (or Hilbert space filling curve) since it has better locality-preserving behavior.

Both Strip and Hilbert are easy to implement and are efficient. However, they only utilize pairwise distances to reduce the total route length, and neglect the overall distribution of all query nodes, which sacrifices accuracy. To improve the accuracy, in every step, there are several strategies that can be adopted to make the final circuit as short as possible. The state-of-the-art approximate algorithm [1] is based on partition. However, it utilizes dynamic programming to connect inner and inter nodes, which is beyond the scope of this work on simple construction heuristics.

3.2 Edge-Based Heuristics

The edge-based heuristics are based on the minimum spanning tree (*MST*). We discuss the greedy (Greedy) which is known as multiple fragment heuristic, double-*MST* (DMST), the Christofides algorithm (Chris) and the savings algorithm (SV).

First, Greedy is designed based on the Kruskal's algorithm [22] to find the minimum spanning tree for a undirected graph. As shown in Algorithm 1, it inserts every pair of u and v in Q as an edge into a min-heap $\mathcal{H}$ with $d(u, v)$. In the while loop, it picks up the edge (u, v) from $\mathcal{H}$, which is with the minimum distance, and checks if such an edge (u, v) can connect two different subtrees as a larger subtree without a cycle. In addition, it further checks if the tree formed can end up a *TSP* by ensuring that the degree of u/v ($deg(u)/deg(v)$) is less than or equal to 2. At the end, it connects the two nodes in T with degree 1 to form a circuit.

Second, DMST is an algorithm which traverses the minimum spanning tree T constructed for the edge-weighted undirected graph representation for Q. To obtain the circuit, it keeps the traversal order and skips the nodes which are traversed before.

Third, the Christofides algorithm (Chris) finds the circuit as follows. (1) Given the edge-weighted undirected graph representation $G = (V, E)$ for Q, it finds the minimum spanning tree $T = (V_T, E_T)$. (2) It identifies a subset of V_T, denoted as V_O, which includes all those nodes in V_T that have an odd degree. (3) It then constructs an induced subgraph $G_O(V_O, E_O)$ from G. (4) It finds a minimum weighted perfect matching M from G_O, where a perfect matching M is a set of edges that do not have any common nodes. (5) It constructs a multigraph $G_H = T \cup M$. (6) It then finds an Eulerian circuit in G_H, because every node in G_H has an even degree. (7) Finally, it obtains the Hamilton circuit by removing the repeated nodes from the Eulerian circuit.

Fourth, the savings algorithm (SV) takes a different approach, and does not build a circuit using a minimum spanning tree. SV starts from a randomly selected node as the central node v_c and then builds a pseudo tour, T_P, from the central node v_c to all other nodes in Q. In order to make the tour short, SV looks for shortcuts in the pseudo tour T_P constructed. In every iteration, SV selects a pair of nodes u

and v that connect with v_c in T_P based on Eq. (3), deletes the edge $(u, v_c), (v, v_c)$, and inserts a new edge (u, v) as shortcut. In order to find the shortcut with maximum benefit, it defines a new cost function as:

$$(u, v) = \underset{u, v \in T_P \land u \neq v \neq v_c}{\operatorname{argmin}} \{c'(u, v)\} \tag{3}$$

where the cost function c' is given in Eq. (4).

$$c'(u, v) = d(u, v) - d(u, v_c) - d(v, v_c) \tag{4}$$

All the edge-based heuristics aim at finding the edge with the smallest distance directly into the circuit. DMST and Chris have a better approximate ratio than most heuristics studied in this work because a *TSP* circuit becomes a tree if any edge is removed from it, whose total length should be smaller than that of *MST*.

3.3 Node-Based Heuristics

The node-based heuristics construct a circuit by expanding the nodes in Q one by one until all of them are visited. There are three main issues in the heuristics, which are (a) how to initialize an initial node(s) and (b) in every iteration, how to select the next node to expand and where it is for the next node to be inserted. Among the node-based heuristics, we discuss the nearest-neighbor heuristics, the insertion heuristics, the convex hull-based insertion heuristics, the addition heuristics, and the augmented addition heuristics. Algorithm 2 shows the framework of node-based heuristics.

Algorithm 2: *TSP*-N(Q)

Input: Q: a *TSP* query of a set of points
Output: T: the *TSP* for Q
1 **begin**
2 $\quad$ $T \leftarrow \text{init}(Q)$;
3 $\quad$ **while** *T does not contain all nodes in Q* **do**
4 $\quad\quad$ $v \leftarrow \text{select}(Q, T)$;
5 $\quad\quad$ $\text{insert}(v, T)$;
6 $\quad$ **return** T;

The Nearest-Neighbor Heuristics [3] The nearest-neighbor heuristics do not spend time on finding an initial *TSP* by init(Q), and randomly picks one node from Q. In other words, T by init(Q) contains only one node randomly selected. Then, in every iteration in the while loop, it picks up a point from the nodes that have not been selected before, namely from $Q \setminus T$, and inserts it into the end of the current partial path computed in the previous iteration. Assume $T_i = (\pi_1, \pi_2, \ldots, \pi_i)$ is the partial path computed at the ith iteration. There are two ends in T_i, namely π_1 and π_i. Consider the $(i+1)$th iteration to expand the path by adding one more node. The nearest-neighbor heuristic (NN) selects the nearest-neighbor node to the node at the position π_i from $Q \setminus T_i$, and inserts the node selected at π_{i+1}. On the

other hand, the double-ended nearest-neighbor heuristic (DENN) considers the nearest-neighbor node to either of the two end points: π_1 and π_i. Assume the node selected is near to the node at π_1, DENN will insert the newly selected node at π_1 in T_{i+1} and place the node at the jth position (π_j) in T_i at $(j+1)$th position π_{j+1} in T_{i+1}. Otherwise, if the node selected is near to the node π_i, DENN behaves like NN. Both NN and DENN expand a path. After the while loop, both obtain the *TSP* by adding one edge from the last node to the first node in T. We omit such post-processing from Algorithm 2. In brief, comparing with NN, DENN considers both ends of the current partial path when expanding and selects the one with shorter length. Consequently, DENN consumes longer time than NN to improve the accuracy.

The Insertion Heuristics [31] Like the nearest-neighbor heuristics, the insertion heuristics randomly pick one node from Q by init(Q). Unlike the nearest-neighbor heuristics which expand the current partial path in every iteration, the insertion heuristics enlarge the current partial circuit in every iteration. Let T_i be the partial circuit over nodes of size i such that $T_i = (\pi_1, \pi_2, \ldots, \pi_i, \pi_1)$. In the $(i+1)$th iteration, the insertion heuristics attempt to add one node into the current circuit by minimizing the increment of the total distance of the circuit. There are two things. One is how to select a node, w, from $Q \setminus T_i$. The other is how to insert w into T_i to obtain T_{i+1}. We first discuss how to insert a new node into T_i, assuming the node to be inserted next is selected from $Q \setminus T_i$. We will discuss the node selection next (Table 1).

Consider an insertion of a node w ($\notin T_i$) between u and v in T_i. Here, for simplicity, we say to insert a node w into an edge (u, v) in T_i, where an edge (u, v) implies that v is next to u in the permutation. In the new circuit to be, T_{i+1}, the edge (u, v) in T_i will be replaced by two edges (u, w) and (w, v). Among all edges in T_i, the edge, (u, v), selected for a given node w is to minimize the incremental cost by Eq. (5).

$$(u, v) = \underset{(u,v) \in T_i}{\operatorname{argmin}} \{c(u, v, w)\} \tag{5}$$

where $c(u, v, w)$ is a cost function to measure the incremental cost of inserting a node between two nodes (an edge) as given in Eq. (6).

$$c(u, v, w) = d(w, u) + d(w, v) - d(u, v) \tag{6}$$

Next consider how to select the next node. There are 4 ways to select the next node w to be inserted into T_i, namely the random insertion (RI), the nearest insertion (NI), the cheapest insertion (CI) and the furthest insertion (FI) [28]. Here, RI randomly picks one as the next node

Table 1 Expansion order of the node-based heuristics

Node-Based	1	2	3	4	5	6	7	8	9	10	11	12	13	14	15	16	17	18	19	20
NN	**v_1**	v_{20}	v_2	v_3	v_4	v_{18}	v_{17}	v_{16}	v_{15}	v_{14}	v_{13}	v_{12}	v_{11}	v_{10}	v_9	v_8	v_7	v_6	v_5	v_{19}
DENN	**v_1**	v_{20}	v_2	v_3	v_4	v_{18}	v_{17}	v_{16}	v_{15}	v_{14}	v_{13}	v_{12}	v_{11}	v_{10}	v_9	v_8	v_{19}	v_7	v_6	v_5
NI	**v_1**	v_{20}	v_2	v_3	v_4	v_{18}	v_7	v_6	v_{17}	v_{16}	v_{15}	v_{14}	v_{13}	v_{12}	v_{11}	v_{10}	v_9	v_8	v_{19}	v_5
CI	**v_1**	v_{20}	v_2	v_3	v_{18}	v_4	v_7	v_6	v_{17}	v_{16}	v_{15}	v_{13}	v_{14}	v_{12}	v_{11}	v_{10}	v_9	v_8	v_5	v_{19}
RI	**v_3**	v_6	v_{17}	v_8	v_2	v_9	v_{12}	v_{19}	v_{16}	v_{11}	v_{20}	v_{15}	v_7	v_5	v_{10}	v_{18}	v_{14}	v_4	v_1	v_{13}
FI	**v_1**	v_8	v_5	v_{19}	v_7	v_4	v_{17}	v_{18}	v_{10}	v_3	v_{20}	v_9	v_{16}	v_{15}	v_{12}	v_6	v_{11}	v_2	v_{14}	v_{13}
CHNI	**v_8**	**v_{10}**	**v_{19}**	**v_5**	v_{11}	v_{12}	v_{13}	v_{14}	v_{15}	v_{16}	v_9	v_{17}	v_7	v_6	v_4	v_3	v_2	v_1	v_{20}	v_{18}
CHCI	**v_8**	**v_{10}**	**v_{19}**	**v_5**	v_{20}	v_{12}	v_9	v_{13}	v_{14}	v_{11}	v_6	v_7	v_1	v_2	v_3	v_4	v_{18}	v_{16}	v_{17}	v_{15}
CHRI	**v_8**	**v_{10}**	**v_{19}**	**v_5**	v_1	v_2	v_3	v_4	v_6	v_7	v_9	v_{11}	v_{12}	v_{13}	v_{14}	v_{15}	v_{16}	v_{17}	v_{18}	v_{20}
CHFI	**v_8**	**v_{10}**	**v_{19}**	**v_5**	v_2	v_7	v_{20}	v_{17}	v_{18}	v_4	v_1	v_9	v_{16}	v_{15}	v_{12}	v_6	v_{11}	v_3	v_{14}	v_{13}
NA	**v_1**	v_{20}	v_2	v_3	v_4	v_{18}	v_7	v_6	v_{17}	v_{16}	v_{15}	v_{14}	v_{13}	v_{12}	v_{11}	v_{10}	v_9	v_8	v_{19}	v_5
RA	**v_3**	v_6	v_{17}	v_8	v_2	v_9	v_{12}	v_{19}	v_{16}	v_{11}	v_{20}	v_{15}	v_7	v_5	v_{10}	v_{18}	v_{14}	v_4	v_1	v_{13}
FA	**v_1**	v_8	v_5	v_{19}	v_7	v_4	v_{17}	v_{18}	v_{10}	v_3	v_{20}	v_9	v_{16}	v_{15}	v_{12}	v_6	v_{11}	v_2	v_{14}	v_{13}
NA+	**v_1**	v_{20}	v_2	v_3	v_4	v_{18}	v_7	v_6	v_{17}	v_{16}	v_{15}	v_{14}	v_{13}	v_{12}	v_{11}	v_{10}	v_9	v_8	v_{19}	v_5
RA+	**v_3**	v_6	v_{17}	v_8	v_2	v_9	v_{12}	v_{19}	v_{16}	v_{11}	v_{20}	v_{15}	v_7	v_5	v_{10}	v_{18}	v_{14}	v_4	v_1	v_{13}
FA+	**v_1**	v_8	v_5	v_{19}	v_7	v_4	v_{17}	v_{18}	v_{10}	v_3	v_{20}	v_9	v_{16}	v_{15}	v_{12}	v_6	v_{11}	v_2	v_{14}	v_{13}

Bold values in each row represent the initial node(s) for the corresponding heuristic

w. NI selects the next node w from $Q \setminus T_i$ that has the smallest distance to a node in T_i (Eq. 7)

$$w = \underset{w \notin T_i}{\operatorname{argmin}}\{d(w, v), \forall v \in T_i\} \qquad (7)$$

Note that NI inserts the nearest node to the current circuit, instead of the end node as done by the nearest-neighbor heuristics (NN or DENN). CI selects the next node based on the cost function.

$$w = \underset{w \notin T_i}{\operatorname{argmin}}\{c(u, v, w), \forall (u, v) \in T_i\} \qquad (8)$$

We discuss the similarity between NI and CI in certain cases. Suppose the next node to be inserted is w. Assume v' is the node in T_i under which w is selected by Eq. (7), and assume (u, v) is the edge under which the next node w is selected by CI based on Eq. (8) As proved in [5], (u, v) should satisfy at least one of the 3 conditions: (1) $u = v'$ or $v = v'$, which means one endpoint of this edge in T_i is the nearest neighbor to w; (2) given a circle C centered at w with the radius $1.5 \times d(w, v')$, then either $u \in C$ or $v \in C$, which means one endpoint of this edge is inside a circle centered at w; and (3) for every pair of (v_i, v_j) in T_i, given a circle C_i centered at v_i with radius $1.5 \times d(v_i, v_j)$, then either $w \in C_i$ or $w \in C_j$, which means w is inside the corresponding circle of u or v. Here, if the condition 1 is satisfied, CI selects the same node as NI does.

Unlike the 3 heuristics to select the next node discussed above, FI picks up the next node which is far away from T_i with a higher priority. It chooses the next node following Eq. (9).

$$w = \underset{w \notin T_i}{\operatorname{argmax}}\{d(w, T_i)\} \qquad (9)$$

where $d(w, T_i)$ is the smallest distance from a node $w \notin T_i$ to a node in the current T_i such that $d(w, T_i) = \min_{v \in T_p} d(v, w)$.

Convex Hull-Based Insertion Heuristics The insertion heuristics pick the start node randomly, which may affect the quality of the result. As pointed out in [27], it is an effective approach to construct an initial circuit for the points Q and then insert the remaining nodes into the initial circuit. It is proved that for the optimal circuit, the nodes lying on the boundary of the convex hull will be visited in their cyclic order [14]. This suggests that the convex hull can serve as a sketch to guide future insertions. The convex hull-based insertions are proposed to find the convex hull of all nodes in Q first using $T \leftarrow init(Q)$ and then compute the circuit using one of the insertion heuristics for the remaining nodes in $Q \setminus T$. Here, we investigate 4 heuristics: convex hull cheapest insertion (CHCI), convex hull nearest insertion (CHNI), convex hull random insertion (CHRI) and convex hull furthest insertion (CHFI). Note that [21] only shows the testing results for CHCI.

The Addition Heuristics [5] The insertion heuristics determine an edge for a node to be inserted among all the edges in T_i. To further reduce the computational cost, for a node w selected from $Q \setminus T_i$, the addition heuristics pick a node v at π_j on the current circuit T_i and only consider the insertion of w either between two nodes at (π_{j-1}, π_j) or between two nodes at (π_j, π_{j+1}). The edge can be selected with the smallest cost by Eq. (6). We study 3 ways to select the next node w, namely random addition (RA), nearest addition (NA) and furthest addition (FA). We do not study cheapest addition, since the insert position by the cheapest heuristic is decided once the next node is determined. Here, RA selects the next node w from $Q \setminus T_i$ randomly, and identifies $v \in T_i$ based on Eq. (10).

$$v = \operatorname*{argmin}_{v \in T_i}\{d(w, v)\} \qquad (10)$$

NA selects a pair of nodes, w and v such that $w \notin T_i$ and $v \in T_i$ in a similar way like the nearest insertion, based on Eq. (11).

$$(v, w) = \operatorname*{argmin}_{v \in T_i, w \notin T_i}\{d(v, w)\} \qquad (11)$$

Here, w is the next node to be selected, and v is the node at π_j position in the current T_i. FA selects the next node w based on Eq. (9), and identifies the insertion position π_j by Eq. (10), and inserts w either between π_{j-1} and π_j or between π_j and π_{j+1} following the minimal incremental cost (Eq. 6).

Augmented Addition Heuristics Consider the insertion heuristics and the addition heuristics. On the one hand, the insertion heuristics explore all edges in T_i to insert a node w between a pair of nodes, u and v, as an edge (u, v). On the other hand, the addition heuristics only consider 2 edges incident to the node v at π_j, when inserting w. Different from insertion/addition heuristics, the augmented additions attempt to explore more than 2 edges up to some extent. Here, like the addition heuristics, they select the node w ($\notin T_i$) and the insertion position v at π_j in T_i using either RA, NA, and FA. Then, the augmented addition heuristics select an edge with the minimum cost from all edges in a circle centered at w with the radius of $\alpha \cdot r$, where $\alpha \geq 1$ and $r = d(w, v)$ in the two-dimensional space. Here, an edge (u, v) is in the circle if u or v appears in the circle. We denote such augmented addition heuristics as random augmented addition (RA+), nearest augmented addition (NA+) and furthest augmented addition (FA+).

3.4 An Example

Figure 2 shows the optimal *TSP*, T, for a *TSP* query Q with 20 points, v_i, for $1 \leq i \leq 20$ sampled from NY. The positions of the 20 points are also given in Fig. 2, which forms 3 clusters, one with 10 points, $\{v_i\}$, for $8 \leq i \leq 17$, one with 2 points, $\{v_7, v_8\}$ and one with 5 points, $\{v_1, v_2, v_3, v_4, v_{20}\}$. There are some points which are at a distance from any of the clusters, such as v_5, v_{18} and v_{19}. Table 2 shows the 22 heuristics in the three categories: space-partitioning-based, edge-based, and node-based. For each heuristic, the approximate ratio is given, if any, which is for a *TSP*, Q,

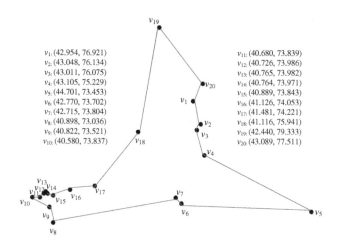

Fig. 2 A *TSP* Example

with n points. Also, in Table 2, the 5th column shows the eratio, for the *TSP* of 20 points shown in Fig. 2. Here, as default, we select v_1 as the first node to start except for the 4 convex hull-based insertion heuristics, which identify a convex hull with nodes, v_8, v_{10}, v_{19}, and v_4, to start. In particular, we also show how the node-based heuristics select the next node in every iteration in Table 1. In terms of the accuracy, among the 22 heuristics, there are 3 heuristics that get the optimal *TSP*.

4 Performance Studies

We study all 22 heuristics covering a large range of datasets: 4 real datasets, 20 datasets from *TSPLIB* benchmark [30], 2 existing synthetic datasets [21] and new synthetic datasets.

Datasets: The 4 real datasets used to test are shown in Table 3. Here, NY (New York) and BJ (Beijing) are real *POI*s of the two cities. LA (Los Angeles) and HK (Hong Kong) are real check-in data we crawled from the location-based social network in the two cities from Twitter (https://twitter.com/) and Gowalla, respectively.

The 20 datasets selected from the *TSPLIB* benchmark [30] cover 3 major types of *TSPLIB* data: ATT, EUD_2D, and GEO, and are summarized in Table 4, where the 1st and 4th columns are the short names, the 2nd and 5th columns are the names used in the benchmark, and the 3rd and 6th columns are the size of points used in the dataset. There are 10 datasets where $n = |Q|$ is selected between 100 and 1000, denoted as TB_H, and there are 10 datasets where $n = |Q|$ is selected between 1000 and 10000, denoted as TB_T.

We discuss our new synthetic datasets generation in this work. Note that the 2 existing synthetic datasets by uniform distribution and normal distribution [21] are not the

Table 2 Twenty-two heuristics (default start node: v_1)

Category		Heuristics	App. ratio	eratio for Fig. 2
Space-partitioning-based		Hilbert [2]	$\Omega(\sqrt{n})$	1.639
		Strip [29]	$O(\sqrt{n})$	0.129
Edge-based		Greedy [21]	$O(\sqrt{n})$	0.132
		DMST [21]	2	0.116
		Chris [11]	1.5	0.145
		SV [21]	–	0.028
Node-based	Nearest neighbor	NN [31]	$O(\lg n)$	0.158
		DENN [5]	–	0.096
	Insertion	NI [31]	2	0.073
		CI [31]	2	0.049
		RI [31]	$O(\lg n)$	0.011
		FI [28]	1.5	0
	Convex hull-based insertion	CHRI [21]	–	0.004
		CHCI [21]	–	0.001
		CHNI [21]	–	0.006
		CHFI [21]	–	0
	Addition	NA [21]	2	0.085
		RA [21]	–	0.160
		FA [21]	–	0.243
	Augmented addition	NA+ [5]	–	0.073
		RA+ [5]	–	0.083
		FA+ [5]	$O(\sqrt{n})$	0

Table 3 Four real datasets

Dataset	Size	Type	Dataset	Size	Type
NY	653,008	*POI*	LA	411,596	check-in
BJ	115,719	*POI*	HK	20,103	check-in

Table 4 Twenty Selected *TSPLIB* Benchmarks

Abbrv.	Name	n	Abbrv.	Name	n
h1	eil101.tsp	101	t1	u1060.tsp	1060
h2	u159.tsp	159	t2	pcb1173.tsp	1173
h3	rat195.tsp	195	t3	rl1304.tsp	1304
h4	ts225.tsp	225	t4	rl1889.tsp	1889
h5	pr299.tsp	299	t5	u2152.tsp	2152
h6	pcb442.tsp	442	t6	pcb3038.tsp	3038
h7	att532.tsp	532	t7	fnl4461.tsp	4461
h8	u574.tsp	574	t8	rl5915.tsp	5915
h9	gr666.tsp	666	t9	rl5934.tsp	5934
h10	rat783.tsp	783	t10	pla7397.tsp	7397

Table 5 Parameters of new synthetic datasets

Parameter	Values
The size of points (N)	**100,000**
The number of clusters (K)	1, 4, 16, **64**, 256, 1,024, 4,096
Inter-cluster distance (l)	1, 5, **10**, 50, 100
Cluster distribution (α)	0.7, 0.8, 0.9, **1**, 2, 3, 4
TSP Query size (n)	20, 40, 60, 80, **100**, 200, 400, 600, 800

Bold represent default values for the parameters during the experiment

Table 6 Average inter-cluster distance (normalized)

l		K		α	
1	1	0.8	9.84	4	9.25
5	4.97	0.9	9.45	16	9.48
10	10.46	1	10.03	64	10.07
50	52.88	2	9.91	256	10.23
100	107.17	3	10.61	1024	10.4

best for *LBS*, since there is a gap between uniform/normal and the real datasets. In this work, we simulate that people visit n *POI*s in a real dataset of N *POI*s, where a small number of hot *POI*s are visited by many people. In brief,

we synthesize large datasets of size N followed by randomly selecting $n = |Q|$ from the large synthetic datasets. A synthetic dataset is generated with $N = 100,000$ points using 3 parameters, namely the number of clusters (K), the inter-cluster distance (l) and the distribution of points in clusters (α). First, the total number of points $N = 100,000$ is used because it is similar to the sizes of the real datasets we use (Table 3). Second, we randomly generate K points, as centers of the clusters, following uniform distribution in a square with size $l \times l$. Let C_i and k_i be the ith cluster and the center of C_i, for $1 \leq i \leq K$. Third, we randomly generate $N_i = \frac{100,000}{K}$ points for each of the K clusters, C_i. The points in a cluster follow Gaussian distribution, which is widely

used to model spatial data/events [13, 32] and user mobility [10]. Let σ_i be the variance for C_i with N_i points centered at k_i. The covariance matrix of the Gaussian distribution will be in the form of $[[\sigma_i^2, 0], [0, \sigma_i^2]]$. All σ_i for all clusters C_i ($1 \leq i \leq K$) follow Pareto distribution (α). The Pareto distribution is used because it is proved in [15] that human mobility patterns follow a power law distribution, which means a small number of places are visited by most people. The corresponding Gaussian distribution will be compact for a small σ, i.e., the small region has high visiting frequency. Table 5 shows the parameters with the default values.

With our synthetic datasets, we can study different settings including **uniform** and **normal**. For the normal distribution, it is by setting $K = 1$. where there is only one cluster. For the uniform distribution, it is by setting K as a large value, e.g., $K = N$. We discuss l and α. Recall that l is a parameter to decide the size of plane. When l is large, the average inter-cluster distance will be large, and the overlap between clusters will be small, as shown in Table 6. We show the average inter-cluster distances by varying three parameters. It is nearly in proportionate to l, and the varying of K and α will have no influence on it. For Pareto distribution, the parameter α decides the skewness. As shown Fig. 3, the larger α is, the more skew the distribution will be.

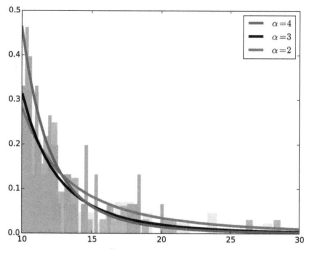

Fig. 3 Pareto distribution

Fig. 4 Data distribution with different parameters.
a $K = 64, l = 10, \alpha = 1$.
b $K = 1, l = 10, \alpha = 1$.
c $K = 64, l = 50, \alpha = 1$.
d $K = 64, l = 10, \alpha = 4$

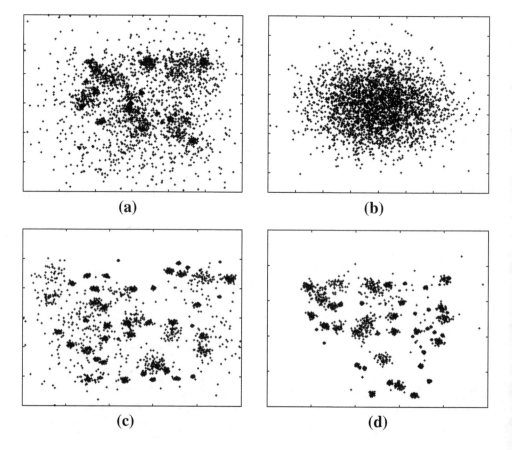

(a)　　　　**(b)**

(c)　　　　**(d)**

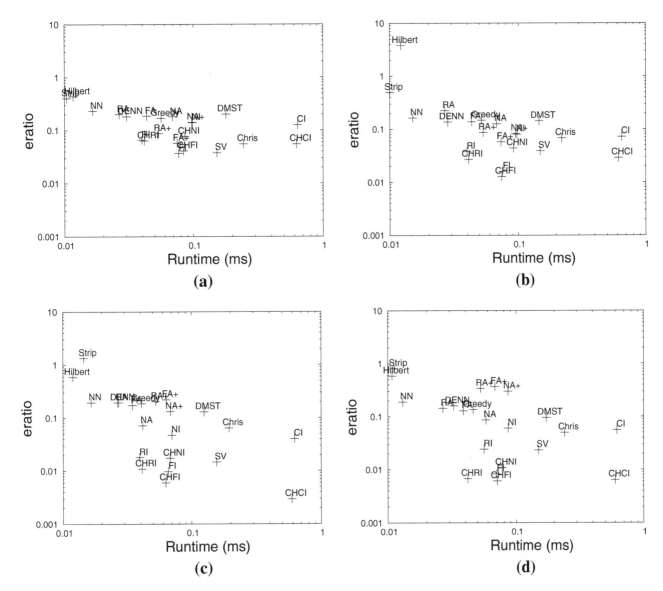

Fig. 5 Accuracy versus Runtime ($|Q| = 60$). **a** BJ. **b** NY. **c** LA. **d** HK

Figure 4 shows the data distributions with different parameters. Each figure contains 3000 points similar to Fig. 1. Figure 4a shows the distribution with default settings, which simulates LA (Fig. 1d). Figure 4b shows the distribution when $K = 1$. It is a normal distribution, similar to the benchmark shown in Fig. 1b. Comparing Fig. 4a, d shows the case when there are more clusters with a smaller variance (larger α). Consequently, it is more skewed. Figure 4d shows how to simulate NY (Fig. 1c). Figure 4c has a larger l.

TSP Queries   For real datasets, the *TSP* query size is $n = |Q|$, where the default is 60. For *TSPLIB* datasets, we test it using the same number of points as given in the benchmark. For the 2 existing synthetic datasets, uniform and normal, used in [21], we generate a set of n points for a given size to test. For both real datasets and our synthetic

datasets generated using the parameters with $N = 100,000$ points, we conduct testing 100 times for a *TSP* query with n points randomly selected, and report the average.

The heuristics   We study the 22 heuristics listed in Table 2, which are implemented in C++ following [5, 21], where *KD tree* [4] is used for efficient search. The convex hull for a *TSP* query is implemented by Graham scan [16]. The implementation details can be found in [5]. We have conducted extensive experiments on a PC with two Intel Xeon X5550@2.67GHz CPU and 48GB main memory.

The Measures   We measure the heuristics by accuracy and efficiency. The accuracy is based on the error-ratio eratio (Eq. 2), and the efficiency is based on CPU time. We focus on the accuracy, since all the heuristics are fast as reported in [5].

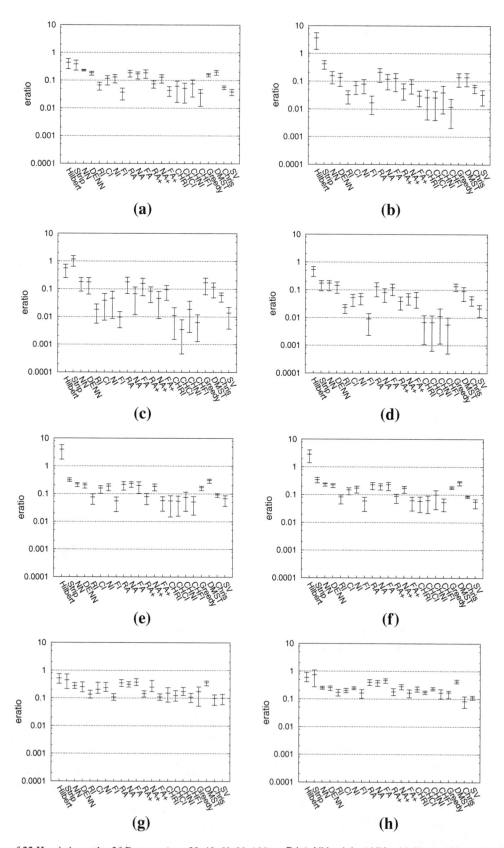

Fig. 6 Accuracy of 22 Heuristics under 26 Datasets ($n = 20, 40, 60, 80, 100$). **a** BJ. **b** NY. **c** LA. **d** HK. **e** Uniform. **f** Normal. **g** TB_H. **h** TB_T

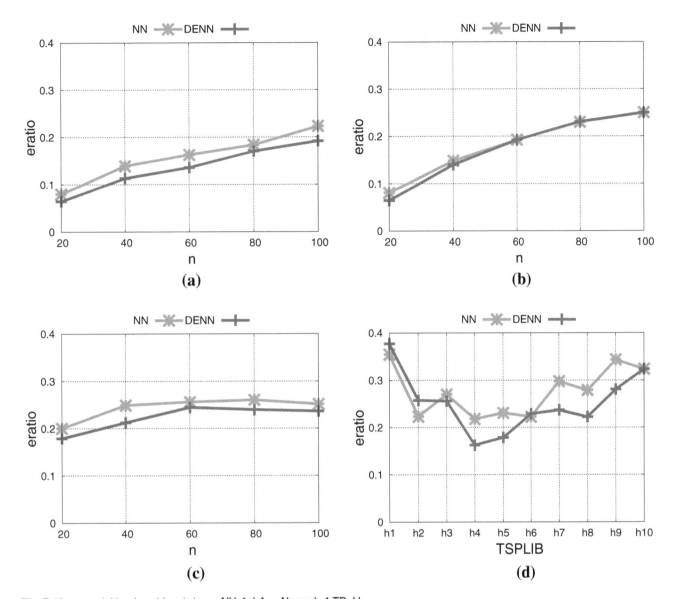

Fig. 7 Nearest-neighbor-based heuristics. **a** NY. **b** LA. **c** Normal. **d** TB_H

Below, we give an overview for the 22 heuristics using real datasets and the existing synthetic datasets in Sect. 4.1. We give details in terms of accuracy in Sect. 4.2, and discuss the issue whether we can find a *TSP* using indexing in Sect. 4.3. Finally, we discuss the heuristics using our new synthetic datasets in Sect. 4.4.

4.1 Accuracy Versus Efficiency

Figure 5 shows CPU time and error-ratio for *TSP* queries of size $n = 60$, for the 4 real datasets. The results shown in Fig. 5 for real datasets highlight the difference from the results conducted in [21] for 9 heuristics with $n = 10,000$ using uniform distributed datasets. On the one hand, as shown in [21], SV has the highest accuracy followed by FI, Greedy is

better than CHCI, and NN is better than NI. On the other hand, for these 4 real datasets, as shown in Fig. 5, the convex hull-based insertion heuristics achieve near-optimal accuracy, especially for NY, LA, and HK, since BJ is close to the normal distribution due to its urban planning. In other words, the results of BJ share the similarity with those reported in [21].

CPU Time The results of using real datasets are similar to the finding given in [21]. Both Strip and Hilbert are the fastest, as they only need to sort n values. NN and DENN are fast, because the nearest neighbors can be found efficiently using *KD tree*. The convex hull-based insertion heuristics spend time to select the initial convex hull as a sketch in $O(n \lg n)$ time, which is cost-effective since it reduces the number of nodes for insertion. Therefore, the

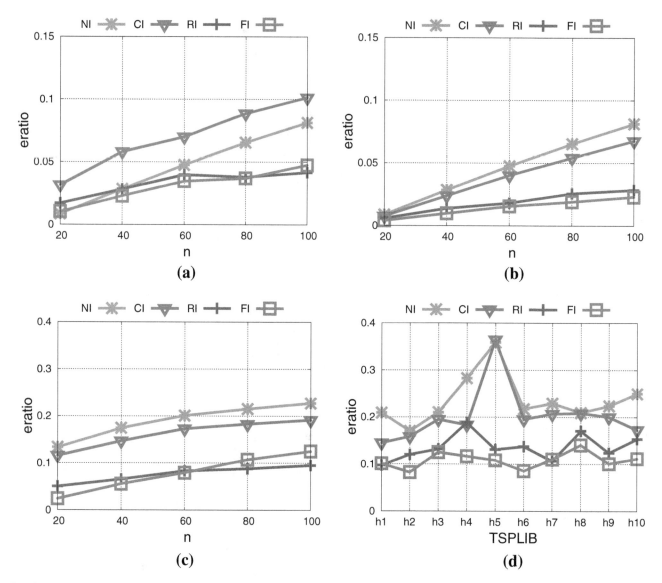

Fig. 8 insertion Heuristics. **a** NY. **b** LA. **c** Normal. **d** TB_H

convex hull-based insertion heuristics can run even faster than the other insertion heuristics which randomly select an initial node to start. For the node-based heuristics, the main CPU cost is to select a node in iterations, and there are 4 expanding orders of nodes in iterations: the random order, the nearest order, the cheapest and the furthest. The random is the fastest, as it picks the next node for insertion randomly. The CPU cost for the nearest and the furthest has only marginal difference, since both can be done using *KD tree*. The cheapest takes the longest time, since it needs to calculate the possible insertion cost for every node and every edge in iterations. For the edge-based heuristics, **Greedy** is the fastest. Its CPU time is comparable to that by the insertion heuristics. **DMST** and **Chris** build a minimum spanning tree before generating the route, and consume more time.

The Error-Ratio In addition to the efficiency (x axis) and the accuracy (y axis) shown in Fig. 5, we further conduct testing for all 22 heuristics over 26 datasets: 4 real datasets (BJ, NY, LA, and HK), 2 synthetic datasets (uniform and normal) and 20 *TSPLIB* benchmarks (10 **TB_H** and 10 **TB_T**) for $n = |Q|$ to be selected over 20, 40, 60, 80, and 100. Figure 6 shows the results using candlesticks for the *TSP* queries tested. The differences among the 22 heuristics in terms of accuracy are more obvious than the differences in terms of efficiency, for the datasets tested. Note that the accuracy is related to the distribution, whereas the efficiency is related to the heuristics. As shown in Fig. 6, in terms of accuracy, the range of eratio is between 0.0001 and 10 (y axis). In a short summary, in general, the error-ratio of the 22 heuristics over the real datasets (BJ, NY, LA, HK) is lower than that of the

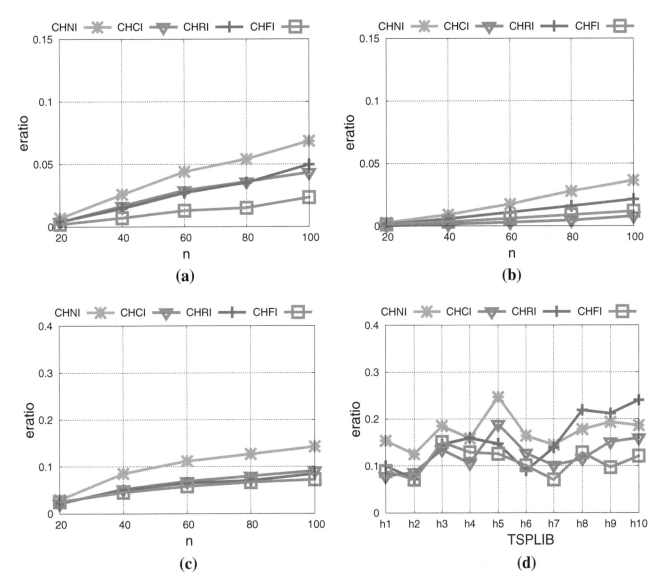

Fig. 9 Convex hull-based insertion heuristics. **a** NY. **b** LA. **c** Normal. **d** TB_H

synthetic datasets by uniform and normal as well as TB, especially for the best cases. Among the 4 real datasets, BJ follows the normal distribution, the error-ratio for the heuristics over BJ is relatively higher. Over NY, LA and HK, most heuristics can generate results with an error-ratio below 0.1 (below 10%). As a comparison, for normal and TB, the error-ratio is larger than 0.1 (10%). Among the 22 heuristics, the convex hull-based insertion heuristics are the best for most cases, whereas the space-partitioning-based heuristics are the worst. The insertion heuristics are better than the augmented addition heuristics which are better than the addition heuristics. For the edge-based heuristics, SV and Chris can be used to obtain accurate answers in some circumstances.

4.2 The Accuracy

In this section, we focus on the accuracy over 2 real datasets, NY and LA, a synthetic dataset by normal, and TB_H benchmarks. The main purpose is to show that the heuristics behave differently in real datasets comparing to normal and TB_H benchmarks. We focus on the node-based and edge-based heuristics, and do not discuss the space-partitioning heuristics since they do not show their advantages in terms of accuracy for *LBS*.

The Nearest-Neighbor Heuristics   Figure 7 shows how the accuracy of NN/DENN changes while increasing query size n. For the real datasets, the error-ratios increase

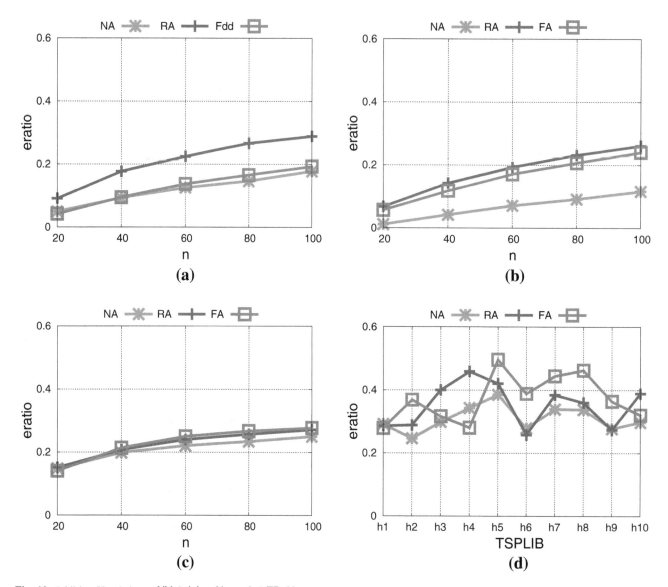

Fig. 10 Addition Heuristics. **a** NY. **b** LA. **c** Normal. **d** TB_H

monotonically. However, it does not hold for non-real datasets, especially for the 10 datasets in TB_H. In TB_H, the first with 101 points has the largest error. This suggests that the accuracy is related to data distribution. In terms of accuracy, DENN is a little better than NN. When n is small, for $n = 20$, the error-ratios for the two over NY and LA are less than 10%, whereas the error-ratio is around 20% for normal, and is even higher than 30% for TB_H. When n becomes larger, the error-ratio for NY and LA increases noticeably, as shown in Fig. 7a, b, which is different from the error-ratios observed from normal.

The Insertion Heuristics Figure 8 shows the error-ratio for the insertion heuristics. Like Fig. 7, the error-ratio

increases with query size for the real datasets (NY and LA). The error-ratios for real datasets are much better than that of non-real datasets. The error-ratios range from 0 to 10% for NY and LA, from 0 to 25% for normal, and can be up to 35% for TB_H. Among the 4 insertion heuristics, CI and NI perform in a similar way. It is surprised to notice that RI can perform better than CI and NI in terms of error-ratio. FI performs the best. Both RI and FI have an error-ratio less than 5% for NY, is even less than 3% for LA for all queries tested on average.

The Convex Hull-Based Insertion Heuristics They are the optimal choices for most cases, as shown in Fig. 6. Different from the insertion-based heuristics (RI, NI, CI, and FI) which randomly pick up a node to start, the convex

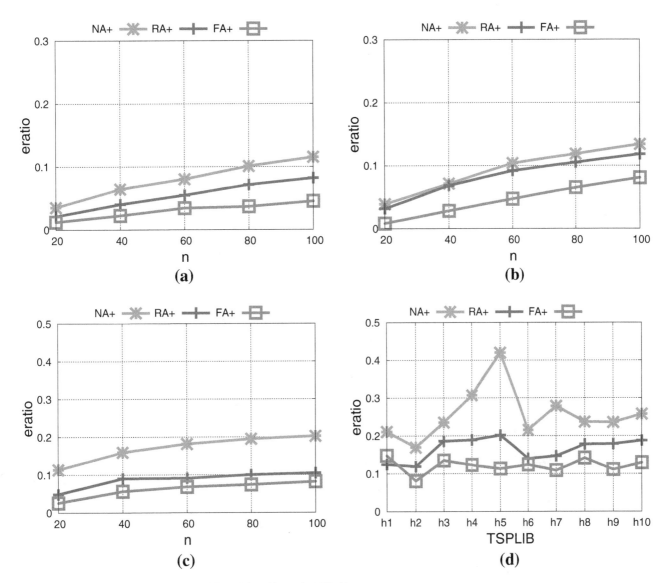

Fig. 11 Augmented addition heuristics. **a** NY. **b** LA. **c** Normal. **d** TB_H

hull-based heuristics find the convex hull as a sketch for a *TSP* query first, and expands the remaining nodes under the guide of the sketch in a similar way as the insertion-based (RI, NI, CI and FI). There are CHRI, CHNI, CHCI, and CHFI. First, comparing Fig. 9 with Fig. 8, the convex hull-based heuristics outperform the corresponding insertion-based heuristics. The error-ratios are noticeably reduced. Second, the reduction on error-ratio by the convex hull changes the order of the heuristics in terms of the accuracy. Consider Figs. 8a and 9a for NY. Without the convex hull, as shown in Fig. 8a, CI performs the worst. Both RI and FI perform in a similar way, and when $n = 100$, RI even outperforms FI. On the other hand, with the convex hull, as shown in Fig. 9a, CHNI (or convex hull plus NI) performs the worst, and CHFI (or convex hull plus FI) outperforms others.

The Addition Heuristics The addition heuristics pick the next node to insert in the same way as the corresponding insertion heuristics. As shown in Table 1 for the *TSP* example in Fig. 2, both FI and FA, and both NI and NA have the same expanding order to select the next node in iterations, respectively. On the other hand, the addition heuristics do not consider all the insertion positions in the current circuit, instead consider only between the two edges that are incident to a node v in the current circuit, where v is the nearest neighbor to the next node selected to insert. As expected, the addition heuristics cannot outperform the corresponding insertion-based heuristics. This is also observed by comparing Fig. 10 with Fig. 8. The advantage of the addition heuristics is the efficiency, since they check much less number of insertion positions on the current circuit in iterations.

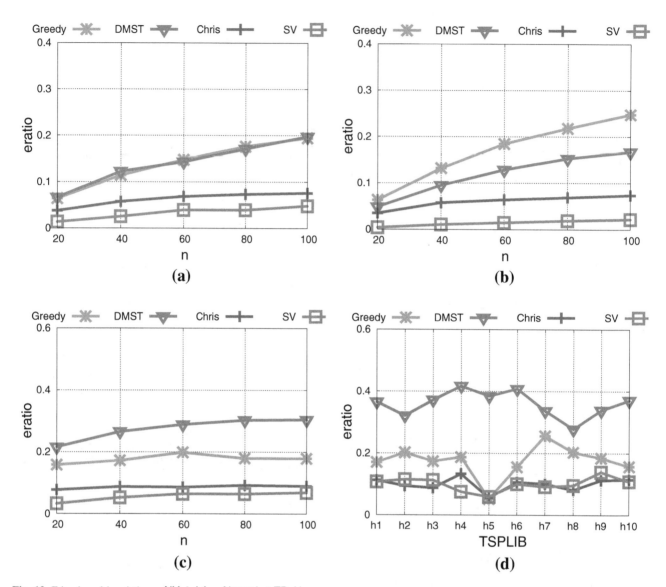

Fig. 12 Edge-based heuristics. **a** NY. **b** LA. **c** Normal. **d** TB_H

It is worth noticing that there are two main things in iterations. One is to select the next node to insert, and the other is to find an insertion position to insert. The following heuristics, RI, CHRI and RA are to select the next node randomly in iterations. As shown in Figs. 8 and 9, RI and CHRI perform well. However, Fig. 10 shows that RA does not perform well, and performs the worst for NY. This suggests that such random heuristics need to explore a certain number of insertion positions on the current circuit, in order to achieve a better accuracy. The same occurs to the furthest heuristics. Both FI and CHFI perform well, but FA does not perform well on the other hand due to the limited number of exploring insertion positions.

The Augmented Addition Heuristics   Such heuristics are positioned between the insertion heuristics and the

addition heuristics, due to the ways of exploring insertion positions on the current circuit. Figure 11 shows the results for NA+, RA+ and FA+. Comparing Fig. 10 and Figs. 8, 11 shows that, by the limited additional number of insertion positions, RA+ and FA+ outperform NA+, in a similar way as the corresponding RI and FI outperform NI and the corresponding CHRI and CHFI outperform CHNI.

The Edge-Based Heuristics   The performance studies done in [21] using $n = 10{,}000$ points under the uniform distribution conclude that SV is the best among all 9 the heuristics tested. FI outperforms Greedy which in turn outperforms CHCI. Different from the results reported in [21] using $n = 10{,}000$ points under the uniform distribution, as shown in Fig. 6, with many different datasets, SV is not the best, even though SV like other edge-based

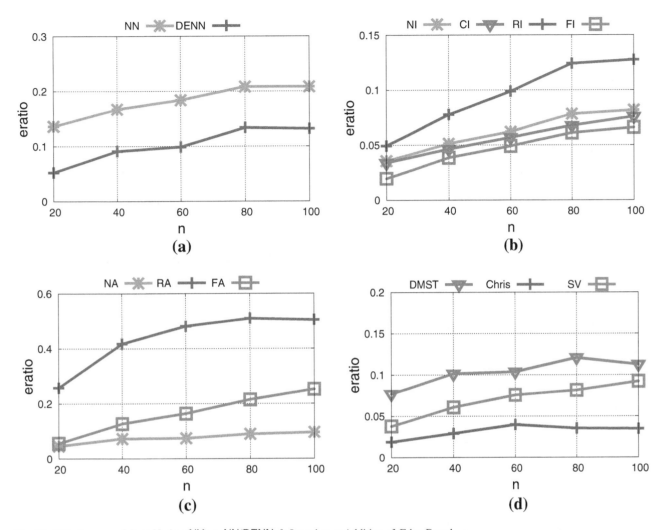

Fig. 13 Effectiveness of Start Nodes (NY). **a** NN/DENN. **b** Insertion. **c** Addition. **d** Edge-Based

heuristics can get better accuracy. Figure 12 shows the details for the edge-based heuristics. SV performs the best. For LA, the error-ratio for SV ranges from 0.2 to 2.3%, which is marginally higher than the error-ratio for CHFI that ranges from 0.1 to 1.2%. Both Chris and DMST are based on *MST*, and Chris outperforms DMST. Note that the approximate ratio is 1.5 for Chris, and is 2 for DMST. As shown in Fig. 5, Chris takes longer CPU time since it needs to find a perfect matching and Euler circuit after generating the minimum spanning tree. Greedy performs well as reported in [21]. However, in our testing settings, Greedy is inferior of Chris in the two synthetic datasets NY and LA, generates similar results with DMST in NY, and is the worst for LA.

The Effectiveness of Start Nodes   All heuristics except for the convex hull-based need to select a start node to start expanding randomly, which may have a great impact on the resulting circuit. We study the selection of start nodes

using the real dataset NY by varying the number of points $n = 20, 40, 60, 80, 100$. For each n value, for example, $n = 60$, we randomly select 100 sets of points of size n from NY. Assume Q is one of the 100 sets for a given n. We test a certain heuristics by selecting every node in Q as a start node. Given a query size n, we record the difference between the shortest and longest routes for every start node in every of the 100 randomly selected sets, and show the average difference in Fig. 13. It shows how the choice of start node affects the quality. As observed, the error-ratios increase monotonically while the query size increases. This suggests that the random selection of the first node to start is more sensitive when there are more node. As shown in Fig. 13, among the 2 nearest-neighbor heuristics, DENN is more stable than NN, given that DENN is only difference from NN by looking at the two ends of the current path in iterations, instead of only one end. For the insertion heuristics, CI, NI, and FI perform in a similar way, whereas RI is more sensitive to the first node selected to start

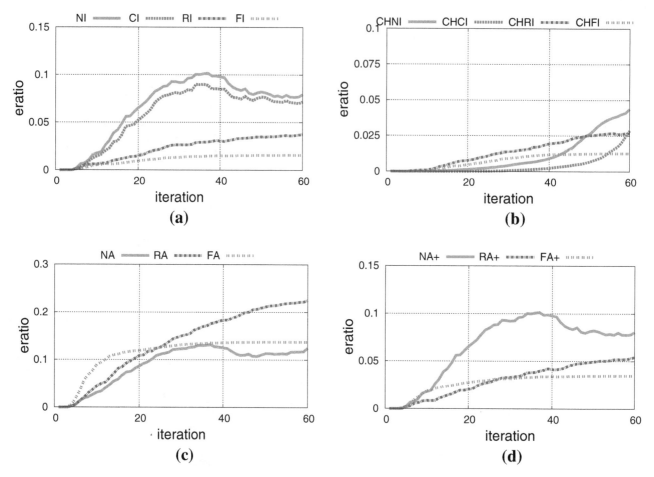

Fig. 14 Error-Ratio in the ith Iteration. **a** Insertion. **b** Convex Hull-based Insertion. **c** Addition. **d** Augmented Addition

(Fig. 13b). The sensitive of the random is also shown in Fig. 13c where RA is the worst, and NA and FA outperform RA significantly. For the edge-based heuristics, Fig. 13d shows that it is less sensitive for the edge-based heuristics to select the start node. Chris is the best among all heuristics, in terms of random selection of the start node.

4.3 More on Accuracy

We further analyze the error-ratios for the insertion, the convex hull-based insertion, the addition, and the augmented addition heuristics, and we focus on three issues: (a) the error-ratios in iterations, (b) the error correlation between the intermediate error-ratios and the final error-ratio and (c) the possibility of reoptimization to obtain the $(i+1)$th expansion by heuristics given the optimal *TSP* for the first i nodes selected. We conduct testing over the real dataset NY, for $n = 60$. We randomly select 100 sets of points of size $n = 60$ from NY, and report the average. Let T_i be a circuit with i nodes, and let T_i^* be the optimal circuit over the same set of nodes.

The Error-Ratio in the ith Iteration The error-ratio eratio(T_i) is computed by Eq. (2) for T_i in the ith iteration. Figure 14 shows the results. Several observations are made. First, for the random methods (RI, CHRI, RA and RA+), the error-ratios increase in the ith iteration when i becomes larger. The error-ratio in the ith iteration becomes comparatively smaller, if it tries to find an insertion position among more choices, i.e., RI is better than RA+, which is better than RA. Among all the random-based methods, CHRI is best given the convex hull computed. Second, the error-ratios for the addition heuristics are high due to the limited insertion positions in iterations. Third, for the nearest-neighbor methods (NI, CHNI, CHCI), the error-ratio increases in the first iterations and then drop in the late iterations. The reason is that in the first iterations, it takes near-to-far approach, whereas in the late iterations it may insert the next node between two nodes to refine the circuit. For CHCI, given the convex hull computed, it increases, and terminates before it finds the position to drop. Fourth, for the furthest methods (FI, CHFI, FA+, and FA), the error-ratios are small and grow slowly. Among all heuristics, CHFI performs the best.

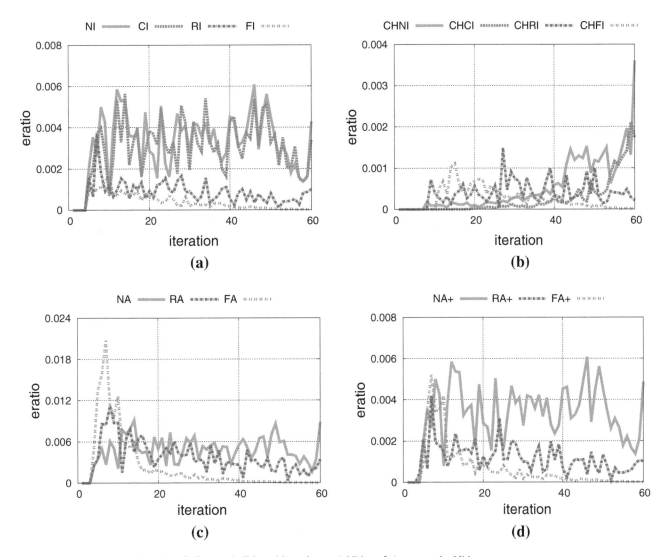

Fig. 15 Reoptimization. **a** Insertion. **b** Convex hull-based insertion. **c** Addition. **d** Augmented addition

The Reoptimization For reoptimization, the rationale behind is whether there is any possibility to answer a *TSP* query based on an indexing to maintain certain length optimal circuit, even though it is known that the local optimal property does not hold. For a given heuristic method to obtain T_{i+1} by expanding a new node from T_i, we consider expanding the new node into the optimal T_i^* over the same set of nodes in T_i generated by the same method. We denote such a circuit obtained as T'_{i+1}, and the error-ratio by $\text{eratio}(T')$ is the error-ratio introduced in the last iteration only. Figure 15 shows the introduced error-ratio for different heuristics. The introduced errors are very small, which indicates that the reoptimization can generate high-quality solutions in most cases. For the addition heuristics, the error-ratio is higher than the others (Fig. 15c). For the insertion heuristics, FI outperforms the others, and RI also performs well. It is worth noting that when T_i becomes longer, the error-ratios become smaller.

When $i > 30$, the error-ratio is below 0.001, and when $i > 40$, the error-ratio is close to zero. In general, the convex hull-based insertion better than the insertion.

4.4 The New Synthetic Datasets

In order to better understand the heuristics in real applications for *LBS*, we study the 22 heuristics in terms of accuracy using the new synthetic datasets proposed in this work.

Figure 16 gives an overview by candlesticks, where each figure is presented by varying the parameter in concern while fixing the other parameters by their default value. In this study, we use $n = 100$ as the default query size. Figure 16a shows that most node-based heuristics are sensitive to the query size, especially of CHCI. The edge-based heuristics are stable with the change of n. The difference between the best case and worst case of Chris is

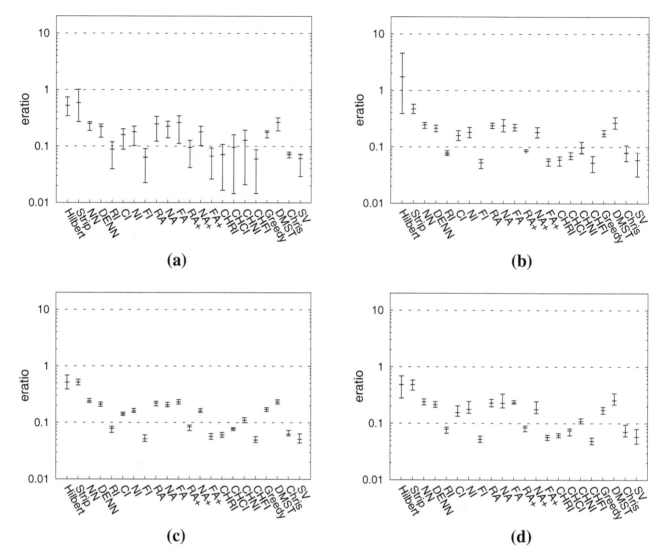

Fig. 16 Impact of parameters: An overview. **a** Query size. **b** Cluster number. **c** Inter-cluster distance. **d** Cluster distribution

just 1.5%. On the other hand, the edge base heuristics are sensitive to the cluster number.

We focus on 6 heuristics in Fig. 17, namely CHFI, CHRI, SV, CHCI, Greedy and DENN, which are selected for the following reasons. CHFI, CHCI and CHRI are the better choices for real datasets tested, SV, CHCI, and Greedy are the better choices as concluded in [21], and DENN is selected as the nearest-neighbor heuristics which is used in *LBS*. Note that DENN outperforms NN in terms of accuracy.

Query Size (n): The error-ratios for all heuristics increase while increasing n. As shown in Fig. 16a, it has higher influence on node-based heuristics (CHCI, CHRI and CHFI). When n is small, CHCI, CHRI and CHFI outperform SV. However, as SV increases slower, SV becomes the best when $n \geq 400$. For Greedy, it looks constant when $n \geq 80$, and will perform well when n is very

large. This explains that Greedy outperforms CHCI in [21].

Cluster Number (K): As shown in Fig. 17b, the cluster number has little influence on the heuristics. The dataset follows a normal distribution when $K = 1$ and gradually changes to uniform distribution when K becomes large. The same can be observed in Fig. 6e and f.

Inter-Cluster Distance (l)   The inter-cluster distance controls the distance between clusters. Note that the overlap between clusters becomes small when l is large. The error-ratios for CHFI and SV increase slightly while increasing l. For DENN, CHRI, CHCI, and Greedy, the error-ratio increases first and then decrease. SV increases faster than CHFI. When $l = 1$, SV outperforms CHFI. However, CHFI outperforms SV when $l \geq 10$ when the boundaries between clusters are more clear.

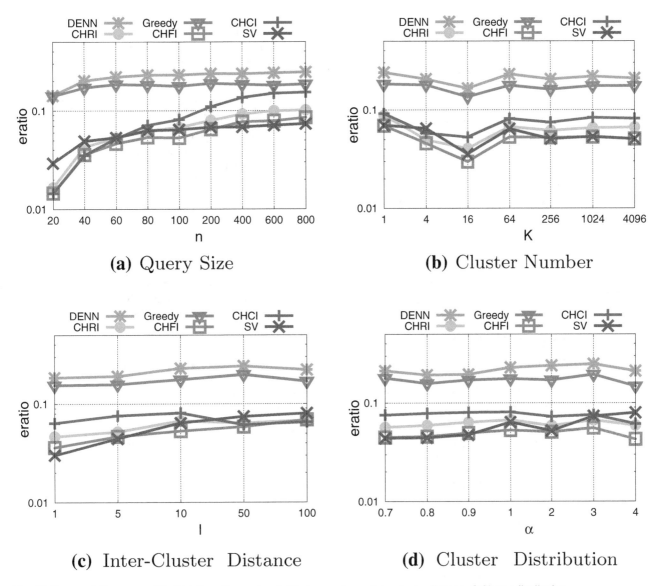

Fig. 17 Impact of Parameters: The Details. **a** Query size. **b** Cluster number. **c** Inter-cluster distance. **d** Cluster distribution

Cluster Distribution (α)   It is to control the variances in clusters. When α is small, the data distribution is highly skewed, and most clusters have a small variance. On the other hand, when α is large, more clusters have a large variance and the distribution over all clusters in terms of variance is more uniform. As shown in Fig. 17d, the error-ratio for CHFI increases while increasing α at the beginning and then decreases. The error-ratio for SV increases monotonously. CHFI is more suitable for the skewed case than SV.

As a summary, we conclude the following. First, CHFI works well for real *LBS* applications, in particular, when the query size is relatively small and the query is highly skewed. Second, SV is a better choice when the query size is large and query distribution is uniform as also observed in the existing work. Third, the nearest-neighbor heuristics

is currently used in *LBS* for the efficiency, and is not the best for accuracy. Fourth, CHRI can generate the near-optimal answers in many cases by randomly selecting next nodes to insert, and shows that the random heuristics is deserved to be investigated.

5 Conclusion

In this work, we investigate 22 construction heuristics for *TSP* in *LBS* by extensive performance studies over 4 real datasets, 20 datasets from *TSPLIB* benchmark, and 2 existing synthetic datasets. In addition, in order to understand real *LBS* setting, we also conduct extensive testing over the new synthetic datasets proposed in this work to simulate that a small number of hot *POIs* are visited by many people. Different from the existing work, we find that CHFI works well for real *LBS* applications, whereas CHCI get a good answer when the query size is small. Also, CHRI can generate the near-optimal answers in many cases by randomly selecting next points to insert. In addition, for the issue of precomputing/indexing, we find that the quality of the circuit T_{i+1} by expanding a new point by heuristics from the optimal T_i^* is high, which shows that it is deserved to study precomputing/indexing to support *TSP* queries.

Acknowledgements This work was supported by grant of the Research Grants Council of the Hong Kong SAR, China 14209314.

References

1. Arora S (1998) Polynomial time approximation schemes for euclidean traveling salesman and other geometric problems. J ACM 45(5):753–782
2. Beardwood J, Halton JH, Hammersley JM (1959) The shortest path through many points. In: Mathematical proceedings of the Cambridge philosophical society. Cambridge University Press, Cambridge, vol 55, pp 299–327
3. Bellmore M, Nemhauser GL (1968) The traveling salesman problem: a survey. Oper Res 16(3):538–558
4. Bentley JL (1975) Multidimensional binary search trees used for associative searching. Commun ACM 18(9):509–517
5. Bentley JL (1992) Fast algorithms for geometric traveling salesman problems. INFORMS J Comput 4(4):387–411
6. Cao X, Chen L, Cong G, Xiao X (2012) Keyword-aware optimal route search. PVLDB 5(11):1136–1147
7. Cao X, Cong G, Jensen CS (2010) Mining significant semantic locations from GPS data. PVLDB 3(1):1009–1020
8. Chen Z, Shen HT, Zhou X (2011) Discovering popular routes from trajectories. In: ICDE, pp 900–911
9. Chen Z, Shen HT, Zhou X, Zheng Y, Xie X (2010) Searching trajectories by locations: an efficiency study. In: SIGMOD, pp 255–266
10. Cho E, Myers SA, Leskovec J (2011) Friendship and mobility: user movement in location-based social networks. In: SIGKDD, pp 1082–1090
11. Christofides N (1976) Worst-case analysis of a new heuristic for the travelling salesman problem. Technical report, DTIC Document
12. Cong G, Jensen CS, Wu D (2009) Efficient retrieval of the top-k most relevant spatial web objects. PVLDB 2(1):337–348
13. Cressie N (2015) Statistics for spatial data. Wiley, New York
14. Flood MM (1956) The traveling-salesman problem. Oper Res 4(1):61–75
15. Gonzalez MC, Hidalgo CA, Barabasi A-L (2008) Understanding individual human mobility patterns. Nature 453(7196):779–782
16. Graham RL (1972) An efficient algorithm for determining the convex hull of a finite planar set. Inf Process Lett 1(4):132–133
17. Guo L, Zhang D, Li G, Tan K, Bao Z (2015) Location-aware pub/sub system: When continuous moving queries meet dynamic event streams. In: SIGMOD, pp 843–857
18. Guo T, Cao X, Cong G (2015) Efficient algorithms for answering the m-closest keywords query. In: SIGMOD, pp 405–418
19. Gutin G, Punnen AP (2002) The traveling salesman problem and its variations, vol 12. Springer Science & Business Media, Berlin
20. Johnson DS, McGeoch LA (1997) The traveling salesman problem: A case study in local optimization. Local search in combinatorial optimization 1:215–310
21. Johnson DS, McGeoch LA (2007) Experimental analysis of heuristics for the stsp. In: The traveling salesman problem and its variations. Springer, Berlin, pp 369–443
22. Kruskal JB (1956) On the shortest spanning subtree of a graph and the traveling salesman problem. Proc Am Math Soc 7(1):48–50
23. Li F, Cheng D, Hadjieleftheriou M, Kollios G, Teng S (2005) On trip planning queries in spatial databases. In: SSTD, pp 273–290
24. Li G, Chen S, Feng J, Tan K, Li W (2014) Efficient location-aware influence maximization. In: SIGMOD, pp 87–98
25. Long C, Wong RC, Wang K, Fu AW (2013) Collective spatial keyword queries: a distance owner-driven approach. In: SIGMOD, pp 689–700
26. Luo W, Tan H, Chen L, Ni LM (2013) Finding time period-based most frequent path in big trajectory data. In: SIGMOD, pp 713–724
27. MacGregor JN, Ormerod T (1996) Human performance on the traveling salesman problem. Percept Psychophys 58(4):527–539
28. Nicholson T (1967) A sequential method for discrete optimization problems and its application to the assignment, travelling salesman, and three machine scheduling problems. IMA J Appl Math 3(4):362–375
29. Platzman LK, Bartholdi JJ III (1989) Spacefilling curves and the planar travelling salesman problem. J ACM (JACM) 36(4):719–737
30. Reinelt G (1991) Tsplib-a traveling salesman problem library. ORSA J Comput 3(4):376–384
31. Rosenkrantz DJ, Stearns RE, P. M. L. II. (1977) An analysis of several heuristics for the traveling salesman problem. SIAM J Comput 6(3):563–581
32. Schabenberger O, Gotway CA (2004) Statistical methods for spatial data analysis. CRC Press, Boca Raton
33. Sharifzadeh M, Kolahdouzan MR, Shahabi C (2008) The optimal sequenced route query. VLDB J 17(4):765–787
34. Sommer C (2014) Shortest-path queries in static networks. ACM Comput Surv 46(4):45:1–45:31
35. Wang S, Lin W, Yang Y, Xiao X, Zhou S (2015) Efficient route planning on public transportation networks: A labelling approach. In: SIGMOD, pp 967–982
36. Xu Z, Jacobsen H (2010) Processing proximity relations in road networks. In: SIGMOD, pp 243–254
37. Yan D, Zhao Z, Ng W (2011) Efficient algorithms for finding optimal meeting point on road networks. PVLDB 4(11):968–979
38. Zhu AD, Ma H, Xiao X, Luo S, Tang Y, Zhou S (2013) Shortest path and distance queries on road networks: towards bridging theory and practice. In: SIGMOD, pp 857–868

14

Distance-Aware Selective Online Query Processing Over Large Distributed Graphs

Xiaofei Zhang[1] · Lei Chen[2]

Abstract Performing online selective queries against graphs is a challenging problem due to the unbounded nature of graph queries which leads to poor computation locality. It becomes even difficult when a graph is too large to be fit in the memory. Although there have been emerging efforts on managing large graphs in a distributed and parallel setting, e.g., Pregel, HaLoop and etc, these computing frameworks are designed from the perspective of scalability instead of the query efficiency. In this work, we present our solution methodology for online selective graph queries based on the shortest path distance semantic, which finds various applications in practice. The essential intuition is to build a distance-aware index for online distance-based query processing and to eliminate redundant graph traversal as much as possible. We discuss how the solution can be applied to two types of research problems, distance join and vertex set bonding, which are distance-based graph pattern discovery and finding the structure-wise bonding of vertices, respectively.

Keywords Graph processing · Shortest path distance · Graph partition

1 Introduction

The tremendous size of real-world graph data raises series of challenges in efficient graph management and query processing. With the generic vertex-centric model [22] applied to practices, there has been a huge advancement in large-scale graph analytic tasks, e.g. PageRank, SCC, subgraph listing and etc. More efficient generic graph processing frameworks, like the subgraph-centric model [33, 35], are emerging to accelerate the graph analytic task. However, online graph query which finds various applications in real practice does not attract much research effort, especially the highly selective queries which has an limited output size. In this work, we study the problem of answering shortest path distance-based selective graph queries in a online fashion, such that *ad hoc* queries of such type can be answered promptly.

Graph queries using the shortest path or shortest path distance semantic are widely used in practices. For example, one popular way to define the similarity of two vertices in the network would be the similarity of their distance vector to a number of pre-selected vertices. Other examples like influential maximization, or adaptive betweenness calculation and etc., are all based on the shortest path semantic. Therefore, effective distance estimation as well as efficient shortest path retrieving are essential for online graph queries. However, one fundamental issue is the unbounded nature of graph queries which often leads to poor computation locality. For example, to find out the shortest path(s) from vertex u to v, a naive BFS would access a large number of vertices in the graph to answer the query. In an extreme case, if graph G is a social network, and the distance between u and v is five, a shortest path query evaluation much likely leads to an entire graph visit due to the six-separation law [13].

✉ Xiaofei Zhang
xiaofei.zhang@uwaterloo.ca

Lei Chen
leichen@cse.ust.hk

[1] University of Waterloo, Waterloo, Canada

[2] Hong Kong University of Science & Technology, Clear Water Bay, Hong Kong

Various graph indexing techniques have been proposed to speed up the query evaluation, like the embedding technique introduced in GStore [39] for efficient SPARQL query processing, independent set-based labeling [10], the distance oracle approach [28] and etc. However, effective generic index structures for *adhoc* graph queries are space-consuming and involve a long setup time. Therefore, answering online selective graph queries with a combination of light-weight indices and fast graph exploration makes it a feasible solution with respect to both time and space efficiency.

In this work, we study both effective distance estimation and efficient graph exploration for shortest path discovery. We apply our methods to two types of online graph queries: distance join and vertex set bonding, which captures interesting graph patterns and structure-wise prominent vertices, respectively. We highlight the contribution of our work as follows:

- We propose a novel partition strategy for web-scaled graphs in the shared-nothing distributed environment to efficiently support the pairwise shortest path estimation;
- We develop a vertex filtering scheme to effectively support guided graph exploration, such that the cost on redundant vertex accessing could be significantly saved;
- We show how our technique can be applied to two types of powerful graph queries;
- We discuss our prototype implementation with extensive experiments over both real and synthetic web-scaled graphs on an in-door cluster.

The rest of this paper is organized as follows: we first formally define the problem in Sect. 2, then we introduce our partition-based distance estimation index in Sect. 3 and guided graph exploration in Sect. 4, respectively. We show how our proposed technique can be applied to accelerate the evaluation of two types of queries in Sect. 5. We report all experiments in Sect. 6 and briefly review the related works in Sect. 7, followed by Sect. 8 which concludes the paper.

2 Problem Definition

In this section, we first clarify the problem definition and notations used in this paper. For comprehensiveness, we present an overview of our solution before diving into the any technical details.

Given graph $G = \langle V, E \rangle, E \subset V \times V$, a path from vertex u to v is a sequence P of edges: $e(x_0, x_1), ..., e(x_{i-1}, x_i)$, where $e(x_i, x_j) \in E$ and $x_0 = u, x_i = v$. Intuitively, the shortest path from u to v, denoted as $SP(u, v)$, is the edge

sequence of the minimum length. The shortest path distance, denoted as $d(u, v)$, is the length of a shortest path. Although one may pre-compute all pairwise shortest path distance by brute-force and materialize all the results, the space cost would be at least $O(n^2)$, which is prohibited in practical usage. On the contrary, we would like to find a quality guaranteed pairwise distance estimation with as less space cost as possible.

Definition 1 (*Distance estimation*) Given a pairwise distance query $Q_D(u, v)$, returning $\hat{d}(u, v)$ in $O(1)$ time using at most $O(c|V|)$ storage, having

$$\hat{d}(u, v) \leq (1 + \epsilon)d(u, v)$$

where $\epsilon \in (0, 1)$, c is a constant factor.

As shown in the definition, all pairwise shortest path distance should be estimated in constant time with quality guarantees. The fundamental challenge is to minimize the space consumption as much as possible. Clearly, if we let ϵ be 0, then the problem can only be solved by pre-compute all pairwise distances. Thus, the problem essentially asks for the space lower bound of a parameter-adjustable solution for distance estimation.

Although finding the shortest path is a well established problem, we define the optimal shortest path computing problem under an exploration semantic as follows:

Definition 2 (*Graph exploration strategy*) Given graph $G = \langle V, E \rangle$, a vertex u is explored only if $\exists e(u, v) \in E$ and v is explored.

Definition 3 (*Atomic graph exploration cost*) Given vertex $u \in V$, the atomic graph exploration cost of u is $|\{e(u, *)\}|$, where $\{e(u, *)\}$ denotes the set of edges going out from u.

Definition 4 (*Optimal shortest path computing*) Given a pairwise shortest path query $Q_{SP}(u, v)$, let $\mathcal{V}$ be a set of vertices to access to answer the query in an exploration manner, then the optimal goal is $\underset{\mathcal{V}}{\text{argmin}} \sum_{|e(v, *)|}$, where $v \in \mathcal{V}$.

Intuitively, the optimal shortest path computing is to locate the minimum set of vertices to access in order to answer the query. Unfortunately, the exploration based path computing has been proven to be untractable in terms of the number of vertex access. Thus, we shall study effective heuristics that eliminate redundant vertex access as much as possible.

The solution we introduced for these two problems are somehow correlated. We first introduce a partition-based distance estimation index, which effectively estimates $d(u, v)$ in constant time. Essentially, we partition the graph into a set of subgraph pairs, such that vertices that are far away enough from each other would be grouped into different partitions. Thus, we can use the distance between partitions to estimate the true pairwise distance. Based on the lightening fast yet accurate (with error guarantee) distance estimation, we can perform a guided graph exploration. Moreover, we introduce the landmark-based guided

[2, 4, 21] to sample V'. The cardinality of V', however, is considered as a customizable parameter in our solution. It would be great to have a larger $|V'|$, but it would be inefficient to compute the partition of $DT(\mathcal{G}_{V'})$ in the main memory. Therefore, we make $|V'|$ reasonably large as long as a $O(|V'|^2)$ matrix can be completely loaded in a server's main memory.

Algorithm 1: Computing $Vor(G_{V'})$

Data: G, V'
Result: $Vor(G_{V'})$

1   Initialize every vertex $v \in V/V'$ to be unmarked;
2   **while** $\exists v \in V/V'$ *does not report termination* **do**
3   **if** v *is unmarked and receives a message (id,len) from an incident edge* **then**
4   Mark v with (id,len);
5   v sends $(id,len+1)$ to all its incident edges;
6   v reports termination;
7   **if** v *is unmarked and receives a set of messages (list(id),len) from incident edges simultaneously* **then**
8   Mark v with (id_{min},len);
9   v sends $(id_{min},len+1)$ to all its incident edges;
10   v reports termination;
11   Bulk Synchronization;
12   **for** *each* $v \in V/V'$ **do**
13   v sends (id) to all its incident edges;
14   Bulk Synchronization;
15   **for** *each* $v \in V/V'$ **do**
16   **if** v's *id is different from the received id* **then**
17   Mark v as a boundary vertex;

---

graph exploration and probe-based graph exploration which requires much less space overhead.

3 Partition-Based Distance Index

Being a crucial criteria of online queries, the latency of query processing should be reduced as much as possible. To address this efficiency issue, we partition graph G based on its summary graph extracted from the Delaunay triangulation of a set of selected vertices. A *Well-Separated-Subgraph Decomposition* method is employed to guarantee a distance-aware partition. Since the partition task is beyond the capability of a single stand-alone server, we first randomly partition G to all computing nodes and compute the summary graph in a distributed manner. As the summary graph is small, a partition schema can be derived in one server. Afterward, a re-partition of G is performed among all computing nodes.

This process includes three steps, selecting a subset of vertices V' from G, building the Voronoi diagrams $Vor(G_{V'})$ and extracting a graph which is the corresponding Delaunay triangulation of V', i.e., $DT(G_{V'})$.

Step 1. Selecting V'. We adopt the betweenness approximation method proposed in a series of work

Step 2. Computing Vor $(G_{V'})$ The pseudo-code given in Algorithm 1 illustrate the computation of $Vor(G_{V'})$. Notice that there could be many different ways to handle conflicts, i.e., a vertex can be of equal distance to different reference points. In our solution, we specifically assign a conflicting vertex to the reference point with a smaller *id* value.

Step 3. Constructing $DT(G_{V'})$. $DT(G_{V'})$ can be easily constructed after *Vor* $(G_{V'})$ is obtained. $DT(G_{V'})$ is a weighted undirected graph. There is an edge between $u, v \in V'$ iff u and v reside in two adjacent Voronoi cells in *Vor* $(G_{V'})$. And the weight of this edge is $diam(u) + diam(v)$, where $diam(\cdot)$ denotes the graph diameter.

3.1 c-WSSD Partition

To partition a graph in a distance-aware fashion, we actually employ a two-layer hierarchical partition method. The bottom layer is constructed with the identification of numbers of distance-preserving Voronoi cells. The top layer is to partition the Delaunay graph $DT(G_{V'})$, which is a summary of the bottom layer. Different from most existing graph partition techniques that aim at reducing cross partition cuts, we would like to have any pairwise distance query be evaluated as quickly as possible. The intuitions are simple: 1) the vertices that are far away from each other should be partitioned into different subgraphs; 2) the vertices that are close to each other should be located in the same or adjacent subgraphs. For clear illustration purpose, we first introduce the concept of *Well-Separated-Subgraph Decomposition*, which serves as a partition constraint for $DT(G_{V'})$.

Definition 5 (*c-WSSD*) Let S be a connected graph of n vertices. Let $\mathcal{F} = \{(A, B) : A \subseteq S, B \subseteq S\}$ be a collection of pairs of subgraphs of S. For any constant $c \geq 1$, we call

subgraph; u, v denote subgraphs of $DT(G_{V'})$; l_u and l_v denote the diameter value of $R(u)$ and $R(v)$, respectively. To elaborate, we first compute $R(DT(G_{V'}))$ and assign it as the root of a binary tree T. T is constructed as follows. For each non-leaf internal (or root) node $u \subseteq V'$, we split it into two children by removing the edge on which the center of $R(u)$ resides. Binary tree T is built along with the subgraph pair extraction process. An internal node u splits only if certain conditions hold, as shown in the *if...then* clauses of Algorithm 2.

Algorithm 2: Constructing c-WSSD of $DT(G_{V'})$

Data: $DT(G_{V'})$, queue Q, binary tree T
Result: $\mathcal{F}$

1 $\mathcal{F} \leftarrow \emptyset$;
2 $T_{\text{root}} \leftarrow R(DT(G_{V'}))$;
3 Add pair $(T_{\text{root}}, T_{\text{root}})$ to Q;
4 **while** $Q \neq \emptyset$ **do**
5   Extract (u, v) from Q;
6   **if** $d(R(u), R(v)) \geq c \times Max\{l_v, l_u\}$ **then**
7   Add pair (u, v) to $\mathcal{F}$;
8   **if** $l_u \geq l_v$ **then**
9   Equal split u into u' and u'' ;
10   Add pairs (u', v) and (u'', v) to Q if they are not in Q;
11   **if** $l_v \geq l_u$ **then**
12   Equal split v into v' and v'' ;
13   Add pairs (u, v') and (u, v'') to Q if they are not in Q;
14   Report $\mathcal{F}$;

$\mathcal{F}$ a c-Well Separated Subgraph Decomposition, c-WSSD in short, if the following conditions are satisfied:

1. For any $x, y \in S$, there exists a unique pair $(A, B) \in \mathcal{F}$ such that $x \in A$ and $y \in B$.
2. $d(A, B) \geq c \times Max\{diam(A), diam(B)\}$.

In the definition, $diam(A)$ refers to the diameter of subgraph A; $d(A, B)$ denotes the shortest path distance between two subgraphs A and B. We reason the c-WSSD graph partition from two aspects. First, such a definition is query oriented. As stated in the first condition, given any two vertices from $DT(G_{V'})$, the distance constraint can be examined on just one machine that holds the corresponding pair of graph partitions. Second, it restricts the distance between partitions to ensure a straightforward query constraint verification. The second condition given in c-WSSD is to guarantee that two clusters of vertices from $\mathcal{G}$ are far apart from each other. As we elaborate later in this section, a c-WSSD graph partition ensures an error-bounded immediate pairwise distance estimation.

We solve the c-WSSD construction problem by employing a comparison-based binary tree traversing procedure presented in Algorithm 2. To be specific, let $R(\cdot)$ denote the minimal spanning tree structure of a given

Essentially, Algorithm 2 constructs the c-WSSD by traversing T with the help of a queue Q. We first initialize Q to store the ordered pair $(T_{\text{root}}, T_{\text{root}})$, where $T_{\text{root}} = R(G_{V'})$. Then we incrementally grow T in a BFS-traversal manner, during which process we compare and discover qualified ordered subgraph pairs and have them be stored in $\mathcal{F}$. We shall first prove the correctness of Algorithm 2 and then explain its running time complexity.

Lemma 1 $\mathcal{F}$ constructed with Algorithm 2 is c-WSSD.

Proof Take any two vertices $x, y \in DT(G_{V'})$, since Q contains $(T_{\text{root}}, T_{\text{root}})$ initially, the traversal algorithm must eventually put a pair of nodes (u, v) into Q such that $R(u) \cap R(v) = \emptyset, x \in u$, and $y \in v$. Afterward, the traversal algorithm expends upon (u, v) and finally put a pair (u', v') into $\mathcal{F}$ such that $x \in R(u')$ and $y \in R(v')$. Notice that (u', v') is inserted into Q exactly once in the algorithm. This guarantees that x and y are not covered by another pair in $\mathcal{F}$. Thus, $\mathcal{F}$ satisfies the first constraint of c-WSSD's definition. Moreover, it is clear that if $(u, v) \in \mathcal{F}, d(R(u), R(v)) \geq c \times Max\{diam(R(u)), diam(R(v))\}$. Thus, $\mathcal{F}$ satisfies the second constraint given in the definition. $\square$

Lemma 2 *The cardinality of $\mathcal{F}$, i.e. $|\mathcal{F}|$, is $O(|V'|)$.*

Proof It suffices to prove that given any internal node u, there are at most $O(1)$ nodes v' such that (u, v') appears in Q. Suppose that (u, v') appears in Q. It holds if $(u, v')=(r, r)$. Otherwise, (u, v') was put into Q because we split the parent of u or the parent of v'. Without loss of generality, assume that we split the parent v of v'. Thus, $l_v \geq l_u$ and $d(R(u), R(v)) < c \times Max\{l_u, l_v\}$. In other words, $R(v)$ lies inside a spanning tree R with the same center of $R(u)$ and length equal to $4c \times l_v$. Then there are no more than $16c^2$ disjoint binary tree segments of width l_v inside R, each of which may generate two children that appear with u in Q. Hence, u appears with at most $32c^2$ nodes in Q. $\square$

Since each pair in $\mathcal{F}$ must appear in Q too, $|\mathcal{F}| = O(n)$. It takes $O(n \log n)$ time to construct $\mathcal{T}(V')$. Then the traversal algorithm runs in $O(m \log m)$, where m is the total number of pairs that appear in Q. Lemma 2 has already shown that $m = O(n)$. Therefore, Algorithm 2 constructs $\mathcal{F}$ in $O(n\log n)$ time ($n = |V'|$). To achieve the $(1 + \epsilon)$ approximation to pairwise shortest path distance, given $0 < \epsilon < 1$, we make $\mathcal{F}$ an error-bounded partition of $DT(G_{V'})$ by making $c = \frac{2(1+\epsilon)}{\epsilon}$. Then we can have the following result:

Lemma 3 *Given any two vertices $x, y \in DT(G_{V'})$, the shortest path distance approximation between x, y is at most $(1 + \epsilon)d(x, y)$.*

Proof Let (u, v) be the pair in $\mathcal{F}$ such that $x \in u$ and $y \in v$. Let path $ab, a \in u$ and $b \in v$, be the shortest path between u and v. Thus, $d(x, y) \geq d(R(u), R(v)) \geq \frac{2(1+\epsilon)}{\epsilon} \times Max\{l_u, l_v\} \geq \frac{2(1+\epsilon)}{\epsilon} \times Max\{d(a, x), d(b, y)\}$. One can inductively assume that a path connecting a and x in u whose length is at most $(1 + \epsilon)d(a, x) \leq \frac{\epsilon}{2}d(x, y)$. The same inductive assumption holds for b and y in v. Thus, the path distance from x to y is at most

$$d(a,b) + (1 + \epsilon)d(a, x) + (1 + \epsilon)d(b, y)$$
$$\leq d(x, y) + (2 + \epsilon)d(a, x) + (2 + \epsilon)d(b, y)$$
$$\leq d(x, y) + \epsilon d(x, y). \quad (1)$$

$\square$

It is worth pointing out that the partition strategy illustrated above also significantly reduces the computation overhead across different storage nodes. Although the c-WSSD computation is sequential and handled centrally, the data re-partition can be easily conducted in parallel.

4 Guided Graph Exploration

In addition to fast and accurate pairwise distance estimation, finding the exact pairwise shortest path efficiently, in terms of minimizing the redundant edge visit, raises a grand challenge as well. In this section, we study a landmark-based guided graph exploration strategy.

4.1 Landmark Selection

Although the technique presented in Sect. 3 gives error-bounded distance estimation in $O(1)$ time, the storage cost of subgraph pair index depends on the underlying graph topology structure. If a graph is extremely dense, the constant factor c could be over 100 which makes it an infeasible solution. Therefore, we consider a more generic strategy to estimate pairwise distance, which is sufficient to perform guided graph exploration.

Selecting landmarks or reference points to facilitate the shortest path distance computation has been adopted in many works [26, 28, 29]. Existing landmark selection criteria are quite biased according to different graph structures and applications. In our solution, we select landmarks not only based on the consideration of graph partition and pairwise shortest distance estimation, but an *evenly coverage* property is desired. To elaborate, we find that given two vertices s and t, the landmark best serves $|p_{st}|$[1] computation is the one closest to p_{st}. Therefore, we define a set of landmarks of evenly coverage as follows:

Definition 6 (δ-*evenly coverage*) Given a graph $G = \langle V, E \rangle$, a set of landmarks, $O = \{o_1, o_2, \ldots, o_d\}$, is said to be an evenly coverage of G, **iff** $\forall v \in V, \exists o_i \in O$ such that $|p_{vo_i}| \leq \delta$, where δ is a customizable parameter.

According to the definition, an interesting question is how to decide an evenly coverage O of a given graph G. Intuitively, if δ is small, the cardinality of O, denoted with parameter d would be large. As a matter of fact, it is easy to derive that in an extreme case, d needs to be at least as large as $\frac{n-1}{2\delta}$. On the other hand, at most 3 landmarks are sufficient if the diameter of G is smaller or equal to 2δ. In practice, we would like to select the minimal number of landmarks that satisfy a δ-evenly coverage of G in order to save index space and computation costs. Algorithm 3 gives a deterministic solution of finding the minimal d, which also helps decide the selection of landmark vertices.

In the first line of Algorithm 3, G_{diam} denotes the diameter of G. We consider G_{diam} as a given input as it can be easily computed following the super step based message passing model. Apparently, the above algorithm is to recursively partition G into a set of small graphs with diameter smaller than 2δ, and report the center vertices of these small graphs as landmarks. Let the level of recursions is h, then the total number of landmarks is $d = 2^h$. The computation cost of Algorithm 3 is $O(h|G|)$, because on

---

[1] For the rest of this paper, we use $|p_{st}|$ and $d(s, t)$ interchangeably, they both denote the shortest path distance from s to t.

each level of recursion the entire graph is traversed. We can save the computation cost using a random algorithm given in Algorithm 4. It is worth pointing out that Algorithm 4 does not need G_{diam} to be pre-computed. On the other hand, as shown on line 3 of the algorithm, we randomly select a path (simply using graph exploration) of length 2δ at each iteration and filter out all vertices that could be evenly covered in δ-hops from the middle vertex of this selected path, until all vertices from G are covered.

Lemma 4 *Algorithm 4 runs at the complexity of $O(|G|)$ and returns an evenly coverage of G with at most $3 \times 2^{h-1}$ landmarks.*

Proof Consider an uncovered subgraph g with a diameter falls in $(2\delta, 4\delta]$, it takes two landmarks to evenly cover g according to Algorithm 3. However, according to Algorithm 4, a subgraph $g' \in g$ could be selected, leaving the remaining part to be sufficiently covered by at most 2 landmarks. Therefore, it takes three landmarks to cover any two adjacent small graphs after partition in Algorithm 3. Therefore, Algorithm 4 reports at most $\frac{3}{2} \times 2^h = 3 \times 2^{h-1}$ landmarks.

With the set of landmarks O determined, we are able to associate each vertex a label vector denoting its distance to all landmarks. Let $l(v)$ be a d-dimensional vector, where $l(v)_i$ denotes v's distance to landmark o_i. Starting from the d landmarks, with one time graph exploration, every $l(v)$ can be determined.

Associating each vertex with a d dimensional vector ideally trades off space cost to empower filtering on graph exploration. However, in real-world scenarios, d could be very large if δ is set to a small value, which could impose infeasible space overhead for graph storage. As a matter of fact, given a vertex u and a landmark o, their shortest path distance can be denoted as $|p_{uo'}| + |p_{o'o}| - \sigma$, where $|p_{uo'}|$ is the distance from u to its nearest landmark o'. As $dist(o, o')$ can be pre-computed during preprocessing, then only the adjusted value σ needs to be stored. Note that the employed graph partition strategy potentially promises a locality-based landmark clustering. It results in the value locality of σ in u's label, where a simple value-based compression technique can be applied to reduce the total space cost significantly.

Algorithm 3: δ-evenly coverage landmarks computation

Data: $G=\langle V, E\rangle, \delta, G_{diam}$
Result: $O=\{o_1, o_2, ..., o_d\}$
Procedure LandMark()
1   **while** $G_{diam} > 2\delta$ **do**
2   LandMark(*HalfSplit(G)*);LandMark(*G-HalfSplit(G)*);
3      $o \leftarrow$ the middle vertex of G's diameter path;
4   **return** o;

Procedure HalfSplit()
5      $e(s, t) \leftarrow$ the middle edge of G's diameter path;
6      $G=G-e(s, t)$;
7      $s.color \leftarrow c_1; t.color \leftarrow c_2$;
8   Mark all vertices active;
9   **while** $\exists v \in V$ *is active* **do**
10   **if** v *receives a color message* c_i **then**
11             $v.color \leftarrow c_i$;
12   **if** v *is active and has a color* **then**
13   v broadcasts its color to all neighbors;
14             $v \leftarrow$ inactive;
15   **return** *the graph colored with* c_1;

Algorithm 4: Fast δ-evenly coverage landmarks computation

Data: $G=\langle V, E\rangle, \delta$
Result: $O=\{o_1, o_2, ..., o_d\}$
1 $O \leftarrow \emptyset$;
2 **while** $G \neq \emptyset$ **do**
3      $p \leftarrow$ randomly select a path of length 2δ from G;
4      $g \leftarrow$ the graph that can be reach from o within δ-hops;
       /* o is the middle point of p */
5      $G \leftarrow G - g$;
6      $O \leftarrow O \cup \{o\}$;
7 **return** O;

4.2 Guided Graph Exploration

To explore the shortest path from s to t, at least $|p_{st}|$ super steps are necessary using a vertex-centric model. Starting from s, a naive graph exploration method like BFS would access all vertices within a distance of $|p_{st}|$ to s. Thus, we would like to investigate a guided graph exploration approach to significantly reduce the redundant vertex access.

Our design is simple and straightforward. Let v_k resides on the shortest path between s and t. Assume $|p_{st}|$ is given, v_k is a k-hop vertex from s, then according to the cosine law, the distance from v_k to a landmark o_i is solely determined on $l(s)_i, l(t)_i$ and k. And such a condition must be hold between every landmark and v_k, which could greatly help filtering out possible candidates for future examination. Plus, as v_k's label has been computed during the preprocessing phase, it is easy to verify whether v_k exists. If negative, it only shows that the assumption on $|p_{st}|$ is wrong.

Given vertex s and t, we can simply bound the $|p_{st}|$ using the triangle inequality. It is easy to verify that $|p_{st}| \in [Max(|l(s)_i - l(t)_i|), Min(|l(s)_i + l(t)_i|)]$, where $1 \leq i \leq d$. For comprehensive presentation, the notation $|p_{st}| \in [LB(|p_{st}|), UB(|p_{st}|)]$ is employed for the rest of this paper. An observation on the determination of $|p_{st}|$ is that an assumption of $|p_{st}|$ is correct **iff** $\forall k \in [1, |p_{st}|) \exists v_k$, such that $\forall o_i \in O, l(v_k)_i$ is valid according to the cosine law. Based on this observation, given a range of possible $|p_{st}|$, a brute-force solution is to check all possible values of $|p_{st}|$ in an ascending order and report the first valid result as the correct $|p_{st}|$, as described in Algorithm 5. Note that the loop given on line 3 indicates an iterative exploration process. In each iteration, we identify a set of valid vertices to be explored according Observation 1. The benefit of Algorithm 5 is that we can get exact p_{st} as a side product. However, the worst case happens when some landmark resides on p_{st}, meaning we get correct $|p_{st}|$ only after checking all the possible values.

Apparently, Algorithm 5 is efficient only for the scenarios where $|p_{st}|$ is very close to its lower bound. In the worst case, it takes $O(|p_{st}|^2)$ iterations to find p_{st}. Therefore, we would like to propose another algorithm which has strict performance guarantees on all possible conditions. The intuition is that by starting from a set of vertices possibly residing on p_{st}, which must be a superset of p_{st}, we perform a guided exploration that iteratively prunes all candidates that do not belong to p_{st}.

Lemma 5 *Given vertices s and t, a vertex v possibly resides on p_{st} if $Max\{|l(v)_i - l(s)_i| + |l(v)_i - l(t)_i|\} \leq UB(|p_{st}|)$, where $1 \leq i \leq d$.*

Proof Let vertices u and v be directly adjacent to each other. Then $Max\{|l(v)_i - l(u)_i|\} = 1$, where $1 \leq i \leq d$, because jumping from u to v, the distances between u and all landmarks alter by at most one. Therefore, given any two vertices u and v, $Max\{|l(v)_i - l(u)_i|\}$ indicates a lower bound of the pairwise shortest path distance between them. Thus, if the sum of lower bounds of a vertex v's distance to s and t is greater than an upper bound of $|p_{st}|$, denoted as $UB(|p_{st}|)$, then v must not reside on p_{st}. □

Although Lemma 5 indicates a filter on the possible vertices to explore, the cost to examine the entire graph set remains unacceptable. We could rule out some candidate vertices based on their distances to all landmarks, as guaranteed by the following:

Lemma 6 *Given s and t, a vertex v possibly resides on p_{st} if for $p_{st} \in [LB(p_{st}), UB(p_{st})]$ and $1 \leq i \leq d$, assuming $l(s)_i \leq l(t)_i$, then*

$$l(v)_i \in \begin{cases} [l(s)_i, l(t)_i] & \text{if} \quad \arccos\dfrac{l(s)_i^2 + l(t)_i^2 - |p_{st}|^2}{2l(s)_i l(t)_i} \leq \dfrac{\pi}{2} \\ [h, l(t)_i] & \text{else} \end{cases}$$

Algorithm 5: A brute-force validation of $|p_{st}|$

Data: $|p_{st}| \in [r_{MIN}, r_{MAX}]$
Result: $|p_{st}|$

1 **for** $i \in [r_{MIN}, r_{MAX}]$ **do**
2      $|p_{st}| = i$;
3   **for** $k \in [1, i]$ **do**
4   Let S_k be the set of vertices that are k-hop neighbors of s;
5   **if** $\nexists v_k \in S_k$ *is valid* **then**
6   continue;

7 **return** $|p_{st}|$;

where

$$h = \frac{2(\alpha(\alpha - l(s)_i)(\alpha - l(t)_i)(\alpha - p_{st}))^{\frac{1}{2}}}{p_{st}},$$

$$\alpha = l(s)_i + l(t)_i + p_{st}$$

Lemma 6 can be easily proved following the cosine law and the Heron's formula. By applying the filtering criteria suggested in Lemmas 5 and 6, we could obtain a subgraph of G, denoted as g_{st}, which must be a superset of p_{st}. Note that $\forall v \in g_{st}$, v's degree is at least 2 and all of v's neighbors belong to g_{st}. This is easy to prove by contradiction. Then, we start an iterative validation process on g_{st} to obtain p_{st} by filtering out unnecessary vertices step by step, as described in Algorithm 6.

Algorithm 6 employs a range label to check whether a vertex resides on the path p_{st}. Each vertex that receives a lower(upper) bound of the range label, it sets up the list to watch if any upper(lower) bound would be sent from the same vertex, e.g. $v.swatch$ and $v.twatch$ in lines 9 and 14, respectively. Initially, s and t are only half bounded, and they pass on the range to its neighbors. Iteratively, if a vertex v finds that it receives both the lower and upper range bounds from the same vertex, as examined in the two **IF** clauses on lines 7 and 11, v definitely does not reside on p_{st}. Therefore, v can be marked as inactive, and it will not participate in any further computation. Finally, all vertices that remains active and closely bounded shall be returned.

Correctness. There are only two cases where v does not reside on p_{st}. One is that v reaches both s and t from a same vertex u. In this case, according to Algorithm 6, v would receive range updates from u only; thus, it will be pruned. The other case is that the sum of two shortest path distances $|p_{uv}| + |p_{u'v}|$ is larger than $|p_{uu'}|$, where u and u' resides on p_{st}. Thus, the algorithm terminates before all vertices on the path p_{uv} and $p_{u'v}$ get closely bounded, and these paths would be removed eventually.

Complexity. Obviously, Algorithm 6 takes the space complexity of up to $O(|g_{st}|)$, and the total iteration step of Algorithm 6 is the same as $|p_{st}|$. And within each step, only vertices with range updates would send out messages to selected neighbors. Therefore, comparing to the naive exploration method, Algorithm 6 reduces the communication cost at each superstep. While comparing with Algorithm 5, Algorithm 6's total number of iteration steps is fixed. It makes Algorithm 6 more generic for all possible workloads.

Note that it is trivial to add a global counter in Algorithm 6 to record each vertex's shortest path distance to s and t. Then the exact $|p_{st}|$ can be obtained after the program execution. The difference between Algorithm 5 and 6 is that the former aims at fast validation of $|p_{st}|$ with as least vertex access as possible under the help of vertex labeling. Algorithm 6 first uses vertex labeling to identify a super set of p_{st} to explore, then conduct the exploration in a way that eliminate communication as much as possible.

Algorithm 6: Graph exploration for p_{st}

Data: g_{st}
Result: p_{st}

1 **for** $v \in g_{st}$ **do**
2     $v.state \leftarrow active$; $v.range \leftarrow (-\infty, +\infty)$;

3 $s.range \leftarrow (s, +\infty)$; $t.range \leftarrow (-\infty, t)$;
4 s and t broadcast their range to all neighbors;
5 **repeat**
6   **if** v receives lower range update $(s, +\infty)$ **then**
7   **if** the message source vertex is not in $v.twatch$ list **then**
8           $v.range \leftarrow (s, \star)$;
9   add the message source vertex to $v.swatch$ list;
10   v forwards the lower range to neighbors that are not in $v.swatch$;

       else
          $v.state \leftarrow inactive$;

11   **if** v receives upper range update $(-\infty, t)$ **then**
12   **if** the message source vertex is not in $v.swatch$ list **then**
13           $v.range \leftarrow (\star, t)$;
14   add the message source vertex to $v.twatch$ list;
15   v forwards the upper range to neighbors that are not in $v.twatch$;

       else
          $v.state \leftarrow inactive$;

    until s and t are closely bounded;
16 $p_{st} \leftarrow$ all active vertices in g_{st} that are closely bounded;
17 **return** g_{st};

Our guided graph exploration method could serve as a building block to evaluate other distance aware queries. For example, in the network field, there are common requests like routing a package from s to t that must pass or must not pass some given node within a transfer budget. Our vertex label method makes it straightforward to estimate the cost to include or exclude a vertex on the shortest path exploration. Therefore, cost aware solutions can be easily constructed to discover such a constraint routing path efficiently.

5 Apply to Online Graph Queries

The distance estimation and guided graph exploration technique elaborated above can serve as fundamental building blocks for various online graph queries. In this section, we present two different types of selective online queries that can benefit from the proposed technique.

5.1 Distance Join Query

Given a query graph Q and the data graph G, a distance join query returns all the subgraphs from G that satisfy every pairwise distance constraint in Q. Such a kind of query is handy and expressive in social network analysis and Biochemical network investigation [8, 14, 38]. It captures not only the structure information about the query graph, but also implies strong connectivity constraints, i.e. the pairwise distance between any two given vertices. Clearly, a distance join query is more flexible than the subgraph search and especially useful in graph analytic tasks that target on co-relationship discovery. For comprehensiveness, we first define the *distance join query* as follows:

Definition 7 (*distance join*) Given a query graph Q of n vertices $\{v_1, \ldots, v_n\}$ and m edges of weights $\{w(v_i, v_j) | (v_i, v_j) \in Q, 1 \leq i \neq j \leq n\}$, let S denote a set of n vertices selected from a data graph G, we define S is a distance match of Q **iff** the following bijective function f holds:

1. $\forall v_{i,1 \leq i \leq n}, f(v_i) \in S$;
2. $\hat{d}(f(v_i), f(v_j)) \leq w(v_i, v_j)$, if $(v_i, v_j) \in Q(1 \leq i \neq j \leq n)$, where function $\hat{d}(\cdot, \cdot)$ denotes the pairwise shortest path distance of two vertices in $\mathcal{G}$.

Then the distance join of Q and G, denoted as $DJ(Q, G)$, is to find all the distance matches of Q in G.

According to the definition, function f can be defined as any bijective mapping, e.g. label matching, similarity matching and etc. And $\hat{d}(\cdot, \cdot)$ can be any distance metric

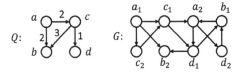

Fig. 1 An example of $DJ(Q, G)$

depending on the application scenario. In this work, we adopt the exact label matching as function f, and the shortest path distance as the distance function $\hat{d}(\cdot, \cdot)$, which satisfies the triangle inequality. An example of $DJ(Q, G)$ is given in Fig. 1. In the example, the weight of each edge in G is one. Based on the query, a vertex c must be adjacent to a vertex d, which makes c_1 and d_1 the only option. Considering $\hat{d}(a_1, b_1) > 2$ and a_2 does not reach c_1, $\{a_1, b_2, c_1, d_1\}$ is the only valid result.

Note that $DJ(Q, G)$ allows different pairwise distance constraints, which makes the query introduced in [38] a special case of our study (as the query in [38] restricts all pairwise distance constraints to a same value Δ). Such a generalized query semantic implies at least the same computational complexity as the query defined in [38], which is reported to be #$\mathcal{P}$-complete.

5.1.1 Evaluation Overview

Intuitively, it is the join order selection problem to generate a good query plan for $DJ(Q, G)$. First of all, we need a cost model to evaluate different query plans. There have been many literatures studying the cost metric of a distributed jobs *w.r.t* various constraints. We omit the details on cost model construction as it is beyond the scope of this paper. For the rest of this paper, we use $C^*(\cdot)$ to denote the cost function.[2]

Given the cost-driven query evaluation plan, which is a sequence of subqueries to evaluate, the join condition validation falls into two categories: (1) validate two vertices that do not reside on the same machine; (2) validate two vertices that are co-located on the same machine. As elaborated in Sect. 3, the distance-aware graph partition particularly favors the distance approximation of vertices that are far away from each other. Thus, it only takes constant time to justify a join condition for the case (1). However, for the query inputs of two vertices that are *not far away* from each other, i.e., they fall into the same set of Voronoi cells after partition, we need further computation on each computing node to answer the query. The essential challenge is to minimize the I/O operation as much as

---

[2] The cost model we employed is elaborated in [36]. As a matter of fact, any off-shelf cost models can be applied.

possible such that queries can be answered more efficiently.

5.1.2 Data Block Construction

We discuss how we organize graph data locally according to the *c-WSSD* property. Let $F_i \subset \mathcal{F}$ be the set of subgraph partitions distributed to a computing node *i*. As it is infeasible to keep F_i completely in the main memory, F_i must be written back to the file system in a certain manner. Since we employ HDFS as the underlying file system, challenge rises because HDFS, like other Cloud file systems, is managed on the block basis. First, the data loading from disk is at the level of blocks. Second, HDFS demonstrates unsatisfactory performance in random block access. Therefore, it is not a trivial task to write F_i back to HDFS. A data block needs to be carefully constructed.

Since $F_i = \{(A, B), \ldots\}$ is a set of subgraph pairs, where both *A* and *B* are sets of Voronoi cells. Therefore, the storage structure should be designed on the basis of Voronoi cells. Without loss of generality, we consider the storage of subgraph *A* from $(A, B) \in F_i$. Let *A* compose *r* Voronoi cells, i.e., $A = \{vc_1, vc_2, \ldots, vc_r\}$. Assume *A* needs *s* disk blocks. It matters the way to assign *r* Voronoi cells to *s* data blocks. Because if two query vertices fall into *A*, intuitively we would not want to load all *s* data blocks to explore *A* for the answer. Our solution is as follows. We first compute the group betweenness of each Voronoi cell, and select the Voronoi cells of high betweenness than all adjacent neighbors, which are named as *peaks*. Starting from these *peaks*, we expand the region of each *peak* by progressively including its adjacent Voronoi cells to form a *mountain*. After all the Voronoi cells are covered by this process, we derive a partition of this subgraph. Each *mountain* corresponds to one or more consecutive data blocks. Like the visual example shown in Fig. 2, we simplify each Voronoi cell as a square, and the number within each cell represents its group betweenness in the subgraph. We consider a 6×8 matrix of Voronoi cells. Clearly, there are some *peak* cells (marked with circles) that have high group betweenness, surrounded by Voronoi cells of relatively low group betweenness, which visually forms three *mountains* in Fig. 2a.[3] Given any two query points *p* and *q*, intuitively, the shortest path between them are most likely to reside on a path passing through some of the peaks, as shown in the figure. Therefore, if we group the Voronoi cells according to the *mountain* areas, we can achieve more efficient disk I/O on average.

Moreover, we introduce redundancies for cell clustering in our implementation, as the three large overlapping

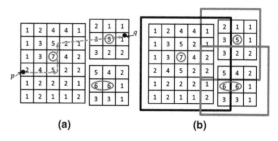

(a)   **(b)**

Fig. 2 An example of Voronoi cell grouping

rectangles shown in Fig. 2(b), such that it reduces the probability of involving more groups of Voronoi cells for the query evaluation. Although the factor of redundancy itself can be a research topic if more data statistics and query patterns are presented, in our prototype system, we only include the two-hop neighbor cells. For each group of Voronoi cells, we write them back to the disk on the basis of Voronoi cells. For each cell, it is organized as the (*key, value*) data model, although we need to add special links from *values* to *keys*, such that when it is loaded in the main memory, it serves as an auxiliary index structure for shortest path computing.

As elaborated above, we now have the power to validate the distance join conditions effectively for both cases: (1) vertices that are far away from each other; (2) vertices that are close by each other. Although to generate the *optimal* query plan remains an open question, fast and accurate distance estimation always serves as a fundamental building block.

5.2 Vertex Set Bonding

Vertex Set Bonding query (VSB query for short) extracts the most prominent vertices, called bonding agents, in connecting two sets of input vertices. The prominence of a vertex is defined on its contribution to the shortest path connectivity between input vertex sets. Intuitively, given two input sets of vertices *X* and *Y*, the desired bonding agents are the minimum set of vertices to remove in order to enlarge every pair of shortest path distance between *X* and *Y*. Such type of query finds various applications in practice, for example, network monitoring [7], community bonding [5, 13] and etc. In this section, we formally define the VSB query and then show how the query evaluation can benefit from our guided graph exploration. For comprehensiveness, we first introduce the vertex-path and vertex–vertex dominance concept.

Definition 8 (*v–p Dominance*) A vertex *v* dominates a path p_{st}, denoted as $v \vdash p_{st}$, **iff** $|p_{st}|$ increases by removing *v* from the graph. $\{v \vdash\}^P$ denotes the set of shortest paths dominated by *v*.

---

[3] Figure 2 is to provide a visual aid, and the boundaries are not specifically defined.

If there exists multiple shortest paths between s and t, then p_{st} may not be dominated by any single vertex. Instead, p_{st} is dominated by a vertex set U, denoted as $U \vdash p_{st}$, where $|p_{st}|$ increases if U is removed from the graph.

Definition 9 *(u-v Dominance)* A vertex u dominates another vertex v, denoted as $u \vdash v$, **iff** $\{v_\vdash\}^P \subseteq \{u_\vdash\}^P$. The set of vertices dominated by vertex u is denoted as $\{u_\vdash\}^V$.

Given two sets of vertices X and Y, let $P_{XY} = \{p_{xy} | x \in X, y \in Y\}$ denote the set of all pairwise shortest paths between the elements of X and Y, we further define closed dominance and minimum closed dominance as follows:

Definition 10 *(Closed dominance)* A vertex set U is said to be a closed dominance of P_{XY}, **iff** $P_{XY} \subset \bigcup_{u \in U} \{u_\vdash\}^P$.

Definition 11 *(Minimum closed dominance)* A vertex set U is a minimum closed dominance of P_{XY} **iff** U is no longer a closed dominance of P_{XY} after removing any element in U.

Definition 12 *(Optimal minimum closed dominance)* A vertex set U is an optimal minimum closed dominance of P_{XY} **iff** U is a minimum closed dominance of P_{XY}, $\nexists U'$ which is another minimum closed dominance of P_{XY} that $\exists u' \in U', \exists u \in U$ having $u'_\vdash u$.

Based on the terminology introduced above, now we formally define the vertex set bonding query, *a.k.a* the VSB query.

Definition 13 *(VSB Query)* Given an undirected graph $G = \langle V, E \rangle$ and two input sets of vertices X and Y, a vertex set bonding query $Q = \langle G, X, Y, R \rangle$ asks for a set of vertices $R \subset V - \{X, Y\}$, such that 1) R forms an optimal minimum closed dominance of P_{XY}; 2) $AB(R) = \sum_{v \in R} C_B(v | X, Y)$ is maximized, where

$$C_B(v | X, Y) = \sum_{x \in X, y \in Y} \frac{\sigma_{xy}(v)}{\sigma_{xy}}$$

In the above definition, $\sigma_{xy}(v)$ denotes the number of shortest paths between x and y that pass through v, σ_{xy} denotes the total number of shortest paths between x and y.

From the problem definition, one can easily tell that the VSB problem is a variation of the weighted set cover problem, which has been proven to be NP-hard. However, one upfront problem is that X and Y are given at *ad hoc*, no vertex-path dominance relation is determined until the run time. In other words, for any vertex $v \in V$, $\{v_\vdash\}^V$ is unpredictable until X and Y are determined and $\mathcal{G}$ is extracted. More importantly, the essential difficulty of the VSB problem is that there could be exponential number of vertex sets for the minimum closed dominance verification, which makes none of the existing solutions for weighted set cover problem applicable.

Our general solution framework works as follows. We label all vertices according to their distances to selected landmarks. Then the guided graph exploration building block would effectively filter unnecessary vertices when a VSB query is submitted to the query engine. Later, we shall perform the betweenness ranking computation on exploring only the valid vertices[4]. To show how guided graph exploration helps with the query evaluation, we highlight two building blocks: path sharing and probe-based communication.

5.2.1 Naive Plan Versus Path Sharing

A naive query plan is to apply the same computation procedure on each p_{xy}, where $x \in X, y \in Y$, and assemble the final results based on a reduction of every p_{xy}'s dominance vertices, as described in Algorithm 7. Note that a temporary data set D_{xy} is employed in the algorithm to store all the dominant vertices of p_{xy} (on Line 4). As Line 1-3 applies the same computing procedure to all pairwise paths between X and Y, this part can be executed in parallel. The reduction process on Line 4 is to reduce the dominance vertices of each path to a single set $\mathcal{D}$ and then compute centrally.

Algorithm 7: Naive VSB query evaluation

Data: $, Q = \langle G, X, Y, R \rangle$
Result: R
1 **for** $x \in X, y \in Y$ **do**
2     $D_{xy} \leftarrow \emptyset$; Explore for p_{xy};
3     $D_{xy} \leftarrow D_{xy} + \{u\}, \forall u \in p_{xy}$ and $u \vdash p_{xy}$;
4 Reduction $\mathcal{D} = \bigcup \{D_{xy}\}$;
5 **for** $D_{xy} \in \mathcal{D}$ **do**
6   **for** $D_{x'y'} \in \mathcal{D}, x' \neq x, y' \neq y$ **do**
7   **if** $\exists u \in D_{xy} \cap D_{x'y'}$ **then**
8   Push(u, q); /* q is a priority queue based on the size of $\{u_\vdash\}^P$ */
9     $u \leftarrow$ Pop(q);
10     $R \leftarrow R + \{u\}$;
11     $\mathcal{D} \leftarrow \mathcal{D} - \bigcup \{D_{x'y'}\}$, where $u \vdash p_{x'y'}$;
12 **return** R;

---

[4] As a matter of fact, we can perform approximated betweenness ranking on exploration as presented in work [37].

Theorem 1 *Algorithm 7 takes up $O(|X||Y||p_{xy}|)$ space, communicates at $O(|X||Y||p_{xy}|)$ volume of data, and runs at the time complexity of $O(|X|^2|Y|^2)$, returns an optimal minimum dominance of $P_{XY}R$ having $AB(R) > \frac{1}{2}AB(R^*)$, where R^* is the optimal answer,.*

Proof For each pairwise shortest path p_{xy}, the temporary dominance vertex set D_{xy} computed on Line 4 can be as large as $|p_{xy}|$, which explains the space and communication complexity. The nested loop structure indicates a comparison between a path against every other path, which is of complexity $O(|X|^2|Y|^2)$.

We prove R is an optimal minimum dominant set of P_{XY} by contradictory. Assume there exists another vertex $u \in p_{xy}$ that dominates $v \in R$. As $v \vdash p_{xy}$ holds, therefore, both u and v are pushed into the priority queue (Line 9). However, v is returned only if it is the vertex of the largest dominance in the priority queue, meaning $\{v_\vdash\}^P \supseteq \{u_\vdash\}^P$, which indicates the assumption must be invalid. As we elaborated before, a vertex u's betweenness $C_B(u)$ equals to $|\{u_\vdash\}^P| + f$, where f is u's contribution to other shortest paths that it resides on but does not dominate. Clearly f cannot exceed 1, therefore, at each step a returned result's betweenness is at least $\frac{1}{2}$ of the optimal choice. Accumulatively, the final $AB(R) \geq AB(R^*)$. $\square$

Algorithm 7 is straightforward and easy to implement, and it works for all query workload. However, its efficiency can suffer from the all-to-one large volume of data copy in the reduction step (Line 4). Meanwhile, the efficacy of Algorithm 7 can be further improved if we take the f part of a vertex's betweenness estimation into consideration. Thus, we develop several optimization techniques to improve the performance of VSB query processing.

In contrast to naively compute the pairwise shortest path between two sets of input vertices X and Y, an optimization opportunity lies in taking the advantage of vertex distribution in X and Y. As the VSB query can be applied to find the bonding between communities, where a community must be composed of vertices that are close to each other. It implies the potential of shortest path sharing property. Thus, there are two problems to solve: (1) how to quickly decide the input vertex distribution, as X and Y are given at *ad hoc*; (2) how to make the best of path sharing.

We solve the first problem with group prediction using vertex labels. Note that all vertices are labeled by their distances to landmarks. Graph G is partitioned into a number of small graphs that have a diameter restriction. Thus, given two vertices u and v, if both $l(u)_i$ and $l(v)_i$ is smaller or equal to δ (the graph partition parameter discussed in Sect. 4), it is certain that u and v are in the same partition graph. Intuitively, if u and v share similar

distances to multiple landmarks, they are close to each other. Given a VSB query $Q = \langle G, X, Y, R \rangle$, we first partition vertices in X and Y according to their labels. With so many distance-based clustering algorithms off-the-shelf, we choose the simplest one. We groups vertices of the same small graph partition together to obtain long shared paths, such that the exploration cost can be greatly saved.

The second problem essentially concerns how to identify the shared paths when vertices are grouped. As a matter of fact, such shared paths can only be determined during the runtime. Sometimes, vertices that are close to each other may not share an single edge to destinations at all. Therefore, we only need to identify the region or the boundary of shared paths to save the exploration cost. Given a set of grouped vertices, denoted as X', we simply add a virtual node x_v to the graph to represent X'. The trick is how we decide $l(x_v)$.

Lemma 7 *Given a set of vertices X', a virtual vertex x_v of label $l(x_v)_i$, having*

$$l(x_v)_i = \left\lceil \frac{Max\{l(x')_i\} - Min\{l(x')_i\}}{2} \right\rceil$$

where $x' \in X'$, guarantees $\forall x' \in X'$ s.t.: 1) if $|p_{x'y}| < |p_{x_vy}|, p_{x'y} \subset p_{x_vy}$; 2) if $|p_{x'y}| > |p_{x_vy}|, p_{x_vy} \subset p_{x'y}$.

Proof Consider the case when $|p_{x'y}| < |p_{x_vy}|$. Clearly, two adjacent vertex's label difference on every dimension is at most one, where the label is a d-dimensional vector. Thus, the label of $l(x_v)$ defined in the Lemma indicates the center of X', which reaches every vertex x' in X' with minimum hops. Therefore, the path p_{x_vy} must passes x', implying $p_{x'y} \subset p_{x_vy}$. Similarly, the case when $|p_{x'y}| > |p_{x_vy}|$ can be easily verified. $\square$

By employing the path sharing, we could greatly save the concurrent exploration cost of Algorithm 7, as well as the space and communication cost on D_{xy}, since the total number of such dominant vertex set are reduced.

5.2.2 Probe-Based Communication

A main bottleneck of Algorithm 7 is its all-to-one communication at the reduction part, which brings about a burst of data copying over network. Instead of such a brute-force solution, we develop a probe-based lookup strategy which could greatly save the overall communication cost. Let each graph vertex be associated with a set of independent hash functions, denoted by H. We could use H to build up a bloom filter for the element-in-set test, which is essential to our probe-based communication. To elaborate, instead of directly copying D_{xy} over network (Line 5 in Algorithm 7), we first compute the bloom filter of each D_{xy} for p_{xy}, denoted as $\mathcal{F}_{xy}$, which is a m_f bits vector. Then we pass m_f

to threads examining other pairwise shortest paths. In this way, each thread can check whether any dominant vertex it finds could also be dominant vertex on other paths. Although the bloom filter may introduce false positive, it greatly reduces the size of data to transfer for verification. Another benefit of using probe-based communication is that most computation is local, such that the centralized computing workload (Lines 5-11 in Algorithm 7) could be reduced. Following the same context of Algorithm 7, we show how the probe-based communication is employed to evaluate a VSB query in Algorithm 8.

challenges in evaluating such queries. For example, adaptive query plan generation, as well as taking the query structure feature into consideration would yield better performance of distance join processing. As VSB query use the betweenness semantic for bonding vertices, online betweenness approximation and ranking technique would greatly contribute to efficient query processing. However, the two techniques discussed in Sects. 3 and 4 are orthogonal research problems and applicable to any distance-aware graph queries.

Algorithm 8: VSB query evaluation with probe-based comm.

Data: $, Q = \langle G, X, Y, R \rangle$
Result: R
1 **for** $x \in X, y \in Y$ **do**
2      $D_{xy} \leftarrow \emptyset$; Explore for p_{xy};
3      $D_{xy} \leftarrow D_{xy} + \{u\}, \forall u \in p_{xy}$ and $u \vdash p_{xy}$;
4      $\mathcal{F}_{xy} \leftarrow \text{BloomFilter}(D_{xy}, H)$; Broadcast$(\mathcal{F}_{xy})$;
5   **for** $u \in D_{xy}$ **do**
6   Push(u, q); /* q is a priority queue based on the number of filters u hits */
7   **while** $q \neq \emptyset$ **do**
8          $u \leftarrow \text{Pop}(q)$;
9   **if** u *is valid* **then**
10   **if** $\nexists r \in R, r \vdash u \&\& \{R_\vdash\}^P \supseteq \{u_\vdash\}^P$ **then**
11                  $R \leftarrow R + \{u\}$;Break;
12 **return** R;

In Algorithm 8, we eliminated the centralized computation. Although R is a shared variable, a distributed lock can be employed for synchronous updates. As the algorithm shows, it is easy to be executed in parallel, e.g., each computing thread computes for each pairwise shortest path. Apparently, the communication cost is much reduced comparing to Algorithm 7, since only the bloom filter vector is transferred in the first place. The verification later on (Line 9) transfers one vertex's label at a time. More importantly, each thread aborts as soon as it contributes a dominance vertex to R, or finds out that a residing path is already in R. This early stop property leads to a fast convergence of the final answer. It is worth pointing out that Algorithm 8 achieves the same approximation ratio on $AB(R)$ as Algorithm 7, as long as R greedily chooses a vertex u of the largest $|\{u_\vdash\}^P|$ at each synchronous update. Comparing to the path sharing technique, which only benefits when input vertices tend to be close to each other, this probe-based solution is generic for all kinds of workloads.

In this section we show how to apply the distance estimation and guided graph exploration to two types of graph queries. As a matter of fact, there are other technical

6 Experiments

We report two sets of experiments in this section: 1) testing the effectiveness of c-WSSD partition method on reducing the computation cost of pairwise join validation for distance join queries; 2) how guided graph exploration accelerates shortest path computing and the VSB query evaluation.

6.1 Setup

6.1.1 c-WSSD Partition for Distance Join

Testbed We built up the test bed on a cluster of 16 servers. Every server has 4 Intel(R) Xeon(R) CPU E5-2650 of 2.0GHz, each of which has two cores and supports 16 threads, 12 GB memory and 1 TB hard disk storage. The running operating system is 2.6.35-22-server #35-Ubuntu SMP.

Datasets Brief statistics of the four employed data sets are summarized in Table 1. In the table $d_{\max}$ denotes the diameter of a graph. Data set A is the US patents data. Data set B is the web graph of the TREC 2009 Category B data set, which is the set of the first 50 million English pages

Table 1 Graph data used for c-WSSD partition and distance join

ID	# of nodes	# of edges	# of labels	d_{max}
A	3,774,768	16,522,438	481	22
B	428,136,613	454,075,638	1,325	78
C	500,000,000	4,287,029,468	1,000,000	1,052
D	10,000,000,000	23,946,452,156	1,000,000	1,927

Table 2 General statistics of employed graph data sets

ID	No. of nodes (million)	No. of edges (million)	d_{max}	Size (GB)
A	~428	~454	78	3.6
B	~1,825	~65,219	5328	869.2
C	~33	~1108	7	25.6
D	10,000	23,946	2,927	42.2

collected in January and February 2009 by the Language Technologies Institute at CMU. Synthetic data sets C and D are random graphs generated with the *igraph*[5] package.

Query Workload Given a data set, we randomly select $10 \sim 20$ labels and generate three types of query graphs: star-shaped, path-shaped and circled graph. Meanwhile, we randomly assign the pairwise distance constraints. We generate 300 distance queries for each data set and evaluate the batch one by one. We run every job batch with 3 cold-start and report the average execution time.

6.1.2 Guided Graph Exploration for VSB Queries

Testbed We build up the test bed using the Google Cloud platform, using 6 servers of the n1-highmem-8 type. Each server has 8 virtual CPUs, 52GB memory and 1TB persistent disk, running Debian 7 of Linux kernel 3.2.0-4-amd64. We choose GraphLab [19] to build the prototype system, as it supports both BSP-based graph computation model and the message passing model. Our program is written in C++ and compiled with gcc 4.7.2(switch O3 is on).

Datasets We employ four data sets of different scales and topologies in the experiments, as briefly summarized in Table 2. Data set A describes the web graph of the TREC 2009 Category B data set. Data set B comes from the WebGraph 2012 project [23], which is extracted from the Web cropus released by the Common Crawl Foundation in August 2012. Data set C is a crawled social graph from twitter [18]. Note that we only employ the largest connected component of graph data B and C and make the

graphs undirected. Synthetic data sets D is a random graph generated with *igraph*.

Query Workload For each VSB query, we randomly select $10 \sim 100$ vertices as input X and Y. We generate three types of queries, which essentially represent different kinds of workloads: (1) $\forall x \in X, l(x)_i \leq \delta, \forall y \in Y, l(y)_j \leq \delta$, where $i, j \in [1, d]$ are randomly selected, i.e., both vertices in X and Y are close to each other, denoted as XLYL; (2) $\forall x \in X, l(x)_i \leq \delta$, where $i \in [1, d]$ is randomly selected, $\forall y \in Y$ is randomly selected, denoted as XLYR; (3) both X and Y are randomly generated from G, denoted as XRYR. We would like to show that our solution works well for all kinds of workloads, and the optimization techniques we proposed would be very useful for certain kind of workload. We generate 100 VSB queries for each type of workload, and evaluate the batch one by one. We run every job batch with 3 cold-start and report the average execution time.

6.2 c-WSSD Partition

c-WSSD partition method provides a distance-aware partition of a large graph, which makes it possible to estimate the pairwise shortest path distance in constant time. In the experiments we study from two aspects: (1) the effectiveness of c-WSSD method in terms of query evaluation time cost as well as the I/O and network cost; (2) the scalability of c-WSSD method under different scales of data and parameter.

Effectiveness To validate the effectiveness of c-WSSD, we randomly generate 100 pairwise shortest path distance queries for each data set. In Fig. 3, we report the experiment results on the largest real and synthetic data set B and D, respectively. We measure the query evaluation cost in terms of disk I/O (swap) volume, network volume and the time efficiency. We employed two other intuitive graph partition strategies for comparison: random partition and the k-minimal cut partition using **METIS** [16]. Note that on each individual computing node, we set up the same data block layout and in-memory index structure. Therefore, only the graph data distribution matters in this experiment.

As shown in Fig. 3a, c-WSSD and random partition have about the same cost, while k-minimal cut can introduce high I/O cost. The rationale behind is that k-minimal cut tends to group large number of connected vertices in one partition. Therefore, the queried two vertices are very much likely fall into the same storage node where graph exploration method needs to be adopted. It is not surprising that, as shown in Fig. 3b, k-minimal cut greatly saves the network traffic. However, c-WSSD is the winner of query evaluation time, as shown in Fig. 3c. Because it does not

---

[5] http://igraph.sourceforge.net/index.html.

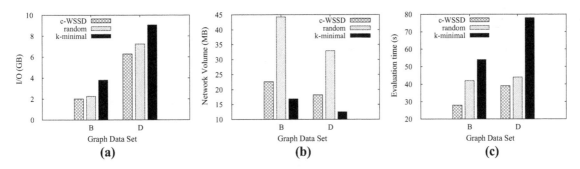

Fig. 3 Pairwise shortest path distance computation: *c*-WSSD versus random versus *k*-minimal cut. **a** I/O cost. **b** Network cost. **c** Time cost

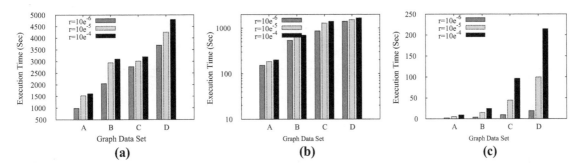

Fig. 4 Scalability test: preprocessing cost of the Voronoi diagram construction and the partition computation. **a** Cost of V' selection. **b** Cost of Voronoi diagram computation. **c** Cost of computing $\mathcal{F}$

introduce much network traffic or I/O cost during the query evaluation. The extra cost of *c*-WSSD is paid during the preprocessing stage of graph partition.

Scalability As introduced in Sect. 3, the preprocessing steps include selecting the initial vertices of high global betweenness, computing the Voronoi diagram, and repartition the graph which involves large volumes of data copying over the network. As discussed before, the cardinality of initial vertex set serves as a trade-off point between query efficiency and system complexity. Therefore, we conduct experiments based on different sizes of initial vertex sets to demonstrate its affection on the final solution.

Figure 4a gives the time cost evaluation on four data sets with respect to the initial vertices selection based on different selection ratios, where $r = \frac{|V'|}{|V|}$ denotes the percentage of employed vertices to partition the graph. We have two main observations. First, for a given r, along with the size of a graph grows, the selection cost increases dramatically. Second, given a data set, when r increases in the order of magnitude, the selection cost also increases, however, following a Logarithm level growth.

Figure 4b demonstrates the time cost of computing Voronoi diagram with Algorithm 1 given in Sect. 3. Given a data set, when r increases in the order of magnitude, the time cost to compute the Voronoi diagram does not grow in

the same pace. Since the computing process is essentially in the BSP (*Bulk Synchronous Processing*) style; therefore, more initial vertices actually help to explore the entire graph faster. However, extra cost to maintain the boundary vertices cannot be neglected.

The time cost to compute the partition set $\mathcal{F}$ is presented in Fig. 4c. The results are obtained when ϵ is set to 0.05, similar trends of results are observed when $\epsilon = 0.01$ and $\epsilon = 0.1$. As proved in Sect. 3, the cardinality of final $\mathcal{F}$ is only subjected to the size of initial vertex set V'. We observe the same trend in the experiment that the time cost to compute $\mathcal{F}$ is closely related to the selection of r.

6.3 Guided Graph Exploration for VSB Query

Our experiment study mainly includes three parts: 1) how the proposed guided graph exploration and betweenness ranking on-exploration help VSB query processing; 2) how different query processing algorithms work under different query workloads.

Preprocessing As presented in Sect. 3.1, we can select d landmarks using either a deterministic or a random algorithm. δ is the crucial parameter to choose. Intuitively, the larger δ is, the number of vertices covered by a single landmark gets larger, which leads to a smaller d. Experiments also validate this point. In Table 3, we report the

Table 3 Graph preprocessing using different algorithms

ID	d			T(sec)		Size(GB)	
	δ	dm.	rd.	dm.	rd.	dm.	rd.
A	4	64	98	146	39	33.2	57.7
	8	36	78	129	32	22.4	41.3
	16	8	42	89	27	8.2	23.6
B	8	2231	3029	549	227	4216	4248
	16	1429	2574	531	189	4094	4225
	32	879	1782	492	141	2709	2799
C	1	126	145	329	124	1139	1178
	2	10	26	69.2	36.4	95.6	105.4
	4	3	59	2.3	78.5	78.9	131.7
D	8	1576	2109	421	179	1465	1509
	16	1206	2005	392	164	1437	1486
	32	457	1324	354	139	1128	1305

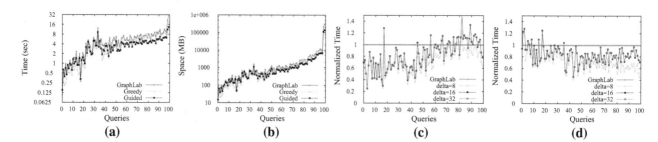

Fig. 5 The speed up of evaluating p_{st} queries. **a** Time ($\delta = 8$). **b** Space ($\delta = 8$). **c** (T) Greedy versus GraphLab. **d** (T) Guided versus GraphLab

time efficiency of graph preprocessing and the value of d accordingly, as well as the total disk space cost after preprocessing.

Regarding time efficiency, we have two observations from the results. First, by increasing δ, d drops more significantly if a deterministic algorithm is employed comparing to using a random algorithm. For example, when δ increases from 16 to 32 in graph B, d drops from 1429 to 879, which almost drops a half using the deterministic algorithm. On the contrary, by using the random algorithm, it only drops from 2574 to 1782. Second, although a random algorithm always generates more partitions, it is still a winner w.r.t. time efficiency. Meanwhile, as shown in Table 2, the extra space cost of vertex labeling turns to be manageable even δ is set to a small value. Although each vertex is presented with a d bytes vector during query processing, the label vectors are initially compressed and recovered only upon data access. The reported data sizes in Table refvsb:datasets are the ones with vertex label compression applied, as elaborated in Sect. 3.1.2. A straightforward observation is that if G is power-law graph with

large G_{diam}, like graph B and D, smaller δ promises better compression ratio. For example, the sizes of graph B with δ set to 8 and 16 are very close. This property is guaranteed by the characteristic of value-based compression. Moreover, if the data graph is extremely dense with a small diameter, like graph C, the extra space cost on vertex labeling drops significantly when δ increases, as the number of landmarks would be very limited.

Fast shortest path computing To validate the guided graph exploration for shortest path, we randomly pick 100 pairs of vertices from each graph and ask for p_{xy}, and rank the betweenness of two random vertices from p_{xy}. As a comparison, we employ the GraphLab's shortest path utility implementation and the parallel betweenness computing algorithm introduced in [2]. Due to the space limit, we highlight our findings on graph B.

Figure 5 shows how our methods, greedy (Algorithm 5) and guided exploration (Algorithm 6), compare to the GraphLab's shortest path in p_{st} evaluation. Figure 5a, b shows the time and space cost respectively. Space cost is the total size of data access on the distributed storage. Note

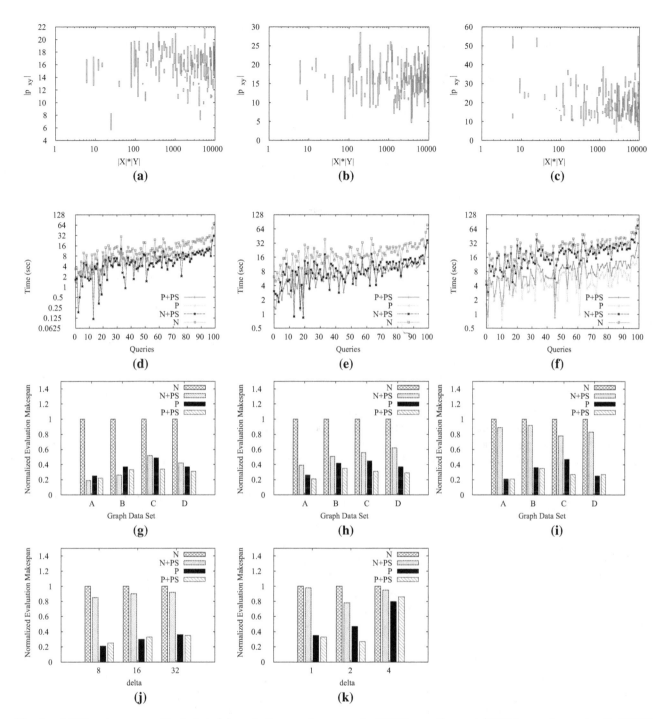

Fig. 6 a–i Different query workloads test; **j–k** evaluation speedup using different δ (Graph B & C). **a** XLYL query distribution. **b** XLYR query distribution. **c** XRYR query distribution. **d** XLYL query time cost. **e** XLYR query time cost. **f** XRYR query time cost. **g** Q of XLYL workload. **h** Q of XLYR workload. **i** Q of XRYR workload. **j** δ & efficiency (Graph B). **k** δ & efficiency (Graph C)

that the queries of x axis are sorted in an ascending order of $|p_{st}|$, and y axis is presented in logarithm scale. As shown in Fig. 5a, when $|p_{st}|$ is small, the greedy method's execution time is only about half of the GraphLab's method. The reason is that Algorithm 5 terminates quickly with less vertex access. With the increasing of $|p_{st}|$, the greedy algorithm's efficiency drops and sometimes even performs worse than the GraphLab's method. Because when $|p_{st}|$ grows, it takes the greedy algorithm more iterations to guess the correct $|p_{st}|$. On the contrary, guided exploration performs stable and achieves more time saving when $|p_{st}|$ grows.

To investigate how δ affects our algorithm, we present time cost of greedy and guided exploration with different δ setting on the same workload in Fig. 5c, d. Note that we normalize all the time cost using GraphLab's result, as it does not rely on the setting of δ. Apparently, our algorithm achieves more speedup when δ is smaller, which is reasonable as it promises better pruning power. Another observation from the result is that, comparing to the guided exploration, the greedy algorithm is more resistent to different δ. It is because greedy algorithm uses vertex label pruning in a passive way, while the guided exploration employs the pruning actively before making a decision on the next hop. Clearly, as shown in Fig. 5d, when $|p_{st}|$ is large, the guided exploration is more sensitive to the setting of δ. Although smaller δ works better for the path query, there is the greater extra space overhead to trade off.

VSB query evaluation We evaluate our proposed solution from the efficiency perspectives. We first set δ for the four data sets as 8, 32, 2 and 32, respectively, to compare the effectiveness of our proposed query processing solution. In Sect. 5.2, we introduce a naive VSB query processing solution (Algorithm 7) and two optimization techniques to improve the time efficiency. To validate the proposed solution, we report how the combination of optimization techniques serve the query evaluation, particularly, on different query workloads. Due to the space limit, we highlight our results on graph B in Fig. 6. Figure 6a–c show the distribution of random queries we generated, where queries are sorted according to their input size ($|X| \times |Y|$ as x axis). Figure 6d–f shows the time costs for different query evaluation methods over different workloads, where N stands for the naive algorithm, P stands for the probe-based communication solution (Algorithm 8), PS stands for path sharing. Apparently, if input vertices are close to each other, path sharing would achieve great time saving, as shown in Fig. 6d. On the contrary, when query inputs are randomly selected, as shown in Fig. 6f, probe-based method performs better.

We report the normalized query processing makespan of different methods on all data sets in Fig. 6g–i. We have made two observations from the efficiency experiments. First, given the same query workload, the underlying graph structure would greatly affect algorithm performance. Take graphs A for example, it is much more sparse than graph C. As shown in Fig. 6g, over the same query workload, the best evaluation strategy for graph A is path sharing, while for graph C it is a combination of path sharing and probe-based communication. Clearly, reducing network communication as much as possible for a dense network brings more benefits than packing shared paths. Second, path sharing clearly helps a lot when the vertices in X or Y are close to each other. For example, for the XLYL workload, comparing to the naive algorithm, we can obtain almost 5x

speed up on graph A by applying path sharing. On the contrary, the probe-based communication method performs more stable on different workloads. One thing to notice is that combining path sharing with probe-based solution does not double the speedup. The reason is that path sharing reduces the concurrent computing threads itself, but makes the computing workload of each thread unbalanced. Note that in Algorithm 8, R is updated with synchronization, which could easily suffer from unbalanced current computing workloads.

Another critical concern is that how δ affects the query evaluation performance. As the algorithms, we proposed are based on the guided graph exploration method, therefore, we observe the similar trend of efficiency improvement when δ decreases as shown in Fig. 5d. We highlight our findings using the results from graph B and C. For graph B, as shown in Fig. 6j, the path sharing optimization method is closely bounded with the total number of vertices to explore. Therefore, the probe-based method is essential to the performance improvement. For graph C, as shown in Fig. 6k, due to the density property, path sharing is desirable when δ is set to a proper value, like $\delta=2$. When *delta* equals to 1, there is not much optimization space left after a probe-based method is employed, as the pruning power on vertex exploration is sufficiently strong. On the contrary, when δ equals to 4, almost the entire graph needs to be considered to extract the shared path, which would result in severe performance decay. The hints we learn from the results are that if the query workload is unknown, smaller δ is preferred for fast query processing as long as the extra space cost is manageable; the crucial performance optimization lies in reducing the total number of vertices to access and compute; path sharing does not help with the speedup if δ is too small or too large.

7 Related Work

Distributed graph processing models and systems General purpose large graph management has drawn great research interest. Early work [20] illustrates the challenging issues of large graph management. Proposals in [3] and [22] are two well recognized models for parallel large graph processing, which are MPI(*Message Passing Interface*)-based and BSP, respectively. Although MPI usually gains more time efficiency, it is relatively complicated and puts a heavy burden of system implementation on programmers. Pregel [22] is a vertex-centric computing model, which is more flexible and relatively easy to program. However, it has to sacrifice time efficiency due to inevitable synchronization costs at each iteration step. Work [24] conducts an empirical comparison of three computing diagrams for large graph processing, which are RDBMS-like approaches, data parallel approach (e.g. Pregel) and in-memory graph exploration approach. Improvement works over Pregel, like Pregelix [6], Blogel [35] targets on network cost reduction to yield better performance. Trinity [31] and GBase [15] are two other state-of-art distributed general purpose graph management systems with substantially different designs. GBase models graphs using adjacent matrices. It transforms nearly all the graph analytic functions into matrix manipulations using iterative MapReduce jobs. On the contrary, Trinity employs an in-memory *key-value* store in a distributed shared memory environment. It models graph data following the vertex-centric model, i.e., each vertex is associated with its one-hop neighbor(s), such that all the classical graph exploring algorithms can be directly plugged in.

Distance-based query over distributed graph Employing landmarks to approximate the shortest path distance is a widely adopted technique [17, 25, 27]. The basic idea is to pre-compute the shortest distances between all the nodes and selected landmarks and then apply the triangle inequality to help estimate the shortest path distance. Work [27] investigates finding the optimal set of landmarks. In particular, they target on answering the pairwise shortest path distance query. They introduce the LandMark-Cover problem, which is to find a minimum number of points such that given any pair of vertices u and v, there exists at least one landmark residing on the shortest path from u to v. This problem is proven to be closely related with the 2-hop labeling scheme [9]. Landmark-based methods do not aim to provide the exact distance. Instead, they use a small number of landmarks to do estimation. Tao et al. [32] introduce the k-skip shortest path, which is a natural substantial of returning the exact shortest path. Intuitively, it reports a set of vertices V that consecutively reside on a shortest path from s to t, having every vertex on this path is at most k-hop away from at least one vertex in V. Follow-up works, like graph simplification [30], shortest path discovery over road network [11, 34], employ similar concepts to perform a distance-preserving graph partition. The δ-evenly coverage landmark selection defined in this work, however, is orthogonal to the k-skip concept. Because shortest path is not the substantial concern in our problem. We select landmarks to serve online graph exploration. There is no sequence semantic of our landmarks. In other words, k-skip returns more vertices residing on the shortest path of two query points when k decreases. On the contrast, given a smaller δ, the δ-evenly coverage serves better in reducing redundant vertex access on exploration step by step. Vertex labeling is another line of research to answer distance queries. Gavoille et al. show that general graphs support an exact distance labeling scheme with labels of $O(n)$ bits [12]. Several special graph families, including trees or graphs with bounded tree-

width, have distance labeling schemes with $O(log_2 n)$ bit labels [1]. However, it is infeasible to directly apply these theory results to a large graph of billion nodes, as the space overhead of labeling would be unaccepted. Our solution, on the other hand, simply targets on vertex pruning using distance labels. And due to the δ-evenly coverage landmark selection scheme, the locality of vertices' label vectors is well preserved. Therefore, a simple value-based compression could greatly help to reduce the overall space cost on vertex labeling.

8 Conclusion

In this paper, we study two fundamental building blocks for distance-aware online graph query: fast and accurate distance estimation, as well as guided graph exploration. A c-WSSD partition method is introduced to generate the index structure to produce error-bounded shortest path distance estimation in $O(1)$ time with space complexity of $O(c|V|)$, where c is a constant factor. Furthermore, we discuss how to perform guided graph exploration with landmark referencing. We validate the proposed technique with distance join and VSB query workload over both real and synthetic graph data in real Cloud environment.

References

1. Alstrup S, Bille P, Rauhe T (2005) Labeling schemes for small distances in trees. SIAM J Discrete Math 19(2):448–462
2. Bader DA, Madduri K (2006) Parallel algorithms for evaluating centrality indices in real-world networks. In: ICPP, pp 539–550
3. Bader DA, Madduri K (2008) Snap, small-world network analysis and partitioning: an open-source parallel graph framework for the exploration of large-scale networks. In: IPDPS, pp 1–12
4. Bader DA, Kintali S, Madduri K, Mihail M (2007) Approximating betweenness centrality. In: WAW, pp 124–137
5. Brandtzæg PB, Heim J, Kaare BH (2010) Bridging and bonding in social network sites—investigating family-based capital. IJWBC 6(3):231–253
6. Bu Y, Borkar VR, Jia J, Carey MJ, Condie T (2014) Pregelix: big(ger) graph analytics on a dataflow engine. PVLDB 8(2):161–172
7. Castro M et al (2003) Future directions in distributed computing. In: Topology-aware routing in structured peer-to-peer overlay networks, pp 103–107
8. Cheng J, Yu JX, Yu PS (2011) Graph pattern matching: a join/semijoin approach. IEEE Trans Knowl Data Eng 23(7):1006–1021
9. Cohen E, Halperin E, Kaplan H, Zwick U (2003) Reachability and distance queries via 2-hop labels. SIAM J Comput 32(5):1338–1355
10. Fu AW, Wu H, Cheng J, Wong RC (2013) IS-LABEL: an independent-set based labeling scheme for point-to-point distance querying. PVLDB 6(6):457–468
11. Funke S, Nusser A, Storandt S (2014) On k-path covers and their applications. PVLDB 7(10):893–902
12. Gavoille C, Peleg D, Pérennes S, Raz R (2004) Distance labeling in graphs. J Algorithms 53(1):85–112

13. Guille A, Hacid H, Favre C, Zighed DA (2013) Information diffusion in online social networks: a survey. SIGMOD Rec 42(2):17–28

14. Jin W, Yang J (2011) A flexible graph pattern matching framework via indexing. In: SSDBM, pp 293–311

15. Kang U, Tong H, Sun J, Lin CY, Faloutsos C (2011) Gbase: a scalable and general graph management system. In: KDD, pp 1091–1099

16. Karypis G et al (1998) A fast and high quality multilevel scheme for partitioning irregular graphs. SIAM J Sci Comput 20(1):359–392

17. Kleinberg JM, Slivkins A, Wexler T (2004) Triangulation and embedding using small sets of beacons. In: FOCS 17–19, pp 444–453

18. Kwak H, Lee C, Park H, Moon SB (2010) What is twitter, a social network or a news media? In: WWW, pp 591–600

19. Low Y, et al (2010) Graphlab: a new framework for parallel machine learning. In: UAI, pp 340–349

20. Lumsdaine A, Gregor D, Hendrickson B, Berry JW (2007) Challenges in parallel graph processing. Parallel Process Lett 17(1):5–20

21. Madduri K, et al (2009) A faster parallel algorithm and efficient multithreaded implementations for evaluating betweenness centrality on massive datasets. In: IPDPS, pp 1–8

22. Malewicz G, et al (2010) Pregel: a system for large-scale graph processing. In: SIGMOD, pp 135–146

23. Meusel R, et al (2014) Graph structure in the web - revisited: a trick of the heavy tail. In: WWW, pp 427–432

24. Najork M, et al (2012) Of hammers and nails: an empirical comparison of three paradigms for processing large graphs. In: WSDM, pp 103–112

25. Ng TSE, Zhang H (2002) Predicting internet network distance with coordinates-based approaches. In: INFOCOM

26. Potamias M, Bonchi F, Castillo C, Gionis A (2009a) Fast shortest path distance estimation in large networks. CIKM, pp 867–876

27. Potamias M, Bonchi F, Castillo C, Gionis A (2009b) Fast shortest path distance estimation in large networks. In: CIKM, pp 867–876

28. Qi Z, Xiao Y, Shao B, Wang H (2013) Toward a distance oracle for billion-node graphs. PVLDB 7(1):61–72

29. Qiao M, Cheng H, Yu JX (2011) Querying shortest path distance with bounded errors in large graphs. In: SSDBM, pp 255–273

30. Ruan N, Jin R, Huang Y (2011) Distance preserving graph simplification. In: ICDM, pp 1200–1205

31. Shao B, Wang H, Li Y (2012) The trinity graph engine. Technical Report 161291, Microsoft Research

32. Tao Y, Sheng C, Pei J (2011) On k-skip shortest paths. In: SIGMOD, pp 421–432

33. Tian Y, Balmin A, Corsten SA, Tatikonda S, McPherson J (2013) From "think like a vertex" to "think like a graph". PVLDB 7(3):193–204

34. Yan D, Cheng J, Ng W, Liu S (2013) Finding distance-preserving subgraphs in large road networks. In: ICDE, pp 625–636

35. Yan D, Cheng J, Lu Y, Ng W (2014) Blogel: a block-centric framework for distributed computation on real-world graphs. PVLDB 7(14):1981–1992

36. Zhang X, Chen L, Wang M (2015a) Efficient parallel processing of distance join queries over distributed graphs. IEEE Trans Knowl Data Eng 27(3):740–754

37. Zhang X, Cheng H, Chen L (2015b) Bonding vertex sets over distributed graph: a betweenness aware approach. PVLDB 8(12):1418–1429

38. Zou L, Chen L, Özsu MT (2009) Distancejoin: pattern match query in a large graph database. PVLDB 2(1):886–897

39. Zou L, Özsu MT, Chen L, Shen X, Huang R, Zhao D (2014) gstore: a graph-based SPARQL query engine. VLDB J 23(4):565–590

Permissions

The contributors of this book come from diverse backgrounds, making this book a truly international effort. This book will bring forth new frontiers with its revolutionizing research information and detailed analysis of the nascent developments around the world.

We would like to thank all the contributing authors for lending their expertise to make the book truly unique. They have played a crucial role in the development of this book. Without their invaluable contributions this book wouldn't have been possible. They have made vital efforts to compile up to date information on the varied aspects of this subject to make this book a valuable addition to the collection of many professionals and students.

This book was conceptualized with the vision of imparting up-to-date information and advanced data in this field. To ensure the same, a matchless editorial board was set up. Every individual on the board went through rigorous rounds of assessment to prove their worth. After which they invested a large part of their time researching and compiling the most relevant data for our readers.

The editorial board has been involved in producing this book since its inception. They have spent rigorous hours researching and exploring the diverse topics which have resulted in the successful publishing of this book. They have passed on their knowledge of decades through this book. To expedite this challenging task, the publisher supported the team at every step. A small team of assistant editors was also appointed to further simplify the editing procedure and attain best results for the readers.

Apart from the editorial board, the designing team has also invested a significant amount of their time in understanding the subject and creating the most relevant covers. They scrutinized every image to scout for the most suitable representation of the subject and create an appropriate cover for the book.

The publishing team has been an ardent support to the editorial, designing and production team. Their endless efforts to recruit the best for this project, has resulted in the accomplishment of this book. They are a veteran in the field of academics and their pool of knowledge is as vast as their experience in printing. Their expertise and guidance has proved useful at every step. Their uncompromising quality standards have made this book an exceptional effort. Their encouragement from time to time has been an inspiration for everyone.

The publisher and the editorial board hope that this book will prove to be a valuable piece of knowledge for researchers, students, practitioners and scholars across the globe.

List of Contributors

Jianfeng Wang and Xiaofeng Chen
State Key Laboratory of Integrated Service Networks (ISN), Xidian University, Xi'an, People's Republic of China

Fatimah Akeel
University of Southampton, Southampton, UK
King Saud University, Riyadh, Saudi Arabia

Asieh Salehi Fathabadi, Federica Paci, Andrew Gravell and Gary Wills
University of Southampton, Southampton, UK

Koji Ueno
Tokyo Institute of Technology, Tokyo, Japan

Toyotaro Suzumura
IBM T.J. Watson Research Center, Westchester County, NY, USA

Naoya Maruyama
RIKEN, Kobe, Japan

Katsuki Fujisawa
Kyushu University, Fukuoka, Japan

Satoshi Matsuoka
Tokyo Institute of Technology/AIST, Tokyo, Japan

Boyi Hou, Zhuo Wang, Qun Chen, Bo Suo, Chao Fang and Zhanhuai Li
School of Computer Science, Northwestern Polytechnical University, Xi'an, China

Zachary G. Ives
Department of Computer and Information Systems, University of Pennsylvania, Philadelphia, PA, USA

Shaoqing Wang
Key Lab of Data Engineering and Knowledge Engineering of MOE, Beijing, China
Renmin University of China, Beijing, China
School of Computer Science and Technology, Shandong University of Technology, Zibo, China

Cuiping Li, Kankan Zhao and Hong Chen
Key Lab of Data Engineering and Knowledge Engineering of MOE, Beijing, China
Renmin University of China, Beijing, China

Muhammad Habib ur Rehman, Chee Sun Liew and Teh Ying Wah
Faculty of Computer Science and Information Technology, University of Malaya, Kuala Lumpur, Malaysia

Assad Abbas and Samee U. Khan
Department of Electrical and Computer Engineering, North Dakota State University, Fargo, ND, USA

Prem Prakash Jayaraman
Department of Computer Science and Software Engineering, Swinburne University of Technology, Melbourne, Australia

Pietro Colombo and Elena Ferrari
DiSTA, University of Insubria, Via Mazzini, 5, Varese, Italy

Makoto Onizuka and Toshimasa Fujimori
Graduate School of Information Science and Technology, Osaka University, 1-5, Yamadaoka, Suita, Osaka 565-0871, Japan

Hiroaki Shiokawa
Center of Computational Sciences, University of Tsukuba, 1-1-1, Tennoudai, Tsukuba, Ibaraki 305-8573, Japan

Shumin Han, Derong Shen, Tiezheng Nie, Yue Kou and Ge Yu
College of Computer Science and Engineering, Northeastern University, Shenyang, China

Ningnan Zhou, Xuan Zhou, Xiao Zhang and Shan Wang
MOE Key Laboratory of DEKE, Renmin University of China, Haidian, China
School of Information, Renmin University of China, Beijing 100872, China

Lotfi Ben Othmane, Golriz Chehrazi and Eric Bodden
Fraunhofer Institute for Secure Information Technology, Darmstadt, Germany

Petar Tsalovski and Achim D. Brucker
SAP SE, Walldorf, Germany

Xiaoying Wu
State Key Laboratory of Software Engineering, Wuhan University, Wuhan, China

Dimitri Theodoratos
New Jersey Institute of Technology, Newark, NJ, USA

Weihuang Huang and Jeffrey Xu Yu
The Chinese University of Hong Kong, Hong Kong, China

Xiaofei Zhang
University of Waterloo, Waterloo, Canada

Lei Chen
Hong Kong University of Science & Technology, Clear Water Bay, Hong Kong

Index

A

Access Control, 10, 12, 14, 17, 20-21, 79-89

Access Control Solutions, 79

B

Batch Replacement, 112-116, 118-121

Big Data, 12, 57, 59-78, 89, 102, 121, 140-141

Bitmaps, 26-27, 140, 142, 147-149, 151, 153-154

Breadth-first Search, 22, 26, 34-35

Buffer Manager, 112-121

Buffer Managers, 112, 114

C

Computational Model, 112-113

Computing Frameworks, 62, 179

Confidentiality, 7-8, 12-14, 16, 19-21, 102

Context-aware Recommendations, 48-51, 53, 55, 57-58

D

Data Auditing, 1, 3

Data Complexity, 59-62, 70, 72-73, 76

Data Compression, 6, 26, 59-60, 64-65, 74, 77

Data Management Platforms, 112

Data Mining, 47, 57-59, 61, 70-71, 76-78, 89, 100, 121, 138, 140, 154-155

Data Organization, 80, 82, 112-114, 120

Data Protection Mechanisms, 79-80

Data Reduction, 59-62, 64-78

Database Management Systems, 79, 81, 89

Development Groups, 122-123, 135-137

Dimensionality Reduction, 59, 69, 72, 75, 77

Distributed Computers, 90-91, 95

Distributed Engines, 90

Distributed Processing, 22, 34-35, 77, 90

Distributed-memory, 22-23, 26, 34-35

Document Stores, 79, 82

E

Embedded Patterns, 140-143, 147-149, 151-154

Event-b, 12-15, 19-21

F

Factorization Machines, 48-51, 57-58

Fine-grained Access Control, 79-81, 84, 89

Fixing Processes, 122

Formal Method, 12-14, 20

G

Graph500, 22-23, 26-28, 31-32, 34-35

Graph Database, 112-115, 118-119, 198

Graph Mining, 36, 90

Graph Partition, 179, 181-184, 187, 190, 192-193, 197

Graph Partitioning, 34, 36-38, 41-42, 45-46, 90-92, 94-95, 99-100

Graph Processing, 33, 36, 90-92, 94, 99-101, 121, 179, 196, 198

Graph Queries, 113, 179-180, 187, 191

Graph-based Applications, 112

H

Heuristics, 156-163, 165-178, 180

Hierarchical Information, 48-49

Homomorphic Patterns, 140-144, 146, 148-152, 154-155

Human Factors, 122

I

I/o Access, 112, 114, 120

Individual Improvements, 122, 136

Internal Development Processes, 122

Issue Fix Time, 122-125, 127, 129-138

Iterative Graph Partitioning, 36, 41

K

K-anonymity, 102, 104-106, 109, 111

L

Large-scale Graph Data, 90

Learning Organizations, 122

Load Balance, 90-96, 98-100

Location-based Services (LBS), 156

Low Communication Cost, 90-92

M

Machine Learning Methods, 59, 75-76, 122, 124

Mapreduce, 36-38, 41-43, 45, 47, 65, 87, 197

Maximal Clique Enumeration, 36-38, 45, 47

Maximal Sequential I/o, 112

Modelling, 12-20

Modularity-based Clustering, 90-93, 99-100

Mongodb, 79-81, 86-89
Multi-core Environment, 112, 121

N
Nosql, 79-86, 89, 140

O
Optimal Replacement Plan, 112-113, 115-119, 121
Outsourced Storage, 1

P
Paillier Cryptosystem, 102-108, 110-111
Parallel Graph Processing, 36, 198
Potential Vulnerability, 122
Powergraph, 90-91, 94-96, 100
Privacy, 1, 7-10, 12-14, 17-21, 62, 65-66, 74, 77, 81, 89, 102-106, 108-109, 111
Privacy-preserving Record Linkage, 102, 111
Private Blocking, 102-105, 108-111
Programming Languages, 86, 122, 124, 137
Public Dataset, 102

Q
Quality of Blocking, 102, 104-105, 109
Query Processing, 4, 67, 75, 156, 179-181, 190-191, 193-194, 196

R
Random Decision Trees, 48-51, 55, 57
Rbac, 12, 14, 16
Record Linkage, 102, 104, 111
Redundant Graph Traversal, 179

S
Scalability, 20, 25-26, 35, 67, 71, 74, 79, 83, 86, 89, 95, 97-100, 102-103, 105, 108, 114, 140, 142, 148-149, 151-152, 154, 179, 192-193
Secure Data Deduplication, 1-2, 9-10
Secure Software, 122-123, 125, 136, 138
Security Issues., 122, 127, 134-136
Security Policy, 12-20, 89
Shortest Path Distance, 179-180, 182-188, 192-193, 197-198
Sketch, 65-66, 68, 74, 156, 161, 167, 171
Social Network Management, 112
Software Structure, 122, 135-136
Synthetic Datasets, 43-44, 88, 112-113, 118, 121, 140, 156-158, 162-165, 167-169, 173, 175, 177

T
Trust, 12-15, 18-21
Trust Model, 12, 18, 20
Tsp, 156-160, 162-163, 165, 167-168, 171, 174-175, 177-178

U
Unstructured Data, 61-63, 76, 79

V
Verifiable Search, 1

W
Web Structure Mining, 112